The Physical and
the Digital City

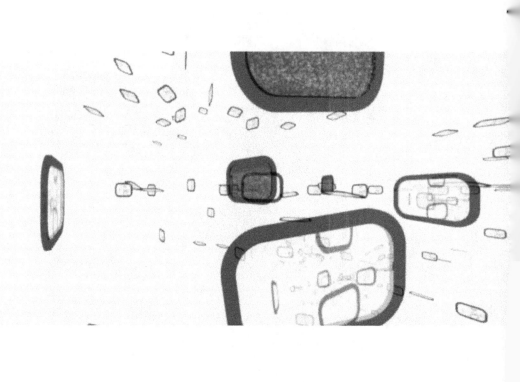

The Physical and the Digital City

Invisible Forces, Data, and Manifestations

EDITED BY

Silvio Carta

Bristol, UK / Chicago, USA

First published in the UK in 2024 by
Intellect, The Mill, Parnall Road, Fishponds, Bristol, BS16 3JG, UK

First published in the USA in 2024 by
Intellect, The University of Chicago Press, 1427 E. 60th Street,
Chicago, IL 60637, USA

Copyright © 2024 Intellect Ltd
All rights reserved. No part of this publication may be reproduced, stored in a retrieval system, or transmitted, in any form or by any means, electronic, mechanical, photocopying, recording, or otherwise, without written permission.

A catalogue record for this book is available from
the British Library.

Copy editor: MPS Limited
Cover designer: Tanya Montefusco
Cover image: Victorian Quaker Centre (Worship Space),
Nervegna Reed Architecture + pH Architects. Photo John Gollings.
Frontispiece image: *Architecture at 25 Frames per Second*.
Video Still. 1998. Toby Reed.
Production manager: Debora Nicosia
Typesetter: MPS Limited

Hardback ISBN 978-1-83595-032-6
ePDF ISBN 978-1-83595-034-0
ePUB ISBN 978-1-83595-033-3

To find out about all our publications, please visit our website. There you can subscribe to our e-newsletter, browse or download our current catalogue and buy any titles that are in print.

www.intellectbooks.com

This is a peer-reviewed publication.

Mediated Cities

Series Editor: Dr. Graham Cairns | **Print ISSN:** 2058–9409

The Mediated Cities series explores the contemporary city as a hybrid phenomenon of digital technologies, new media, digital art practices and physical infrastructure. It is an inherently interdisciplinary series around intersecting issues related to the city of today and tomorrow.

As Marshall McLuhan identified in 1964, today's global village is a place of simultaneous experience; a site for overlapping material and electronic effects; a place not so much altered by the content of a medium, but rather, a space transformed by the very nature of medias themselves. For some, this is little more than the inevitable evolution of urban space in the digital age. For others, it represents the city's liberation from the condition of stasis. For scaremongers, it's a nightmare scenario in which the difference between the virtual and the real, the electronic and the material, the recorded and the lived, becomes impossible to identify.

The series editor is the director of the Architecture Media Politics Society (AMPS).

In this series:

Watch This Space: Exploring Cinematic Intersections Between the Body, Architecture and the City, edited by Howard Griffin and Maciej Stasiowski (2024)

The Physical and the Digital City: Invisible Forces, Data, and Manifestations, edited by Silvio Carta (2024)

Reframing Berlin: Architecture, Memory-Making and Film Locations, by Christopher S. Wilson and Gul Kacmaz Erk (2024)

Equality in the City: Imaginaries of the Smart Future, edited by Susan Flynn (2023)

Narrating the City: Mediated Representations of Architecture, Urban Forms and Social Life, edited by Ayşegül Akçay Kavakoğlu, Türkan Nihan Hacıömeroğlu and Lisa Landrum (2023)

Transformations: Art and the City, edited by Elizabeth Grierson (2017)

Digital Futures and the City of Today: New Technologies and Physical Spaces, edited by Glenda Amayo Caldwell, Carl H. Smith and Edward M. Clift (2016)

Imaging the City: Art, Creative Practices and Media Speculations, edited by Steve Hawley, Edward Clift and Kevin O'Brien (2016)

Filming the City: Urban Documents, Design Practices and Social Criticism through the Lens, edited by Edward M. Clift, by Mirko Guaralda and Ari Mattes (2016)

Contents

List of Figures — ix

Introduction — 1
Silvio Carta

1. Good Game Peace Out — 9
   David Capener
2. Screenness — 24
   Toby Reed
3. Mood-Sensitive Spaces: Inspiration from Ambient Assisted Living and Affective Computing — 43
   Liz Felton
4. Smooth Invisible: Liquid Surveillance and Architecture — 61
   Hüsnü Yegenoglu and Justin Agyin
5. Mediated Participatory Urban Planning and Design: An Interdisciplinary Framework — 79
   David Harris Smith, Frauke Zeller, Emily Eyles, John Eyles, Debora Silva De Jesus, and Calvin Hillis
6. Digital Zoning: From Hippodamus to Mixed Reality — 94
   Kai Reaver
7. Pattern Recognition—The Big Smart Transactional City — 122
   Ian Nazareth and David Schwarzman
8. Outsmarting the City—How Queer Subcultures in Queensborough Used Public Infrastructure for Community, Cruising, and Queering Car Culture, 1890–2000 — 142
   Patricia Silva

9. The Influence of Artificial Intelligence on Autonomous   161
   Vehicle Design and Users' Lifestyle within Responsive
   Urban Environments
   Marco Zilvetti, Matteo Conti, and Fausto Brevi
10. Understanding Postmetropolis in the Latest Virtual City: 188
    Urban Analysis of Night City in *Cyberpunk 2077*
    Yulin Li
11. Parkour, the City, and Mediated Subjectivities   205
    Fidelia Lam
12. Apple Town Square: Digital Placemaking and Digital   222
    Transformation of Urban Public Spaces
    Isabel Fangyi Lu
13. Decoding the Phygital Space: Exploring How Youths Produce   236
    New Urban Festival Spaces through Social Interactions
    Rebecca Onafuye
14. Airbnb Plus Filter: Creating Strategic and Photogenic Interiors   252
    Esra Duygun and Duygu Koca
15. The Smart City in the Smaller Context: Digital Subjectivities and   268
    Smart City Development in Rural Conditions
    Daniel Koch

Note of Contributors   285

Figures

2.1:   A diagram of a classic TV screen as a black hole vortex to 25
       alternate time and spatiality, causing space–time disjuncture
       in everyday life. Toby Reed, 2003–14.
2.2:   *Demolition d'un Mur*, 1896 (film). Auguste and Louis Lumière. 26
       France, consecutive film stills. 27
2.3:   Central Goldfields Art Gallery, Maryborough, Dja Wurrung
       Country. Nervegna Reed Architecture, 2022.
2.4:   Precinct Energy Project. Nervegna Reed Architecture + pH Architects, 30
       2012.
2.5:   Arrow Studio, Nervegna Reed Architecture + pH Architects, 2013. 30
       Photos: Sam Reed.
2.6:   *Prenom Carmen*, 1983 (film). Directed by Jean-Luc Godard. 31
       France. Television tuned to a dead channel. Permission StudioCanal.
2.7:   Total House, Melbourne 1964, Bogle and Banfield Assoc. 32
       TV Building. Photo: Toby Reed.
2.8:   *Videodrome*, 1983 (film). Directed by David Cronenberg. Canada: 35
       CFDC. Permission NBC Universal and David Cronenberg.
2.9:   *SPONGE / SURFACE / SPACE*, Toby Reed, 2018. 36
2.10: Judo House, Nervegna Reed Architecture, 2021. Photos: John
       Gollings. 37
2.11: Victorian Quaker Centre, Nervegna Reed Architecture + pH 38
       Architects, 2020. Photos: John Gollings.
2.12: *Architecture at 25 Frames Per Second*. Video still. Toby Reed, 1998. 40
3.1:   A smart home illustration. "Smart Home House Technology— 45
       Free Vector Graphic on Pixabay." n.d. Accessed July 13, 2022.
3.2:   The sense–compute–act cycle. Liz Felton, 2022. 46

3.3:	An example of AAL space. Liz Felton with icons from icon8 (https://icons8.com/, accessed June 16, 2023), 2023.	47
3.4:	Extending the sense–compute–act cycle to include mood data. Liz Felton, 2022.	50
4.1:	The former AT&T Long Lines Building at 33 Thomas Street, New York, USA, 1974. Architect John Carl Warnecke & Associates. Source: Flickr/Wally Gobetz.	68
4.2:	B 018, Beirut, Lebanon, 1994. Architect Bernard Khoury. Copyright: Jane Alhawat.	69
4.3:	Maison Fibre at the 2021 Architecture Biennale, Venice, Italy. Design by ICD/ITKE/IntCDC, University of Stuttgart. Copyright: ICD/ITKE/IntCDC, University of Stuttgart, 2021.	70
4.4:	Datacenter AM4, Amsterdam, The Netherlands. Architect: Benthem Crouwel Architects. Copyright: Justin Agyin, 2018.	72
4.5:	New Care Center, 2020. Rendering courtesy of Flad Architects // Flad.com. Copyright: Flad Architects.	73
5.1:	Planning charrette combining analog and digital 3D planning environments. Participant used both paper and digital design tools to propose street renovations. David Harris Smith, 2020.	84
5.2:	Interaction design cycle in urban planning. Framework for participatory planning with interaction design approach. David Harris Smith, 2020.	85
6.1:	BorderGO system by Norkart and the Norwegian Mapping Authority, 2016. Source: norkart.no. Accessed October 19, 2021.	96
6.2:	TriO system in Oslo during the COVID-19 pandemic. Oslo from March 17 to May 4, 2020. Oslo Municipality, Department of Emergency Services (*Beredskapsetaten*).	96
6.3:	Case study displaying AR object placement in an urban context, 2021. Source: Reaver, K. (2023). Augmented reality as a participation tool for youth in urban planning processes: Case study in Oslo, Norway. *Frontiers in Virtual Reality*, 4.	98
6.4:	Hippodamus' Plan of Miletus *c.*470 BC. Burns, A. (1976). "Hippodamus and the Planned City." *Historia: Zeitschrift für Alte Geschichte*, 25(4), 414–28.	100

FIGURES

6.5:	Zeltzer, 1992: AIP cube. Zeltzer, D. (1992). "Autonomy, Interaction, and Presence." *Presence: Teleoperators and Virtual Environments*, 1(1), 127–32.	102
6.6:	Technologically mediated experience. Robinett, W. (1992). "Synthetic Experience: A Proposed Taxonomy." *Presence: Teleoperators and Virtual Environments*, Bd. 1, s. 229–47.	104
6.7:	Data flow for types of mediated experience. Robinett, W. (1992). "Synthetic Experience: A Proposed Taxonomy." *Presence: Teleoperators and Virtual Environments*, Bd. 1, s. 229–47.	107
6.8:	City Planning Prototype by Arup / Dan Hill and Chris Green, 2018. Reproduced with permission from Hill, Dan, "Augmented Planning Notice," December 13, 2022, YouTube video. Accessed June 22, 2020.	108
6.9:	UN Habitat and Ericsson experiment with a *Minecraft*-like gaming environment in AR, 2019. Source: UN Habitat & Ericsson, 2019. Habitat, U. N. & Ericsson. (2019). "Mixed Reality for Public Participation in Urban and Public Space Design Towards a New Way of Crowdsourcing More Inclusive Smart Cities."	108
6.10:	Early 2018 case study involving student proposals in Oslo placed in a real-world context through AR. Source: author.	109
6.11:	Case study work on AR for participatory planning in Oslo, 2020–21. Source: author.	111
6.12:	Case study work on AR for participatory planning in Oslo, 2020–21. Source: author.	113
6.13:	Geofencing illustration. Source: Argustracking. Last accessed June 21, 2021.	115
7.1:	Realtime Car Parking. Credit: David Schwarzman and Ian Nazareth.	128
7.2:	Realtime Car Speeds. Image Credit: David Schwarzman and Ian Nazareth.	129
7.3:	Melbourne Functional Mix. Image Credit: David Schwarzman and Ian Nazareth.	131
7.4:	Realtime Crowd Sensing. Image Credit: David Schwarzman and Ian Nazareth.	132
7.5:	Rearranging a Liveable City. Image Credit: Chaitali Bhanushali, Harshitha Mruthyunjaya and Shalome Pinto with Ian Nazareth and David Schwarzman, Firmware 2020.	134

7.6:	Urban Performance Measures. Image Credit: Zecong Tan, Mengzhen Li and Tszto Leung with Ian Nazareth and David Schwarzman, Firmware 2020.	135
7.7:	Pestilential Cities. Image Credit: Tess Nettlefold, Matthew Samson, and Michael Cuccovia with Ian Nazareth and David Schwarzman, Firmware 2020.	136
8.1:	Former site of Backstreet, now a strip club across from auto repair shop, 2019. Source: Patricia Silva Studio.	144
8.2:	Historic photograph, circa 1980, site of a Queer disco on Route 25A. Copyright: New York City Department of Records and Information Services.	149
8.3:	World's Fair Marina grounds, 2015 and 2019. Source: Patricia Silva Studio.	150
8.4:	Site of the 1969 vigilante attack, 2018. Source: Patricia Silva Studio.	151
8.5:	Public park south of World's Fair grounds, 2020. Source: Patricia Silva Studio.	152
8.6:	Near remnants of Vanderbilt Parkway, 2017. Source: Patricia Silva Studio.	155
9.1:	Options for urban commutes and multi-modal mobility. Marco Zilvetti, 2021.	165
9.2:	SAE levels of vehicle automation (adapted from SAE J3016 levels of automation for on-road vehicles). Marco Zilvetti, 2021.	167
9.3:	Visual comparison between the urban assemblage of Milan (left) and London (right). Marco Zilvetti, 2021.	169
9.4:	Research project process. Marco Zilvetti, 2021.	169
9.5:	Key future urban mobility insights in Milan and London (as derived from the expert interviews). Marco Zilvetti, 2021.	171
9.6:	Priorities in car design R&D for the foreseeable future (as derived from the expert interviews). Marco Zilvetti, 2021.	172
9.7:	Key aspects about car-sharing design (as derived from the expert interviews). Marco Zilvetti, 2021.	173
9.8:	Key insights about ideal shared driverless cars (as derived from the survey). Marco Zilvetti, 2021.	175

FIGURES

9.9:	Relevance of key interior design features for 2030 driverless cars in Milan and London (as derived from the survey). Marco Zilvetti, 2021.	176
9.10:	Examples of multisensorial mood-boards showing designers' insights through keywords and multiple images collected by participants. Marco Zilvetti, 2021.	177
9.11:	Key features and types of driverless vehicles in 2030. Marco Zilvetti, 2021.	178
9.12:	Information about respondents to the survey and travel habits. Marco Zilvetti, 2022.	180
9.13:	Key insights about vehicle preferences and use (as per survey). Marco Zilvetti, 2022.	181
10.1:	North Oak Sign in Night City of the game *Cyberpunk 2077*. CD Projekt Red, 2020.	189
10.2:	Japantown in Night City of the game *Cyberpunk 2077*. CD Projekt Red, 2020.	194
10.3:	The location of different neighbourhoods on the elevation of Night City. Graphic created by the author. Pictures credited to CD Projekt Red, 2020.	196
10.4:	The processed reality seen by the protagonist "V." Screenshot from the game *Cyberpunk 2077*. CD Projekt Red, 2020.	199
11.1:	Parkour athlete jumping over a gap while recording with an FPV camera in their mouth, 2021. Image used with permission from the copyright holder. Source: Scott Bass.	209
11.2:	Parkour athlete using a 360-degree camera to record a line, 2021. Image used with permission from the copyright holder.	210
12.1:	A panorama of Melbourne's Federation Square, 2020. Author's photo.	223
13.1:	Visual diagram of Phygital space, and the dissection of physical interaction, digital interaction, and the intersection of physical and digital within the festival landscape. Rebecca Onafuye, 2021.	246
13.2:	Mapping of physical interaction within the festival landscape. Rebecca Onafuye, 2021.	246

13.3:	Exploded visual of phygital space. Rebecca Onafuye, 2021.	247
14.1 a–c:	(a) Pinterest, "Elements of Cohesive Home: 80's Pop / Farmhouse," n.d. © Airbnb Incorporated. (b) Pinterest, "Tips for arranging a living room," n.d. © Airbnb Incorporated. (c) Pinterest, "Tips for styling a mental / Three ways to style a credenza," n.d. © Airbnb Incorporated.	257
14.2 a–c:	(a) Pinterest, "Arranging art over a couch / Three ways to hang art over beds," n.d. © Airbnb Incorporated. (b) Pinterest, "Tips for styling couch pillows," n.d. © Airbnb Incorporated. (c) Pinterest, "Easy upgrade: couch legs / Tips for hanging curtains," n.d. © Airbnb Incorporated.	259
14.3 a–c:	(a) Pinterest, "Design Essentials	Visual Impact: Alternative art [left] / Find art everywhere [right]," n.d. © Airbnb Incorporated. (b) Pinterest, "Design Essentials	Quality Materials: Paint with paper / Groundwork," n.d. © Airbnb Incorporated.	261
14.4 a–c:	(a) Pinterest, "Design Essentials	Personality: Elements of surprise / Gallery wall," n.d. © Airbnb Incorporated. (b) Pinterest, "Bare to Plus / Bedroom," n.d. © Airbnb Incorporated.	262
14.5:	Duygun, "Airbnb Plus Filters: Interior Fragments," 2021, Ankara. © Airbnb Incorporated.	264
15.1:	Duved's main street and centre, 2009. Photo: Matti Paavola (CC).	269
15.2:	Demographic change in Åre municipality per administrative unit (2012–17) with Duved part of the third set. Åre kommun, 2017.	270
15.3:	"Places I use a lot" and "places I avoid" in the Duved-Åre valley. Maps by Ann Legeby, 2021.	271

Introduction

Silvio Carta

Physical and Digital

The relationship between the physical and the digital within the urban context has been extensively studied and debated over the past decades. In particular, the idea of Urban Assemblages[1,2] has gradually come to the fore in key areas of urban studies, architecture, and human geography. The theoretical framework of the assemblage theory[3] applied to the physical–digital relationship suggests that cities today can be read through the lens of a flat ontology:[4] a system by which there is no hierarchy between what is physical and what is digital.[5] The physical and digital are continuously interconnected and their extent is always evolving and mutating, as they are the complex result of the ongoing relationships amongst open systems.[6] The main forces behind this continuous shaping of the urban environment are data and information technologies.

Invisible Forces

Intangible factors in the city pose different difficulties, whereas tangible forces like buildings, roads, and infrastructure are easily apparent and architects and designers are well-trained to observe their qualities using conventional methods of architectural study. It is common practice to ignore invisible forces such as power dynamics, societal conventions, cultural beliefs, or, more especially for this study, data and information technology. These imperceptible factors are fundamental in forming the urban environment and can significantly affect how people perceive and engage with their surroundings.

The urban environment has been profoundly altered by the growth of data and information technologies. Such influences are now pervasive in today's urban scene, from smart cities to intelligent transportation systems. However, to city dwellers, they are frequently unseen.

Cities can now gather and evaluate enormous volumes of data on everything from traffic patterns to energy consumption thanks to information technologies.

This information can be used to guide decision-making, enabling city planners to choose more wisely how to distribute resources and plan infrastructure. Cities might, for instance, use data on traffic patterns to enhance their transport networks, resulting in less congestion and more system efficiency. To improve city services and raise citizen involvement, smart cities use data from numerous sources, including traffic sensors, weather stations, and social media. Smart cities, for instance, employ data to optimize waste management, lower energy use, and improve public safety.

We examine a number of ideas that support the notion of visible and unseen forces in the city within the context of this book. More precisely, we are examining the direct and/or indirect effects that unseen drivers have on urban physical features. Perhaps the smart city, which evolved as a result of the explosion of data and information technology, is the broader concept that comes to mind. These technologies are used by smart cities to gather data on a variety of urban issues, such as energy use and air pollution, in an effort to make cities more sustainable and productive. These data can be used by smart cities to optimize their waste management, transportation, and energy systems. In order to optimize their routes and cut down on pointless journeys, waste management firms can, for instance, utilize sensors to identify when trash cans are full.

The way that cities function has changed as a result of data-driven approaches to the urban environment. They have made it possible to gather, analyse, and share massive volumes of data in real-time, which has improved sustainability, safety, and efficiency. DITs are used, for instance, by smart transportation systems to optimize traffic flow, lessen congestion, and improve safety. Intelligent transportation systems use information from sensors and cameras to track traffic patterns, spot congested locations, and modify the timing of traffic signals to ease congestion.

Transportation and mobility have a direct impact on smart cities. Urban transport networks have been significantly impacted by data and information technologies. The introduction of ride-sharing services like Uber and Lyft has revolutionized how individuals get about urban areas. These apps make transport more effective and convenient by using data to optimize routes and decrease wait times. With the aim of lowering carbon emissions and enhancing safety, the usage of electric and autonomous vehicles is also growing in popularity.

Mobility and transport are closely related in smart cities. Transport systems in metropolitan areas have been greatly impacted by data and information technologies. The way individuals move around cities has changed as a result of the adoption of ride-sharing apps like Uber and Lyft. By using data to optimize routes and shorten wait times, these apps improve the effectiveness and convenience of transportation. In addition, the usage of electric and driverless vehicles

INTRODUCTION

is expanding, with the intention of lowering carbon emissions and enhancing safety.

An improved understanding of energy use and communication (the exchange of data across many systems) is inextricably related to a smart city. Cities were able to optimize energy consumption, lowering expenses and having a smaller negative impact on the environment. Smart grid technologies, for instance, can be used to control energy distribution, enabling more effective and consistent energy delivery. In addition, the use of sensors and data analytics can aid in pinpointing locations with high energy demand, enabling tailored interventions to lower energy consumption. Similar to smart homes, smart buildings maximize energy use and cut costs. They monitor and manage a variety of systems, including lighting, heating, and cooling, using sensors and other data collection tools. Building managers can use this to optimize energy use, cut costs, and maintain ideal interior conditions.

Communication in metropolitan areas has also changed as a result of data and information technology. Real-time communication and cooperation are now possible thanks to the use of social media platforms and messaging applications. Additionally, more and more people are using digital platforms to participate in decision-making processes, enabling inclusive and transparent governance.

However, privacy issues are also brought up by the gathering and use of data. The widespread use of surveillance tools like CCTV cameras and facial recognition software has sparked concerns about how data is used and how it might be abused. As algorithms may be trained on biased data, the use of data in decision-making can also result in bias and discrimination.

The requirements and viewpoints of diverse populations must be taken into account for the creation of smart cities and data-driven urban planning. Future cities must be accessible and valuable to all residents, and inclusive design is essential to achieving this. Diversity must be taken into account at all stages of the design process, including data collecting, algorithm development, and technology implementation. This is known as inclusive design. For instance, there have been questions regarding the possibility of racial prejudice in the use of facial recognition technologies. In order to ensure that the technology is accurate and objective, inclusive design would entail testing it on a variety of groups.

Similar to this, the creation of smart cities should take into account the requirements and viewpoints of various groups in order to guarantee that the technologies are available to and helpful for all residents.

The creation of technology that can increase citizen participation and engagement in urban systems is another important field. In order to make sure that urban systems are usable and helpful to larger communities, citizen engagement is essential.

Data and information technology have developed into an invisible force that has a wide range of effects on urban environments. These technologies are altering how we interact with our cities in all areas, from communication and transportation to energy use and trash disposal. The utilization of data and information technologies will become even more crucial as cities continue to expand and face new problems in building efficient, sustainable, and liveable urban environments. However, it is crucial to understand that these technologies have limitations and that there may be risks and drawbacks to using them. As a result, it is crucial to carefully analyse the effects of data and information technologies in urban settings and to make sure they are used in an ethical and responsible way.

Thinkers vs. Doers

These forces or agencies are studied by a growing number of researchers and designers internationally and the work done so far on the subject can often be categorized in two main groups: those who observe, theorize and offer new understating of how cities are evolving (theorists, human and urban geographers, and sociologists); and those who concentrate on application of methods and models to actual design (computational designers, data scientists, urban analysts and, increasingly, architects and urban designers). In general terms, while designers involved in implementing projects on the ground are actively changing our cities, from the urban scale to the building, their engagement with the analytic and speculative work of theory is often limited. As a result, the theoretical frameworks and notions developed in the conceptual realm are not very often translated into spatial terms and, consequently, there are few projects to date through which to understand the relationship between the theory and application of "assemblage" in the urban context.

This book responds to this current gap in the field by presenting essays that combine theoretical studies and practical applications and whose case studies can be seen as operative across different spatial scales, from territories and cities to buildings and interiors. In doing so, it offers a fluid approach where theory and practice are presented as a whole and concepts such as De Landa's assemblage theory and Marston's flat ontology are directly linked to "concrete" applications and practices in the city, including digital zoning, hybrid physical and digital retail, autonomous vehicles, digital placemaking, phygital spaces, and more. Through this combination of theory and practice, the book offers a direct way to bridge the gap between academics and scholars and designers and practitioners, in the context of digital and physical city.

INTRODUCTION

Book Structure

This work is organized in three sections where we gradually take the readers from general considerations of space (Section I—Space), through urban questions (Section II—City Space) to finally address physical and digital aspects at the building scale (Section III—Building Space). The idea is to present a variety of positions and perspectives on urban space gradually moving from broad spatial concepts to applications to cities and buildings, combining theoretical stances with case studies.

In Section I, David Capener explores the idea of Production of Space in an age of Planetary Computation (Chapter 1), discussing the importance of well-established thinkers like Lefebvre and Stiegler and the production of space. Toby Reed (Chapter 2—Screenness) is concerned with the analysis of the screen as an architectural and media device, to understand if the screen can be used to shed light on the ideological/spatial implications of the contemporary wall/surface. In their "Mood-Sensitive Spaces: Inspiration from Ambient Assisted Living and Affective Computing" (Chapter 3), Liz Felton explores the intersection between affective, pervasive computing and techniques from ambient-assisted living to create mood-sensitive spaces that adapt to the betterment of their inhabitants. Finally, in Chapter 4 Hüsnü Yegenoglu and Justin Agyin ("Smooth Invisible: Liquid Surveillance and Architecture") offer an account on accurate interpretation of urban surveillance and the aesthetics that characterized it.

In Section II David Harris Smith, Frauke Zeller, Emily Eyles, John Eyles, Debora Silva De Jesus, and Calvin Hillis describe a theoretical, interdisciplinary framework for mediated participatory urban planning and design in "Mediated Participatory Urban Planning and Design: An Interdisciplinary Framework" (Chapter 5). Next, in "Digital Zoning—In the Age of Surveillance Capitalism, Can Urban Planning help Regulate Technology?" (Chapter 6), Kai Reaver elaborates on the term "Digital Zoning" discussing the use of urban planning procedures as a form of technology regulation. In Chapter 7 "Pattern Recognition—The Big Smart Transactional City," Ian Nazareth and David Schwarzman explore a concrete case study that deals with urban patterns. Their project is empowered by a process of data scraping—where geo-referenced information and data from web-based Application Programming Interfaces (APIs) is extracted into design environments. In Chapter 8 "Outsmarting the City—How Queer Subcultures in Queensborough Used Public Infrastructure for Community, Cruising, and Queering Car Culture, 1890–2000," Patricia Silva examines—through photography—LGBTQ subculture as an undercurrent of "smart city" networks from 1890 to 2000 in a working-class section of New York City. Marco Zilvetti and Matteo Conti, in their "The Influence of Artificial Intelligence on Autonomous Vehicle Design and Users'

Lifestyle within Responsive Urban Environments" (Chapter 9) suggest a set of key recommendations for the design of the next generation autonomous vehicles (AVs) which are founded on human-centred research and design principles rather than on the systematic implementation of cutting-edge information and communication technologies (ICTs). Finally, in Chapter 10 "Understanding Postmetropolis in the Latest Virtual City: Urban Analysis of Night City in *Cyberpunk 2077*," Yulin Li explores the significance of the Night City: a virtual environment of the video game *Cyberpunk 2077* released in September 2020, for the contemporary city.

Section III starts with "Parkour, the City, and Mediated Subjectivities" (Chapter 11), where Fidelia Lam analyses instances of parkour media that utilize digital technologies to capture media assemblages of bodies and architecture, focusing on how various cameras as sensors are deployed at and imply multiple levels of scale and distance in relation to both bodies and architectures. Isabel Fangyi Lu in Chapter 12 ("Apple Town Square: Digital Placemaking and Digital Transformation of Urban Public Space") argues that re-understanding the contemporary urban governance needs to account for both the affordances of the sociotechnical assemblage and the various modes of public participation. In doing so, her chapter contributes to a contextualized discussion concerning the duality between structure and agency, as well as the relational and the territorial features of urban public spaces. Rebecca Onafuye with "Phygital Spaces" (Chapter 13) suggests that phygital space is socially produced, whilst providing a means to bridge between the physical and the digital space which are made up of symbolic socio-cultural representations. Esra Duygun and Duygu Koca in Chapter 14—"Airbnb Plus Filter: Creating Strategic and Photogenic Interiors" discuss the interiors of Airbnb properties to see whether they affect the design process, content and context of the future interior spaces. Lastly, in his "The Smart City in the Smaller Context" (Chapter 15), Daniel Koch discusses the case of Duved in Sweden, where a research and innovation project has been developed as a way to explore the relationship between local buildings and smart technologies.

Future Cities

With the development of digital technology, the urban environment has undergone a profound upheaval that has had a significant impact on how people live, work, and interact there. Innovative urban applications, smart cities, and complex urban infrastructures that offer new opportunities for urban planning, design, and management have all been made possible by digital technologies. In this regard, *The Physical and the Digital City* presents a singular selection of initiatives and ideas that investigate the nexus between digital technology and the urban setting.

INTRODUCTION

Researchers and designers who looked into the spatial and practical ramifications of the technological ideas that support the digital urban environment collaborated to create this book. The ideas and projects discussed in the book address a wide variety of subjects, including the design of smart structures and intelligent transportation systems as well as the development of interactive public spaces and immersive urban experiences. The book stands out for its attention to the point where the physical and digital worlds converge, portraying them as an ever-more-entwined and entangled sort of assemblage.

The book's emphasis on the practical application of academic principles is one of its key contributions. In designing and implementing digital urban infrastructures, the authors demonstrate how theories of technology like actor-network theory, posthumanism, and assemblage theory can be implemented. The book argues that an in-depth knowledge of the social, cultural, and economic settings in which they are employed is necessary for the successful integration of digital technologies into urban environments. The authors contend that rather than being objective instruments, digital technologies are entangled in intricate social and political relationships that influence how they are used and how they affect the urban environment.

The book's second major issue is the contested nature of urban digital assemblages. The authors paint a picture of how integrating digital technology into urban environments is not a simple process, but rather one that entails negotiation and struggle between various parties with opposing interests and beliefs. The book examines how social and environmental sustainability can be promoted by digital technologies, as well as how these technologies can worsen inequality and exclusion. In order to ensure that digital urban infrastructures are inclusive, democratic, and responsive to the needs and ambitions of all parts of society, it is crucial to involve a variety of stakeholders in their design and implementation, as is stressed in the articles that are provided in the pages that follow.

The significance of design in influencing the digital urban environment is also highlighted in *The Physical and the Digital City*. It becomes clear from the studies and projects given here that design involves more than just building things or spaces for aesthetic purposes; it also involves reshaping social relations and power structures. They demonstrate how design can be used to encourage innovation and creativity, to support social and environmental sustainability, and to give communities the capacity to create their own urban settings. Numerous case examples are included in the book to show how design may be utilized to develop inclusive and sustainable digital urban environments.

Overall, *The Physical and the Digital City* underlines the contested character of digital urban assemblages and provides a unique viewpoint on the spatial and practical implications of the technological ideas underlying the digital urban

environment. In addition, the book emphasizes how design influences the digital urban environment and offers various case studies that show how design can be applied to develop inclusive and sustainable digital urban environments. This book is a significant resource for anybody interested in the future of urban environments in the digital era, and we think that readers from a wide range of disciplines, including urban planning, architecture, design, sociology, and computer science, will find it important.

NOTES

1. Ignacio Farías and Thomas Bender, eds. *Urban Assemblages: How Actor–Network Theory Changes Urban Studies.* (Abingdon, UK: Routledge, 2012).
2. R. Kitchin et al., *Data and the City* (Abingdon, UK: Routledge, 2017), 1–13.
3. M. DeLanda, "Deleuzian Social Ontology and Assemblage Theory." In *Deleuze and the Social*, eds. M. Fuglsang. and B. M. Sørensen (Edinburgh: Edinburgh University Press, 2006), 250–66.
4. S. A. Marston et al. "Human Geography without Scale," *Transactions of the Institute of British Geographers* 30, no. 4 (2005): 416–32.
5. Kim Dovey and Mirjana Ristic "Mapping Urban Assemblages: The Production of Spatial Knowledge," *Journal of Urbanism: International Research on Placemaking and Urban Sustainability* 10, no. 1 (2017): 16.
6. S. Carta, *Big Data, Code and the Discrete City: Shaping Public Realms* (Abingdon, UK: Routledge, 2019), 61.

BIBLIOGRAPHY

Carta, S. *Big Data, Code and the Discrete City: Shaping Public Realms.* Abingdon, UK: Routledge, 2019.

DeLanda, M. "Deleuzian Social Ontology and Assemblage Theory." In *Deleuze and the Social*, edited by M. Fuglsang. and B. M. Sørensen, 250–66. Edinburgh: Edinburgh University Press, 2006.

Dovey, Kim, and Mirjana Ristic. "Mapping Urban Assemblages: The Production of Spatial Knowledge." *Journal of Urbanism: International Research on Placemaking and Urban Sustainability* 10, no. 1 (2017): 15–28.

Farías, Ignacio, and Thomas Bender, eds. *Urban Assemblages: How Actor–Network Theory Changes Urban Studies.* Abingdon, UK: Routledge, 2012.

Kitchin, R., T. P. Lauriault, and G. McArdle. *Data and the City*, 1–13. Abingdon, UK: Routledge, 2017.

Marston, S. A., J. P. Jones III, and K. Woodward. "Human Geography without Scale." *Transactions of the Institute of British Geographers* 30, no. 4 (2005): 416–32.

1

Good Game Peace Out

David Capener

Introduction

This chapter argues that the processes of urbanization have reached a new stage—the infrasomatic city. The infrasomatic city foregrounds the way that contemporary digital technologies are producing new multi-scalar circuits between the body and the infrastructures of everyday life.[1] I propose that a technology central to the infrasomatic city is automated image production which is increasingly operating below the threshold of human perception. I suggest that these technologies call into question the extent to which, what Henri Lefebrve called the right to the city, is possible. This is so because I propose that our access to the world is always-already technologically mediated and that any "suspension of the world, of the thesis of the world, that is, of the spontaneous belief in the existence of the world," can only take place through changes in the systems of retention and representation by and through which we access the world and the world increasingly accesses us.[2] Thus, technics is the condition of the world and technological representations of the world are the condition of our experience of everyday life. Our only access to the world are representations of it and those representations are now technologically mediated in ways that have fundamentally changed what an image is and does. A new human–machine "collaboration" is at play where production consumption and circulation become mixed up "to the point of becoming indistinguishable."[3] Therefore, I suggest that the extent to which the right to the *infrasomatic city* is curtailed is a question of how an algorithmic logic of visualization produces everyday life.

I interpret the right to the city as being the right to the production of spaces. The right to the production of spaces is the right to the production of spaces of difference—spaces that are not "abstract space."[4] The right to the city is the antithesis of abstract space. The logic of abstract spatial production is optical and geometric—these are two terms in Lefebvre's underexplored triadic of abstract

space: optical/geometric/phallic. The question of the extent to which the right to the city is curtailed is also a question of the extent to which an adequate methodology is possible by which these complex entanglements might be understood. I argue that one such adequate methodology is a multi-dimensional reading of Lefebvre's triadic of spatial production.

I propose that my advancement of the triadics of spatial production offer a multi-dimensional reading that could be useful as a methodology for understanding the complex entanglements of spatial production in the infrasomatic city and the multiple levels upon which they operate. This is so because to understand the extent that the right to the city is curtailed in the infrasomatic city is to understand the multi-scalar entanglements across which technologies of algorithmic image production operate—I argue that my reading of the triadic does this. I propose that one-dimensional conceptions of space will not suffice nor will linear conceptions of scale as a means by which this new logic of visualization—which I argue is the predominant characteristic of our technological epoch—might be understood. A non-linear simultaneity of space and scale is required to understand the ways that the processes of algorithmic image production operate simultaneously at scales of neurological flows to planetary scale data infrastructure and multiple other scales. An example of these processes can be found in the deployment of a predictive algorithm called Good Game Peace Out (GGPO) deployed in some online one-on-one fighting games. This example is useful for my argument as it foregrounds how algorithms of automated image production are producing new logics of visualization in the form of automated representations of space which, following Lefebvre I understand, are central to the production of abstract space.

Automated Representations of Space

In one frame of a typical fighting game like *Mortal Kombat* a lot happens. In approximately the 16 milliseconds duration of a frame, a circuit of information is computed. Players are asked for inputs, the network is checked for new information, AI is used to run CPU players, characters are animated, the current game state is assessed—who is getting hit? What move have they just made? If latency drops then this circuit is interrupted and gameplay is affected. If two players are playing locally then delay is not an issue. However, when two players are playing over the internet then the game needs to account for network instability. Simply put, the information from one player's input will take time to travel through the network and arrive at the other player whose input will take time to travel back. The distance between two players is measured in ping which is the round trip of information from one player to another and back again. For example, at the time of writing the ping time between Dublin

and Boston is 84.35 milliseconds.[5] This means that a packet of data will travel the 9,620 km round trip between Dublin and Boston in 0.08 seconds.

For ease let's assume that Dublin to Boston ping time is 90 milliseconds. This means that, on average, it will take a packet of data 45 milliseconds to travel from Dublin to Boston. Assuming that this is represented with a 16-millisecond framerate, this would mean that three-game frames will have elapsed by the time a packet of data leaves Dublin and lands in Boston. This presents a problem. Central to the gameplay of any fighting game is speed. To play a fighting game well requires muscle memory, twitch reflexes, and very fast player reactions. The instability of networks means that information sent between players may be delayed, packets might drop or arrive in the wrong order. Network instability is unpredictable in ways that a game cannot predict. For fighting games, the instability of networks is a particular challenge. This game genre cannot function correctly without consistent latency. The question then is how does a game handle uncertainty?

Latency

Latency is particularly an issue in online gaming and can be the difference between winning and losing a match. This is because the threshold of human perception in gaming is much lower than it is for other mediums. For example, when watching online streaming content such as Netflix it is unlikely that a person would notice if the audio was out of sync with the video providing the delay is no less than 45 milliseconds or no more than 125 milliseconds. In fact, people will continue to watch the content even if the audio arrives 90 milliseconds early or 185 milliseconds too late. Likewise on YouTube, it is only if there is a delay of more than 250 milliseconds between clicking the pause button and the content pausing do we think that something has gone wrong. However, in online gaming, the threshold is significantly lower. Regular gamers will become frustrated with delays over 50 milliseconds, non-gamers at 110 milliseconds with games becoming unplayable at 150 milliseconds. In fact, weekly gameplay reduces by up to 6% if there is a 10-millisecond increase or decrease in latency. Networks require hardware and software solutions to try and overcome the volatility of latency.

Geopolitics of Latency

One such hardware solution (what Lefebrve would call a spatial practice) is the use of server regions that aim to minimize latency on a geographical basis.[6] Players are grouped together into geographical regions—for example, Western Europe,

Midwest America, and Southeast Asia—thereby minimizing latency. For example, in online play in the car racing game *Mario Kart 8*, players can select to race against other players in their "region" or "globally."[7] From experience, when racing globally latency spikes occur regularly, the game ends and a screen is displayed stating that a "communication error has occurred."[8] The glitching of games like *Mario Kart 8* is at one level relatively inconsequential yet at another level reveals the complex infrastructural entanglements of the geopolitics of latency.

The geographical distribution of server regions is a geopolitical issue. According to the developer Subspace "three quarters of all internet connections in the Middle East are outside playable latency levels for dynamic multiplayer games," compared to a quarter in the United States and Europe.[9] This is not simply a matter of server location nor an issue of broadband connection but of a global disparity of speed. For example, it is predicted that in Latin America, by 2026, "44% of the population will have access to fixed broadband services […] but only 5.3% will be on a connection delivering 500Mbps or more, and only 1% will have speeds of more than 1Gbps."[10] Hardware solutions that attempt to overcome the volatility of latency are geopolitical but in the infrasomatic city must also be thought infrasomatically. To think the volatility of latency infrasomatically is to understand it not simply as a geopolitics of the earth but as a geopolitics of the body. The infrasomatic nature of latency as geopolitics of the body can be seen in the following example of a software solution called Rollback Netcode deployed in some online one-on-one fighting games in the form of a predictive algorithm called GGPO.

GGPO

GGPO uses a delay-based netcode (e.g., a three-frame delay applied to both players) but to account for latency spikes that exceed the delay, Rollback allows the game to continue by predicting what the next move might be. For example, a player in Dublin inputs a command to punch their opponent, this appears on their opponent's screen three frames later and the game runs smoothly. However, what if there is a spike in latency and the players are now out of sync? The player in Dublin does not receive their opponent's next move. Rather than the game glitching or stopping, GGPO predicts what the player in Boston's move is going to be. The game continues with the predicted move. Five frames later the Boston-based player's move arrives in Dublin. If the prediction was correct the game continues. If the prediction was not correct the game rolls back five frames and replays the move based on the actual input. In short, GGPO simulates gameplay predicting the future to adjust the past to change the present while maintaining a coherent experience of a temporal object.

GGPO does this by being able to convert objects in the computer's memory into a format that can save different game states and load them—this is called serialization. For Rollback Netcode to work successfully two things must be in place: serialization and the separation of game logic from game rendering. First, to be able to roll back and correct the game every single frame of gameplay must be serialized—converted into a storable stream of bytes that can be recalled and rendered when needed. Second, the game logic—simply put the code that runs the game—must be separated from the rendering of individual game frames. This means that in theory the game could continue to run without any of the gameplay being rendered and that at speeds below the threshold of human perception different game states and game logic are being continually simulated in the background.[11] Importantly, when the game rolls back to a frame where a prediction error was made what is seen on the screen is not a rendering of the actual move but a resimulation of a move that was previously made—importantly rollback is not rendering but resimulation of an actual past that was serialized but not rendered and is resimulated in the future in order to correct the past. This resimulation produces what Denson calls discorrelated images—images that operate below the threshold of human cognition calling into question the relationship of the subject and the object and therefore body-centric notions of phenomenology.[12]

Between the act of producing a representation of space in the form of image code and the representation of space itself as code image a space is opened out for image manipulation to take place at speeds that often operate below the threshold of human consciousness. In GGPO this discorrelation occurs mostly below the threshold of human perception. However, on the occasion where a significant spike in latency occurs and the game must roll back a number of frames some glitching can occur—a player who was predicted to be walking forward but had in fact stopped walking will suddenly jolt back and the gameplay will not appear smooth. In terms of gameplay, this glitching is usually inconsequential. While gameplay is usually unaffected, this glitching is useful as it foregrounds some processes that are important for my argument such as the realization of being caught up in a different and technically manufactured temporality. It also dispels the myth of the immateriality of the network, and foregrounds the entangled web of physical infrastructures and digital codes that facilitate the production of space.

The Crisis of Representation

Shane Denson describes this kind of automated image production as the migration of conventional forms of cinematic techniques, production and dissemination, analogue and digital, to "algorithms, software, networks and codecs."[13] These

shifts, and the new speeds at which these technologies operate, and the new perceptual regimes that they produce are transforming both the subject and the object. "[N]ew relations are being forged in the microtemporal intervals of algorithmic processing."[14] "With new objects of computational images emerge new subjectivities, new affects, and uncertain potentials for perception and action."[15] In the infrasomatic city, we have entered a new epoch of "the logic of visualization" and the logic of geometricization.[16] A logic whose history can be traced back to the advent of the Renaissance perspective gaze and the "algorithmic character" of Alberti's screen, but one whose logic has been fundamentally changed by the algorithmic automation of computational representation. This shift in the perspectival gaze is not simply one that produces a more efficient technological object for image production but produces an entirely new relationship between the viewing subject and the viewed. As Gaboury writes, "[t]he perspective that computer graphics offers is algorithmically rendered by a virtual camera decoupled from any connection with the embodied position of a viewing subject, let alone optics or the physical properties of light."[17] In computational representation "we find a new set of relations structured not by vision but instead by a theory of the nature of objects, a computational ontology for which the rendered image is only one of many possible expressions."[18] Kittler writes that

> [c]omputers must calculate all optical or acoustic data on their own precisely because they are born dimensionless and thus imageless. For this reason, images on computer monitors [...] do not reproduce any extant things, surfaces or space at all. They emerge on the surface of the monitor through the application of mathematical systems of equations.[19]

Unlike a hand-drawn image based on a single-point perspective, computational images exist "prior to their manifestation as a visible image."[20] They are nonphenomenological and can be "known" as code "prior to our perception of them."[21] Computational images are "decoupled from any connection with the embodied position of a viewing subject."[22] The fundamental basis of automated image production in our age of digital technology is the separation between the image as captured and the image as rendered. The image as captured is simulated, the image as rendered is a representation of that simulation. I suggest that it is the rupturing of the image away from its material substrate that opens images out to all manners of manipulation. As such, algorithms "defeat" our images "they pass through our human representations, categories, cosmetics, as if none of these even existed."[23]

This means that a fundamental break has occurred in the logic of visualization whereby "[c]omputer graphics is a medium engaged in a disavowal of its technical apparatus."[24] In short, this means that in order to produce a representation

"a graphical program must first produce a simulation of that scene [...] and then extract from that scene those parts that should be rendered visible."[25] In the infrasomatic city, it is between simulation and rendering that the possibility exists for the manipulation of images. As Hansen writes,

> [w]ith the material fruition of the form of computer vision [...] we witnessed a marked deprivileging of the particular perspectival image in favour of a total and fully manipulable grasp of the entire dataspace, the whole repertoire of possible images it could be said to contain.[26]

This logic of visualization and geometricization cannot be thought apart. The relationship between the two has taken on a new significance in our age of contemporary digital technology and has contributed to producing a "crisis of visibility" and a crisis of representation.[27] I suggest that this crisis of representation is a result of a fundamental change in the relationship between the visual and geometric which by following Lefebvre's triadic of abstract spatial production is a new logic of abstract space.

How then might we understand the production of space in an age marked by a crisis of representation? What kind of methodology might be capable of understanding the multiple scales—from neurological flows to planetary scale infrastructure—across which these technologies operate? I propose that one such methodology is my advancement of Henri Lefebvre's triadic of spatial production.

The Multi-Dimensional Triadic

The development of Lefebvre's triadic begins as early as his 1936 text *La Conscience Mystifiée* and ends with his final text *Rhythmanalysis* (1992). The two most well-known of the triadics are found in *The Production of Space*.[28] They are spatial practice/representations of space/spaces of representation and perceived/conceived/lived space.[29] In making a multi-dimensional reading of the triadic I stay with, go through and go beyond Lefebvre. I stay with Lefebvre by following his triadic method and understanding space as a multiplicity of processes that cannot be thought apart from each other. I go through Lefebvre by proposing a multi-dimensional reading of the triadics and conclude that to fully understand the three triadics that Lefebvre develops in *The Production of Space* one must read them through the prism of the four other triadics. I go beyond Lefebvre by proposing that while all terms of the triadic have equal value there are two terms and one triadic that in the context of automated image production in the infrasomatic city has particular relevance—representations of space, spatial practice, and the triadic

of abstract spatial production. Representations of space are images produced of or about space or images of proposals for interventions in space but, for Lefebvre, following Heidegger, representations of space are also representing-producing images. They do not just represent space but they also produce space. Spatial practice is the network of infrastructures such as communication networks, or networks of places such as the house, the workplace, or networks of finance, production and exchange. Abstract space is now introduced.

Automated Abstract Space

The sovereign ruler of capitalism produces a very particular kind of space, a space, without which it could not survive, this Lefebvre calls abstract space. Abstract space, writes Lefebvre, is "founded on the vast network of banks, business centres and major productive entities, as also on motorways, airports and information lattices."[30] In the infrasomatic city, these information lattices are the complex infrastructural entanglements that facilitate and mediate the supply chains of perception that produce and manipulate automated images. Extending Lefebvre's concept of spatial practice to the infrasomatic city it could be argued that our age is marked by a new kind of abstract space—algorithmically produced, automated abstract space.

In *The Production of Space* Lefebvre introduces the triadic of abstract spatial production. One rarely discussed in Lefebvre literature—geometric/phallic/optical.[31] This triadic is used to articulate the image-based, geometric, and ideological processes at play in the production of abstract space. Abstract space is a central concept in the production of space. It is "[t]he predominance of the visual (or more precisely of the geometric-visual-spatial)."[32] It is a coding of space, a "mesh thrown over society"—a Euclidian framework of cartesian coordinates, carving space up into measurable, calculable, and analysable space. In Heideggerian terms it is the "enframing" of space, the production of space as "standing reserve."[33] But this abstracting of space "was not arrived at without a struggle." It is a struggle for the abstraction of space as calculable, the visual representation of space, and the distribution of power in space, which is spatial practice.[34]

In the triadic of abstract space, the optical denotes a particular "logic of visualization" that is central to the production of abstract space. This logic is produced by certain representations of space which, following Martin Heidegger, do not just represent space but are "representing-producing" and as such produce abstract space.[35] The logic of geometricization that is central to the production of abstract space is produced when "lived space" is overcome by mental space that is based on the mathematical logic of Cartesian geometry which "reduces the world [...]

to a homogeneous grid where all that matters is the relative position of the centre, which in turn determines the value of each location."[36]

Lefebvre's primary argument was that capitalist societies produce abstract space. But how is this abstract space produced? Abstract space is produced when mental space becomes dominant over natural and social space.[37] Mental space is based on a mathematical logic that "reduces the world around us to a homogeneous grid where all that matters is the relative position of the centre, which in turn determines the value of each location."[38] The logic of abstract space is Cartesian geometry which is also the logic that underpins the entire prehistory of computer graphics from its earliest days with Martin Newell's "Utah Teapot" all the way to our age of the real-time algorithmic manipulation of images.[39]

For Lefebvre, these were the spatial practice infrastructures of early twentieth-century capitalism—planes, trains, automobiles, etc. Cartesian grid-space produced by the rational mathematical logic of capitalism. In our age of automated abstract space, real-time infrastructures, overcoming latency, and bandwidth in the name of reliability produce representations of space based on the same Cartesian principles. It was the "development of Cartesian coordinates of analytical geometry [that] made it possible to define points, lines, and shapes in abstract space using mathematical formulae."[40] These mathematically produced points, lines, and shapes which are abstract spatial configurations open to geometric modification are easily replicated in computer code and can therefore be graphically represented. The same Cartesian principles that were used to produce and render the Utah Teapot are the same that produce representations of everyday life. Everyday life is now lived through and mediated by automated image production to the extent that the line between the two is becoming increasingly blurred. These automated representations require that in the infrasomatic city we suspend "the visible as our primary mode of analysis."[41]

The Infrasomatic City

It is in the infrasomatic city where we are beginning to realize the possibilities that these kinds of automated images can be deployed in ways that produce new regimes and supply chains of perceptions. Infrastructural configurations of automated image production are creating new cognitive entanglements between technological infrastructures and the body. Therefore our current urban condition is marked by "social structuring technologies that inscribe new forms of the social (or sometimes the anti-social) onto the bodies and minds of humans" and create "cognitive infrastructures that proletarianize our cognitive faculties."[42] Infrasomatic infrastructures, suggests Berry, are "not just the production of tools or

instruments" but are "the production of constitutive infrastructures" that combine and produce "endosomatic capacities and exosomatic technics."[43] They are not simply the production and use of tools but rather fuse together "endosomatic capacities and exosomatic technics." This means that algorithmic infrastructures are not simply tools for acting in or upon the world, or indeed tools in the Stieglerian sense of technical prostheses but are themselves infrastructures that produce the very conditions for the possibility of thought and action.

The idea of the city as infrasomatic is not specific to our age of contemporary digital technologies. Spatial practices such as roads, rail networks, sewage systems, etc. entangled the body in new ways with technological infrastructures.[44] However, in our age of digital contemporary technology these entanglements have become increasingly more complex as algorithmic technologies are deployed in the form of techniques of urban governance—this, Antoinette Rouvroy (sometimes with Thomas Berns) calls algorithmic governmentality—the governance of "the social world that is based on the algorithmic processing of big data sets rather than on politics, law, and social norms."[45] Rouvroy follows Foucault's understanding of Governmentality as

> the ensemble formed by institutions, procedures, analyses and relections, calculations, and tactics that allow the exercise of [...] power that has the population as its target, political economy as its major form of knowledge, and apparatuses of security as its essential technological instrument.[46]

However with her concept of algorithmic governmentality Rouvroy wants to turn Foucault on his head and show that in algorithmic governmentality it is no longer a matter of producing docile bodies according to a norm, but of making the norms docile according to the body.[47] Thus algorithmic governmentality in this sense is infrasomatic.

Algorithmic governmentality is comprised of three stages. Firstly, the "collection and automated storage of unfiltered mass data." Secondly, "the automated processing of these big data to identify subtle correlations between them" which is "a matter of knowledge production." Thirdly, the deployment of data to "anticipate individual behaviours and associate them with profiles defined on the basis of correlations discovered through datamining."[48] Algorithms, like roads, rail networks, and sewage systems, are infrasomatic organs which are infrastructures that are increasingly becoming integral to the functioning of everyday life in the city.

As such algorithmic governance is, proposes Rouvroy, a matter of the "colonization of public space by a hypertrophied private sphere."[49] It colonizes public space by

"producing" peculiar subjectivities: fragmented, the subject comes in the form of a myriad of data that link him or her to a multitude of profiles (as a consumer, a potential fraudster, a more or less trustable and productive employee and so on).[50]

Therefore if algorithmic governance is a matter of the production of public and private space it is also a matter of the extent to which a right to the city is possible in the infrasomatic city.

Conclusions

The infrastructures of the infrasomatic city cannot be thought apart from the regimes of perception that they produce—the geopolitics of the body. Regimes of perception cannot be thought apart from the materiality of the infrastructures that facilitate them—spatial practices. The algorithmic processing of data in the form of automated image techniques that produce representations of space cannot be thought apart from the material forms of storage and the networks of transmission which cannot be thought apart from the body which must be thought alongside the volatility of networks and their associated geopolitics. I suggest that the complexity of the problem posed by our contemporary technological condition requires a multidisciplinary response which requires a methodology around which different disciplines can coalesce. I argue that one such methodology is a multi-dimensional reading of Henri Lefevre's triadic of spatial production.

NOTES

1. David Berry, "Infrasomatization, the Datanthropocene and the Negantropic University." Stunlaw, September 22, 2018. http://stunlaw.blogspot.com/2018/09/infrasomatization-and-datanthropocene_22.html; David Berry. "Against Infrasomatization, Towards a Critical Theory of Algorithms," in *Data Politics: Worlds, Subjects, Rights*, by Didier Bigo, Engin Isin, and Evelyn Ruppert (Oxford: Routledge, 2019), 48.
2. Bernard Stiegler, *Technics and Time: 2. Disorientation*, trans. Stephen Barker (Stanford: Stanford University Press, 2009), 22.
3. Hito Steyerl, "Too Much World: Is the Internet Dead?" in *The Flood of Rights*, by T. Keenan, S. Malik, and T. Zolghadr (Cambridge: MIT Press, 2015), 220.
4. Henri Lefebvre, *The Production of Space*, trans. Donald Nicholson-Smith (Malden, MA: Blackwell, 1991), 33, 49–53, 60.
5. "Global Ping Statistics." Wondernetwork, accessed March 30, 2022, https://wondernetwork.com/pings/Dublin.

6. "Networking and the Metaverse," Michael Ball, accessed March 30, 2022, https://www.matthewball.vc/all/networkingmetaverse/. Also see Nicole Starosielski, *The Undersea Network (Sign, Storage, Transmission)* (Durham: Duke University Press, 2015).
7. Nintendo. *Mario Kart 8*. Nintendo Entertainment Analysis & Development. 2014.
8. Ibid.
9. Joe O'Halloran, "Global Broadband Divide Is Closing but Speed Inequalities Widen." *Computer Weekly*, accessed May 3, 2022, https://www.computerweekly.com/news/252512375/Global-broadband-divide-is-closing-but-speed-inequalities-are-widening.
10. Ibid.
11. Ricky Pusch, "Explaining How Fighting Games Use Delay-Based and Rollback Netcode," *Ars Technica* (October 18, 2019), accessed June 2023, https://arstechnica.com/gaming/2019/10/explaining-how-fighting-games-use-delay-based-and-rollback-netcode/.
12. Shane Denson, *Discorrelated Images* (Durham: Duke University Press, 2020).
13. Ibid., 1.
14. Ibid.
15. Ibid.
16. Henri Lefebvre, *The Production of Space*, trans. Donald Nicholson-Smith (Malden, MA: Blackwell, 1991), 285–89.
17. Jacob Gaboury, *Image Objects: An Archaeology of Computer Graphics* (Boston, MA: MIT Press, 2021), 38.
18. Ibid.
19. Ibid., 36
20. Ibid., 38.
21. Ibid.
22. Ibid.
23. Antoinette Rouvroy, "Algorithmic Governmentality and the Death of Politics." *Green European Journal* (2020), https://www.greeneuropeanjournal.eu/algorithmic-governmentalityand-the-death-of-politics/.
24. Ibid.
25. Ibid.
26. Mark Hansen, *New Philosophy for New Media* (Cambridge: MIT Press, 2004), 95. See also Anne Friedberg, *Virtual Window* (Cambridge: MIT Press, 2006).
27. Gaboury, *Image Objects*, 36.
28. There is also a third underexplored triadic in *The Production of Space* which is the triadic of abstract spatial production. In Lefebvre literature, this triadic has been largely ignored. It appears that the only text which deals with this triadic in any significant way is Gardiner's *The Dictatorship of the Eye* (2012) where he explores the implications of what Lefebvre calls "the logic of visualization."

29. Henri Lefebvre, *The Production of Space*, trans. Donald Nicholson-Smith (Cambridge, MA: Blackwell, 1991), 38–39, https://d1wqtxts1xzle7.cloudfront.net/47828054/Lefebvre_Henri_The_Production_of_Space-libre.pdf?1470448871=&response-content-disposition=inline%3B+filename%3DThe_Production_of_Space.pdf&Expires=1697711104&Signature=YR2~SI3M1YeVQfjYCbV2XF1FtlQ-A6dsfV0UhxB
30. Ibid.
31. Michael E. Gardiner, "The 'Dictatorship of the Eye': Henri Lefebvre on Vision, Space and Modernity," in *The Handbook of Visual Culture*, by Ian Heywood and Barry Sandywell (London: Bloomsbury, 2012), 512.
32. Henri Lefebvre, *The Production of Space*, trans. Donald Nicholson-Smith (Malden, MA: Blackwell, 1991), 284.
33. In a world in which the panopticon has been replaced by the screens of social media, it would seem worthwhile to analyse the structure of the viewer/screen relationship to see if it sheds light on modern architectural surface and our experience of boundary. This is a constantly mutating and evolving situation. Although the cinema is dying fast, it can be instructive to go back to this modern primal scene to help understand the situation we are now in and how it has evolved.

    One of the first and most important writings about viewer/screen relations in the cinema is Jean-Louis Baudry's 1970 article "Ideological Effects of the Basic Cinematographic Apparatus." Baudry utilized a number of theoretical systems to help us understand our relationship to the screen, combining the diagrams of Plato's Cave (with Platonic metaphysics and representation) Jacques Lacan's psychoanalytic Mirror Stage, with Marxist ideology with semiotic theory. Baudry related how the false impression of movement of still images that appear to move relates to Marxist theories on the masking of difference and true social relations in order to create an impression that reinforces dominant ideology. Baudry's diagram exposes conscious and unconscious viewer/screen relations which can be explored in relation to architectural surface, politics, and power relations within society.
34. Ibid.
35. Martin Heidegger, "The Age of the World Picture", in *Martin Heidegger, Off the Beaten Track*, trans. and ed. Julian Young and Kenneth Haynes (Cambridge: Cambridge University Press, 2002), 57–85.
36. "The Production of Space, Urban Design Library #36." Urban Design Group, accessed May 3, 2022, https://www.udg.org.uk/publications/udlibrary/production-space.
37. Lefebvre, *The Production of Space*, 229–91.
38. "The Production of Space, Urban Design Library #36." Urban Design Group, accessed May 3, 2022, https://www.udg.org.uk/publications/udlibrary/production-space.
39. See Jacob Gaboury, *Image*.
40. Grant Tavinor, *The Aesthetics of Virtual Reality* (London: Routledge, 2022), 44.
41. Ibid., 195.

42. David Berry, "Infrasomatization." Berry, "Against Infrasomatization," 48.
43. David Berry, "Infrasomatization."
44. See David Berry, "Infrasomatization."
45. Antoinette Rouvroy, "Algorithmic Governmentality and the Death of Politics," *Green European Journal* (2020), https://www.greeneuropeanjournal.eu/algorithmic-governmentality-and-the-death-of-politics/. Last accessed October 19, 2023.
46. Michel Foucault, *Security, Territory, Population: Lectures at the Collège de France 1977–1978*, trans. Graham Burchell (New York: Palgrave Macmillan, 2007), 108.
47. Antoinette Rouvroy and Bernard Stiegler, "The Digital Regime of Truth: From the Algorithmic Governmentality to a New Rule of Law." *La Deleuziana—Online Journal of Philosophy*, no. 3 (2016).
48. Antoinette Rouvroy and Thomas Berns, trans. Liz Carey Libbrecht, "Algorithmic Governmentality and Prospects of Emancipation." *Reseaux* 117, no 1 (January 2013): 163–96.
49. Ibid. See also Rouvroy, "Algorithmic Governmentality."
50. Rouvroy and Stiegler, "The Digital Regime," 34, 6–29.

BIBLIOGRAPHY

Andermatt Conley, Verena. *Spatial Ecologies, Urban Sites, State and World-Space in French Cultural Theory*. Liverpool: Liverpool University Press, 2012.

Ball, Michael. "Networking and the Metaverse." Accessed March 30, 2022. https://www.matthewball.vc/all/networkingmetaverse.

Berry, David. "Infrasomatization." Accessed May 7, 2018. http://stunlaw.blogspot.com/2016/12/infrasomatization.html.

Berry, David. "Infrasomatization, the Datanthropocene and the Negantropic University." Accessed September 22, 2018. http://stunlaw.blogspot.com/2018/09/infrasomatization-and-datanthropocene_22.html.

Bigo, Didier, Engin Isin, and Evelyn Ruppert, eds. *Data Politics: Worlds, Subjects, Rights*. Oxford: Routledge, 2019.

Computer Weekly. "Global Broadband Divide Is Closing but Speed Inequalities Widen." Accessed May 3, 2022. https://www.computerweekly.com/news/252512375/Global-broadband-divide-is-closing-but-speed-inequalities-are-widening.

Crang, Mike, and Nigel Thrift, eds. *Thinking Space*. London: Routledge, 2000.

Denson, Shane. *Discorrelated Images*. Durham: Duke University Press, 2022.

Gaboury, Jacob. *Image Objects: An Archaeology of Computer Graphics*. Boston: MIT Press, 2021.

Goonewardena, Kanishka, Stefan Kipfer, Richard Milgram, and Christian Schmid, eds. *Space, Difference, Everyday Life: Reading Henri Lefebvre*. New York: Routledge, 2008.

Hansen, Mark. *New Philosophy for New Media*. Cambridge: MIT Press, 2004.

Heidegger, Martin. *Off the Beaten Track*. Translated and edited by Julian Young and Kenneth Haynes. Cambridge: Cambridge University Press, 2002.

Heywood, Ian, and Barry Sandywell, eds. *The Handbook of Visual Culture*. London: Bloomsbury, 2012.

Keenan, Thomas, S. Malik, and T. Zolghadr, eds. *The Flood of Rights*. Cambridge: MIT Press, 2015.

Kittler, Fredrich. *Optical Media*. Translated by Anthony Enns. Cambridge: Polity, 2010.

Lefebvre, Henri. *The Production of Space*. Cambridge: Blackwell, 1991.

Pusch, Ricky. "Explaining How Fighting Games Use Delay-Based and Rollback Netcode." Accessed April 10, 2022. https://arstechnica.com/gaming/2019/10/explaining-how-fighting-games-use-delay-based-and-rollback-netcode.

Rouvroy, Antoinette. "Algorithmic Governmentality and the Death of Politics." Accessed June 1, 2021. https://www.greeneuropeanjournal.eu/algorithmic-governmentality-and-the-death-of-politics.

Rouvroy, Antoinette, and Bernard Stiegler. "The Digital Regime of Truth: From the Algorithmic Governmentality to a New Rule of Law." *La Deleuziana—Online Journal of Philosophy*, no. 3 (2016): 6–29

Rouvroy, Antoinette, and Thomas Berns. "Algorithmic Governmentality and Prospects of Emancipation." *Reseaux* 177, no. 1 (2013): 163–96.

Stiegler, Bernard. *Technics and Time: 2. Disorientation*. Translated by Stephen Barker, Stanford: Stanford University Press, 2009.

Tavinor, Grant. *The Aesthetics of Virtual Reality*. London: Routledge, 2022.

Urban Design Group. "The Production of Space, Urban Design Library #36." Accessed May 3, 2022. https://www.udg.org.uk/publications/udlibrary/production-space.

Wondernetwork. "Global Ping Statistics." Accessed March 30, 2022. https://wondernetwork.com/pings/Dublin.

2

Screenness

Toby Reed

Enter the Cathode Ray

If our constant exposure to screens over the last 125 years has had a deep impact on our optic subconscious (as Walter Benjamin might have put it), then one of those sub-optic influences must be on our relation to objects and space, including surface, image, and form. This chapter attempts to explore the influence of the cinematic apparatus and particularly the screen, on our experience (and the design) of space, objects, and surface. The primary condition of the wall, and the spaces they traditionally enclose, once the solid spatial boundary of architecture and the city, through the influence of media and particularly the screen, have slowly dissolved into a state of what could be termed as "screenness."

The effects are twofold: first, architects were influenced by the screen and the screen apparatus to produce new screen-like architectural surface and space. Second, our constant exposure to screens in all their mutations has likely changed our spatial and surface conditioning so we experience surface, space, objects, and the city in different ways.

What are the characteristics of the screen and our relation to screens that can help explain our current spatial/surface relations in the contemporary city: false movement and cinematic spatial depth on a paper-thin screen? Can an analysis of the screen and the cinematic apparatus that produced it shed light on the spatiality of the contemporary city and the ideological implications of the wall and surface?

This is a cinematic journey through architectural space, exploring some of the screen's influences as they have affected architecture since the advent of the cinema, and how architects have responded to these new spatial possibilities, as well as how our conditioning and proximity to media may have influenced the way we experience everyday space, surface, and objects.

This investigation began through an expanded practice that includes writing film and architectural theory, the production of video works, and (primarily) the design

of architectural projects. Slowly noting the effects that one has upon the other has allowed for an analysis of this situation in a theoretical manner but at the same time note the very real effects and influences of the screen and its offspring upon the everyday design process, noting how the influence of the screen has permeated every aspect of the design of our environment, particularly space, surface, and objects.

The End of the Wall

The wall as a defined boundary has for a long time been mutating towards a state of screenness. Until recently, the construction of the Berlin Wall in 1961 would have appeared to be the last symbolic gasp of the dying concept of the wall as a solid boundary. Although this concept persists, its conditions have changed. For most of the twentieth century, the wall has been slowly mutating towards new conditions in which the once-solid wall becomes permeable or semi-transparent and more screen-like, or even a zone of surveillance. This is a transformation that is parallel to the growing proliferation and influence of the screen within our everyday environment. Both the wall and screen share certain qualities and effects. To understand the contemporary surface/wall we must also understand the screen in all its manifestations.

The screen is like a black hole in our living room (Figure 2.1). It brings far away space (and spatial morphologies) and alternate time zones into close proximity, causing a perceptual space-time disjuncture into our living room via the flat-screen television on the wall.

FIGURE 2.1: A diagram of a classic TV screen as a black hole vortex to alternate time and spatiality, causing space–time disjuncture in everyday life. Toby Reed, 2003–14.

Besides the materiality of the wall transforming, its function has also been affected by and sometimes taken over by the camera. Because of this, the wall as a signifier has mutated in various ways, to sometimes include the conventional solid image, the modern X-ray style screen, and the prison wall with cameras.

Not only has the wall changed but the way we experience and relate to surface has most likely altered through living in a society surrounded by screens of all sizes. If there is a link between our spatial relation to the screen and the illusion of space, depth, and time within the screen, and an effect on our experience of surface and space, then we must look at all the possible ways of understanding this spatiality. This must include an analysis of the structure of the screen as well as the media in general.

Sub-Optic Surface

The birth of cinema in 1895 was the beginning of a slow but steady mutation of the condition of the wall as a boundary and our relation to architectural surface—the beginning of a type of "screenness." The Lumière's *Demolition d'un Mur* (1896), a reverse motion film of a wall falling down (Figure 2.2), exposed an actual optic subconscious for the first time. This image of a wall reverse-collapsing is prophetic of the mutations that architectural surface would undergo over the next century. This is what Walter Benjamin called the optical subconscious.[1]

Can we find an origin for this sense of screenness? The first official X-ray took place on December 22, 1895, just six days before the first film screening. Experiments with the cathode ray dated from around 1875. The Schlieren camera dates from 1864 and was a technique to photograph air flow. The thermographic camera (also called an infrared camera) uses wavelengths to record. These

FIGURE 2.2: *Demolition d'un Mur*, 1896 (film). Auguste and Louis Lumière. France. Consecutive film stills showing the wall collapsing, collapsed, and then the wall "moving" backwards into place, in reverse motion. Benjamin noted that the film revealed sub-optic phenomena for the first time. Interestingly this cinematic trick was performed first on a wall and aims directly at the traditional phenomena associated with the wall: solidity and permanence.

SCREENNESS

techniques along with photography, cinema, radio, and television all inhabit and express the immaterial. We could say that before 1895 was the age of the material, whereas 1895 ushered in the age of the immaterial.

Mies collected X-rays. His experiments in the X-ray nature of reflections and architectural structure in the Friedrichstrasse skyscraper project and the 1922 Glass skyscraper project were early studies of this sense of screenness and the potential of an X-ray-like semi-transparency in architecture. Even the curtain wall of late Mies plays out as ultimate screenness with its serial repetition mixed with transparency and reflections.

Many modernist architects experimented with new conditions of the once solid wall: total transparency with accompanying reflections and overlapping was the most common. Often the aim was to obliterate the boundary between inside and outside. Architects used mirror (Loos), opacity (Mies), and the X-ray (Chareau), and others. So how do these coincide with a cinematic reading of the wall and a tendency towards cinematic surface in architecture?

FIGURE 2.3: Central Goldfields Art Gallery, Maryborough, Dja Wurrung Country. Nervegna Reed Architecture, 2022. A circular iris within the translucent wall forms a screen wall and projection at different times throughout the day and night, the effect alternating in the interior and exterior. Left image: Toby Reed. Right image: John Gollings.

The Free Plan as Cinematic Diagram

We can see an early move towards infecting the wall with the cinematic in the use of the white wall by Adolf Loos and Le Corbusier. The Raumplan of Loos and then the Free Plan of Le Corbusier work as diagrams of cinematic spatial disjuncture par excellence. Both concepts embody the space–time shifts that are an integral element of the screen, between interior and exterior, as well as space to space. We can see the white cube exterior of their 1920s houses as a three-dimensional empty white cinema screen, with a dis-associative relation to a chaotic or picturesque interior, like the multi-spaces in the projected film. This is the pre-television experience of the cinema screen as a white surface with other spaces and temporalities inside it when projected upon. The white wall of early modernism would seem to also negotiate a very modern and early conceptual sense of space–time overlap and spatial disjuncture (particularly between inside and outside) that is intrinsic to the cinema screen (Sigfried Giedion wrote about experiencing Le Corbusier's work in terms of space–time in the 1940s).[2] This relates closely to Paul Virilio's analysis of the relation between space, surface, and screen in "The Overexposed City."[3] It is the beginning of the infecting of the boundary with the overlapping zones of the camera and surveillance.

White Walls and Black Holes

In "Year Zero: Faciality"[4] Deleuze and Guattari describe the white wall of signification and the black hole of consciousness and subjectivity. The model for this is the face, which de-territorializes over the landscape, the orifices (eyes, mouth) becoming black holes of consciousness. We can easily relate this notion to the white walls and shadowed windows of 1920s modernism, particularly the free plan buildings of Le Corbusier and Raumplan buildings of Loos with their interior experiences distinctly separate from the outside field. The perceptiveness towards screens and the development of varying new wall types that relate to screens opens up a multitude of variations on this facial de territorialization which forms a black hole node of consciousness on the surface. The recent perforated white wall now gradates the white wall of signification and the black holes into the abstract blur of the void like the blur of a television on the blink, and countless other variations. In certain situations, the house becomes a screen for living in.

Becoming Television (Towards a Cathode Ray Surface)

Architecture has been moving towards a cathode-ray-like surface for some time. The free façade as envisaged by Le Corbusier in point 5 of his "Les Cinq Points

d'une architecture nouvelle"[5] (1926), has now slipped out of the confines of traditional masonry construction and the slab and column diagram of the Maison Dom-ino. The wall has mutated as its various functions have separated in space and become distinct layers of function: inside boundary, outside barrier, internal and external abstract shape, semi-solid wall and transparent window, sunshade, signifying skin.

The purity of the single modern skin where structure, shelter, protection, boundary, and signification are all wrapped into a single element, was a short-lived modernist ideal.

To understand the mutation of the building skin we need to take into account the history of the cavity wall, the role of poché, the screen and the veil in traditional architectures. These all play their part in the transformations that have happened to the buildings skin up until now and in the development in walls and the current tendency towards screenness.

The optical metal facade, which we first saw in Herzog & de Meuron's Signal Box (1988–95) helps dissolve the separateness of the wall's functions. The wall begins to separate out and is no longer the one single defined boundary as indicated by a thick black line on the plan. In buildings following on from this, the cavity wall slowly expanded to become many layers, the gap between the wall and outer skin expanding and contracting at will, embracing the screen as layer (and brise soleil), surface expanding, and absorbing space. Relations such as that between window and wall began dissolving to become the one slightly out-of-focus experience, as windows began to frequently hide behind abstract patterned skins. In the metal half-tone screen wall, the solid and transparent have become a gradient favouring the in-between as the prevalent experience, creating a new sense of screenspace with a resultant shift in architectural image. In this expanded cavity wall, we get a blurring of opacity levels from both outside and inside.

The old poché space of the classical and the baroque carved-out room shapes from a layering of different geometries (e.g. square container with circular interior) has mutated. The new perforated metal wall often reverses this situation to place the abstract shape on the outside, interacting with the city, with a more normalized interior, as we can see in Gehry's post-Bilbao formula. The poché, which once was a hidden solid between two internal geometries, has now conceptually mutated and become layers of the cavity wall, sometimes semi-transparent like an X-ray screen, and is often blown up in scale. The building now becomes a blow-up "reverse-poché."

The mutation of the cavity wall and poché have helped in the evolution of the surface towards a type of screenness. We can see here how the cavity wall has expanded to slowly absorb space into the surface. This tendency feeds into the impression of "screen depth" sometimes experienced in modern surface which fuses the impact of the cinema and television screens into the skin. Now buildings

can be abstract screens influenced by the static of the television caught between channels, like the Signal Box, or have images on them like OMA's Karlsruhe project (1989–92) and Herzog & de Meuron's Eberswalde Library (1996–99), or buildings can be shaped as images situated in the urban screenscape, like Gehry's Bilbao or OMA's CCTV.

The building with an image or abstract pattern is like a television screen, whereas a building shaped like an image conceives of the world as a screenscape in which the building floats or projects as an image object. The wall in our contemporary city has often evolved into the screen-like state of a credit sequence, hovering between abstraction and sign. These two conditions, the building as a screen (Figure 2.4) and building as image object in a screenscape (Figure 2.5) can be used as creative starting points for projects.

FIGURE 2.4: Precinct Energy Project. Nervegna Reed Architecture + pH Architects, 2012. Situated as part of the urban assemblage of Dandenong, perforated metal skin with optic splatter and images, form a screen surface to the plaza, hovering between abstraction and image. Left: Tom Nervegna-Reed. Right: John Gollings.

FIGURE 2.5: Arrow Studio. Nervegna Reed Architecture + pH Architects, 2013. The building is conceived as an object image in a screenscape with a projection surface. Photos Sam Reed.

SCREENNESS

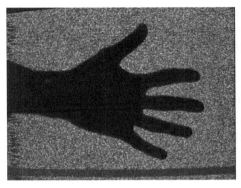

FIGURE 2.6: *Prenom Carmen*, 1983 (film). Directed by Jean-Luc Godard. France. Television tuned to a dead channel. Permission StudioCanal.

Static Voids

For many years in the twentieth century, the static on the screen late at night was one of the most common experiences of the void. The void permeates the appearance of the television screen tuned to a dead channel in movies such as Jean-Luc Godard's *Numero Deux* (1975), *Prenom Carmen* (1983), and *Poltergeist* (Hooper 1982) where we contemplate static voids. In the screen void lies a sliding scale between image and abstraction that reverberates optically and psychically. Deleuze discussed the relation of the chaos of abstraction to the screen which creates a "something" out of chaos.[6] This could be possibly an optic abstraction or image.

With the recent popularity of the perforated metal skin, we have the whole façade, in many instances, taking on the static of channel surfing, like the TV sky in William Gibson's *Neuromancer*.[7] Even if we ignore the obvious use of "media walls" in the urban environment, the overriding new status of the skin is that of an information surface, even when there is no actual image, just optical abstraction or a void.

Living Inside a Television

Private and social space in our society has been overtaken by screens: smartphones, televisions, computers, and surveillance, like a society of the spectacle. It is only natural that buildings would slowly develop forms and surfaces that responded to this screenness.

In *Privacy and Publicity,* Beatriz Colomina has noted the tendency within early modernism for buildings to be devices for viewing and being viewed, projecting the exterior into the interior like a camera obscura, as well as the interior out to the exterior environment (the window as an eye to the soul).[8] The conceptualization of the building as cinematic, and later as televisual, not only happened from within architecture (Le Corbusier) but also notably from within the cinema.

Alfred Hitchcock, in his 1954 film *Rear Window*, conceived of the standard apartment window as a TV and/or cinema screen. In the train sequence of the 1931 film *Possessed*, the windows of the train become cinema screens with mini scenes taking place in each one.[9] Eisenstein conceptualized a whole apartment block made of glass where every surface is like a crystalline screen in his unrealized *Glass House* (1947) film project.[10]

In Le Corbusier's Immeubles Villas project (1922) each unit can be seen as a positive and negative screenspace for living. In the axonometric view, the interior and exterior spaces for each unit have a certain screenness, predating Hitchcock's window/screen analogy. The interior view from the main living positions the view as a screenscape.

Architects have consciously conceptualized windows with this metaphor, particularly after the advent of television, producing buildings as readymade televisions, with obvious attached social critique. We can see the early iconic

FIGURE 2.7: Total House, Melbourne 1964, Bogle and Banfield Assoc. TV Building: An office building figured as a television hovers over a "readymade" car park. Photo Toby Reed.

treatment of the television screen as a façade image and building as a stack of televisions in SOM/Gordon Bunshaft's Beineke Library at Yale (1964). Here the screen, in the "TV" frame, is replaced by translucent marble which filters cathode-ray style light into the interior. The screen surface creates an interior screenspace as marble homage to the cathode ray. Even Kisho Kurokawa's Nakagin Capsule Tower (1972) has an obvious reading of an asymmetrical stack of sci-fi TVs. The metabolists were prone to conceiving of the spatial unit as a screen or television. Total House in Melbourne (Bogle and Banfield, 1965) has an office building as TV hovering over a readymade carpark. Modernist architects often made the window a lens or an aperture. Buckminster Fuller's Fly-Eye Dome (1965) rendered the surface a fish-eye lens aperture. Carlo Scarpa's iconic double moon window in his Brion Cemetery (1968–77) is also an out-of-focus aperture about to click into focus like a 007 credit sequence. Le Corbusier's windows at Ronchamp (1954) filter the light like a cinema projection booth. Marcel Breuer's windows in his Whitney Museum (1966) imply a projection box.

The Camera Replaces the Wall

The camera has now replaced the wall. The ancient function of the wall as a boundary has evolved and has often been taken over by the camera. The boundary wall, one of the most primitive architectural and political acts, has been replaced by (often overlapping) surveillance zones. This is Virilio's position in "The Overexposed City" in which he describes the camera surveillance boundary of the modern city and the space/time disjuncture of the screen as the new city wall. The contemporary "smart" border wall, like those being developed by the Israeli defence company Elbit, makes the line in the sand a blurred surveillance zone that surrounds the actual wall in close circuit television zones and can potentially eradicate the actual physical boundary wall in places where it might not be possible to build one.

Virilio wrote that close-circuit television surveillance serves the function of the boundary wall in American suburbs (along with toll booths with surveillance cameras), and that these have replaced the function of the old city wall. With the camera and the screen taking over much of the boundary function of the traditional wall there is a dispersion over space and time in the notion of the boundary, as well the side-effect of a type of global connectedness, that is different from that of the traditional boundary. Virilio wrote: "From here on people can't be separated by physical objects or by temporal distances. With the interfacing of computer terminals and video monitors, distinctions here and there no longer mean anything."[11]

The camera has also replaced the surveillance and boundary function of the wall in many instances. This is a physical change that has affected our understanding

of walls as a barrier. The image of the surveillance camera combined with various wall types is an everyday occurrence and the pairing of the two has become inseparable in our mass psyche.

The Section Elevation

This screen interface has not only affected us deeply in the experience of everyday space but also has affected the way we now design these spaces. Spatial disjunctures are now more likely to occur than spatial flow. In places where previously spatial disjuncture used to happen (the classical boundary wall) we now tend to have the flow of the screen, but a flow that incorporates shifts: a non-chronological flow (and the overlapping zones of multiple surveillance cameras).

In the cinema, the all-seeing camera often travels through walls and sometimes floors. We see the sectional "dolls house" set in *The Night of the Hunter* (Laughton, 1955) and *Tout va Bien* (Godard and Gorin, 1972). In architecture, the "section-elevation" cuts away walls or renders them invisible or opaque to produce camera-like views: an X-ray screen. This is a conceptual shift in spatial composition. The "section" facade exposes new sometimes clashing spatial types to the outside as in OMA's Trés Grande Bibliothéque project (1989), the Jussieu Libraries project (1992), and the Educatorium in Utrecht (1995). The conceptual and actual replacing of the wall by the camera has resulted in these section façades, the X-ray skin, screen and TV buildings, as well as the function of surveillance and separation being partly taken over by cameras.

In this paradoxical spatial flow, the impression of (non-chronological) time as an organizer of space can be dominant over movement. This allows for the impression of disjunctures between spaces, both temporally and spatially, rather than the smooth transition that classical architectures expressed through the dominance of movement through space. Paradoxical flow is now normal. This is both a conditioning by the screen but also a conscious tendency within architecture and an unintentional occurrence in the contemporary city.

Screenspace—Sponge Surface

Videodrome (Cronenberg, 1983) (Figure 2.8) plays with the horror of our psychological sense of screen depth. The image of Deborah Harry's lips on the TV, pushing the screen surface of the television outwards and inwards like a pneumatic pillow connecting two worlds, as James Wood's character, Max, stares transfixed, then plunges his head slowly into the bubbly three-dimensional "depth" of the screen. These images in

FIGURE 2.8: *Videodrome*, 1983 (film). Directed by David Cronenberg. Canada: CFDC. Screen surface as perceptual expanding and contracting spatial zone with unclassifiable depth. Permission NBC Universal and David Cronenberg.

Videodrome show comically how the impression of screen depth works perceptually in the surface. We have seen how throughout the twentieth century there has been a tendency for building's skins to mutate towards a screen-like surface.

The surface appears to absorb space in a television screen (and its various offspring) like an ever-changing perceptual sponge surface (Figure 2.9). This is obviously an explicit screen experience that can be channelled to motivate design disjunctures and distortions in architectural space and objects. Screen surface has a spatial indeterminacy like in-between space, or Kurokawa's Ma Space. The phenomenology of the screen—out-of-focus static blurs, the paradoxical combination of flatness with perceptual sponge surface—has become a starting point in the design process for many architects.

Screenspace (Actual and Perceptual)

Our consciousness of the (sometimes) paper-thin screen with spatial depth has infiltrated our everyday spatial and surface experience, also changing the way we design and conceptualize both space and surface.

FIGURE 2.9: *SPONGE / SURFACE / SPACE*, Toby Reed, 2018. Architectural screen surface is like a sponge, absorbing space into the surface like a television screen.

The screen has "real" space (or depth) and the "impression" of space (or depth). Screen depth is different from normal flatness and blurs this with various regimes of perspective space. The screen often has these characteristics embedded within a primarily fuzzy depth. This is due to the fact that, in the screen there is the perspective that the camera depicts combined with our knowledge that the screen itself is not that deep. The screen has a new slightly blurred sense of space which is sometimes combined with an abrupt space/time shift, sometimes in quick succession.

The screen is like a perceptual void in which the surface appears to absorb space through perceptual impressions. This is explicit in the flat cinema screen and the curved television screen, and often implied in architecture. In OMA's Karlsruhe project, there is a screenness and "screenspace" which is like a television screen, with a sponge-like absorption of space into surface image, combined with an X-ray style wall, which loses its solidity and through transparency becomes spatial.

The space inside the static blur of the screen is partly created by various techniques with their origins in the cinema: lens types and techniques such as deep focus, depth of field, zooms, and camera movements, and editing techniques such as jump-cuts, fades, and titles all help form the space of the screen surface. These techniques are often organized by a system of subliminal cubism which evolves around the blurry cinematic code of the 180-degree rule, which is a basis for the construction of the majority of screen space. These techniques all help create a sense of screenspace and most likely infiltrate our everyday lives, changing the way we see spatially and experience objects.

FIGURE 2.10: Judo House, Nervegna Reed Architecture, 2021. The screen mediates the exterior and interior boundary experience via an expanded triangular zone of screenspace at the entry. Photos John Gollings.

Unlike Cubism and New Wave directors like Godard and Resnais, classic Hollywood film space generally hides the disjunctures. Images are sutured smoothly onto the screen surface via the editing process, cutting up the space using the 180-degree rule. This all happens on a paper-thin screen, but deeply affects our perception of the depth and space of the screen, as well as our spatial experience and perception generally.

Credit Sequence Skin

Driving down a suburban strip at night is often like a noir credit sequence: out-of-focus perspective with signs, reflective glass, and semi-transparent surfaces. The credit sequence has inadvertently become a model for modern architectural surfaces in the city. Billboards add images and text to this scenario like subtitles to our everyday spatiality, exposing subconscious desires and political structures through advertizing and branding.

Architecture and the Screen Apparatus

In a world in which the panopticon has been replaced by the screens of social media, it would seem worthwhile to analyse the structure of the viewer–screen relationship to see if it sheds light on the modern architectural surface and our experience of the boundary. This is a constantly mutating and evolving situation. Although the cinema is dying fast, it can be instructive to go back to this

 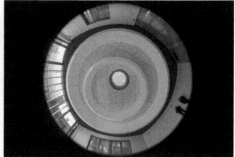

FIGURE 2.11: Victorian Quaker Centre, Nervegna Reed Architecture + pH Architects, 2020. A circular "space object" inscribed by light (and markings) to define a zone for peaceful contemplation. Photos John Gollings.

modern primal scene to help understand the situation we are now in and how it has evolved.

One of the first and most important writings about viewer–screen relations in the cinema is Jean-Louis Baudry's 1970 article "Ideological Effects of the Basic Cinematographic Apparatus."[12] Baudry utilized a number of theoretical systems to help us understand our relationship to the screen, combining the diagrams of Plato's Cave (with Platonic metaphysics and representation) Jacques Lacan's psychoanalytic Mirror Stage, with Marxist ideology with semiotic theory. Baudry related how the false impression of movement of still images that appear to move relates to Marxist theories on the masking of difference and true social relations in order to create an impression that reinforces dominant ideology. Baudry's diagram exposes conscious and unconscious viewer–screen relations which can be explored in relation to architectural surface, politics, and power relations within society.

The Wall as Media Sign

Even if this sub-optic infiltration of the screen into our experience is too subliminal to notice, it is a fact that the wall has mutated, blurred, and expanded. The cavity wall has exploded as if pneumatically injected with space, becoming semi-inhabitable with the surveillance camera often taking over part of its functionality and spreading the effects of the wall outwards into vague surveillance zones. The Chinese internet firewall shows the power of the wall as an ephemeral media boundary, stopping the flow of information, a contemporary Great Wall of China that has proved to be more powerful than a physical wall.

The sign of the wall as a boundary has also mutated. The solid wall persists as an image, but generally, the image has split between the (sometimes pairing of) surveillance camera and an image of the prison or detention centre security wall.

Baudry asserted that the false movement of the screen image masks difference and true social relations and therefore reinforces a dominant ideology. His critique of the cinema is equally applicable to the screen image in all its current forms and particularly to the image (and impression) of the contemporary surface in relation to power and border security. Just as the image on a television screen is a false image of movement, made of still images that appear to move, the modern border wall is a false boundary, an image of a boundary made for the screen.

Donald Trump's US–Mexico border wall is a false image, a sign of a wall for the mass media. In a world in which the camera has replaced the boundary wall with zones of camera surveillance, the actual wall, now porous and immaterial, used as a geopolitical border is anachronistic and contradictory to its contemporary use. Since the collapse of the Berlin Wall and the Cold War, defence companies have been switching from arms manufacturing to marketing border walls as security solutions for a world in peacetime, trying to secure a transference of military expenditure. These walls including Trump's wall are images intended as media propaganda, channelling the ancient function of the wall as separation to simplify political dialogue in an attempt to reinforce the outmoded notions of distinct boundaries. The image of a border wall on a smartphone is more effective as ideological propaganda than the wall is at keeping people separated.

The End

The screen has now multiplied, grown bigger, wider, and smaller, both in internal space and the space of the city. It is everywhere, particularly in the contemporary city, fracturing and distorting space and surface and the boundary between the two. This has forced a change in the way we design surface. Whereas commercial media may hide spatial disjunctures in order to mask difference and reinforce ideologies, a conscious exposing of disjunctures in architecture (and media) could help disrupt the seamlessness of the image exposing cracks in ideology. Our ontological understanding of ourselves within a globally connected world (through camera and screen), has been affected by both the proliferation of screens and the impression of screen depth in surface, particularly in our experience of surface and boundaries in and around the city.

FIGURE 2.12: *Architecture at 25 Frames Per Second*. Video still. Toby Reed, 1998. A video diagram of a zero-gravity space populated with screens each of which is a black hole vortex to another world with other space, time, and spatial morphologies within.

It would seem that the design of space and surface by architects and designers has for a long time been influenced by the screen and the cinematic apparatus. Architects have constantly found inspiration in new media to help them create environments and this will undoubtedly continue. It also seems certain that our experience of space and surface has been conditioned by the screen and the cinematic apparatus and all its mutations. This is particularly true of an apparent sense of non-chronological space-time in relation to surface, space, and objects which occurs in the contemporary city. Our spatial experience now would seem to be a discontinuous flow and experienced in relation to a flow of spatial disjunctures and non-chronological sheets of time, without the continuous movement of classicism as a marker. This has flow on psychological and ideological implications which can be explored theoretically and endlessly in the design process.

ACKNOWLEDGEMENT
Many of these observations came out of research for a PhD in the School of Architecture and Urban Design, RMIT University, Melbourne, Australia (2017).

NOTES
1. Walter Benjamin, "The Work of Art in the Age of Mechanical Reproduction," in *Illuminations: Essays and Reflections*, trans. Harry Zohn and ed. Hannah Arendt (New York: Schocken, 1969).

2. Sigfried Giedion, *Space, Time, and Architecture* (Cambridge, MA: Harvard University Press, 1947), 356.
3. Paul Virilio, "The Overexposed City," in *Zone*, ed. Michel Feher and Sanford Kwinter (Urzone Inc., 1986), 14–31.
4. Gilles Deleuze and Felix Guattari, "Year Zero: Faciality." In *A Thousand Plateaus—Capitalism and Schizophrenia*, trans. Brian Massumi (London: The Athlone Press, 2004), 187.
5. Le Corbusier, *Decorative Arts of Today*, p. 76 quoted in Frampton, Kenneth, *Le Corbusier*, Thames and Hudson, 2001, p. 72.
6. Gilles Deleuze, "What Is an Event." *The Fold—Leibniz and the Baroque* (Minneapolis: University of Minnesota Press, 1993), 76.
7. William Gibson, *Neuromancer*, in the opening paragraph. Ace/ Penguin, 1984.
8. Beatriz Colomina, *Privacy and Publicity—Architecture and Mass Media* (Cambridge: The MIT Press 1994), 1996 edition, 6–13.
9. As pointed out by Slavoj Žižek in *The Perverts Guide to Cinema*.
10. Jay Leyda and Zina Voynow, *Eisenstein at Work* (London: Methuen, 1985), 42–43.
11. Virilio, "The Overexposed City," 14–31.
12. Jean Louis Baudry, "Idealogical Effects of the Basic Cinematographic Apparatus," in *Movies and Methods* 2, ed. Collins, Bill (1974).

BIBLIOGRAPHY

Baudrillard, Jean. *Simulations*. Translated by Paul Foss, Paul Patton, and Phil Beitchman. New York: Philip. Semiotexte, 1983.

Baudry, Jean Louis. "Idealogical Effects of the Basic Cinematographic Apparatus." In *Movies and Methods* 2, edited by Bill Collins. Los Angeles, California: University of California Press, 1985.

Benjamin, Walter. "The Work of Art in the Age of Mechanical Reproduction." In *Illuminations: Essays and Reflections*, translated by Harry Zohn and edited by Hannah Arendt. New York: Schocken, 1969.

Colomina, Beatriz. *Privacy and Publicity*. Woburn, MA: The MIT Press, 1996.

Cronenberg, David. dir. *Videodrome*. Filmplan International, Canada: Guardian Trust Company and CFDC, 1983.

Debord, Guy. *The Society of the Spectacle*, 2021, Unredacted Word. Translation from La société du spectacle, 1967. Buchet-Chastel (in French).

Deleuze, Gilles, and Feliz Guattari. *A Thousand Plateaus—Capitalism and Schizophrenia*. Translated by Brian Massumi. London: The Athlone Press, 1999.

Frampton, Kenneth. *Le Corbusier*. London: Thames and Hudson, 2001.

Gibson, William. *Neuromancer*. London: Ace and Penguin, 1984.

Giedion, Sigfried. *Space, Time, and Architecture*. Cambridge: Harvard University Press, 1947.

Godard, Jean-Luc. dir. *Numero Deux*. France: Anne-age-Bela, Bela Productions and SNC, 1975.

Godard, Jean-Luc. dir. *Prenom Carmen*. France: JLG Films, Sara Films and Films A2, 1983.

Hooper, Tobe. dir. *Poltergeist*. MGM, 1982.
Le Corbusier. *Towards a New Architecture*. New York: Dover, 1986.
Lumière, Auguste, and Louis. dirs. *Demolition d'un Mur*. France: Lumiere, 1896.
MacCabe, Colin, and Laura Mulvey. *Godard: Images, Sounds, Politics*. BFI London, 1980.
McLuhan, Marshall. *Understanding Media: The Extensions of Man*. Cambridge, MA: MIT Press, 1994
Virilio, Paul. "The Overexposed City." In *Zone*, edited by Michel Feher and Sanford Kwinter, 14–31. New York, USA: Urzone Inc., 1986.

3

Mood-Sensitive Spaces: Inspiration from Ambient Assisted Living and Affective Computing

Liz Felton

Introduction

The world of smart technology is rapidly changing, aided by the plethora of data produced by each of us daily and the Internet of Things (IoT) bringing ubiquitous inter-connectivity between us, our devices, and our spaces. The capabilities offered by smart homes vary across multiple modalities; from automatically adjustable lighting and climate control to power management and home security profiles.[1] Ambient assisted living (AAL) systems take this one step further by allowing the smart space to intervene in the presence of danger, for example if it detects an inhabitant has fallen and cannot get up, and to interact with its inhabitants to aid quality of life and independence.[2] The IoT is expanding, with an estimated 19% of people by 2025[3] utilizing smart home technology in their daily lives, which makes the case for full utilization of the technology's potential.

This chapter argues that the next logical step in this process is a "mood-sensitive" smart space which can anticipate and understand the emotional states and needs of its inhabitants, via the integration of affective computing systems into smart spaces, and respond appropriately with its available systems. Then, once these systems are commonly placed in smart homes, it is not difficult to see the progression to larger mood-sensitive spaces, for use in areas with potentially high occupancy, such as theatres or subway stations. This chapter will present a framework for integrating mood data and appropriate responses into already smart spaces and discuss the reasons and benefits for doing so.

Such mood-sensitive spaces would have a positive impact on the mood of their inhabitants by increasing the inhabitants' exposure to mood-boosting stimuli.[4]

This improvement in mood will give a long-term boost to the quality of life of the inhabitants, as their mood will be elevated over time and the burden to improve their own mood is reduced. Mood-sensitive spaces will improve inhabitants' interactions and perceived relationship with their smart home,[5] which will aid in the adoption of AAL technology amongst traditionally resistant user groups.[6]

To create a mood-sensitive space, a high-level understanding of several elements is needed. This chapter will provide this by firstly reviewing state-of-the-art smart home technology ("The Smart Home"), the AAL technology needed to create a reactive smart space ("Reactive Smart Spaces"), and the technology to sense and compute with emotion ("Affective Computing"). These three elements are needed to create a mood-sensitive space, and it is important to understand the considerations and limitations of each technology when designing such a space. The chapter will then present a framework for combining these elements to create mood-sensitive spaces within the smart home ("Creating Mood-Sensitive Spaces"), to aid in the conceptual and technical design of these spaces. The "Future Work" section details the practical first steps one would need to take to implement a mood-sensitive space, as well as areas of further research. Finally, there is a discussion of the benefits of such a system, as well as of potential problems the system might face and future extensions to a smart home with mood-sensitive spaces ("Discussion"). On balance, this chapter finds considerable benefit to the use of mood-sensitive spaces in the home and, further in the future, in public spheres.

The Smart Home

A smart home allows inhabitants to control appliances and environmental settings, and automate household tasks, via the IoT (Figure 3.1). Inhabitants can either choose to activate their home's smart features (e.g. turn off the lights from their phone), or set the home to make decisions autonomously based on a predefined plan of action (e.g. automated climate control based on environmental readings). The purpose of smart homes is to improve the quality of life of their inhabitants by optimizing and automating control of the home's variables, or by allowing the inhabitants more direct and connected control over their home's settings.

Smart homes are capable of monitoring and controlling a large range of inputs and outputs. State-of-the-art smart homes are commonly capable of monitoring light levels, humidity, time of day, and power consumption.[7] From this sensor data, they then act upon various systems to keep the home running in optimal condition, for example by adjusting the lighting, turning appliances on or off, adjusting climate control, and enacting home security protocols. Both of the major players in consumer-accessible cloud computing, Amazon and Google, offer smart home

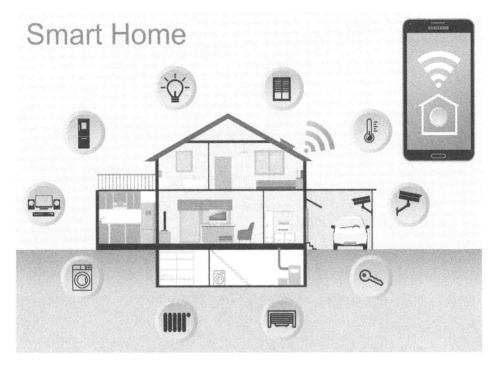

FIGURE 3.1: A smart home illustration. "Smart Home House Technology—Free Vector Graphic on Pixabay." n.d. https://pixabay.com/vectors/smart-home-housetechnology-2005993/. Accessed July 31, 2024.

solutions. Amazon's offering[8] centres around their Alexa smart hub, and gives users options to augment their home with smart appliances, security systems, power management, garden space management, and to automate their lights and power sockets to turn off when not in use. These systems can be set to work autonomously or can be accessed by the Alexa smart voice assistant packaged with the hub. Google's equivalent[9] offering, the Nest, currently offers fewer options for a smart home and the options focus around security, safety, and integration with Google Home products (such as the Chromecast). Even the furniture retailer IKEA is beginning to expand into smart home technology,[10] with their first round of products including smart power and lighting options, as well as smart programmable blinds for a building's windows.

Smart homes follow a sense–compute–act model[11] (Figure 3.2) when deciding on which action to take. The components are defined as follows: sensing (gathering data from the home's array of sensors); computing (interpreting the reading of the sensors and deciding on appropriate action); acting (adjusting some form of output in-line with the decision made in the computing stage). In general, the actions of a smart home are broken into two separate categories: user directed and centrally

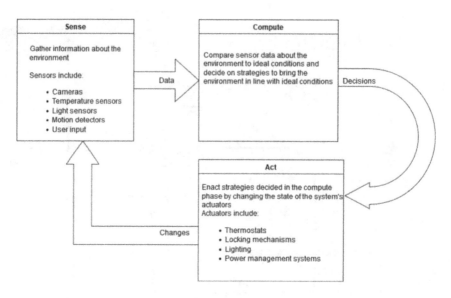

FIGURE 3.2: The sense–compute–act cycle. Liz Felton, 2022.

controlled. User-directed action is the simplest form of smart home technology, in that the user (inhabitant) requests for an action to happen, for example they press a button on their phone to turn down the lights, and the home receives that request and acts upon it. Mood-sensitive spaces would require the second form, centrally controlled actions (actions for which the smart home is responsible). For example, in a smart climate control system the inhabitant does not request that the thermostat be turned up or down, instead the home is capable of sensing changes in temperature and autonomously deciding to adjust the thermostat. In a mood-sensitive smart home, the home would be able to receive the inhabitant's mood as data during the "sense" part of the cycle, then autonomously make decisions about what outputs it should adjust based on that mood data.

ALL is the utilization of technology, including smart home technology, to assist in the care of disabled persons.[12] The goals of AAL are to improve quality of life and patient outcomes by passing some care responsibilities to technology,[13] for example monitoring the person's routine or enabling safer use of smart appliances. This improves the independence of the person whilst reducing the burden on care services,[14] and appropriately monitoring risk.

Perhaps the simplest of AAL technologies is a fall detector, a wearable device which is capable of monitoring and categorizing a person's movement status (e.g. walking, sitting upright, sleeping, prone) and can then alert appropriate care services if it detects the person has fallen and cannot recover. This detection

happens in one of two ways: the person hits a button on the device to call for help, or the device uses AI to interpret the data it has gathered and send out an alert autonomously. The addition of an autonomous aid caller, in this case, improves care outcomes when the person is unconscious and cannot call for help themselves.

There are many sensor modalities an AAL system may utilize.[15] A wearable fall detection device may use a gyroscope and accelerometer to compute a person's body position,[16] whereas a smart environment may achieve the same outcomes by using cameras about the home and a computer vision system to interpret the person's body position.[17] Other AAL technologies about the person may interface with worn diagnostic equipment to aid in a person's care, for example by monitoring blood glucose and insulin levels in a diabetic person. The smart home environment may include cameras, microphones, and temperature sensors to monitor a person's state, as well as feeding that information back to their care team. Figure 3.3 provides an example of an AAL smart home.

Once an AAL system can monitor a person's state, it is then simple to integrate that with smart home technologies to further improve quality of life. For example, doors that can provide an auditory warning if they are closed to a blind occupant approaching, or bathroom fittings that can be activated from a person's wheelchair controls if they lack the dexterity to operate taps and levers.[18] AAL systems can also be integrated into smart spaces outside of the home, with one of the most common usages being induction loops for persons with hearing aids in public buildings and businesses.

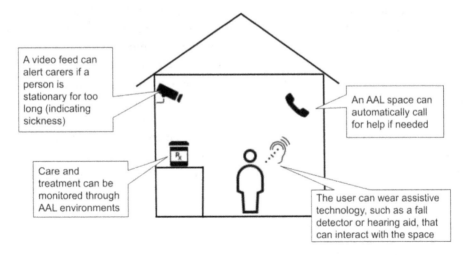

FIGURE 3.3: An example of AAL space. Liz Felton with icons from icon8 (https://icons8.com/, accessed June 16, 2023), 2023.

Affective Computing

Affective computing is a subfield of artificial intelligence (AI), concerned with encoding human mood and emotion in a machine-understandable way. The main goal of affective computing is to enable AI systems to be able to use emotion data to facilitate better, smarter interactions with human users.[19] There are two types of affective computing problems: classification, where an AI can correctly assign an emotion label to human-generated data; and prediction, where an AI can predict a future emotion state based on current data. A classification problem might be an e-learning system which can identify a student's motivation levels and adjust content accordingly, whereas a prediction problem might involve a meditation app capable of proactively suggesting content to the user based on their predicted future mood state.

There are three main data groups used to determine mood in affective computing: text,[20] audio-visual,[21] and biometric.[22] The first, text, is not directly relevant to the purposes presented here, and works by using natural language processing to analyse sentiments in written text. The second two are far more readily available to integrate into smart environments. Audio-visual emotion data comes from microphones and cameras which record the participants' voices and, commonly, facial expressions These data sources are the most human-understandable, as it is how humans commonly interpret each other's emotions. Biometric data sources involve measuring and monitoring various bodily signals from participants, which have been proven linked to emotion expression. Biometric sources commonly include electro-dermal activity, heart rate and electrocardiogram, and electromyogram (muscle activity).[23]

State-of-the-art affective computing techniques are able to classify emotions with between 80% and 90% accuracy, and predict emotions with between 70% and 80% accuracy.[24] Classification techniques include modified pattern recognition AI such as deep learning, and traditional AI classification techniques such as support-vector machines. Prediction techniques are often ensemble machines using multiple elements to complete their task, such as a classification technique to understand current emotion data and a modelling component such as time-series analysis to perform the prediction. Another key element in many successful affective computing systems is transfer learning, where data points from other, similar, participants can be used to help understand the data for the current participant.

Creating Mood-Sensitive Spaces

From the above elements presented—smart home technology, AAL technology, and affective computing—a model for mood-sensitive spaces can be constructed.

The goals of mood-sensitive spaces are to integrate mood data into smart environments in order to improve the usability and adaptability of the smart environments, whilst also improving user health and satisfaction.

Broadly, the model follows the smart home sense–compute–act cycle to deliver smart services appropriate to the inhabitant's mood. The affective computing sensors, including audio-visual and biometric, will be integrated into the "sense" part of the cycle. The classification and prediction of the mood data form part of the "compute" step. Elements from AAL will be used in the "act" portion of the cycle to enable the smart space to react appropriately to emotion data.

A framework for mood-sensitive smart homes

A framework for a mood-sensitive space must consider two elements: the sense–compute–act cycle, and the addition of affective sensors and actuators (technology that has an effect on the state of the smart environment, e.g. changing the lighting, or increasing the temperature) into the smart space. The framework presented here focuses on adding affective capability to existing smart spaces; however, building mood-sensitive spaces from the ground-up is also considered.

Extending the sense–compute–act cycle for affective computing

A smart home can be broadly abstracted into its sense–compute–act cycle, as explained in the previous section ("The Smart Home"). When adding affective capabilities to create a mood-sensitive space, extra information is needed in each part of the sense–compute–act cycle. The design of a mood-sensitive space must insert its required functionality at each appropriate stage. A mood-sensitive space will need to sense information about the inhabitant, either through existing sensors within the smart space or through adding new sensors to the existing space. For example, a smart home may already be equipped with facial recognition capabilities to aid in security, so during the "sense" part of the cycle it may be possible to store images of the inhabitant's current facial expression. During the "compute" phase, an affective computing method for extracting the inhabitant's current mood from their facial expression can be added. Then, during the "act" part of the cycle, existing actuators and outputs in the smart home may include connected lighting and a stereo system, so the smart home can activate those in response to the inhabitant's mood. Figure 3.4 provides an example of this new sense-compute-act cycle. It is also possible to add new sensors and actuators into the smart home ecosystem. Many affective computing applications use bodily-worn sensors to detect biometrics which relate to the wearer's mood, so once the inhabitant is wearing such a sensing device then part of the "sense" cycle of the smart home becomes pulling

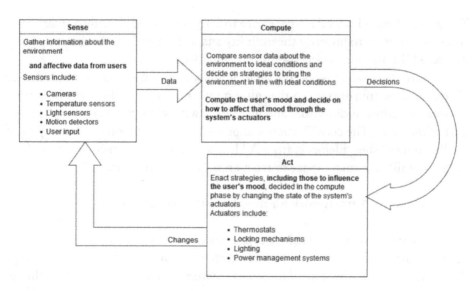

FIGURE 3.4: Extending the sense–compute–act cycle to include mood data. Liz Felton, 2022.

biometric data from the inhabitant's device. The addition to the "compute" part of the cycle remains similar; using the biometrics to compute the inhabitant's mood. Actuators can also be added into smart home ecosystems and can be leveraged in a mood-sensitive space, for example replacing existing smart lightbulbs with lightbulbs with RGB colour capability so that the hue and saturation of the lights can be changed in accordance with the inhabitant's mood.

Safety considerations

The addition of sensor and actuator modalities to a smart space is limited to the available computing power of the smart space, and while this is discussed in more depth in the next section on design considerations, safety-critical systems should be considered as part of the core framework and not as a design consideration. When discussing safety in physical computing, there are three broad areas to consider: the safety of the user, safety of the system, and the safety of the environment. When implementing affective systems into a smart home space, the designer should take care to ensure their added elements do not accidentally obscure or override any safety system. In the example above, a smart home with facial recognition capabilities has an affective system added to its "compute" cycle, where it analyses the facial expression of the captured face to compute the emotion being expressed. The designer should ensure that this is only taking place after the safety-critical parts of the "compute" cycle have been executed, in this case checking to see if

any of the captured faces are intruders before it tries to compute their emotion. The safety-critical behaviour of engaging the security protocols, occurring inside the "act" part of the cycle, should then also take place either before, or instead of, any affective protocols. It may seem like common sense to ensure safety-critical behaviours take precedence over other behaviours of the smart home; however, it is important to keep this at the forefront of designing smart spaces when you are adding new modalities into existing smart ecosystems. It is easy to accidentally disrupt the order of behaviours inside a smart ecosystem, especially when adding to an existing system rather than building a system from scratch, so the preservation of safety-critical behaviours should form the first part of your systems testing.

Design considerations

There are several design considerations which must be taken into account when designing mood-sensitive spaces, no matter if an existing smart space is being adapted or a new smart space is being built from scratch. This section will discuss computing limitations and modalities, the physical space, the purpose of the mood-sensitive space, the skills a team needs to build a mood-sensitive space, and finally the willingness of inhabitants to live within mood-sensitive smart spaces.

Computing limitations

The computing power available to smart homes is often significantly restricted, due to the hardware being used. Smart homes are coordinated centrally through a "hub" device which will have a limited number of slots for sensors or actuators to be attached, or may be restricted to proprietary devices, or approved third-party devices, only (e.g. use of Amazon Alexa as a smart hub requires Amazon-branded smart sockets). Assuming that there are no such proprietary restrictions, the device used as the smart hub still has a physical limit to the number of devices (including sensors and actuators) that may be attached to it. A common connection for smart devices is Bluetooth, and the current Bluetooth 5.0 protocol limits the number of devices which can connect to a singular device (the hub in this instance) to seven.[25] In complex smart spaces, more than one hub may be needed to accommodate all the connections needed, and those hubs will need to communicate with each other to provide a ubiquitous experience. Hub devices are also subject to physical computing limitations due to their maximum power consumption and storage capabilities. For example, the popular Raspberry Pi Model 4 B has a maximum of 8GB of RAM and is powered by a USB-C connection (3A at 5V).[26] Whilst programmers who do not commonly work with ubiquitous platforms may be used to as little as 8GB of RAM, the relatively low power draw of

the USB-C connection will place limits on the amount of processing the Raspberry Pi is able to do. It is important, when designing any system using IoT or embedded hardware, to consider the computing resources available and the resources that the project needs.

Sensors, actuators, and their modalities

It is important to consider the sensors and actuators that are available to the designer of the smart space, as well as their modalities (the types of data they produce or consume, and how often). It is a design task in itself to synchronize sensors and actuators with each other across a smart space so that the actuators update their outputs as new sensor information comes in. It is rare for sensors of different types to sample from the environment at the same rate; a camera might take video at 60 frames per second to capture someone walking across a room, whereas a temperature sensor may only be sampled once per minute since ambient temperature changes on a much slower scale. As multiple sensors and actuators may be involved with one smart decision in a mood-sensitive space (e.g. wishing to change the output of multiple actuators based on multiple mood sensors) it is important to make sure they align properly to produce the expected result. It is also important to read the documentation carefully for any sensors and actuators in the space, as not all sensors and actuators of the same type work in the same ways (e.g., different cameras have different frames-per-second capability, different pixel density, or different colour sensitivity).

The physical space

As much as the technology is important, the physical space that is available is just as important in designing a successful smart space. A perfect smart space would be large, square, evenly lit and sparsely populated by both people and furniture; however such spaces rarely exist in the real world. When designing a smart space, particularly a mood-sensitive space which may rely on multiple sensors and actuators working together and at once, one must consider the advantages and constraints of the physical space available. A non-exhaustive list of physical features to consider includes:

- The position of the walls and the material they are made of, as some sensors require line-of-sight (such as cameras), and Bluetooth connectivity is affected by denser building materials.
- Windows, natural light, and the placement of artificial lights: is the space well-lit? Is it evenly lit? Are there any areas that are too bright, or too dark, for the

components to function? Are there any areas that get strong sunlight, which may cause components to overheat or give inaccurate readings (e.g., a room temperature sensor shouldn't be placed in direct sunlight)?
- Ceiling height, for sensors or actuators that may need to be ceiling-mounted (or adapted to be wall-mounted, if the ceiling is too high to be practical).
- The size of the space: a smaller space will be able to accommodate fewer components, but in a large space the components should not be spaced too far apart (e.g., so that they are not placed in areas that inhabitants rarely go).
- Surface textures, especially those that may cause light and sound reflection.
- The placement and availability of power sources.

The shape and size of the space should be considered either when adding mood-sensitive elements to an existing smart space, or when designing a mood-sensitive space from the ground up.

The purpose of the mood-sensitive space

The purpose of the mood-sensitive space encompasses both the goals of the mood-sensitive space and how inhabitants will interact with the space, and both will have an effect on how the space is designed. One thing to consider is if the space is passive or active, and if the space is autonomous or not. "Passive" spaces do not require interaction from the inhabitant, and as such their processes must be fully autonomous. "Active" spaces, such as mood-sensitive exhibition spaces, rely on interaction from inhabitants of the space as one of the system's inputs (e.g., pressing a button to indicate how they feel about a piece of art). Active spaces may be autonomous, or they may also rely on inhabitants to activate the smart or mood-sensitive processes.

It is important to consider the desired effect that the mood-sensitive space will have on inhabitants. It is expected a mood-sensitive space will have some effect on the inhabitants' emotions, but how and when the emotions are to be elicited will affect which sensors and actuators are chosen in the design phase. It is often worth testing the space and getting feedback from inhabitants about which elements they found had the most effect on their mental state, and then refining the design around those elements.

Building a team to build a mood-sensitive space

A diverse and multi-talented team is needed to successfully build and operate a mood-sensitive space. A list of recommended skills is presented below. It is not exhaustive, and members of the team may be capable of fulfilling many of the roles.

Above all, a willingness to learn new skills and work with unfamiliar technologies is paramount, as no one person can be expected to be an expert in all available smart technologies. The basic skills for building a mood-sensitive space are:

- architectural knowledge (for assessing the space available);
- hardware and software skills, in particular prototyping and testing;
- IoT knowledge;
- a basic psychological understanding of mood and emotion (to have the space correctly adapt to inhabitants' psychological expressions).

As well as team members that can adapt their existing knowledge and learn new skills, knowledge and expertise may come from contractors, consultants, existing literature, and any stakeholders in the space (e.g., the building's owners).

Usability and user willingness to engage

A successful mood-sensitive smart space is intrinsically linked to the engagement of the inhabitants with the space. As such, the usability of the space must be one of the foremost design considerations. A user-friendly smart space is one that maximizes the gains for those using it, whilst minimizing the obligations of the inhabitant to the space to ensure its functioning. Smart spaces should utilize their autonomy to reduce the amount of input required from inhabitants, which increases the usability of the space, while also allowing for inhabitants to override the smart space's choices if desired. As a rule of thumb, the less intrusive the smart space is into the experiences of the inhabitants, the more user-friendly the space will be. This rule should be considered when placing sensors in the space, and if the space needs to ask for input from the inhabitants. For example, a camera for detecting an inhabitant's mood through their facial expression may facilitate a mood-sensitive space; however, the space is not usable if the inhabitant has to walk up to the camera and stand perfectly still every few minutes to get their facial expression recorded. It should also be stated that a usable smart space must be fully accessible to inhabitants and considerate of any physical, mental, or emotional needs.

The other important factor to consider when designing for usability is the willingness of the inhabitants to use the space at all. Demographics such as age are strongly correlated with an unwillingness to engage with technology, as discussed in the previous section on AAL, and are compounded by the fact that an autonomous mood-sensitive space must record and process biometric information about its inhabitants in order to compute their emotion. Biometric information is extremely sensitive and should be stored and used in a secure manner, and having a plan for data security that inhabitants can access and understand can help increase their

willingness to engage with the space. However, it is important that designers of potential mood-sensitive spaces consult with potential users of the space to establish that the space is useful, usable, and welcomed. It is important to note that for this that "users" does not just include inhabitants of the space, but encompasses other people who would potentially be in the space, such as carers or cleaning staff.

An Example of a Mood-Sensitive Space

An example of how a mood-sensitive smart home might utilize mood data is presented here. This example assumes that the smart home can collect audio-visual mood data from its inhabitant, and has the ability to control lighting, climate controls, entertainment systems, and home security. In this example, the inhabitant of the home returns after a stressful day at work feeling particularly burnt out. This behaviour is evident in their facial expression and their body posture, which is analysed during the "sense" cycle of their smart home. During the "compute" cycle, the home ascribes the "stressed" emotion label to the inhabitant using an affective computing classifier. The smart home is now able to make decisions based on this classification label. The user has previously set up a music playlist that they wish to listen to when stressed, so the smart home begins the playlist on the entertainment system. The smart home also dims the lights and changes their hue, based on previously learnt information that softer lighting helps alleviate a stressed mood. Finally, the smart home has learnt that from previous times the inhabitant has been "stressed," the inhabitant has a tendency to forget to lock the doors and set the burglar alarm when in a "stressed" state, so the smart home is able to perform those actions for them.

From a smart home with one inhabitant, the system could be expanded to multiple inhabitants[27] with each room reacting appropriately to its inhabitant's mood (clashes caused by inhabitants being in the same space are discussed in the following section). When multi-person mood-sensitive spaces are possible, it is then a short stretch to envisage an enclosed public space that is also mood-sensitive. For example, consider a smart theatre that is putting on a dramatic performance; the theatre could utilize visual data, for example cameras facing the audience, to determine the aggregate audience mood and then change elements of the performance to aid in swaying the audience's mood and perception (perhaps by adjusting ambient sounds and lighting in the space).

Discussion

Mood-sensitive spaces as presented above are complex both computationally and socially, and have a variety of benefits and drawbacks associated with

them. It is worth reiterating at this stage that such spaces are currently only theoretical, so any discussion of their pros and cons must be read with the understanding that these are speculation based on similar use cases.[28] However, even with that caveat, the potential gains from mood-sensitive spaces are significant.

The benefits of mood-sensitive smart homes are centred around the health, well-being, and happiness of the inhabitants. The ability of the smart home to automatically take action to improve the inhabitants' moods will reduce stress, improve mental health, and subsequently improve the general health of the inhabitants. Increasing the number of actions that can be automated by the home, particularly pertaining to health and wellness, will also reduce the burden of the system on the inhabitants. This will improve the general usability of the system and the likelihood of further adoption of smart home technologies. Multi-user mood-sensitive public spaces, for example theatres or subway stations, will improve user experience by adapting to the emotional needs of the users. Such spaces will also be able to aid public health and safety, for example by aiding with emotional management for crowd control.

The drawbacks to mood-sensitive spaces, both public and in the home, fall into two camps: privacy concerns and computational concerns. The first, privacy, must be paramount in mood-sensitive spaces, given the systems' inherent access to personal and potentially identifiable information (e.g. biometric readings). Within the smart home, privacy is already a well-monitored concern; however, there is always the risk of a data breach. This risk increases in public spaces due to the visibility of the space (making the spaces more viable targets for malicious attacks) and the large amount of individuals' data being processed. The second set of drawbacks, computational, relates to wider concerns with big data and computational complexity; mainly, how such a large volume of data can be processed in an efficient and timely fashion. The continuous classification of mood and prediction of further mood, from a wide array of sensors, is a complex task that requires many computational resources that may simply not be available in some smart homes. This processing could be outsourced to a central service hosted away from the individual's home; however that then increases the risk of privacy violations. There is not currently an answer to the optimal way to deal with this complexity. Since this work is theoretical, there is also no current model for a multi-user mood-sensitive space. When designing such a space, differences between the users' moods (and, subsequently, how they wish the space to react to those moods) must be taken into account and some form of conflict resolution put into place. AI-driven conflict resolution can make suboptimal decisions and may require training for the home's specific inhabitants. This means that further research is required before a truly multi-user space can become available.

Future Work

The concept of a mood-sensitive space is, at this point, largely theoretical. Each of the required elements exists, as outlined in the previous sections of this chapter; however, they have not yet been combined into one ubiquitous solution. This makes the prospect of future work in this area both exciting and daunting. The first practical steps would be to take the framework and recommendations presented here and create a smart space that is reactive to a single inhabitant's emotions. This task is not only technical and would need to include studies on how the space affects the inhabitant's mood, as well as the inhabitant's opinions about the space. Research into, and application of, privacy and security concerns arising from using biometric information in a smart home system should also take place. From there, a mood-sensitive space could be further refined as more research is carried out.

There is computational research that needs to be done in order to facilitate a multi-user mood-sensitive space. In the previous section, computational concerns were outlined in regard to affective computing, and a mood-sensitive space would need to rely on lightweight, dynamic models of inhabitants' moods in order to compute the most appropriate action for the smart space to take. Currently, even affective computing models that can learn from multiple users are highly personalized to a specific user. Lightweight and generalized affective models need to be researched and developed for multi-user mood-sensitive spaces. The previous section also outlined the issue of aggregating mood across multiple space users, and the limitations of current AI-based conflict resolution algorithms for deciding between actions to take (in this case, deciding between conflicting mood states so that the space can take action). Specific aggregation and conflict resolution algorithms for affective computing need to be developed before a multi-user mood-sensitive space can be fully realized.

Finally, more research into the design, usability, and habitability of smart spaces needs to take place before mood-sensitive spaces become commonplace. Creating seamless, comfortable, usable, and liveable smart spaces should be looked at from both a human–computer interaction standpoint and an architectural standpoint. This should include developing frameworks of best practice for adapting different types of spaces into both smart spaces and specifically mood-sensitive spaces.

Conclusion

This chapter has reviewed technologies currently available and how they may be adapted to create mood-sensitive spaces, both private and public, and has presented arguments for the benefits of such spaces. There are privacy and computational

concerns with such spaces that are not insignificant but also not insurmountable. There is also further research required before such spaces can be completely realized. On the whole, mood-sensitive spaces have the capacity to offer sizable benefits to health, well-being, and user satisfaction and deserve to be explored further.

NOTES

1. Marie Chan, Daniel Estève, Christophe Escriba, and Eric Campo, "A Review of Smart Homes—Present State and Future Challenges." *Computer Methods and Programs in Biomedicine* 91, no. 1 (2008): 55–81. https://doi.org/10.1016/j.cmpb.2008.02.001.
2. Ju Wang, Nicolai Spicher, Joana M. Warnecke, Mostafa Haghi, Jonas Schwartze, and Thomas M. Deserno, "Unobtrusive Health Monitoring in Private Spaces: The Smart Home." *Sensors (Switzerland)* (2021). MDPI AG. https://doi.org/10.3390/s21030864.
3. Rasha El-Azab, "Smart Homes: Potentials and Challenges." *Clean Energy* 5, no. 2 (2021): 302–15. https://doi.org/10.1093/CE/ZKAB010.
4. Suriya Priya R. Asaithambi, Sitalakshmi Venkatraman, and Ramanathan Venkatraman, "Big Data and Personalisation for Non-Intrusive Smart Home Automation." *Big Data and Cognitive Computing* 5, no. 1 (2021): 6. https://doi.org/10.3390/BDCC5010006.
5. Wenda Li, Tan Yigitcanlar, Isil Erol, and Aaron Liu, "Motivations, Barriers and Risks of Smart Home Adoption: From Systematic Literature Review to Conceptual Framework." *Energy Research & Social Science* 80 (October 2021): 102211. https://doi.org/10.1016/J.ERSS.2021.102211.
6. W. A. Rogers, T. L. Mitzner, W. R. Boot, N. H. Charness, S. J. Czaja, and J. Sharit, "Understanding Individual and Age-Related Differences in Technology Adoption." *Innovation in Aging* 1 (suppl_1) (2017): 1026. https://doi.org/10.1093/geroni/igx004.3733.
7. Mehedi Hasan, Parag Biswas, Md Toufiqul Islam Bilash, and Md Ashik Zafar Dipto, "Smart Home Systems: Overview and Comparative Analysis," in *Proceedings – 2018 4th IEEE International Conference on Research in Computational Intelligence and Communication Networks, ICRCICN 2018* (Institute of Electrical and Electronics Engineers Inc., 2018), 264–68. https://doi.org/10.1109/ICRCICN.2018.8718722.
8. "Amazon.Co.Uk: Amazon Smart Home." n.d., accessed July 13, 2022. https://www.amazon.co.uk/b?node=14526211031.
9. "Google Nest, Build Your Connected Home—Google Store." n.d., accessed July 13, 2022. https://store.google.com/gb/category/connected_home?pli=1&hl=en-GB.
10. "Smart Home & Smart Home Systems—IKEA." n.d., accessed July 13, 2022. https://www.ikea.com/gb/en/product-guides/ikea-home-smart-system/.
11. Sense–compute–act models are a common design paradigm for reactive systems which use hardware to interact with their environment.
12. Stephanie Blackman, Claudine Matlo, Charisse Bobrovitskiy, Ashley Waldoch, Mei Lan Fang, Piper Jackson, Alex Mihailidis, Louise Nygård, Arlene Astell, and Andrew Sixsmith,

"Ambient Assisted Living Technologies for Aging Well: A Scoping Review." *Journal of Intelligent Systems* 25 (2016): 55–69. https://doi.org/10.1515/jisys-2014-0136.
13. Ju Wang et al., "Unobtrusive Health Monitoring."
14. Luis M. Camarinha-Matos, Joao Rosas, Ana Ines Oliveira, and Filipa Ferrada, "Care Services Ecosystem for Ambient Assisted Living." *Enterprise Information Systems* 9, no. 5–6 (2015): 607–33. https://doi.org/10.1080/17517575.2013.852693.
15. Aristodemos Pnevmatikakis, "Recognising Daily Functioning Activities in Smart Homes." *Wireless Personal Communications* 96, no. 3 (October 2017): 3639–54. https://doi.org/10.1007/s11277-017-4060-3.
16. Aras R. Dargazany, Paolo Stegagno, and Kunal Mankodiya, "WearableDL: Wearable Internet-of-Things and Deep Learning for Big Data Analytics—Concept, Literature, and Future." *Mobile Information Systems* (Hindawi Limited, 2018). https://doi.org/10.1155/2018/8125126.
17. Giovanni Diraco, Alessandro Leone, and Pietro Siciliano, "A Radar-Based Smart Sensor for Unobtrusive Elderly Monitoring in Ambient Assisted Living Applications." *Biosensors* 7, no. 4 (November 2017): 55. https://doi.org/10.3390/bios7040055.
18. Rubén Blasco, Álvaro Marco, Roberto Casas, Diego Cirujano, and Richard Picking, "A Smart Kitchen for Ambient Assisted Living." *Sensors (Switzerland)* 14, no. 1 (January 2014): 1629–53. https://doi.org/10.3390/s140101629.
19. Soujanya Poria, Erik Cambria, Rajiv Bajpai, and Amir Hussain, "A Review of Affective Computing: From Unimodal Analysis to Multimodal Fusion." *Information Fusion* 37 (September 2017): 98–125. https://doi.org/10.1016/j.inffus.2017.02.003.
20. Charalampos Karyotis, Faiyaz Doctor, Rahat Iqbal, Anne James, and Victor Chang, "A Fuzzy Computational Model of Emotion for Cloud Based Sentiment Analysis." *Information Sciences* 433–34 (April 2018): 448–63. https://doi.org/10.1016/j.ins.2017.02.004.
21. Ali Mollahosseini, Behzad Hasani, and Mohammad H. Mahoor, "AffectNet: A Database for Facial Expression, Valence, and Arousal Computing in the Wild." *IEEE Transactions on Affective Computing* 10, no. 1 (January 2019): 18–31. https://doi.org/10.1109/TAFFC.2017.2740923.
22. Yuan Pin Lin, "Constructing a Personalized Cross-Day EEG-Based Emotion-Classification Model Using Transfer Learning." *IEEE Journal of Biomedical and Health Informatics* 24, no. 5 (May 2020): 1255–64. https://doi.org/10.1109/JBHI.2019.2934172.
23. Philip Schmidt, Attila Reiss, Robert Dürichen, and Kristof Van Laerhoven, "Wearable-Based Affect Recognition—A Review." *Sensors (Switzerland)* (September 20, 2019). https://doi.org/10.3390/s19194079.
24. Sara Ann Taylor, Natasha Jaques, Ehimwenma Nosakhare, Akane Sano, and Rosalind Picard, "Personalized Multitask Learning for Predicting Tomorrow's Mood, Stress, and Health." *IEEE Transactions on Affective Computing* (2017): 1–1. https://doi.org/10.1109/TAFFC.2017.2784832.

25. "Core Specification 5.0 – Bluetooth® Technology Website." n.d., accessed July 4, 2022. https://www.bluetooth.com/specifications/specs/core-specification-5/.
26. "Raspberry Pi 4 Model B Specifications—Raspberry Pi." n.d., accessed July 4, 2022. https://www.raspberrypi.com/products/raspberry-pi-4-model-b/specifications/.
27. Tinghui Wang and Diane J. Cook, "Multi-Person Activity Recognition in Continuously Monitored Smart Homes." *IEEE Transactions on Emerging Topics in Computing* (2021). https://doi.org/10.1109/TETC.2021.3072980.
28. Charlie Wilson, Tom Hargreaves, and Richard Hauxwell-Baldwin, "Benefits and Risks of Smart Home Technologies." *Energy Policy* 103 (April 2017): 72–83. https://doi.org/10.1016/j.enpol.2016.12.047.

BIBLIOGRAPHY

Anonymous. "USB Type-C | USB-IF." n.d. Accessed July 4, 2022. https://usb.org/usbc.

Asaithambi, Suriya Priya R., Sitalakshmi Venkatraman, and Ramanathan Venkatraman. "Big Data and Personalisation for Non-Intrusive Smart Home Automation." *Big Data and Cognitive Computing* 5, no. 1 (2021): 6. https://doi.org/10.3390/BDCC5010006.

Chadborn, Neil H., Krista Blair, Helen Creswick, Nancy Hughes, Liz Dowthwaite, Oluwafunmilade Adenekan, and Elvira Pérez Vallejos. "Citizens' Juries: When Older Adults Deliberate on the Benefits and Risks of Smart Health and Smart Homes." *Healthcare* 7, no. 2 (April 2019): 54. https://doi.org/10.3390/healthcare7020054.

Dong, Bowei, Qiongfeng Shi, Yanqin Yang, Feng Wen, Zixuan Zhang, and Chengkuo Lee. "Technology Evolution from Self-Powered Sensors to AIoT Enabled Smart Homes." *Nano Energy* 79, January (2021): 105414. https://doi.org/10.1016/J.NANOEN.2020.105414.

4

Smooth Invisible: Liquid Surveillance and Architecture

Hüsnü Yegenoglu and Justin Agyin

Introduction

The collection, extraction, processing, and interpretation of big data, increasingly executed by algorithms and artificial intelligence, might have various advantages for individuals, companies, governments, and society at large. However, the processing of data also presents an inherent societal danger of control and surveillance that threatens notions such as privacy, self-determination, and independence. This leads to the vagueness of the classical demarcations and intermediaries between public and private domains. Contemporary surveillance technologies contribute to this increasing interpenetration of domains, leading to the erosion of traditional spatial boundaries and thresholds, whilst creating new kinds of surveillance aesthetics in architecture. What might the spatial impact of the transforming conditions of transparency be, and what might the role of the discipline of architecture be, at a time when the definition of the boundaries between private and public domains are increasingly becoming blurred at a virtual rather than physical level? The key hypothesis of this chapter is that the contemporary architectural manifestations of surveillance are not driven by physical restrictions but that they are being taken over by virtual structures of information, access, exchange, and smooth invisible control embedded in our built environments.

We assume that "the sheltering eyes of privacy" will increasingly be digitally dissolved by advanced types of data-based surveillance systems that manifest themselves in new architectural aesthetics.[1] This development will lead to new categories of watching and being watched, and revaluations of the balance between the digital gaze and the physical gaze. This ongoing process is examined by a discussion of relevant literature and a concise analyses of a selection of buildings that are representative of the ongoing transformations. Hence, this chapter is composed

of three parts. In the first part a selection of architectural and power-related interpretations of the twentieth-century emergence of constant mobility and change, also known as "liquid spaces," is explored.[2] Second, the influence of the latest technological advances on contemporary strategies of surveillance in architecture will be discussed. Lastly, the practical application of this development is discussed through a speculative exploration of three hypermodern architectural tactics. In a concluding critical and speculative reflection, the parts are synthesized, and the key hypothesis of this chapter is explicated.

The Architecture of Lethargic Transparency

The transition from opacity to transparency has been pivotal in twentieth-century modernist architecture. Architecture historian Siegfried Giedion, one of the most influential interpreters of modernist architecture, has discussed this subject intensively throughout his career. Gideon was strongly inspired by Paul Scheerbart's book *Glass Architecture* (1914) which contained a sequence of inspiring aphorisms about the advantage of a future development designed with iron and glass.[3] According to Scheerbart, our culture is to a certain extent the product of our architecture.

> If we want our culture to rise to a higher level, we are obliged, for better or for worse, to change our architecture [...]. We can only do that by introducing glass architecture, which lets in the light of the sun, the moon, and the stars, not merely through a few windows, but through every possible wall, which will be made entirely of glass—of coloured glass. The new environment, which we thus create, must bring us a new culture.[4,5]

Giedion described the attendance of spatial transparency as something that occurs via the interstitial constitution of a composition, "a fluid transition of things," which is characterized by "a great indivisible space in which relations and interpenetrations, rather than boundaries, reign."[6] For Giedion, transparent architecture should overcome traditional concepts of spatial division and tectonic solidity, and should consist of one indivisible, continuous space where interior and exterior merge into one another. In this way, a direct link is forged between glass as an architectural material and as an aesthetic instrument to shape modern society. In 1963, Giedion's perspective on spatial interpenetration was further examined by architectural theorists Colin Rowe and Robert Slutzky, who distinguished two types of transparency: *literal* transparency, a kind of perceptual experience that engages the eye, and *phenomenal* transparency, which can be understood as a cognitive experience that engages the intellect of the viewer.[7,8]

Moreover, transparency has been embedded in modernist architecture by systematically propagating it in the avant-garde design education at the influential Bauhaus School of Art and Architecture. Its founder and director Walter Gropius designed the first large glass façade in Europe for the Fagus Factory in Lower Saxony in 1911, and his successor Mies van der Rohe created an unprecedented design for a fully glass-sheathed skyscraper in Berlin in 1921. Hence, at the beginning of the twentieth century, the artistic potential of transparency was discovered and illustrated on a hitherto unprecedented scale, as was its ability to liberate the suffocating traditional interior space characterized by seclusion and separateness. Despite the substantive differences between the interpretations, these and many other examples attest to transparency being a particular strategy in modernist architecture as powerfully representing the openness of the modern human to "overcome space and time fixations," and to "transpose insignificant singularities into meaningful complexities."[9] Nevertheless, it is striking that the heroes of modern architecture as Giedion, Gropius, and Van der Rohe exclusively described the architectural and aesthetical features of transparency in their discourses, but not its deeper social, cultural and ethical impacts on aspects of public and private lives, such as the notion of privacy. For instance, Edith Farnsworth, commissioner of Van der Rohe's seminal Farnsworth House in Plano, Illinois, once famously said: "No one knows what it is like to live in a glass house," thereby expressing her frustration and fear of the constant feeling of surveillance that was induced by the exposure through the large transparent glass planes of the house. This feeling was exacerbated by the rigid placement of furniture as per Van der Rohe's design and ideas of what transparent modern architecture should be.[10]

The Emergence of Disciplinary Surveillance

These impacts manifest themselves in architectural projects and proposals, as transparency in modern architecture is often diametrically opposed to traditional conceptions of privacy. It can be argued that there is no overarching concept or singular understanding of privacy, but that there are, rather, several distinct core notions that have been lumped together.[11] Traditionally, privacy has been determined "as the right to be left alone."[12] Within this classical perspective, "the right to privacy is essentially the right of individuals to have their own domain, separated from the public."[13] Despite the different readings of privacy that have emerged over time, they are consistent in their concern about the fragility of private spaces, and therefore advocate for a maximum insight into the benefits of spatial transparency together with its panoptical characteristics.

The spatial conditions of the modern panopticon were worked out by the philosopher and social theorist Jeremy Bentham in *A Plan of Management for a*

Panopticon Penitentiary-House, written in 1791.[14] As a prison, the panopticon allows, by way of its design with a central observation tower, a single watchman to observe and surveil all cells and inmates in its perimeter ring without the latter knowing whether they are being watched. This structure creates a permanent and unobstructed transparency into the activities of the prisoners while inspectors are invisible from view.[15] Hence, it is an effective system of omnipresent control, a machine for self-discipline, and a humanist perspective on punishment. In 1975, philosopher Michel Foucault used Bentham's panopticon concept in his influential book *Discipline and Punish: The Birth of the Prison* as a metaphor for modern society's "disciplinary capacity and [as] a hierarchical network that created what he [Foucault] describes as a dystopian unfreedom."[16] For Foucault, Bentham's Panopticon is the architectural figure of omnipresent control mechanisms of societies, in which the transparent gaze of power is under the permanent invisible authority of a minority.[17]

Probably the most imaginative damning of spatial transparency has, however, not emerged in architectural discourses, but in the domain of literature. The origin of this development can be found in Yevgeny Zamyatin's dystopic novel *We* from 1921.[18] In *We*, the identity and behaviour of the protagonist D-503 and the other citizens of *One State* are moulded by a transparent world that is characterized by tall glass buildings, which restrict and expose personal space to subject everyday life to continuous surveillance. All spaces are always visible to everyone, especially to the "ciphers," the omnipresent agents of state control, who are assumed to be always watching, creating an architectural landscape of constant observation.[19] The internalized surveillance of the One State is not applied exclusively by ciphers and snitches. Trained as a mathematician-engineer, D-503 is aware of the power of machines in the development of new controlling techniques that never existed before. It may be surprising, but according to D-503 machines are meant to be more than just serving and functional objects of control. Because of their ability to create an *interspace* between humans and technology, they illuminate the aesthetics of sublime rationalism "by light blue rays of sunshine."[20]

In his book *1984*, which is heavily influenced by Zamyatin's *We*, George Orwell describes the rise of a system in which people are continuously monitored by an all-knowing authority: *Big Brother*. This authority regulates and controls every facet of people's lives and accomplishes its dominance "by targeting the private life, employing various techniques of power to eliminate any sense of privacy."[21] Different from Bentham's, Foucault's, and Zamyetin's systems of control, where people are intensely monitored by other people, the primary surveillance device in Orwell's superstate *Oceania* is a technological device called the *telescreen*. Telescreens are installed in each private house and public space as a control tool that achieves its power through an ingenious technique of virtual visual communication. As a

live screen interface, it is not only a new mode of representation of power, but it also institutes a new order of control, which we could now recognize as the rise of digital surveillance at the beginning of the twenty-first century.[22]

Orwell indicates the rise of new information systems driven by the advancement of profound technologies that radically change the *solid* relation of spatial boundaries between inside and outside, the visible and the invisible, and the viewer and the viewed, into a state of permanent *liquid* change, which can be considered as "the rise of a condition of mental and physical flexibility that replaced solidity as the ideal order to be pursued."[23] Orwell's prophecy from 1949 was long considered a cultural and social science fiction rather than a concrete spatial reality. However, the current rapid development of digital technologies such as artificial intelligence (AI), the Internet of things (IoT), augmented reality (AR), virtual reality (VR), and robotics demand a more radical questioning of the established readings of the relation between transparency and surveillance. This should also be done from the discipline of architecture, as claimed in contemporary literature which includes David Lyon's *The Electronic Eye*, "where invisible observers track our footprints," and Shoshana Zuboff's *High Tech Is Watching You*, discussing the preoccupation of the Late-Anthropocene man with "total information," leading to "the unilateral claiming of private human experience as free raw material for translation into behavioral data."[24,25]

The Emergence of One State 2.0

In *The Transparent Society* (1998), philosopher David Brin discusses how new technological advances affect our physical private domain and erode our conception of privacy, as we are getting used to it being encroached on. He introduces the concept of *reciprocal* transparency through which surveillance technology is controlled by many instead of a few. Nevertheless, he stresses that in an era of cameras and sensors, "it will be more vital than ever for us to watch the watchers."[26] According to the lawyer Daniel J. Solove, we are in an ongoing information revolution, and we are only beginning to understand its implications for surveillance. He argues in his book *The Digital Person* (2004) for an adjusted architecture between protecting privacy and the control of data flows, and therefore "to reconcile the tension between transparency and privacy." Information scientist Helen Nissenbaum has also taken up the deeply problematic subject of privacy in relation to information technology in her book *Privacy in Content* (2010). However, she objects to the classical argument that protecting privacy means "people's right to control information about themselves."[27] What can be concluded from these and other examples of the increasingly blurring boundaries between private and

public domains is that the dizzying speed with which digital systems of information technology are being developed has an equally swift and powerful effect on social and spatial transformations in our built and experienced environments. Consequently, Ray Kurzweil's book *The Age of Spiritual Machines* (1999) now seems almost prophetic, as he argues that at the end of twenty-first century machine-based intelligences will be derived entirely from extended models of human intelligence that will affect all physical and virtual realms of the human experience.

Luciano Floridi, professor of ethics of information, describes the current increasing impact an interactive and virtual environment, also known as the *cybersphere*, on the physical sphere by means of an architectural metaphor:

> As in a classic Renaissance house, we now inhabit a piano nobile, the upper, noble floor, not even knowing what happens on the ground floor below us, where technologies are humming in the service rooms. Unless there is some malfunctioning, we may not even know that such technologies are in place. But, if something goes wrong, it is the specialist who will now have to take care of both sides of the interface, with the result that specialists are the new priests in Janus' temple. They will become increasingly powerful and influential the more we rely on higher-order technologies.[28]

If that is the case, this development will also have a radical impact on the field of architecture.

The Space of Tactics

The ongoing evolutionary process of artificial intelligence is challenging architecture's long-lasting ability to depict strategic changes, as future alternations are increasingly determined by virtual rather than by physical conditions. In this respect, the fate of contemporary architecture resonates with the verdict of theoretician Manfredo Tafuri who already claimed four decades ago that the architectural designs of his day "speak very much fluently precisely of that in which it has no part."[29] Here, we assume that architecture's capacity to reflect on the key phenomena of the twenty-first century will be *tactical* instead of *strategic*. The scholar Michel de Certeau distinguishes these two terms as follows: a strategy describes the principles of leading developments "that can be observed and measured [...] within its scope of vision." In contrast:

> the space of the tactic is the space of the other. Thus, it must play on and with a terrain imposed on it and organized by the law of a foreign power [...]. It operates in isolated actions, blow by blow.[30]

Hence, we can ask: What is the effect of the transforming conditions of transparency on surveillance aesthetics in architecture, and the role of architecture as a discipline, at a time where the definition of the boundaries between the private and the public are blurred on a virtual rather than a physical level? From this perspective, three potential lines of architectural tactics are put forward through built and unbuilt projects that serve as examples of what architectural concepts in an age of *smooth liquid surveillance* might be. Each of the six examples put forward creates different spatial conditions for the experience of surveillance and control. The differences in the designs lead to a different impact on surveillance and hence an array of perceptions and expressions of surveillance aesthetics in architecture, ranging from autonomous, stringent architecture to smooth or even hedonistic architecture. Hedonistic in the sense of an architecture that maskerades and covers the smooth surveillance operations behind its awe inspiring aesthetic surface or entertaining programme.

The first tactic exacerbates the dominance of real space through iconic physical manifestations. These are the boxy, windowless landscapes that are (almost) devoid of humans and the places where surveillance materializes in impenetrable fortresses, inverting the notion of architectural transparency with "blind spaces" hosted in the interiors. An example of this approach is the former *AT&T Long Lines Building* at 33 Thomas Street, New York, which was designed as a wire centre for interexchange telephony. The building is shaped as a heavy, stepped monolithic mass. Its completely closed façade conveys a message of "nothing to see here," and the only, yet monumental, architectural details are the ventilation ducts and vents that serve the needs of the machines inside rather than public or private lives.[31] Its visible and invisible stratified security systems exude a message of "you have no business being here," aiming to be hidden in plain sight. In doing so, architecture might be reduced to self-sustaining machines without any human interaction or intervention. It is a closed box that accommodates its content within its opaque walls, representing the ultimate tectonics of physical surveillance (Figure 4.1).

B 018 is a nightclub in Beirut, a place of nocturnal survival, designed by architect Bernard Khoury in 1998. The project is built below ground and its façade is pressed into the ground to avoid the overexposure of a mass that could act as a rhetorical monument. During the Civil War, which took place from 1975 to 1990, the area where the club is now sited was completely wiped out. Sunk into the ground like a cross between a military bunker and a mine shaft, B 018 is covered by a huge circular metal plate roof that resembles a helicopter landing pad.[32] Most famously, this roof is retractable so clubbers can dance underground yet beneath the open night sky. The bunker can be considered as a powerful architectural metaphor that mitigates the tension between the violent history of its location and people's desire for extensive entertainment and coming together to celebrate in a way to see and be seen: to surveil and to be surveilled (Figure 4.2).

FIGURE 4.1: The former AT&T Long Lines Building at 33 Thomas Street, New York, USA, 1974. Architect John Carl Warnecke & Associates. Source: Flickr/Wally Gobetz.

FIGURE 4.2: B 018, Beirut, Lebanon, 1994. Architect Bernard Khoury. Copyright: Jane Alhawat.

Voyeuristic architecture: The pleasure of the gaze

Voyeuristic architecture might be considered as that which does the exact opposite of the architecture from the bunker. By accepting the idleness of trying to retreat or hide in no longer existing private spaces, it portrays what goes on inside a building as a permanent exhibition. It traps people in glazed, reflective interiors that are explicitly visible from the outside and make the most public interior spaces possible, resulting in confusion, estrangement, and a feeling of being somewhere and nowhere simultaneously. It is the tension between the watcher and the watched, the presence of the objectifying penetrative gaze of the other, which makes one aware of being seen or judged. The new Shanghai office of *SOHO*, a major Chinese property developer, can be considered an example of voyeuristic design as its interior has been transformed into a labyrinthine, illusionary maze, also known as the *Escher Room*. The architecture's extreme transparency, lack of spatial limitations, and boundaries with a completely glazed interior creates dizzying spatial experiences to anyone who enters it and generates the discomforting feeling of total

surveillance. This is the liquid space of the Late-Anthropocene period inhabited by the *visible man*.[33]

Maison Fibre is a two-storey structure designed by the Institute for Computational Design and Construction at the University of Stuttgart and robotically manufactured from anisotropic materials, such as glass and carbon fibre systems. The size of the installation refers to Le Corbusier's *Dom-Ino*. However, it weighs about 1/50th of Corbusier's iconic artefact, which was designed with heavy, isotropic building materials. The purpose of the project is to express the possibilities of low material consumption in a building process that is performed by robots, which could mean carrying out "the entire production on-site without a significant amount of noise or waste."[34] The design aims to offer humans an ecologically balanced future, driven by artificial intelligence and technological devices. The synthetic substance of the building pushes the observer into a new sensibility by synthesizing the real world and the virtual world, as well as the interior and exterior spaces, into an indistinguishable amalgam. The lightness and openness of the design, as well as its ambiguous position between the physical and digital, constitutes an aesthetic and subtle perspective on the classic subject of voyeuristic architecture (Figure 4.3).

FIGURE 4.3: Maison Fibre at the 2021 Architecture Biennale, Venice, Italy. Design by ICD/ITKE/IntCDC, University of Stuttgart. Copyright: ICD/ITKE/IntCDC, University of Stuttgart, 2021.

The architecture of Cybertopia: The simultaneity of physical and virtual space

Cybertopia represents an early adaptation of a future inevitably dominated by technology in a society struggling to abandon analogue methods. In Cybertopia, scale is irrelevant and skylines and recognizable forms bear no relation to their original functions. The virtual becomes spatial through readings of the structure of computers and their networks. Entire neighbourhoods and cities are built and deleted, moved, transformed, and morphed in Cybertopia, where limits are inconceivable and reality is undefined, making landscapes of computer games an integral part of the city.[35] The world of Cybertopia is a metaphysical realm of information and data, though it could not exist without physical infrastructures, such as data centres. The *AM4 Datacenter*, designed by Benthem & Crouwel Architects in Amsterdam, is in essence a big box full of electronic devices, as routers, switches, firewalls, storage systems, servers, and application-delivery controllers. No daylight, which could indicate changes in time, enters the server rooms. Access to the building is completely restricted because of the need for the highest level of security. It is a hypermodern castellum, a physical artefact of Cyberspace that protects the domains of the infosphere and metaverse. The abstract, patterned façade that glistens under the sunlight emphasizes the abstractness and complete interiority of the design, giving it a surrealistic gaze. The advent of shiny data centres represents the beginning of the final geological epoch, also known as the *Post-Anthropocene*, where it is not humans who are the dominant force shaping the planet, but machines of data surveillance driven by artificial intelligence and machine learning, which is step-by-step transforming the way humans live and interact with machines (Figure 4.4).

Flad Architects' *New Care Center* is a new type of healthcare architecture. It is driven by information technology transforming patient care and disease management. The rise of digital health includes mobile health apps, electronic records, virtual disease management, and digital twins.[36] The new care centre should be seen as no less than the beginning of a revolutionary alteration of healthcare, which was once based on the physical communication between physician and patient. The healthcare of the twenty-first century will presumably take place in the world of 3D mixed reality to a large extent, characterized by a synthesis of augmented reality (AR), virtual reality (VR), and artificial intelligence (AI). This kind of treatment will be another step on the road to virtuality, and the vanishing of physical communication, as patients will no longer be bound to their physical location to consult clinicians.[37] In the world of digital health, the patient may live in Amsterdam and the specialist treating that patient may be a resident of Shanghai, whilst they can meet effectively in the same room by putting on headsets. In the care centre of the future, the human body will become transparent in all its

FIGURE 4.4: Datacenter AM4, Amsterdam, The Netherlands. Architect: Benthem Crouwel Architects. Copyright: Justin Agyin, 2018.

FIGURE 4.5: New Care Center, 2020. Rendering courtesy of Flad Architects // Flad.com. Copyright: Flad Architects.

details without being chained to any physical conditions of specific healthcare architecture. Within the clash of the physical infosphere and digital cybersphere, the human body becomes the subject of a surveillance architecture that is geared towards omnipresent data accumulation (Figure 4.5).

Conclusion

Reflecting on the central thesis of this chapter, it could be argued that the physical threshold between the private and public realms is eroded by new kinds of virtual surveillance technologies that seem to dissolve "the sheltering walls of privacy digitally."[38] Moreover, the ongoing evolutionary process of computational technology, AI, AR, and VR have a radical impact on architecture's traditional and long-lasting ability to depict strategic changes, since future alternations will be determined by virtual rather than physical conditions. The unlimited flow of artificial data generates very powerful new interventions that nobody plans or controls. Consequently, "as the global data-processing system becomes all-knowing and all-powerful, so connecting to the system becomes the source of all meaning."[39] This increasing impact of digital technologies will have an impact on (spatial) transparency, surveillance, and privacy. Hence, it could be assumed that architecture's capacity to reflect critically on these contemporary phenomena will be rather tactical than

strategic. Architecture, including its theory and praxis, has to accept that its strategic role is lost, forcing it to explore its remaining possibilities and relative independence on a tactical level.[40] Consequently, architecture should take an artful and devious position that reflects on the rapidly changing physical and virtual world.

While the examples outlined above are by no means exhaustive, and range from built edifices to speculative future scenarios, they serve to illustrate how smooth invisible surveillance might be and is being embedded in architectural objects. We consider this development as irreversible. It is precisely in exploring this breadth of architectural concepts from an artful stance that the very real notions of digital surveillance and control, as well as their effect on the demarcations between public and private domains need to be understood, thematized, and critically countered by the discipline of architecture in order to retain its cultural and intellectual significance instead of becoming meaningless. The architectural tactics as examined in this chapter have yielded some of the most eye-catching designs that are incorporated in the world of surveillance in some way or other, but in an alienating and distorted way. The nightclub B 018, SOHO's glass office, and the Long Lines Building, for instance, all have eliciting qualities from the perspective of spatial scenography. They are highly theatrical and entertaining by combining surveillance with the pleasure of the gaze, the space of panoptic control with the blurry voyeuristic fantasies of the flâneur, and the curiosity of watching with the hidden pleasure of being watched. In our view, there is no doubt that all the projects outlined are hedonistic and scopophilic shells that accommodate smart systems of surveillance. They surprise and please the observer because of their aesthetics appearance and may even create doubts regarding the inexorably power of smooth invisible surveillance in architectural space. In any case, it is clear that Jeremy Bentham's concept of the panopticon and Michel Foucault's perspective on dystopias have entered an evolved era, characterized by a new fusion of private and public space that is increasingly controlled by invisible virtual realities. The notion of architectural transparency is gaining new meanings at the beginning of the twenty-first century. It is no longer dependent on real space but is progressively dominated by virtual space and the world of artificial reality. A phenomenon that may cause the advancement of total transparency. Instead of being just a passive spectator, this radical progress opens up new perspectives for self-reflection and reconsideration in the field of architectural design and critique.

NOTES

1. Daniel J. Solove, "The Meaning and Value of Privacy," in *Social Dimensions of Privacy: 5 Interdisciplinary Perspectives*, eds B. Roessler and D. Mokrosinska (Cambridge: Cambridge 6 University Press, 2015), 71–82.

2. Zygmunt Bauman, *Liquid Modernity* (Cambridge: Polity Press, 2000).
3. Paul Scheerbart and Bruno Taut, *Glass Architecture & Alpine Architecture* (Westport: Praeger, 1972).
4. Sigfried Giedion, *Building in France, Building in Iron, Building in Ferro-Concrete*, trans. J. Duncan Berry (Santa Monica: The Getty Center for the History of Art and the Humanities, 1995).
5. Owen Hatherley, "Without a Palace of Glass, Life Is a Burdensome Task, Paul Scheebarts's Utopian Fantasies." *Apollo: The International Art Magazine* (November 28, 2015), accessed March 18, 2022, https://www.apollo-magazine.com/without-a-palace-of-glass-life-is-a-burdensome-task-paul-scheerbarts-utopian-fantasies/.
6. Giedion, *Building in France*.
7. Colin Rowe and Robert Slutzky, "Transparency: Literal and Phenomenal." *Perspecta* 8 (1963), 45–54.
8. ALO, "Transparency II: Layering of Planes / Layering of Spaces." *Architecturality* (February 24, 2011), accessed August 3, 2021, https://architecturality.wordpress.com/2011/02/24/transparency-ii-layering-of-planeslayering-of-spaces/.
9. Rowe, *Transparency*, 45.
10. Amy M. Haddad, "Life in a Glass House." *Medium* (2016), accessed August 20, 2021, https://amymhaddad.medium.com/life-in-a-glass-house-c2ab280711e6.
11. Adam D. Moore, "Privacy: Its Meaning and Value." *American Philosophical Quarterly* 40 (2003): 215.
12. Samuel D. Warren and Louis D. Brandeis, "The Right to Privacy." *Harvard Law Review* 4 (1890): 193–220.
13. Solove, "The Meaning and Value," 71–82.
14. Jeremy Bentham, *Panopticon: Postscript; Part II: A Plan of Management for a Panopticon Penitentiary-House* (London: Printed for T. Payne, at the News-Gate, 1791).
15. Joseph M. Prio, "Foucault and the Architecture of Surveillance: Creating Regimes of Power in Schools, Shrines, and Society." *Educational Studies* 1 (2008): 35.
16. Ibid., 35.
17. Michel Foucault, *Discipline and Punish: The Birth of the Prison* (New York: Vintage books, 1995), 196.
18. Scott McQuire, "From Glass Architecture to Big Brother: Scenes from a Cultural History of Transparency." *Cultural Studies Review* 9 (2013), 109.
19. Yevgeny Zamyatin, *We*, trans. Gregory Zilboorg (Boston: E.P. Dutton, 1924), 19, accessed August 3, 2021, https://www.gutenberg.org/files/61963/61963-h/61963-h.htm#rec02.
20. Ibid., 4.
21. Solove, "The Meaning and Value," 8–29.
22. McQuire, "From Glass Architecture," 111.
23. Bauman, *Liquid Modernity*.

24. Shoshana Zuboff, *The Age of Surveillance Capitalism* (London: Profile Books, 2019).
25. David Lyon, *The Electronic Eye: The Rise of Surveillance Society* (Minneapolis: University of Minnesota Press, 1994).
26. David Brin, "The Transparent Society: Will Technology Force Us to Choose Between Privacy and Freedom?," n.d., 2021, accessed August 3, 2021, https://www.davidbrin.com/transparentsociety.html.
27. Helen Nissenbaum, *Privacy in Content: Technology, Policy, and the Integrity of Social Life* (Redwood City: Stanford University Press, 2010), 9.
28. Luciano Floridi, *The 4th Revolution: How the Infosphere Is Reshaping Human Reality* (Oxford: Oxford University Press, 2014), 37.
29. Manfredo Tafuri and Francesco Dal Co, *Modern Architecture*, trans. R. E. Wolf (New York: Harry N. Abrams, 1979), 391.
30. Michel de Certeau, *The Practice of Everyday Life* (Berkeley: University of California Press, 1988), 36–37.
31. Ryan Gallagher and Henrik Moltke, "Titanpointe: The NSA's Spy Hub in New York, Hidden in Plain Sight." *The Intercept* (November 16, 2020), accessed March 1, 2022, https://theintercept.com/2016/11/16/the-nsas-spy-hub-in-new-york-hidden-in-plain-sight/.
32. India Block, "Bernard Khoury Gives Beirut's B018 Nightclub an Even Darker Upgrade." *Dezeen* (March 3, 2019), accessed March 1, 2022, https://www.dezeen.com/2019/03/03/bernard-khoury-b018-beirut-nightclub-architecture/.
33. Chuck Klosterman, *The Visible Man* (New York: Scribner, 2011).
34. Geyer Hans-Herwig, "Living and Working in the Future: Maison Fibre of the University of Stuttgart at Biennale Architectura 2021." University of Stuttgart (May 20, 2021), accessed February 23, 2022, https://www.uni-stuttgart.de/en/university/news/all/Living-and-working-in-the-future-Maison-Fibre-of-the-University-of-Stuttgart-at-Biennale-Architettura-2021/.
35. Finn MacLeod, "Cybertopia: The Digital Future of Analog Architectural Space." *ArchDaily* (December 7, 2014), accessed August 1, 2021, https://www.archdaily.com/575874/cybertopia-the-digital-future-of-analog-architectural-space.
36. Laura Stillman, "Virtual and Physical Space Reinvention: New Care Centers of the Future." *Flad Architects* (July 13, 2020), accessed March 1, 2022, https://www.flad.com/ideas/rethinking-virtual-physical-space.php.
37. Bernard Marr, "The Amazing Possibilities of Healthcare in the Metaverse." *Forbes* (February 23, 2022), accessed March 1, 2022, https://www.forbes.com/sites/bernardmarr/2022/02/23/the-amazing-possibilities-of-healthcare-in-the-metaverse/.
38. Eric Howeler, "Anxious Architectures: The Aesthetics of Surveillance," *Archis* 3 (2002).
39. Harari, Yuval Noah, *Homo Deus: A Brief History of Tomorrow* (London: Vintage books 2017) 449.
40. Bernard Colenbrander and Hüsnü Yegenoglu, *The Instrumental Building: Architecture in the Age of Total Control* (Eindhoven: Eindhoven University of Technology, 2020), 20.

BIBLIOGRAPHY

ALO. "Transparency II: Layering of Planes / Layering of Spaces." *Architecturality* (February 24, 2011). Accessed August 3, 2021. https://architecturality.wordpress.com/2011/02/24/transparency-ii-layering-of-planeslayering-of-spaces/.

Bauman, Zygmunt. *Liquid Modernity*. Cambridge: Polity Press, 2000.

Bentham, Jeremy. *Panopticon: Postscript; Part II: A Plan of Management for a Panopticon Penitentiary-House*. London: Printed for T. Payne, at the News-Gate, 1791.

Block, India. "Bernard Khoury Gives Beirut's B018 Nightclub an Even Darker Upgrade." *Dezeen* (March 3, 2019). Accessed March 1, 2022. https://www.dezeen.com/2019/03/03/bernard-khoury-b018-beirut-nightclub-architecture/.

Brin, David. "The Transparent Society: Will Technology Force Us to Choose Between Privacy and Freedom?" 2021. Accessed August 3, 2021. https://www.davidbrin.com/transparent-society.html.

Certeau, Michel de. *The Practice of Everyday Life*. Berkeley: University of California Press, 1988, 36–37.

Colenbrander, Bernard, and Hüsnü Yegenoglu. *The Instrumental Building: Architecture in the Age of Total Control*. Eindhoven: Eindhoven University of Technology, 2020, 20.

Floridi, Luciano. *The 4th Revolution: How the Infosphere Is Reshaping Human Reality*. Oxford: Oxford University Press, 2014, 37.

Foucault, Michel. *Discipline and Punish: The Birth of the Prison*. New York: Vintage Books, 1995, 196.

Gallagher, Ryan, and Henrik Moltke. "Titanpointe, The NSA's Spy Hub in New York, Hidden in Plain Sight." *The Intercept* (November 16, 2016). Accessed March 1, 2022. https://theintercept.com/2016/11/16/the-nsas-spy-hub-in-new-york-hidden-in-plain-sight/.

Giedion, Sigfried. *Building in France, Building in Iron, Building in Ferro-Concrete*. Translated by J. Duncan Berry. Santa Monica: The Getty Center for the History of Art and the Humanities, 1995.

Haddad, Amy M. "Life in a Glass House." *Medium* (2016). Accessed August 20, 2021. https://amymhaddad.medium.com/life-in-a-glass-house-c2ab280711e6.

Hans-Herwig, Geyer. "Living and Working in the Future: Maison Fibre of the University of Stuttgart at Biennale Architectura 2021." University of Stuttgart, May 20, 2021. Accessed 23 February 2022. https://www.uni-stuttgart.de/en/university/news/all/Living-and-working-in-the-future-Maison-Fibre-of-the-University-of-Stuttgart-at-Biennale-Architettura-2021/.

Hatherley, Owen. "Without a Palace of Glass, Life Is a Burdensome Task, Paul Scheebarts's Utopian Fantasies." *Apollo: The International Art Magazine* (November 28, 2015). Accessed March 18, 2022. https://www.apollo-magazine.com/without-a-palace-of-glass-life-is-a-burdensome-task-paul-scheerbarts-utopian-fantasies/.

Howeler, Eric. "Anxious Architectures: The Aesthetics of Surveillance." *Archis* 3 (2002).

Klosterman, Chuck. *The Visible Man*. New York: Scribner, 2011.

Lyon, David. *The Electronic Eye: The Rise of Surveillance Society*. Minneapolis: University of Minnesota Press, 1994.

MacLeod, Finn. "Cybertopia: The Digital Future of Analog Architectural Space." *ArchDaily* (December 7, 2014). Accessed August 1, 2021. https://www.archdaily.com/575874/cybertopia-the-digital-future-of-analog-architectural-space.

Marr, Bernard. "The Amazing Possibilities of Healthcare in the Metaverse." *Forbes* (February 23, 2022). Accessed March 1, 2022. https://www.forbes.com/sites/bernardmarr/2022/02/23/the-amazing-possibilities-of-healthcare-in-the-metaverse/.

McQuire, Scott. "From Glass Architecture to Big Brother: Scenes from a Cultural History of Transparency." *Cultural Studies Review* 9 (2013): 109. https://search.informit.org/doi/pdf/10.3316/ielapa.200310728.

Moore, Adam D. "Privacy: Its Meaning and Value." *American Philosophical Quarterly* 40, no. 3 (2003): 215.

Nissenbaum, Helen. *Privacy in Content. Technology, Policy, and the Integrity of Social Life*, Redwood City: Stanford University Press, 2010, 9.

Prio, Joseph M. "Foucault and the Architecture of Surveillance: Creating Regimes of Power in Schools, Shrines, and Society." *Educational Studies* 44, no. 1 (2008): 35.

Rowe, Colin, and Robert Slutzky. "Transparency: Literal and Phenomenal." *Perspecta* 8 (1963): 45–54.

Scheerbart, Paul, and Bruno Taut. *Glass Architecture & Alpine Architecture*. Westport: Praeger, 1972.

Solove, Daniel J. *The Digital Person: Technology and Privacy in the Information Age*. New York: New York University Press, 2004, 8–29.

Solove, Daniel J. "The Meaning and Value of Privacy." In *Social Dimensions of Privacy: Interdisciplinary Perspectives*, edited by B. Roessler and D. Mokrosinska, Cambridge: Cambridge University Press, 2015, 71–82.

Stillman, Laura. "Virtual and Physical Space Reinvention: New Care Centers of the Future." *Flad Architects* (July 13, 2020). Accessed March 1, 2022. https://www.flad.com/ideas/rethinking-virtual-physical-space.php.

Tafuri, Manfredo, and Francesco Dal Co. *Modern Architecture*. Translated by R. E. Wolf, New York: Harry N. Abrams, 1979, 391.

Warren, Samuel D., and Louis D. Brandeis. "The Right to Privacy." *Harvard Law Review* 4(1890): 193–220.

Zamyatin, Yevgeny. *We*. Translated by Gregory Zilboorg, Boston: E.P. Dutton, 1924, 19. Accessed August 3, 2021. https://www.gutenberg.org/files/61963/61963-h/61963-h.htm#rec02.

Zuboff, Shoshana. *The Age of Surveillance Capitalism*. London: Profile Books, 2019.

5

Mediated Participatory Urban Planning and Design: An Interdisciplinary Framework

*David Harris Smith, Frauke Zeller, Emily Eyles,
John Eyles, Debora Silva De Jesus, and Calvin Hillis*

Introduction

This chapter introduces a theoretical framework for interdisciplinary mediated participatory urban planning and design. Our framework is derived from a multidisciplinary project using virtual environment technologies for participatory urban planning. As digital technologies have come to shape the city and the daily lives of its citizenry,[1] it is timely and necessary that the means by which we envision the future city are enabled by these same technologies.[2] Batty[3] suggested "that computers will have to be used to understand cities which are built of computers. There will be no other way."[4] Yet, in the digital age, planning activities are not easily communicated, nor readily understood by all stakeholders.[5,6] Furthermore, there is a gap in the research on how digital technologies, and especially, virtual environments, may be effectively utilized to achieve fuller civic participation in planning communities.

Different research areas can inform and enrich urban planning by combining the sense of place in the urban context[7,8] and the virtual sense of place.[9,10] Documenting and exploring the variation of individual and shared senses of place is critical to an inclusive urban planning paradigm that aims to achieve input and approval from all urban stakeholders. Participation and a shared sense of place is necessary to facilitate consent, collaboration, and cooperation in planning.[11] We propose that the input of urban stakeholders' sense of place can be prioritized through an approach to participatory urban planning that uses social media and multi-user virtual world environments. Moreover, given that our urban experiences include mediated (technological) experiences, the integration of media

and audience focus would help us to better understand the contributions of media to placemaking. An approach incorporating the methods used for user interaction design, typical of digital technology development,[12,13] and methods for audience research[14,15,16] can be integrated in the practices of participatory urban planning, on a theoretical level, an instrumental level, and on a measurement level.

The theoretical level

Participatory urban planning and community building

Urban planning has evolved over the past 50 years from the closed, expert-driven models employed until the late 1960s towards more inclusive, participatory approaches.[17] Participation has, in some respects, been institutionalized since the 1990s, but some researchers claim that participants have become disillusioned, as there are not always clear links between their input and what actually happens.[18,19] There are diverging views on what specifically is a useful participatory urban planning practice, as well as variation in the dissemination of these ideas and practices.[20]

At the theoretical level, a better understanding of the perception and conception of urban contexts is necessary. The fact is that urban context per se does not exist, nor is it an entity that can be discretely defined a priori. On the contrary, urban context(s) consist of variable sets of different concepts that contribute to an individual's sense of place and the perception of shared places, such as physical space, historical engagement, economic and demographic status, locality, and neighbourhood; these contributing concepts may be used to shape a framework for participatory urban planning.

The notion of space

Space is amorphous and intangible and is nearly always associated with other concepts. For example, Lefebvre distinguishes between absolute space and social or meaningful space.[21] According to Tuan, spaces become places as they are given value.[22] Space versus place renders a crude juxtaposition between a physical and a semantic reading of the environment, while it is unlikely that either of these perspectives are capable of standing alone. Relph[8] conceived of geographical space as fragmented, becoming differentiated and claimed for humanity through naming it, making familiar spaces into places. Relph distinguishes different types of space, the primitive space of instinctive behaviour and unselfconscious action, and a perceptual space that has a clearly developed phenomenological structure. Encounters and experiences in perceptual spaces become differentiated into places, which can also be called "centres of special personal significance."[23]

The sense of place

Notions that inform a sense of place often describe the atmosphere and quality of a place, and perhaps what is attractive about that place to the person in question.[24] A person's sense of place is formed by integrating the topography, natural conditions, symbolism, meanings, and built environment.[25] Hay describes the sense of place as "an individually-based but group-informed, place-specific, personal means of relating to the world."[26]

Agnew's structuralist approach parses three components of place: "locale, location, and sense of place."[27] Locale is where social relations are constituted, in essence, the material space in which individuals and communities interact, whereas location is the geographical setting for these interactions, governed by socio-economic processes. Although we often assert that urban change emphasizes location above all else, a sense of place is the common frame of experiences linking location and locale.[28] Places can take on different identities depending on the role an individual plays in a space, as an insider or outsider, or depending on how it is navigated, i.e. by drivers versus pedestrians.[8] Rose argues that the sense of place can be felt so intensely that it can become a central part in the construction of individual identities.[29] Places are interconnected, contributing to the scope and character of actions.[30] It is therefore important to assess the sense of place by conducting research into the varied meanings, beliefs, and experiences behind it:[31] urban spaces always have an identity and sense of place associated with them for individuals and these may be variously shared with or contradicted by others.

Place attachment is an important human need and is the foundation of community and individual identity. Place attachment and identity can influence behaviour, as, according to Stedman,[32] people are willing to fight for places central to their identity, and so the community is strongly linked with place.[33] Place attachments are often best realized when planning and/or development threatens their existence.[34] The challenge is how to integrate shared and individual emotional experiences with more objective, physical community needs in the planning process. One approach might be to use different channels for participation, as a mediated participatory urban planning approach offers: different (media) channels or practices offer a multitude of ways for participation.

Media practices and sense of place in urban contexts

The role of media in urban processes has been an area of increasing interest in urban studies, with a particular focus on information and communication technologies (ICTs). According to Tosoni and Tarantino,[35] the media system and individual practices relating to media have qualitatively shifted through media saturation.

Couldry[36] calls for research approaches that focus on the practice of social actors and audiences rather than solely on the media itself.[37] "Audiencing," according to Waltorp,[38] refers to both an opportunity and activity to see or hear a representation or performance. With new technologies and venues, come new opportunities to act as audiences or to project representations and make meanings. For example, social media platforms are a form of constructed place, featuring intersections of personalized and mass media and public and private spheres.[39] Tosoni and Tarantino's review of the literature on urban conflict and media emphasizes four problematic factors: "(1) a polarisation of 'old' and 'new' media; (2) a single-medium focus; (3) a poor integration of media content with social actors' meaning-making and practices; and (4) preconceived notions of 'media' and 'social actors'."[40] They propose bridging audience studies and urban studies in order to overcome these limitations and to generate more well-rounded research. Adapting the concept and understanding of *audiences*, instead of participants or even merely citizens, can provide a new perspective that explains how media usage has saturated our perception of urban space.

Virtual sense of place

Since Batty's prescient discussion of the computable city,[41] digital technologies have increasingly shaped the city and the everyday lives of its citizenry.[42,43,44] Takeyama[45] proposed that cyberspace and real space are not necessarily two distinct spaces, as our real space is already overlaid and activated with the data resources and products of computation. Individuals, cultural organizations, businesses, and governments use the hybrid real-digital city in their work in commerce, resource and utility distribution, information retrieval and distribution, communication, and entertainment.[46] Furthermore, most citizens use mobile devices, which liberate many of these activities from temporal and spatial constraints.

Kesselring[47] proposes that an individual's or community's important places may no longer be strictly physical, but could, for example, places facilitated by their mobile phone. People go places online, and, according to Cowan,[48] these places are not metaphorical, or imagined, but literal ones; the language of Internet use is that of travel, for example to explore, navigate, or visit websites. People are compelled to form communities and be proximate to one another, but now, with virtual places, this is no longer necessarily physical.[49] Telepresence involves being alone, or together with others, in a virtual environment by means of a communication medium.[50,51] 3D virtual worlds, such as Second Life, SineSpace, Sansar, High Fidelity, OpenSimulator, or Mozilla Hubs, are virtual places where people can be telepresent together, and they include a variety of types of spaces to which users attach meaning. The sense of place individuals derive from these virtual spaces appears to involve similar personalized conceptions to that associated with their

physical spaces, such as the history of engagement, social status, and identity. In their study of a Second Life virtual world community, Bardzell and Odom observed that "the tools used to design and administer these environments need to focus not just on the literal building of spaces (i.e. 3D modelling tools) but also on the building of emotional, personal, and meaningful spaces."[52]

The Instrument Level

With increasing capabilities and diffusion of digital technologies, it is necessary for ongoing review and updating of participatory planning practices in this context.[53] Visualization appears key to public participation, as it is a shared language to which participants can relate.[54] Tress and Tress[55] suggest that the ideal visualization tool for participatory urban planning would be 3D, GIS-based software with dynamic characteristics. Wu, He, and Gong underline the importance of well-designed visualization and engagement tools for planning communication, and specifically the development of a "virtual globe-based 3D visualization framework for publicizing urban planning information"[56] via the internet and suggest four objectives for this environment.[57,58]

> 1. The system should be a distributed computing environment, which is convenient for end users to access from any low-end personal home computer. [...] 2. The system should provide a 3D visualization environment that inherits the visual effects and the operating habits of virtual globes such as Google Earth. [...] 3. The integrated 3D visualization client supports interaction and interoperability. [...] 4. Various other traditional channels are provided for end users to submit online comments about urban planning designs.[59]

There is an increasing amount of user-generated geospatial content online[60] which Sui calls the "wikification" of GIS, creating "geography without geographers."[61] Building upon the distributed authorship of GIS content, users rely upon social media comments from other users and used them more frequently than other navigational aids.[62] Additionally, literature from a number of fields points to user preference for narrative information over statistical information.[63,64,65]

As mobile devices have become ubiquitous, 3D mixed reality (MR) and augmented reality (AR) techniques may contribute to participatory urban planning. Using a mobile viewfinder, participants can visualize developments overlaid onto the streets and buildings in front of them, allowing for an integrated sensory experience of planning proposals. Ghadirian and Bishop[66] tested overlaying panoramic video with modelled temporal changes in Victoria, Australia,

and found that participants did not generally detect a computer element. Thus, visualization and especially 3D visualization environments do not only integrate the possibility of bundling diverse participants' input, but they also provide early multiple channels/practices for participation.[67] However, in order for these participatory planning benefits to be realized, the visualization technologies must be easily accessed and manipulated by people with minimal training; user-friendly interfaces remain a significant challenge.[68]

The digital and virtual technologies in our model provide platforms for stakeholder input, in addition to traditional methods. For example, we can record, measure, and analyse how different participants use 3D visualization environments in a participatory urban planning context. This includes personal preferences related to actual urban planning contexts, but also how they use these environments in general, which (communication) channels they prefer, etc. Thus, these environments do not only offer diverse interaction opportunities in participatory urban planning, they also function as data collection and storage devices essential to the evaluation of stakeholders' attitudes. For example, in Figures 5.1 and 5.2 public planning charrette participants used both paper and digital design tools to propose street renovations. The digital design tools included street layout software integrated with 3D street models which were capable of running pedestrian and traffic simulations as well as calculating renovation costs for the various designs. The planning charrette was also augmented by popular social media such as Twitter, Facebook, and YouTube.

Indeed, through an approach that leverages social media and virtual scenarios, there are opportunities to facilitate the collection and integration of personal narratives regarding a sense of place in planning activities, and affordances for

FIGURE 5.1: Planning charrette combining analog and digital 3D planning environments. Participant used both paper and digital design tools to propose street renovations. The inclusion of 3D virtual environments provides flexible real-time visualization and the ability to run traffic and pedestrian simulations. David Harris Smith, 2020.

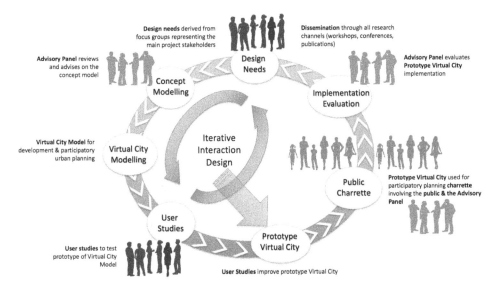

FIGURE 5.2: Interaction design cycle in urban planning. Framework for participatory planning that utilizes an interaction design approach to the mediated city to contribute to equitable changes in a sense of place. David Harris Smith, 2020.

citizens to meaningfully interact with and shape multiple planning scenarios via the digitized virtual environment as a prelude to decisive commitment. The application of 3D virtual worlds to urban modelling and participatory planning facilitates the visualization of alternative proposals and their support of real-time modifications allows for an iterative design process in response to stakeholder inputs (Figure 5.2).

The Measurement Level

We suggest using the theoretical and instrument level for a novel measuring approach: the audience studies approach at the theoretical level can provide a new understanding of the users or participants in 3D-enabled urban planning. Direct consumption or participation in this sort of initiative also falls within the framework of primary audiencing. The model we propose suggests that the inputs of the process and the outputs are often less discrete than one would imagine and create a feedback loop of sorts. Everyday experiences, for example, are useful when participating in a neighbourhood planning exercise, but they may also be shaped by this exercise and any concrete initiative that results from it. At the same time, an audience studies approach also provides methodological instruments, which can be used for measuring participatory urban planning. These instruments include

focus groups, expert interviews, and virtual ethnographies—studying the usage of 3D visualization environments. As many individuals and groups as practicable should be involved, and a mixture of these approaches is helpful to understand the use of the environment from a number of perspectives.

Conclusions

How might a framework for digitized participatory urban planning have special utility for accessing and including the highly personalized and somewhat intangible elements that contribute to a sense of place? Our theoretical, interdisciplinary framework for mediated participatory urban planning and design focused on the theoretical level on notions of sense of place in urban contexts and virtual sense of place. By discussing different notions of both place and space, we aimed to first of all see commonalities in these concepts, but also to understand how a sense of place is an important prerequisite to be able to think about changes of places and space.

The next step is to adapt these theories to a virtual sense of space as a first element at the instrument level. We did this by introducing one of our core areas of the framework—virtual technologies in participatory urban planning. The framework was designed as a multi- or interdisciplinary approach that overcomes certain disciplinary borders for the sake of a holistic approach. For example, addressing questions relating to media studies and in particular urban environments of mediated spaces as well as questions of audiencing, enables us to better understand how to use (virtual) technologies in participatory urban planning. Finally, an overview of the ideas behind and the history of participatory urban planning served as a necessary introduction to more detailed discussions about how specific digital technologies and the iterative cycle of interaction design can be used in participatory urban planning.

To summarize, we hope that this framework provides the necessary theoretical background and overview for future work in participatory urban planning, integrating digital and virtual technologies. Concepts as to perceptions of space and place, community, and mediated spaces play a pivotal role in this field, but they must be combined with a sound understanding of the different digital technologies—such as GIS-3D visualization technologies—in order to provide a successful, applicable planning and discussion approach.

ACKNOWLEDGEMENTS
This chapter has been produced through researched funded by the Social Sciences and Humanities Research Council (SSHRC) and the Ontario Ministry of Research and Innovation, Canada.

NOTES

1. Seija Ridell and Frauke Zeller, "Mediated Urbanism: Navigating an Interdisciplinary Terrain" (2013).
2. David Harris Smith, "Reflexive Design of the Recursive Space of Virtual Worlds" (2013).
3. Michael Batty, *The Computable City* (1997).
4. Ibid., 159.
5. Martin Podevyn, Margaret Horne, and Peter Fisher, "Virtual Cities: Management and Organisational Issues" (2009).
6. Johanna Ylipulli and Tiina Suopajärvi, "Contesting Ubicomp Visions through ICT Practices: Power Negotiations in the Meshwork of a Technologised City" (2013).
7. Jive´n and Larkham, "Sense of Place, Authenticity and Character: A Commentary" (2003).
8. Edward Relph, *Place and Placelessness* (1976).
9. Sven Kesselring, "Pioneering Mobilities: New Patterns of Movement and Motility in a Mobile World" (2006); see also Kevin Morgan, "The Exaggerated Death of Geography: Learning, Proximity and Territorial Innovation Systems" (2004) and Aharon Kellerman, "Social-Spatial Interaction, Proximity, and Distance: From Face-to-face to Virtual Communications" (2022) for the relative value of physical locality compared to digital spaces.
10. Edward Relph, "Spirit of Place and Sense of Place in Virtual Realities" (2007).
11. David Harris Smith, "A Theoretical Basis for Participatory Planning" (1973).
12. Yvonne Rogers, Helen Sharp, and Jenny Preece, "Interaction Design: Beyond Human-Computer Interaction" (2011).
13. David Benyon, "Designing Interactive Systems: A Comprehensive Guide to HCI, UX and Interaction Design" (2014).
14. P. M. Napoli, "Audience Evolution and the Future of Audience Research" (2012).
15. Virginia Nightingale, ed., *The Handbook of Media Audiences* (2013).
16. Brian O'Neill, J. Ignacio Gallego, and Frauke Zeller, "New Perspectives on Audience Activity: 'Prosumption' and Media Activism as Audience Practices" (2013).
17. Richard K. Brail and Richard E. Klosterman, "Planning Support Systems: Integrating Geographic Information Systems, Models, and Visualization Tools" (2001).
18. Karen Bickerstaff and Gordon Walker, "Shared Visions, Unholy Alliances: Power, Governance and Deliberative Processes in Local Transport Planning" (2005).
19. Valeria Monno and Abdul Khakee, "Tokenism or Political Activism? Some Reflections on Participatory Planning" (2012).
20. Andrew Harris and Susan Moore, "Planning Histories and Practices of Circulating Urban Knowledge" (2013).
21. Henri Lefebvre, "Reflections on the Politics of Space" (1991).
22. Yi-Fu Tuan, "The Perspective of Experience" (1977).
23. Relph, *Place and Placelessness*, 11.
24. Miriam Billig, "Sense of Place in the Neighborhood, in Locations of Urban Revitalization" (2005).

25. Jive´n and Larkham, "Sense of Place" (2003).
26. Robert Hay, "A Rooted Sense of Place in Cross-cultural Perspective" (1998), 24.
27. John A. Agnew, "Place and Politics: The Geographical Mediation of State and Society" (1987), 28.
28. Ibid.
29. Gillian Rose, "Place and Identity: A Sense of Place" (1995).
30. Mae A. Davenport and Dorothy H. Anderson, "Getting from Sense of Place to Place-based Management: An Interpretive Investigation of Place Meanings and Perceptions of Landscape Change" (2005).
31. Gerard Kyle and Garry Chick, "The Social Construction of a Sense of Place" (2007).
32. Richard C. Stedman, "Toward a Social Psychology of Place: Predicting Behavior from Place-Based Cognitions, Attitude, and Identity" (2002).
33. Hay, "A Rooted Sense of Place" (1998).
34. Lynne C. Manzo and D. Perkins Douglas, "Finding Common Ground: The Importance of Place Attachment to Community Participation and Planning" (2006).
35. Simone Tosoni and Matteo Tarantino, "Media Territories and Urban Conflict: Exploring Symbolic Tactics and Audience Activities in the Conflict over Paolo Sarpi, Milan" (2013).
36. Nick Couldry, "the Audience … and How to Research It" (2011).
37. Ridell and Zeller, "Mediated Urbanism" (2013).
38. Karen Waltorp, "Public/Private Negotiations in the Media Uses of Young Muslim Women in Copenhagen: Gendered Social Control and the Technology-Enabled Moral Laboratories of a Multicultural City" (2013).
39. Ibid.
40. Tosoni and Tarantino, "Media Territories" (2013), 576.
41. Batty, "The Computable City" (1997).
42. Ridell and Zeller, "Mediated Urbanism" (2013).
43. Eva Thulin and Bertil Vilhelmson, "Virtual Mobility of Urban Youth: ICT-based Communication in Sweden" (2004).
44. See Dong-Hee Shin, "Ubiquitous City: Urban Technologies, Urban Infrastructure and Urban Informatics" (2009); Glenn Lyons, Patricia Mokhtarian, Martin Dijst, and Lars Böcker, "The Dynamics of Urban Metabolism in the Face of Digitalization and Changing Lifestyles: Understanding and Influencing Our Cities" (2018).
45. Masanao Takeyama, "Geographical Conceptualization of Cyberplaces" (2001).
46. Thulin and Vilhelmson, "Virtual Mobility" (2004).
47. Kesselring, "Pioneering Mobilities."
48. Beng-Kiang Tan and Stephen Lim Tsung Yee, "Place and Placelessness in 3D Online Virtual World" (2010).
49. Kesselring, "Pioneering Mobilities."
50. Takeyama, "Geographical Conceptualization" (2001).
51. Relph, "Spirit of Place" (2007).

52. Shaowen Bardzell and William Odom, "The Experience of Embodied Space in Virtual Worlds: An Ethnography of a Second Life Community" (2008), 257. See also Brad McKenna, "Creating Convivial Affordances: A Study of Virtual World Social Movements" (2020).
53. Alenka Poplin, "Playful Public Participation in Urban Planning: A Case Study for Online Serious Games" (2012).
54. Kheir Al-Kodmany, "Using Visualization Techniques for Enhancing Public Participation in Planning and Design: Process, Implementation, and Evaluation" (1999).
55. Bärbel Tress and Gunther Tress, "Scenario Visualisation for Participatory Landscape Planning—A Study from Denmark" (2003). For recent examples of these applications, see Elmira Jamei et al. "Investigating the Role of Virtual Reality in Planning for Sustainable Smart Cities" (2017) and Helmut Schrom-Feiertag et al. "An Interactive and Responsive Virtual Reality Environment for Participatory Urban Planning" (2020).
56. Huayi Wu, Zhengwei He, and Jianya Gong. "A Virtual Globe-Based 3D Visualization and Interactive Framework for Public Participation in Urban Planning Processes." *Computers, Environment and Urban Systems* 34, no. 4 (2010): 293.
57. Christopher J. Pettit, William Cartwright, and Michael Berry, "Geographical Visualization: A Participatory Planning Support Tool for Imagining Landscape Futures" (2006).
58. Toby L. J. Howard and Nicolas Gaborit, "Using Virtual Environment Technology to Improve Public Participation in Urban Planning Process" (2007).
59. Wu, He, and Gong, "A Virtual Globe-Based 3D Visualization."
60. Matthias Baldauf et al., "Comparing Viewing and Filtering Techniques for Mobile Urban Exploration" (2011).
61. Daniel Z. Sui, "The Wikification of GIS and Its Consequences: Or Angelina Jolie's New Tattoo and the Future of GIS" (2008), 5.
62. Geisa Bugs et al., "An Assessment of Public Participation GIS and Web 2.0 Technologies in Urban Planning Practice in Canela, Brazil" (2010).
63. Angela Fagerlin, Catharine Wang, and Peter A. Ubel, "Reducing the Influence of Anecdotal Reasoning on People's Health Care Decisions: Is a Picture Worth a Thousand Statistics?" (2005).
64. Zhiyong Yang, Ritesh Saini, and Traci Freling, "How Anxiety Leads to Suboptimal Decisions under Risky Choice Situations" (2015).
65. John B. F. De Wit, Enny Das, and Raymond Vet, "What Works Best: Objective Statistics or a Personal Testimonial? An Assessment of the Persuasive Effects of Different Types of Message Evidence on Risk Perception" (2008).
66. Payam Ghadirian and Ian D. Bishop, "Integration of Augmented Reality and GIS: A New Approach to Realistic Landscape Visualisation" (2008).
67. For example, Mario Wolf, Heinrich Söbke, and Florian Wehking, "Mixed Reality Media-Enabled Public Participation in Urban Planning" (2020) and Purav Bhardwaj, Cletus Joseph, and Lamha Bijili, "Ikigailand: Gamified Urban Planning Experiences for Improved Participatory Planning. A Gamified Experience as a Tool for Town Planning" (2020).

68. See Eric Gordon and Gene Koo, "Placeworlds: Using Virtual Worlds to Foster Civic Engagement" (2008), 217.

BIBLIOGRAPHY

Agnew, John A. *Place and Politics: The Geographical Mediation of State and Society*. Abingdon, UK: Routledge, 1987.

Al-Kodmany, Kheir. "Using Visualization Techniques for Enhancing Public Participation in Planning and Design: Process, Implementation, and Evaluation." *Landscape and Urban Planning* 45, no. 1 (1999): 37–45.

Baldauf, Matthias, Peter Fröhlich, Kathrin Masuch, and Thomas Grechenig. "Comparing Viewing and Filtering Techniques for Mobile Urban Exploration." *Journal of Location Based Services* 5, no. 1 (2011): 38–57.

Bardzell, Shaowen, and William Odom. "The Experience of Embodied Space in Virtual Worlds: An Ethnography of a Second Life Community." *Space and Culture* 11, no. 3 (2008): 239–59.

Batty, Michael. "The Computable City." *International Planning Studies* 2, no. 2 (1997): 155–73.

Benyon, David. "Designing Interactive Systems: A Comprehensive Guide to HCI." In *UX and Interaction Design*. London: Pearson, 2014.

Bhardwaj, Purav, Cletus Joseph, and Lamha Bijili. "Ikigailand: Gamified Urban Planning Experiences for Improved Participatory Planning. A Gamified Experience as a Tool for Town Planning." In *IndiaHCI'20: Proceedings of the 11th Indian Conference on Human-Computer Interaction*, 104–08. New York, USA: Association for Computing Machinery, November 5–8, 2020.

Bickerstaff, Karen, and Gordon Walker. "Shared Visions, Unholy Alliances: Power, Governance and Deliberative Processes in Local Transport Planning." *Urban Studies* 42, no. 12 (2005): 2123–44.

Billig, Miriam. "Sense of Place in the Neighborhood, in Locations of Urban Revitalization." *GeoJournal* 64, no. 2 (2005): 117–30.

Brail, Richard K., and Richard E. Klosterman. *Planning Support Systems: Integrating Geographic Information Systems, Models, and Visualization Tools*. Redlands, CA: ESRI, Inc., 2001.

Bugs, Geisa, Carlos Granell, Oscar Fonts, Joaquín Huerta, and Marco Painho. "An Assessment of Public Participation GIS and Web 2.0 Technologies in Urban Planning Practice in Canela, Brazil." *Cities* 27, no. 3 (2010): 172–81.

Couldry, Nick. "the Audience ... and How to Research It." In *The Handbook of Media Audiences*, vol. 4, 213–29. Hoboken: Wiley, 2011.

Cowan, Douglas E. "Online u-topia: Cyberspace and the Mythology of Placelessness." *Journal for the Scientific Study of Religion* 44, no. 3 (2005): 257–63.

Davenport, Mae A., and Dorothy H. Anderson. "Getting from Sense of Place to Place-Based Management: An Interpretive Investigation of Place Meanings and Perceptions of Landscape Change." *Society and Natural Resources* 18, no. 7 (2005): 625–41.

De Wit, John B. F., Enny Das, and Raymond Vet. "What Works Best: Objective Statistics or a Personal Testimonial? An Assessment of the Persuasive Effects of Different Types of Message Evidence on Risk Perception." *Health Psychology* 27, no. 1 (2008): 110.

Fagerlin, Angela, Catharine Wang, and Peter A. Ubel. "Reducing the Influence of Anecdotal Reasoning on People's Health care Decisions: Is a Picture Worth a Thousand Statistics?" *Medical Decision Making* 25, no. 4 (2005): 398–405.

Ghadirian, Payam, and Ian D. Bishop. "Integration of Augmented Reality and GIS: A New Approach to Realistic Landscape Visualisation." *Landscape and Urban Planning* 86, no. 3–4 (2008): 226–32.

Gordon, Eric, and Gene Koo. "Placeworlds: Using Virtual Worlds to Foster Civic Engagement." *Space and Culture* 11, no. 3 (2008): 204–21.

Harris, Andrew, and Susan Moore. "Planning Histories and Practices of Circulating Urban Knowledge." *International Journal of Urban and Regional Research* 37, no. 5 (2013): 1499–1509.

Hay, Robert. "A Rooted Sense of Place in Cross-Cultural Perspective." *Canadian Geographer/Le Géographe canadien* 42, no. 3 (1998): 245–66.

Howard, Toby L. J., and Nicolas Gaborit. "Using Virtual Environment Technology to Improve Public Participation in Urban Planning Process." *Journal of Urban Planning and Development* 133, no. 4 (2007): 233–41.

Jamei, Elmira, Michael Mortimer, Mehdi Seyedmahmoudian, Ben Horan, and Alex Stojcevski. "Investigating the Role of Virtual Reality in Planning for Sustainable Smart Cities." *Sustainability* 9, no. 11 (2017). https://www.mdpi.com/2071-1050/9/11/2006.

Jive´n, Gunila, and Peter J. Larkham. "Sense of Place, Authenticity and Character: A Commentary." *Journal of Urban Design* 8, no. 1 (2003): 67–81.

Kellerman, Aharon. "Social-Spatial Interaction, Proximity, and Distance: From Face-to-Face to Virtual Communications." *Applied Mobilities* 7, no. 4 (2022), 394–412, https://doi.org/10.1080/23800127.2021.1928992.

Kesselring, Sven. "Pioneering Mobilities: New Patterns of Movement and Motility in a Mobile World." *Environment and Planning A* 38, no. 2 (2006): 269–79.

Kyle, Gerard, and Garry Chick. "The Social Construction of a Sense of Place." *Leisure Sciences* 29, no. 3 (2007): 209–25.

Lefebvre, Henri. *Reflections on the Politics of Space*. Minneapolis: University of Minnesota Press, 1991.

Lyons, Glenn, Patricia Mokhtarian, Martin Dijst, and Lars Böcker. "The Dynamics of Urban Metabolism in the Face of Digitalization and Changing Lifestyles: Understanding and Influencing Our Cities." *Resources, Conservation and Recycling* 132 (2018): 246–57.

Manzo, Lynne C., and D. Perkins Douglas. "Finding Common Ground: The Importance of Place Attachment to Community Participation and Planning." *Journal of Planning Literature* 20, no. 4 (2006): 335–50.

McKenna, Brad. "Creating Convivial Affordances: A Study of Virtual World Social Movements." *Information Systems Journal* 30, no. 1 (2020): 185–214.

Monno, Valeria, and Abdul Khakee. "Tokenism or Political Activism? Some Reflections on Participatory Planning." *International Planning Studies* 17, no. 1 (2012): 85–101.

Morgan, Kevin. "The Exaggerated Death of Geography: Learning, Proximity and Territorial Innovation Systems." *Journal of Economic Geography* 4, no. 1 (2004): 3–21.

Napoli, P. M. "Audience Evolution and the Future of Audience Research." *International Journal on Media Management* 14, no. 2 (2012): 79–97.

Nightingale, Virginia, ed. *The Handbook of Media Audiences*. Hoboken, NJ: John Wiley & Sons, 2013.

O'Neill, Brian, J. Ignacio Gallego, and Frauke Zeller. "New Perspectives on Audience Activity: 'Prosumption' and Media Activism as Audience Practices." In *Audience Transformations: Shifting Audience Positions in Late Modernity*, edited by K. C. S. Niko Carpentier and L. Hallett, 157–71. London: Routledge, 2013.

Pettit, Christopher J., William Cartwright, and Michael Berry. "Geographical Visualization: A Participatory Planning Support Tool for Imagining Landscape Futures". *Applied GIS* 2, no. 3 (2006): 1–17.

Podevyn, Martin, Margaret Horne, and Peter Fisher. "Virtual Cities: Management and Organisational Issues." In *CUPUM 2009 11th International Conference on Computers in Urban Planning and Urban Management*, Hong Kong, June 2009, 1–13.

Poplin, Alenka. "Playful Public Participation in Urban Planning: A Case Study for Online Serious Games." *Computers, Environment and Urban Systems* 36, no. 3 (2012): 195–206.

Relph, Edward. *Place and Placelessness*, vol. 67. London: Pion, 1976.

Relph, Edward. "Spirit of Place and Sense of Place in Virtual Realities." *Techné: Research in Philosophy and Technology* 10, no. 3 (2007): 17–25.

Ridell, Seija, and Frauke Zeller. "Mediated Urbanism: Navigating an Interdisciplinary Terrain." *International Communication Gazette* 75, no. 5–6 (August 2013): 437–51, https://doi.org/10.1177/1748048513491891.

Rogers, Yvonne, Helen Sharp, and Jenny Preece. *Interaction Design: Beyond Human–Computer Interaction*. Hoboken, NJ: John Wiley & Sons, 2011.

Rose, Gillian. "Place and Identity: A Sense of Place." *A Place in the World?: Places, Cultures and Globalization* (1995): 87–132.

Schrom-Feiertag, Helmut, Martin Stubenschrott, Georg Regal, Thomas Matyus, and Stefan Seer. "An Interactive and Responsive Virtual Reality Environment for Participatory Urban Planning." In *Proceedings of the Symposium on Simulation for Architecture and Urban Design SimAUD*, 119–25. San Diego, CA: Society for Computer Simulation International, Virtual Event Austria May 25–27, 2020.

Shin, Dong-Hee. "Ubiquitous City: Urban Technologies, Urban Infrastructure and Urban Informatics." *Journal of Information Science* 35, no. 5 (2009): 515–26.

Smith, David Harris. "Reflexive Design of the Recursive Space of Virtual Worlds: macGRID Art and Cyberscience Network as an Example of Mediated Urbanism." *International Communication Gazette* 75, no. 5–6 (2013): 452–69.

Smith, Richard Warren. "A Theoretical Basis for Participatory Planning." *Policy Sciences* 4, no. 3 (1973): 275–95.

Stedman, Richard C. "Toward a Social Psychology of Place: Predicting Behavior from Place-Based Cognitions, Attitude, and Identity." *Environment and Behavior* 34, no. 5 (2002): 561–81.

Sui, Daniel Z. "The Wikification of GIS and Its Consequences: Or Angelina Jolie's New Tattoo and the Future of GIS." *Computers, Environment and Urban Systems* 1, no. 32 (2008): 1–5.

Takeyama, Masanao. "Geographical Conceptualization of Cyberplaces." *GeoJournal* 53, no. 4 (2001): 419–26.

Tan, Beng-Kiang, and Stephen Lim Tsung Yee. "Place and Placelessness in 3D Online Virtual World." In *New Frontiers: Proceedings of the 15th International Conference on Computer-Aided Architectural Design Research in Asia*, 103–12. Hong Kong: CAADRIA, April 7–10, 2010.

Thulin, Eva, and Bertil Vilhelmson. "Virtual Mobility of Urban Youth: ICT-Based Communication in Sweden." *Tijdschrift voor economische en sociale geografie* 96, no. 5 (2005): 477–87.

Tosoni, Simone, and Matteo Tarantino. "Media Territories and Urban Conflict: Exploring Symbolic Tactics and Audience Activities in the Conflict over Paolo Sarpi, Milan." *International Communication Gazette* 75, no. 5–6 (2013): 573–94.

Tress, Bärbel, and Gunther Tress. "Scenario Visualisation for Participatory Landscape Planning—A Study from Denmark." *Landscape and Urban Planning* 64, no. 3 (2003): 161–78.

Tuan, Yi-Fu. *Space and Place: The Perspective of Experience*. Minneapolis, MI: University of Minnesota Press, 1977.

Waltorp, Karen. "Public/Private Negotiations in the Media Uses of Young Muslim Women in Copenhagen: Gendered Social Control and the Technology-Enabled Moral Laboratories of a Multicultural City." *International Communication Gazette* 75, no. 5–6 (2013): 555–72.

Wolf, Mario, Heinrich Söbke, and Florian Wehking. "Mixed Reality Media-Enabled Public Participation in Urban Planning." In *Augmented Reality and Virtual Reality*, edited by Timothy Jung, M. Claudia tom Dieck, and Philipp A. Rauschnabel, 125–38. Cham: Springer, 2020.

Wu, Huayi, Zhengwei He, and Jianya Gong. "A Virtual Globe-Based 3D Visualization and Interactive Framework for Public Participation in Urban Planning Processes." *Computers, Environment and Urban Systems* 34, no. 4 (2010): 291–98.

Yang, Zhiyong, Ritesh Saini, and Traci Freling. "How Anxiety Leads to Suboptimal Decisions under Risky Choice Situations." *Risk Analysis* 35, no. 10 (2015): 1789–1800.

Ylipulli, Johanna, and Tiina Suopajärvi. "Contesting Ubicomp Visions through ICT Practices: Power Negotiations in the Meshwork of a Technologised City." *International Communication Gazette* 75, no. 5–6 (2013): 538–54.

6

Digital Zoning: From Hippodamus to Mixed Reality

Kai Reaver

Introduction

With regard to our current discussion on digitization, there is certainly the feeling that we lack proper coordination between our digital and physical worlds. This chapter proposes that the digitization of physical space and cities would benefit from being more closely connected to the history of spatial design and planning— particularly through the use of zoning. We present the term *digital zoning* as a manner in which to encapsulate a range of recent research findings concerning the relationship between new digital technologies and their intersection with the city and urban planning. We utilize an analysis of Greek antiquity's approach to zoning, particularly the writings of Aristotle, on the "first political philosopher and urban planner," Hippodamus. Through Hippodamus' invention of the zoning grid for the prototypical city of Miletus, we recount the philosophical underpinnings of zoning in the western planning canon. This analysis is then utilized to frame findings from a range of recent case studies on applying mixed reality to urban design and planning. Recent literature on topics spanning smart and digital cities, surveillance capitalism, and mixed reality contextualize this research. Digital zoning is then presented as both a necessity for interweaving planning conventions with digital technologies such as mixed reality, and as a manner in which to regulate the use of technology in physical space based on a prescribed use of land. We conclude by speculating on how the integration of digital services with urban regulation and planning, through digital zoning, may fill a range of technical and conceptual gaps within current digital cities development.

Digital zoning

Smart and digital cities research focus on the relationship between digitization and urbanization. As the ubiquitous use of smartphones and wearable devices within urban environments increasingly brings technology into our everyday life, the overlaying of technology-driven concepts into cities and urban environments simultaneously heightens debate on various forms of possible new risks such as the fragmentation of individual privacy and the loss of democratic societal norms. From our perspective of architecture, design, and planning research, we have found that smart and digital cities discourse offer a framework to contextualize some of the more noticeable changes we have witnessed in the past decades in the built environment, particularly regarding the use of smartphones and ICTs in cities and the impact these technologies have on the everyday life of urban inhabitants. This framework has been particularly useful in analysing why some forms of digital technologies in urban environments have been more readily adopted, while others have failed to acquire mass adoption. From this standpoint we are able to utilize this framework both in creating evaluation criteria and design guidelines for possible new applications, buildings and services, and in developing analysis and critique of digitization and urbanization challenges and trends.

This digital cities research framework has also helped us develop theory and critique regarding the relationship between municipal data and the use of this data for digital urban services, which has also become a topic in the design of services and products focused towards on the digitization of the Nordic welfare state, for example the use of public mapping data in mixed reality (Figure 6.1). This has been a particular concern from our context of Norway and the Nordic region which in recent years has sought to develop a "Norwegian" definition for smart or digital cities. More recently, this research framework helped us analyse the use of surveillance and tracking technologies we saw in Oslo, Norway during the COVID-19 pandemic (Figure 6.2). This allowed us to understand not only the capabilities for ICTs to influence product and service development but also the very real manner in which inhabitants are becoming increasingly interweaved with their environments through urban digitization.

While digital city theory provides researchers with concepts to understand some of these phenomena, case studies and field work allow theories to be evaluated in real-world settings. In response to the highly speculative and theoretical nature of digital cities research, recent smart and digital cities literature has expressed the need for conducting more detailed fieldwork in a number of carefully selected cities to study the actual social, economic, and environmental impacts of digitization projects, and to monitor their short- and long-term impacts of digitization. Glasmeier and Christopherson, Carvalho, and Kitchin alike suggest that we need more

FIGURE 6.1: BorderGO system by Norkart and the Norwegian Mapping Authority, 2016, was a prototype for showing property lines and map data in augmented reality. Source: norkart.no. Accessed October 19, 2021.

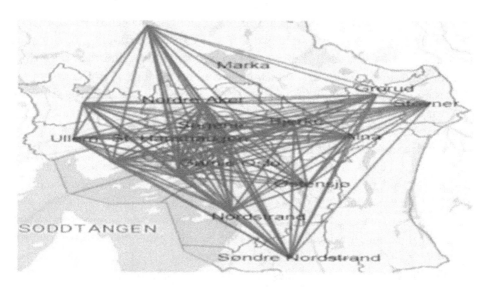

FIGURE 6.2: The TriO system in Oslo which was used during the COVID-19 pandemic to track individual inhabitants throughout the city. Oslo from March 17 to May 4, 2020. Oslo Municipality, Department of Emergency Services (*Beredskapsetaten*).

thoughtful comparative work in order to understand actually existing digital city developments. Experiments such as Kitchen et al.'s case studies in Dublin, testing citizen participation through the ladder of participation showcase the role of such

case work in understanding the digital cities model in interaction with citizens. In addition, the UN Habitat recommended more closely integrated case studies with municipalities and local governments in studying the effects of technologies such as mixed reality. Following this observation, we have recently concentrated on conducting field work in the form of real-world case studies in order to study the intersection of technology development with urban planning. One of the more prevalent findings across our research concerns the way zoning interacts with new digital services and spaces within the smart or digital city context. The term we have landed upon to describe these findings is *digital zoning*.

As we will now elaborate, our research documents that digital information, in the form of augmented reality models or digital services—when placed within the physical world—have a frequent tendency to display what we have begun to consider as a lack of integration between the digital technologies' internal spatial navigation and the underlying zoning of physical space (Figure 6.3). We argue that this gap between digitization and urban zoning can be viewed as a general phenomenon that can be found across multiple domains of emerging technology, and thus requires specific terminology in order to explore the concept holistically. Our hope is that this term will help researcher and practitioners discuss common aspects of the physical–digital discrepancies and possibilities amongst a variety of emerging technology trends, including augmented and virtual reality, new mobility services, privacy and surveillance through various forms of tracking, and even the technologies involved with COVID-19 pandemic, such as infection tracking. As a whole, we believe there is sufficient cause to point to *digital zoning* as an emerging area of research considering the unification of physical spatial planning and regulation with the digitization of urban environments and the development of new technological services. In the following sections, we will develop this argument first by recontextualizing the origins of zoning through the foundations of the western planning canon.

Zoning and the Hippodamian grid

Urban planning is concerned with the design and planning of urban environments and cities, concentrating on the development of land use and the built environment. In urban planning, zoning is the manner in which physical space is planned, organized, and regulated. The method of zoning divides land into areas called zones, each of which has a set of regulations that differs from other zones. Zones may be defined for single use such as public, or private; or more detailed specifications such as residential, industrial, parks, roadways, protected areas, etc. Zoning may also specify conditional uses of land, and thus specify how land may or may not be used. Zones may also combine several compatible activities in the form of mixed-use zoning.

FIGURE 6.3: Case study displaying AR object placement in an urban context, 2021. Source: Reaver, K. (2023). Augmented reality as a participation tool for youth in urban planning processes: Case study in Oslo, Norway. *Frontiers in Virtual Reality*, 4.

The planning rules for each zone determine whether planning permission for a given development may be granted. Thus, planners can specify land use for future scenarios, which can guide architects and developers towards desired uses. Because zoning specifies not only land planning but also conditional land use, it thus functions as a legal regulatory tool. In this manner zoning concepts underlie the foundations of not only

urban planning, but also territorial law. An example of this can be found in the way public assembly and protest are regulated spatially based on an area's zoning code.

The origins of zoning can be traced back to Greek antiquity, to the work of the Greek political philosopher and urban planner Hippodamus (c. 498–c. 408 BC). The primary written account can be found in Aristotle's *Politics* (c. 350 BC), which references Hippodamus and his lost document "The Urban Planning Study for Piraeus" which scholars argue formed the first basis for city planning standards. Aristotle discusses the political and social ideas of Hippodamus, while attributing the invention of formal city planning, including the invention of zoning, to his work. Hippodamus is frequently associated with the orthogonally planned towns of Olynthus, Priene, and Miletus. Though his direct involvement in these cases remains unproven, the evidence provided through Aristotle has instantiated his name as permanently associated with this type of zoned grid plan that we now call Hippodamian. This Hippodamian system has been replicated as a planning standard throughout the western world over the past 2,500 years.

As far as we understand, in ancient Greece, philosophy and planning were closely linked, and Hippodamus was here tasked with designing prototypical cities that would represent philosophical concepts for the governance of society. Among the literature concerning Hippodamus' works, we find the first idea that a town plan might formally "embody and clarify a rational social order" through the study of "functional problems of cities being linked to the state administration system." For example, in Hippodamus' plans, citizens are divided into classes, such as soldiers, peasants, and administration and clergy, while the land is divided into zoned functions, such as sacred, public, and private. This concept is based on the necessity for mobility of all classes across public land whereas private land would offer explicit legal domain over the private residence. Therefore, for the prototypical city of Miletus, Hippodamus designed the grid system, with private residences bordered by public streets; thus creating public and private zoning where all classes would interact freely in the streets. Additionally, temples and other spaces dedicated to worship were given a third zone designated for "sacred" space. The Hippodamian grid plan is further elaborated by organizing citizens and zones flexibly across the topography of the site, as topographical features are to be used for specific functions, such as atria, which require inclination in the terrain.

The work of Hippodamus brings a few important ideas to the table. Note the manner in which Hippodamus' design philosophy seems to extend spatial functions to their conceptual extremes. For example, In the plan for Miletus (Figure 6.4), a prototypical city for 10,000 inhabitants, the main feature is a wide central area known as the *agora*, a public space for the centre of the city—and thus the centre society—which is dimensioned to fit the entirety of the populace of 10,000 people. In this manner, the *agora* is representative of the maximal public space and

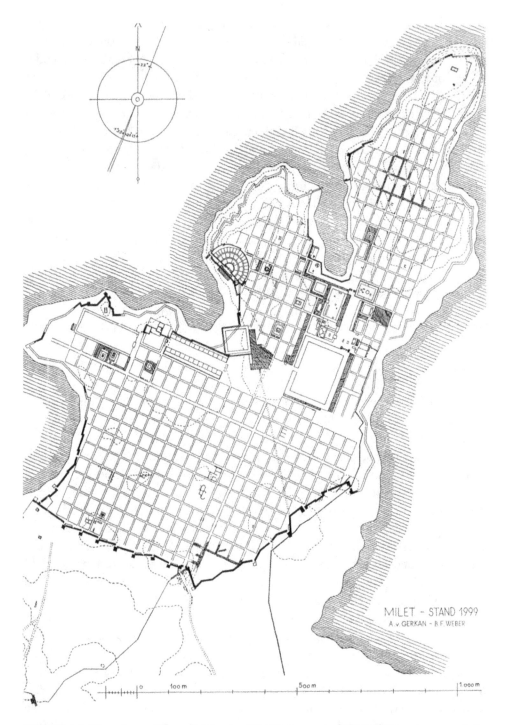

FIGURE 6.4: Hippodamus' Plan of Miletus c.470 BC. Burns, A. (1976). "Hippodamus and the Planned City." *Historia: Zeitschrift für Alte Geschichte*, 25(4), 414–28.

was thus meant to conceptualize this notion by being the centre of the athletic, artistic, spiritual, and political life in the city. The *agora* eventually became attributed to both the acts of public speech and open trade, which again can account to the concepts of public space being foundational to basic democratic concepts in the western canon. Here we may assert that the concepts invented by Hippodamus are not merely spatial in nature, but have conceptual roots to foundational aspects of human organization and spatial experience. It is for the reason that the Hippodamian plan, and its use of zoning, has important relevance to our contemporary discussion concerning digitization in urban environments.

From "smart" to "digital"

Fast forward a few thousand years to our current situation. We live in a period of both unprecedented digitization and rapid urban growth. Among prevalent models to explain and conceptualize these two trends we find the "digital city" model. The digital city is defined "as a city that integrates urban information (both achievable and real time) and creates public spaces for people living in the cities." Digital cities were initially seen as one of several various sub-concepts within smart or ubiquitous cities research (Figure 6.5). However, scholars argue that in recent years, smart and digital cities models have bifurcated between the two concepts. While it is argued that the concept of "smart" cities has proven particularly popular in terms of investment opportunities for physical urban and infrastructure development, the smart city model has received widespread criticism due to the model's failure to "put people first." The digital city, in more recent literature, refers more broadly to the possibility to place with digitization of urban environments within an understanding of "bigger values." Current literature argues that "the digital" cities model may have the capacity to place humans at the centre of urban culture in a manner which allows human activities to drive technology development, rather than allowing technologies to shape human potential. Thus, whereas the "smart city" discusses the need for providing integrated building and technological fixes, and reflects the substantial capital needs involved in building new and/or maintaining existing urban infrastructure, the digital city concept has begun to function as a critique of the technologically centred smart city model, offering the potential to refocus research towards more holistically oriented studies of the digitization of urban environments and the impact of such digitization upon people.

We have noticed that within this bifurcation between smart and digital cities models, digital cities literature has argued that some of the failures of smart city projects have been due to these types of projects' lack of integration with the design of the physical spaces they are placed within. This has prompted some of

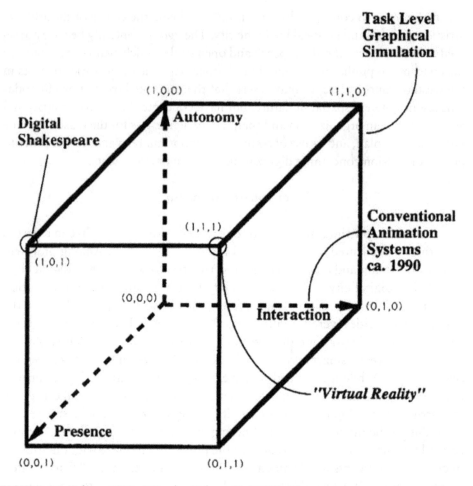

FIGURE 6.5: Zeltzer, 1992: AIP cube. Zeltzer, D. (1992). "Autonomy, Interaction, and Presence." *Presence: Teleoperators and Virtual Environments*, 1(1), 127–32.

our initial inquiries into how the practices of physical spatial design are organized and regulated. We notice that while proponents of the smart city model emphasize possibilities for improved efficiency in public services through new technologies, slimmer administrations as well as new departments, in addition to being drivers for innovation, and extended public ownership and control over data—perhaps even driving new funding sources for investments—many scholars argue that smart cities tend to "struggle with putting people first" due to the phenomenon of "Tech goggles"—meaning that technology becomes the primary focus of a project or solution rather than the social or cultural context. This phenomenon is also reported to be linked to a contradiction between "placemaking strategies

initiated through technologies," and "placemaking strategies coded into the design of physical spaces." Here, designer and urbanist Dan Hill (2018) notes that technology developers could potentially create more citizen-centric services by learning from urban planning methods, which tend to incorporate participation while conducting early-stage planning. We ask ourselves therefore if there may be alternative models to the smart city that are able to set citizens more in the centre of projects, and perhaps more embedded within traditions of urban planning.

Surveillance capitalism

In parallel to the ongoing research on digital cities, we have recently witnessed a growth in the related discourse on so-called "surveillance capitalism," meaning a form of capitalism which relies upon surveillance to generate profit. Harvard scholar Shoshana Zuboff (2018) found the growth of private tech companies, particularly through the use of social media and related cloud services, to be a threat to democratic society due to the use of antidemocratic surveillance practices. Zuboff found surveillance capitalism to be detrimental to individual privacy while utilizing psychology and technology to create behaviourally manipulative services that could then generate revenue through targeted advertising. Surveillance capitalism discourse has been widely supported by a general unease we witness in smart and digital cities research regarding topics such as user privacy, data harvesting, and technological monopolization. These concerns have been further elaborated in view of recent smart and digital city projects demonstrating ways in which combinations of surveillance technology, such as facial recognition and other automated systems which are designed to modify human behaviour in the direction of preferred outcomes. The central concern is the manner in which such surveillance practices may reconfigure urban environments into systems with an unprecedented degree of control over inhabitants.

As we have discussed, Silicon Valley tech companies have begun to experiment with urban planning and real estate development. This prompted Zuboff to write that smart cities such as Alphabet's Sidewalk Labs project in Toronto should be viewed as the "frontier" of surveillance capitalism (Figure 6.6). Here, Zuboff claimed that Sidewalk Labs had unilaterally declared that "all public and private experience occurring within this experimental zone would be deemed 'urban data' available for monitoring and actuation" with the real outcome being the "privatization of the city." Zuboff argued here that computational revenue streams would replace democratic municipal governance. While certainly alarmist in tone, Zuboff does point to real deficiencies in the Silicon Valley tech business model being based primarily on private data and advertising revenue, leading both to a reliance on data harvesting in order to create more tailored personal ads, but

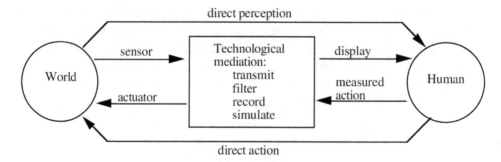

FIGURE 6.6: Technologically mediated experience. Robinett, W. (1992). "Synthetic Experience: A Proposed Taxonomy." *Presence: Teleoperators and Virtual Environments*, Bd. 1, s. 229–47.

also leading to technology services focusing primarily on individual data, rather than public data sets. Importantly, this logic led to the necessity to privatize all land within the Quayside development, including road and service infrastructure which traditionally may have been deemed public.

A likely related issue can be seen as various cities and public venues around the world have begun to experiment with "tech-free zones." In 2019, the city of Hobart, Tasmania, discussed the implementation of tech-free parks. The director of city innovation, Peter Carr, stated he was looking at how to create tech freeze areas in the city at how a park can turn off Wi-Fi and 4G for "personal and social well-being." Similarly, the city of San Francisco recently banned facial recognition, stating privacy concerns. Relatedly, in 2017, the London Design festival began experimenting with a tech-free café. These developments signalled for us a growing need in developing coherent theories and techniques for technology regulation in physical space. Of course, there remains some disagreement as to whether such "tech-free zones" are feasible. Under most telecommunications regulations, it is illegal to install a device to block a telecommunications signal. For this reason, it is often illegal to install Wi-Fi or 4G blockers. For tech-free zones to be implemented in a future urban governance scenario we would likely need 5G to be understood as a public infrastructure that could be legally governed by local city councils and officials.

Surveillance capitalism and related discourse have played the important role of exposing the many ways in which the ambitions of tech companies were far removed from the traditions of design and planning of the built environment, even when proposing actual urban developments such as Quayside. The entanglement we have observed between the seemingly innocuous ambitions of Silicon Valley and the deeper cultural challenges regarding technology's role in contemporary society as a whole, suggests for us that the digital city could in actuality

be a troublingly unfavourable, and potentially even dangerous model. To put this more generally, the digital city presents the paradox that if managed incorrectly, its lofty goals and ambitions could potentially create the exact opposite results as its stated intention at a massive, global scale. The implementation of the digital city could then potentially create an irreparable rift between the historic city and its continuous development, by both radically breaking with the traditions and histories of urban planning and design while eroding the trust between users and their governments. Therefore, it is argued that current digital city doctrines of technological determinism alone will not solve its stated goals, and that the careful insertion of technology within the city needs to be rigorously evaluated and tested within the structure of existing governmental frameworks and the history of its applicable disciplines, before smart city proposals are implemented into policy. In this manner, finding an applicable context in which to test and evaluate digital city technologies within an existing governmental framework seemed to be the most useful step forward.

Mixed reality

Some of the more interesting convergences between zoning, Silicon Valley tech development, and smartphone and wearable technology use can be observed within mixed reality research. Mixed reality is a technology involving the merging of real and virtual space where physical and digital objects co-exist and interact with users in real time. Augmented reality (AR) is a subset of mixed reality, which allows digital objects to be placed within the physical world through a screen such as glasses, smartphones, and tablets. Mixed reality emerges from the cybernetics culture of the 1960s, notable in the paper on "A Conceptual Framework for the Augmentation of Man's Intellect" in which Doug Englebart proposed that computers could be used to increase human understanding and problem-solving ability. He foresaw this as being an interactive process, involving computer-controlled changing images on cathode-ray tubes and controlled by the human with interactive manual input devices. Similarly, Ivan Sutherland proposed that a computer-based, multi-sensory, interactive simulated world could be created with the ultimate goal that it "look real, feel real, and act real." Some following work used video cameras to capture images of the user, and real-time image processing on the user's silhouette to allow the user's gestures to control events in a computer graphic world.

The late 1980s and early 1990s saw a consolidation of concepts and the development of taxonomic systems for understanding virtual and augmented reality. Fred Brooks made a case for interactive computer graphic simulation as a "potent tool [...] in man's on-going scientific enterprise in the understanding of the physical

universe." Brooks had earlier explored interactive 3D graphical simulations to represent the interior of buildings and built a see-through HMD for various applications. In his 1991 paper on "Autonomy, Interaction, and Presence," David Zeltzer proposed a taxonomy of graphical simulation systems that consisted of three independent scalar dimensions that defined a space of possibilities, as the "AIP cube"—standing for autonomy, interaction, and presence. The dimension "autonomy" describes the sophistication and dynamics of the model defining the virtual world. The "interaction" dimension measured the degree to which user actions could affect what happened in the virtual world, and the "presence" dimension measured the degree to which users were bodily immersed within the system (Figure 6.6). For Zeltzer, Virtual Reality represented the pinnacle of the three AIP scalar dimensions.

Some of the more interesting conceptual ground of mixed reality stems from Robinette's series of mixed reality taxonomies from his 1992 paper on *Synthetic experiences*. By analysing the first diagram of Robinette's "Technologically-mediated experience" taxonomies (Figure 6.7) we can see a few core arguments. The first is that technological mediation is placed between direct perception and action between humans and the world. The mediation is then facilitated between the world through sensors, to humans through display systems. Humans then influence the world through actions imposed upon the technological mediation system, which in turn performs actions upon the world. Note how in Figure 6.8 we differentiate between recorded, transmitted, simulated, and robotically mediated experiences. Whereas a recorded or simulated experience merely instantiates human participation with a technologically mediated model, either with or without active input from the real world, a transmitted experience instantiates the active influence of humans upon the world through a technologically mediated model.

It is therefore important to understand the conceptual roots of AR not only as a visualization technology but as a manner in which humans enact real changes upon the real world as a transmitted experience. Early research stated that AR for urban planning represented a potential breakthrough in how we interact with the built environment because in city planning it is very important to arrange the layout of 3D objects such as buildings or trees and to see the relationship among them. An initial prototype by Kato et al. demonstrated some of the first work within this area, in which a tabletop AR setting enabled users to consider city plans in AR and manipulate 3D structures that are displayed as virtual objects in a sandbox setting. These early researchers understood that potential AR applications required giving the user the ability to walk around large environments, even outdoors which required making the equipment self-contained and portable. However, it was only with the invention of smartphone AR in the past years that it became

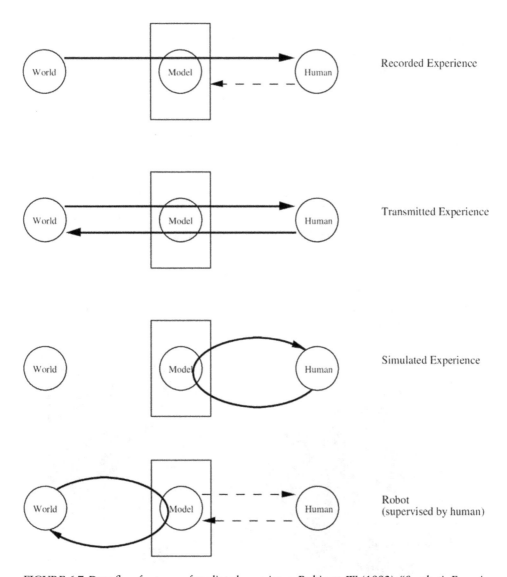

FIGURE 6.7: Data flow for types of mediated experience. Robinett, W. (1992). "Synthetic Experience: A Proposed Taxonomy." *Presence: Teleoperators and Virtual Environments*, Bd. 1, s. 229–47.

capable of tracking a user outdoors at the required accuracy, allowing researchers to study the adoption of the smartphone-wide audience to AR. This led to the aforementioned prototype called BorderGO, made by NorKart and The Norwegian Mapping Authority, which depicts property boundaries transposed onto the real world in real time through the Google Tango smartphone system. Similarly, in 2018, a prototype was demonstrated by ARUP and Dan Hill (Figure 6.9)

FIGURE 6.8: The City Planning Prototype made by Arup / Dan Hill and Chris Green (2018) depicts how users could interact with planning proposals on site through AR. Reproduced with permission from Dan Hill, "Augmented Planning Notice," December 13, 2022, YouTube Video, 01:00. Url: https://www.youtube.com/watch?v=zrJkUht9ywI&ab_channel=DanHill. Accessed June 22, 2020.

FIGURE 6.9: UN Habitat and Ericsson experiment utilizing a *Minecraft*-like gaming environment in AR which allowed youth participants to envision and place designs within the real-world setting of Johannesburg, SA. Source: UN Habitat & Ericsson, 2019. "Mixed Reality for Public Participation in Urban and Public Space Design Towards a New Way of Crowdsourcing More Inclusive Smart Cities."

which depicted how users could interact with planning proposals on site through AR with a tablet.

There is much speculation on how urban planning and the use of mixed reality may intersect. For example, a UN Habitat and Ericsson report from 2019 documented the use of smartphones and a local Wi-Fi hub to do enact free-form scenario planning with local youth in Johannesburg, South Africa. The report stated that

> mixed reality holds tremendous potential for real-time digital visualizations, both at the street and neighbourhood level and the overall urban skyline and city grid [...] pulling users into the process of design and strengthening the long-term viability and buy-in of urban projects.

The project they created allowed users to sketch their own fantasies through a Minecraft-like computer game which then could be imported into AR and then placed within the real-world setting (Figure 6.10).

Case studies

Within digital cities discourse, architecture, design, and planning encompass the role of not only analysis and reflection on the digitization of urban environments, but also the design of services, products, buildings, or urban plans within this context. Architecture and design research, often in close connection to architecture and design pedagogy, has traditionally followed a studio-based model in which students develop design proposals within an appropriate context, and here, the digital city is an interesting context for study. Here, a common research approach is through analysing this context and prototyping products, buildings,

FIGURE 6.10: Early 2018 case study involving student proposals in Oslo placed in a real-world context through AR. Source: author.

and services in which students and design practitioners participate within this digital city context. For these reasons, understanding what new possibilities or risks may arise in the space of the smart or digital city is of particular importance not only when considering the application and evaluation of design proposals within an urban or city context, but also when providing insight into how the design and architecture fields may approach topics such as regulation and governance.

The question of the digital city as an emerging research has spawned several case studies, both in the lab and in the field. These cases have been designed with the goal of studying what such a digital city may entail, and help understand how it is experienced by real people. An important component of the case studies has been their integration with planning institutions. Through testing digital technologies within planning institutions such as design and planning authorities, architectural heritage authorities, municipal and state agencies, and local city districts and councils, we have been able to get some insight into how the digital city may take shape in the real world. This has also offered a perspective to help us understand the needs and goals of users, institutions, and governmental bodies at the intersection of the digitization of services for citizens and the broader digitization of their urban context. Through these opportunities, we have been able to test real-world applications of technology with citizens and inhabitants of the city. Through this work, we have been able to generalize some of the findings across case studies and to make some assumptions about new concepts and frameworks worth further study and investigation in the digital city context.

The aforementioned cases with AR in planning by UN Habitat and others were performed in a free-form environment without any technical links to the underlying zoning of the context they were within. However, as Robinette's diagrams entail, the real world should in theory be able to input relevant information into the mediated experience in order to facilitate mediated actions between human users and the world. This brings us again to a discussion on zoning and planning. In contemporary planning, zoning is often conducted within geographic information system (GIS) software which allows for zones to be tightly connected to a digital map. These zoning tools form the basis of planning, permitting, regulation, as well as legal disputes and complaints over land use and planning decisions. Thus, we see that a closer relationship between digitization and zoning could mean much more than digital services having an accurate placement in physical space. Especially for AR, we noticed that there was an abundance of latent and exciting possibilities for digital services if connected more closely to the physical environment through interweaving zoning protocols with digital services and products within a mediated environment such as AR (Figure 6.11).

With the expansion of digital city research, a discussion regarding digital zoning arises from several vantage points. First of all, the lack of reliable and accurate

FIGURE 6.11: Case study work on AR for participatory planning in Oslo, 2020–21. Source: author.

positioning in physical space, for example with augmented reality (AR) through GPS, creates real barriers to professional use of AR technology in its current state. This is due to the fact that because AR objects lack a common infrastructure or map in which to exchange object information across devices, making any device its own ecosystem and thus unable to share 3D information with other devices. However, the current trajectory in emerging technologies' ability to position accurately in physical space, through the development of location services such as the 5G network or the so-called "AR Cloud," will at some theoretical point be more or less fully accurate. This means that a digital service or object's position in physical space will be known at a high enough level of accuracy for the underlying zoning code to provide information or operating protocols upwards to the service. Such a relationship would entail a closer link between city planning and digitization in several key manners.

AR in urban planning

One very concrete example of this phenomenon of location-zoning discrepancy was witnessed when performing a case study on the use of AR for planning new

trees in Oslo. This case was done with the Oslo Planning and Building Agency and was performed by youth participants tasked with planning new trees in their local neighbourhood. This work was done by "planting" the trees with a tablet through AR (Figure 6.12). For the study, participants would choose between a list of available trees, and by using the tablet, would place a tree in a desired location. In this manner the Planning and Building Agency was able to collect data on where new trees were desired through user-generated proposals, and simultaneously perform their responsibility for citizen participation, a legal requirement within planning in Norway. Here, we found that in order to facilitate the AR tree planning work, participants needed to understand where or where not a tree was allowed to be planted. In urban planning, the differences between public and private land become very important for precisely this reason. However, the lack of a digital map in which to coordinate which zones were acceptable for trees and which were not, became very apparent. Additionally, manners in which to coordinate tree placement within the municipal GIS became difficult and had to be done manually, based on screenshots rather than actual AR data. Across the board, we found a lack of coordination between the technology and the underlying zoning logic of planning.

Understanding the complexity of real-world planning in relation to which elements should be included in an AR gave us some valuable feedback to consider, such as the necessity for a future iteration of the tool to contain zoning data. This was particularly important because areas where trees can and cannot be planted, based on private or public land, zoned for greenery or other uses, would become determinant at later stages for whether or not a plan could be enacted in the real world. With these aspects taken into account, we concluded that we are surprised at the high level of design quality achieved by the participants. This leads to a further conclusion that AR in urban planning could perhaps break down barriers between experts and the general citizenry, if the underlying infrastructure was consistent and manageable from a public planning perspective. We also found that such a use of AR could point at a level of intuitive knowledge that local citizens can have about their environment and its planning. However, there may not be enough relevant information within the interface to incorporate all stages of planning law and bureaucracy.

In the case study, we wanted to know more about the experience of AR in order to understand the feasibility of AR for urban planning. In our findings, we find that AR can be a good tool for AR, perhaps even especially for youth groups like the groups we conducted research on for this case study. Findings related to the use of AR in a real-world scenario show that our initial expectation of the technology being difficult to use was highly overestimated. On the contrary, we see that with this user group the technology was much easier than expected. We also expected

FIGURE 6.12: Case study work on AR for participatory planning in Oslo, 2020–21. Source: author.

there to be a significant difference between the experience of digital objects in space and physical objects in real life. A major finding in the case study is that there seems to have been little difference for the participants in the experience of AR in relation to the experience of the real world, rather, participants present the AR trees as if they indeed are "real." While this finding seems to conflict with existing models in architectural theory, it does correlate with some of the assumptions of early mixed reality pioneers as discussed in the previous section.

A future research inquiry regards concrete plans for further implementation of the research case studies into a holistic system for integration of AR in planning. Following the case studies, we have had multiple meetings within the research team and with the municipality of Oslo to help plan any steps forward. A central discussion has regarded how to coordinate planning with AR into a GIS mapping system, which was discussed in the previous section. There is also plenty of further work to be done in structuring planning steps and youth participation within that planning. We also will conduct further participation scenarios in 2022 which will give new tree data and more user experience data to help build upon this initial case. Our overall conclusion so far is that the facilitation of a multiuser planning application will require a common zoning data platform, preferably a direct copy of the municipal GIS plan, to be integrated directly within the AR planning tool in a manner that allows AR data to be distributed, coordinated, and integrated into the procedural planning system. This has further highlighted the need to consolidate terminology around common concepts such as digital zoning in order to link various disparate technical and conceptual ideas together towards understanding and addressing the problems at hand.

Geofencing

One manner to discuss the feasibility of digital zoning at a technical level is to invoke the concept of *geofencing*, and apply this concept to urban planning and mixed reality. A geofence is a virtual perimeter for a real-world geographic area. Geofences can be dynamically generated around a point location, and can also be generated based on a predefined set of boundaries (Figure 6.13). An example of the use of a geofence could be seen in triggering a response on a location-aware device such as a smartphone application or an electric scooter. Entering or exiting a geofenced zone can trigger a response on the device as well as message the geofence operator. Such methods are commonly used with bike rental services which require bikes to be parked in specific zones, for example, or for monitoring vehicles. One can imagine such methods being used for a large number of products and services. Because geofencing allows administrators to set up triggers based on physical–digital boundaries, services, and products can be connected to real-world

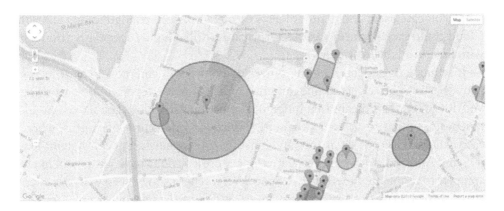

FIGURE 6.13: Geofencing illustration. Source: Argustracking. https://argustracking.co.nz/geo-fencing. Last accessed June 21, 2021.

coordinates with corresponding trigger actions to their position in space. So far, geofencing is used primarily in private services. Now, let us consider the implications of the zoning plan of the city actively functioning with geofencing protocols as a common infrastructure within the city.

As mentioned earlier, geofences have many uses in cities and urban environments. These uses include seeing when vehicles have entered a particular zone and for how long, or for monitoring vehicles within certain zones. Geofencing is also used for security purposes. However, geofencing has had limited use in urban planning, and it is unclear whether current geofencing technology, with an accuracy threshold of up to 3 m, has high enough accuracy to be used in a manner that can correspond accurately enough with positioning in the physical world.

The AR Cloud

Another developing technology with similar implications to digital zoning is the concept of the AR Cloud. The AR Cloud is an infrastructural system for augmented reality that is scalable, shareable, and understands the geometry and shapes of the real world. The purpose of the AR Cloud is to be an instant, ubiquitous localizer that works from any angle on multiple AR devices simultaneously, allowing for real-time multi-user interaction, even with remote users. Since AR Clouds will require precise geo-positioning to function properly, various types of positioning technology are necessary for them to function. Some technology companies are developing the use of machine learning algorithms in order to construct AR Clouds based on real-time imagery through smartphone camera. From another manner in which to create an AR Cloud is through Telecom companies and ISPs

who geolocate users and digital objects through network triangulation. The AR Cloud could take shape in various forms and is still a highly speculative domain with little available research.

It remains to be seen how the power dynamics will emerge and shift in AR Clouds. Multiple tech companies and research groups are reported to be working on AR Clouds. This means that different competing AR Clouds could exist simultaneously, similar to content streaming services or video game platforms, where each cloud has its own set of apps and functions. As we have seen with systems like iOS and Android, with their respective app stores, various tech actors will likely compete to dominate the AR Cloud space. Yet it remains to be seen who will exercise disproportionate power in AR Clouds. Will it be the telecom companies, the various device manufacturers, games and social platforms, or some other group of application providers? Microsoft, Facebook, and Snapchat already have AR and VR headsets available, which enable users to experience the respective networks and applications interactively.

A digital zoning protocol

Having outlined the various conceptual, technological, and functional aspects of digital zoning, we may finally sketch out what digital zoning may entail. By drawing on conclusions based on the previous sections, we can outline specifications for a hypothetical future digital zoning protocol. As we have seen within the smart and digital city bifurcation, one important aspect of the digital city is the manner in which it may invert a tech-centric logic to be citizen or user-oriented. From the surveillance capitalism section, we saw the manner in which private data harvesting through personalized advertising incentives possibly necessitates the use of public of municipal oversight to govern digital services and products based on spatial use. Here we have argued that recontextualizing the discussion on planning standards from the western canon, as we have seen from Aristotle's writings on Hippodamus, allows for concepts related to societal functions and goals to be seen as interconnected with urban planning and zoning. We thus posit that digital zoning embodies the following concepts:

- Utilization of GIS and mapping data to plan and designate uses of land upon digital products and services, thus reinforcing spatial use up to the digital level.
- Through location-based systems such as 5G (and future iterations) as well as GPS and telecon-related tracking systems, digital zoning relies upon a more or less accurate interaction between physical coordinates and corresponding digital information.

- By utilizing the "transmitted experience" diagram, digital zoning functions as an interactive layer in which services and products can interact and compete within a common infrastructural layer.
- By functioning across municipal or state-level infrastructure, within designated areas, it facilitates and secures public digital functions such as market transactions, free speech, etc. across public domains within an AR Cloud-like environment.

Concluding remarks

The chapter has discussed the concept of digital zoning as a means in which to distribute, plan, and regulate technology services and products within the physical and digital city. This is proposed as a necessary step in developing holistic digital city projects, both conceptually and technically. We see the digital zoning concept as a response to several conceptual, regulatory, and technical problems related to the merging of physical and digital space that sooner or later will need to be dealt with. We have speculated that as technology companies' activities within physical space and cities continue to be developed, we can expect spatial technologies such as augmented reality, facial recognition, location-based services, and similar developments to become further integrated into the fabric of everyday life, and thus the logic of physical space and spatial planning. The question we have posed is whether spatial technologies have the capacity to be regulated within the zoning system in urban planning regulation. This has argued that the democratic procedures within urban planning, particularly zoning, can be useful tools to test the capacity to regulate spatial technologies, specifically in the manner in which zoning can specify the use of land, while also performing the vital role of creating a common infrastructural platform in which services and products can communicate across domains and borders.

We have argued that the digital city model may allow for a closer development of digital urban services and products in line with the everyday needs of citizens and inhabitants. In may be the case the digital city can be a helpful model in informing new ways of designing and governing cities and urban space in the convergence with technology, and in providing valuable clues for the merging of technology with existing urban planning traditions. However, such a model simultaneously calls for new forms of regulation and protection in order to secure the rights of its users, and an evaluation of the robustness of existing codes and doctrines within urban governance, especially in relation to surveillance and privacy concerns. From our perspective of Oslo, Norway, we see that the intentions in creating such a holistic model have been encapsulated in the ongoing work towards a Norwegian or Nordic smart city approach. As all of this is still up in the air for now, all of these possibilities point to a need for more rigorous and embedded case work.

Is digital zoning possible? We notice here that some of the more interesting digital city literature suggests that cities need technologies and infrastructure that can connect different sectors together in a more iterative and modular manner, with components provided by multiple vendors by sharing enough core protocols and data to be interoperable. The challenge in seems, as de Waal argues, is that "cities lack competence in understanding digitisation, experimenting with technologies and approaching challenges flexibly," and that "business models, funding models and procurement practices are underdeveloped, do not support technological innovation and are often unsuitable for multi-stakeholder strategic collaboration." This identifies a clear set of problems to be tackled. We believe that this opens up the opportunity for architects to planners to create new cooperatives and forms of dialogue in order to embrace the novel opportunities for cooperation and creativity these new technologies can provide.

There is some room for real optimism regarding the potential for the digital cities model to enhance urban life through digitization. As we have seen, recent advancements within a range of digital technologies, including spatial positioning systems, mobile communications networks such as 5G, wearable computing devices, 3D scanning, and mixed reality, demonstrate the possibility for the merging of physical and digital space into a single, continuous, lived experience. This is particularly applicable to urban spaces, which can apply these technologies to large public user audiences with a high degree of coordinated and accurate data. This technological advancement presents a vast range of new services offering potentially ground-breaking improvements to urban life, including the capacity for the digital city to increase access to participatory planning and decision-making if placed within established frameworks for democratic governance. This context provides a range of interesting new conceptual frameworks for understanding architectural space and could present a range of new aesthetic and spatial opportunities in making a more interactive and richer urban environment. Here we argue that this holistic approach requires that such technologies are implemented within coherent urban planning doctrines, such as digital zoning in order to secure bureaucratic procedures in accordance with the governing principles of the physical space and the city.

The digital zoning concept seeks to address the potential usefulness of technologies like AR in urban planning if the accuracy of AR models proposals could be precisely tethered to their physical location. Our case studies in this area so far have indicated that location data, in its current iteration of the technology, is not precise enough for planning purposes and thus required manual positioning. For this reason, the actual position of AR objects that were placed during our case studies had to be configured manually after the fact. However, we have seen that with future technologies in the form of accurate geofencing, the AR Cloud, or

similar solutions, the real possibility of including very accurate position data in the planning ecosystem. We see from this experience that in a future iteration (such as with 5G) it would be valuable to find a system that would allow object positioning to be registered automatically in a digital coordinate system that was linked with a planning map or system at a very accurate level. It does seem that further iterations with AR in urban planning, alongside future technology developments alongside digital zoning, could find ways to position digital objects as accurately as needed in a real-world coordinate system, further merging the physical and digital city.

Finally, the support for the research work we have conducted on digital zoning and similar topics has been overwhelming at times, suggesting that the topics addressed are relevant to a variety of contexts and research considerations outside of this immediate context. Within the digital city discourse, we have been given expert technical guidance on how to coordinate various coordinate systems, and will continue our work on prototyping such as system in close connection to Oslo Municipality and our work on AR. We have also seen a particular emphasis on the idea of local community engagement and the empowerment of citizens that this type of work entails. This will certainly be an interesting avenue to consider while moving forward either in Oslo with this case work, or in other contexts around the world and with other audiences as these research topics continue to be explored.

BIBLIOGRAPHY

AfricaLtd, MiX Telematics. n.d. "Get Geofence Alerts with GPS Geofencing Technology & Tracking." *Matrix Vehicle Tracking*. Accessed May 22, 2023. https://www.matrix.co.za/geo-fencing-tracking.

Airey, J., J. Rohlf, and F. Brooks. "Towards Image Realism with Interactive Update Rates in Complex Virtual Building Enviro-ments." *ACM SIGGRAPH Computer Graphics* 24 (1990): 41–50. https://doi.org/10.1145/91385.91416.

Albino, Vito, Umberto Berardi, and Rosa Dangelico. "Smart Cities: Definitions, Dimensions, Performance, and Initiatives." *Journal of Urban Technology* 22 (February 2015): 2015. https://doi.org/10.1080/10630732.2014.942092.

Anastasiu, Irina. "Unpacking the Smart City through the Lens of the Right to the City: A Taxonomy as a Way Forward in Participatory City-Making." In *The Hackable City: Digital Media and Collaborative City-Making in the Network Society*, edited by Michiel de Lange and Martijn de Waal, 239–60. Singapore: Springer, 2019. https://doi.org/10.1007/978-981-13-2694-3_13.

Argus Tracking. "Geofencing." *Argus Tracking*. Accessed May 22, 2023. https://argustracking.co.nz/geo-fencing. n.d.

Aristotle. *Aristotle's Politics*. Oxford: Clarendon Press, 1905.

Aspen, Jonny, Peter Hemmersam, Jørn Knutsen, and Einar Martinussen. "Challenges of the 'Urban Digital': Addressing Interdisciplinarity and Power in the Planning and Design of the

Digital City." *Nordes Conference Series*, June 2017. https://dl.designresearchsociety.org/nordes/nordes2017/researchpapers/3.

Azuma, Ronald T. "A Survey of Augmented Reality." *Presence: Teleoperators and Virtual Environments* 6, no. 4 (1997): 355–85. https://doi.org/10.1162/pres.1997.6.4.355.

Barfield, Woodrow. *Fundamentals of Wearable Computers and Augmented Reality*, 2nd ed. Boca Raton: CRC Press, Inc., 2017.

Beckwith, Richard, John Sherry, and David Prendergast. "Data Flow in the Smart City: Open Data Versus the Commons." In *The Hackable City: Digital Media and Collaborative City-Making in the Network Society*, edited by Michiel de Lange and Martijn de Waal, 205–21. Singapore: Springer, 2019. https://doi.org/10.1007/978-981-13-2694-3_11.

BorderGO project by Norkart and the Norwegian Mapping Authority. Accessed October 19, 2021. https://www.norkart.no/wp-content/uploads/2018/06/BorderGO-Erik-Landsnes-Norkart.pdf.

Brooks, R. "A Robust Layered Control System for a Mobile Robot." *IEEE Journal on Robotics and Automation* 2, no. 1 (1986): 14–23, https://doi.org/10.1109/JRA.1986.1087032.

Burns, Alfred. "Hippodamus and the Planned City." *Historia: Zeitschrift Für Alte Geschichte* 25, no. 4 (1976): 414–28.

Cardullo, P., and R. Kitchin. "Being a 'Citizen' in the Smart City: Up and Down the Scaffold of Smart Citizen Participation in Dublin, Ireland." *GeoJournal* 84, no. 1 (2019): 1–13.

Englebart, D. "A Conceptual Framework for the Augmentation of Man's Intellect." I Contract AF 49(638)-1024 • SRI Project (Nummer 3578). Air Force Office of Scientific Research, 1963.

Glasmeier, Amy, and Susan Christopherson. "Thinking about Smart Cities." *Cambridge Journal of Regions, Economy and Society* 8, no. 1 (2015): 3–12. https://doi.org/10.1093/cjres/rsu034.

Green, Ben. *Smart Enough City*. Cambridge, MA: MIT Press, 2019. https://smartenoughcity.mitpress.mit.edu/.

Halegoua, Germaine. *Smart Cities: MIT Essential Knowledge Series*. MIT Press Cambridge, MA, 2020. https://mitpress.mit.edu/books/smart-cities.

Hemmersam, Peter, Einar Martinussen, Jonny Aspen, and Jørn Knutsen. "Challenges of the 'Urban Digital': Addressing Interdisciplinarity and Power in the Planning and Design of the Digital City" (2017). https://doi.org/10.21606/nordes.2017.003.

Höhl, W., and D. Broschart. "Augmented Reality in Architecture and Urban Planning." *gisScience*, 1 (2015): 20–29.

Ishida, Toru, and Katherine Isbister. *Digital Cities: Technologies, Experiences, and Future Perspectives*, vol. 1765. Springer, NY, 2000. https://doi.org/10.1007/3-540-46422-0.

Jong, Martin de, Simon Joss, Daan Schraven, Changjie Zhan, and Margot Weijnen. "Sustainable–Smart–Resilient–Low Carbon–Eco–Knowledge Cities; Making Sense of a Multitude of Concepts Promoting Sustainable Urbanization." *Journal of Cleaner Production*, Special Issue: "Toward a Regenerative Sustainability Paradigm for the Built Environment: From Vision to Reality," 109 (December2015): 25–38. https://doi.org/10.1016/j.jclepro.2015.02.004.

Kato, H., K. Tachibana, M. Tanabe, T. Nakajima, and Y. Fukuda. "A City-Planning System Based on Augmented Reality with a Tangible Interface." *The Second IEEE and ACM International Symposium on Mixed and Augmented Reality*, 340–41, 2003.

Landry, Charles. *The Digitized City: Influence & Impact*. Stroud: Comedia, 2016.

Landsnes, Erik. "Norkart: 'Visualizations of Borderlines in AR.'" 2018. Accessed May 22, 2023. https://www.norkart.no/wp-content/uploads/2018/06/BorderGO-Erik-Landsnes-Norkart.pdf.

MacDonald, Nancy. "How Can We Build Smart Cities of the Future?" n.d. Accessed May 22, 2023. https://www.stantec.com/en/ideas/topic/cities/how-can-we-build-smart-cities-of-the-future-start-now-by-bringing-the-best-ideas-to-bear.html.

Martinussen, Einar S. "TRUST IS WORK." *Digital Urban Living* (November 9, 2020). Accessed May 22, 2023. https://medium.com/digital-urban-living/trust-is-work-3716059013e5.

Mora, L., M. Deakin, and R. Bolici. "The First Two Decades of Smart-City Research: A Bibliometric Analysis." *Journal of Urban Technology*, no. 24 (2017): 3–27. https://doi.org/10.1080/10630732.2017.1285123.

Picon, Antoine. *Smart Cities: A Spatialised Intelligence*. Hoboken, NJ: John Wiley & Sons, 2015.

Reaver, Kai. "Evaluating the Use of Mixed Reality (MR) in Urban Planning." *eCaade Conference Proceedings, 2019*. 2020.

Reaver, Kai. "After Imagery: Evaluating the Use of Mixed Reality (MR) in Urban Planning." In *Anthropologic: Architecture and Fabrication in the Cognitive Age—Proceedings of the 38th ECAADe Conference*, vol. 1, edited by L. Werner and D. Koering, TU Berlin, Berlin, Germany, September 16–18, 2020, 187–96. CUMINCAD. Accessed October 12, 2022. http://papers.cumincad.org/cgi-bin/works/paper/ecaade2020_009.

Robinett, Warren. "Synthetic Experience: A Proposed Taxonomy." *Presence: Teleoperators and Virtual Environments* 1, no. 2 (1992): 229–47. https://doi.org/10.1162/pres.1992.1.2.229.

Sutherland, I. "The Ultimate Display." *Proceedings of the Congress of the International Federation of Information Processing (IFIP)*, 2, 506–508. New York City, 1965.

UN Habitat and Ericsson. "Mixed Reality for Public Participation in Urban and Public Space Design Towards a New Way of Crowdsourcing More Inclusive Smart Cities." *U.N. Habitat, Johannesburg, SA*, 2019.

Zeltzer, David. "Autonomy, Interaction, and Presence." *Presence: Teleoperators and Virtual Environments* 1, no. 1 (1992): 127–32. https://doi.org/10.1162/pres.1992.1.1.127.

Zuboff, Shoshana. *The Age of Surveillance Capitalism: The Fight for a Human Future at the New Frontier of Power*. New York: PublicAffairs, 2019.

7

Pattern Recognition—
The Big Smart Transactional City

Ian Nazareth and David Schwarzman

Introduction

The future is already here—it is just not evenly distributed.

(William Gibson)

Cities are in a constant state of flux. These anomalous characteristics and behaviours are a product of its interaction with local governmental policies, market forces, social and economic practices, as well as fluctuations on the global dais. These uncertainties make any attempt to distinguish or intervene within their complex organization, precarious. Unsuccessful or flailing modernist enterprise, the rise of nation states and unbound exuberance of the free market economy, has coincided with the retreat of creative disciplines from the civic realm and public imagination. Collectively, the models and tools of engagement of architects, urban designers, and planners with the city remain didactic and hierarchical, and arguably have not adapted to the plurality of the urban environment, its variables, and utter hybridity.

The increasing decentralized forces—from transformation of workforces amid post-industrial paradigms, ecological and environmental change and migration, that have reshaped contemporary metropolitan regions, compel a new manner of engagement. The urban debate centres around regulating population growth and consequently ways of moving people and goods over increasing distances. While crucial and generic concerns, cities continue to operate within contested spaces, disputed forms of urban renewal, and antiquated models of real estate speculation. These cannot be addressed as static, parochial identities, and call for acute, nimble tactile responses with overarching strategic foresight.

Overall, the productivity of infrastructure has declined[1] and the relative pace of transformation of the "soft infrastructures" of the city has created a schism, prompting an evaluation of design and the agency of creative disciplines in the city.

This chapter navigates a series of paradigms, thematic agendas, and projects—to locate the research interest, describe a series of patterns and emergent conditions, tools, techniques, and practices that collectively capture the domain of inquiry. The chapter examines the role of precedent, data, and emulation in informing the city while constructing a potential design briefing document. Precedent and best practice are determined to establish a narrative and conceptual focus for the potential transformation of the fabric of the city.

Transactional Urbanism

A reframing or repositioning of the attributes of the city in order to comprehend its potential.

In *Megalopolis* (1961), Jean Gottmann began to describe transactional forces that stemmed from a labour pool once engaged primarily in the production of goods and tangible products, that were rapidly moving to a model of processing and managing intangibles like information and knowledge.[2] In assessing the role of cities, it became apparent that cities were still the "principal loci"[3] for activities that were now akin to transactions. The shift into intangible domains was elaborated through *The Coming of the Transactional City* (1983). While the paradigm was rather nascent, Gottmann posits cities as hosting environments for transactional activities. Access (in a broader sense) to nodes of hyper-connectivity is a vital force in globalization. As a counterpoint to Thomas Friedman's "flat world" dictum, which describes the levelling effects of technology on a global scale, urban theorist Richard Florida observed that from an economic, consumption, and innovation standpoint the world is "spiky"[4]—a view that is ratified by the explosive growth of cities, manufacturing hubs, and nodes of service activities.

In the intervening decades, digital transformation has continued to be an imperious force driving the metamorphosis of cities and regions, where de-spatialized dynamics and variables increasingly effect how cities are described, understood, and valued, fundamentally increasing pressure for deeper societal change.

"Transactional Urbanism" is a protraction of the flat, spiky, decentralized city, expressing the significance and influence of ubiquitous transactional exchanges on the form of the city. It presents the techno-social spatial domains that engender the city—an urban realm that is remote, dispersed yet kinetic and all-pervading

and responds to a subtle relative pace of change. The transformational shifts are simultaneously incremental and rapid, and adjust, occupy, and insert themselves within the fabric of the city. The "sharing" or "peer-to-peer" economy has accelerated the distribution and division of individual transactions, altering the form and order of the city.

Disruptive Sharing

Platform technologies and new economic practices, catalyse a shift in patterns of ownership.

The now ubiquitous term "sharing economy," also described as "collaborative consumption" and the "gig economy," is a decentralized platform for commerce and transactions, that operates from peer-to-peer (P2P).

While the sharing economy is a product of capitalism, it signifies a new, possibly novel economic system, and the first since capitalism and socialism.[5] Economist Jeremy Rifkin places the sharing economy at the centre of the current epoch he refers to as "The Third Industrial Revolution." The "cloud" (cloud computing), big data and the Internet of Things (IoT) have fuelled a "planetary digital interconnected platform."[6] The convergence of new communication technologies, energy regimes, renewables, and mobility—i.e. an unfolding of a matrix of co-dependent "internets" has collectively energized fundamental economic change.

The sharing economy is still a rather ambiguous term, as it is not explicitly sharing in an altruistic or charitable sense but is focused on monetization. It enables the commodification of personal assets—this could be a villa, an apartment, a spare bedroom, the rear seat of a car, or one's indefinite time. People have had not dissimilar interactions prior to the pervasive IoT. The P2P economy is perhaps unique, insofar that it has numerous centralities and terminals of exchanges within a decentralized landscape.

On one hand, it is plausible that this economy is catalysed by the technological backbone, but simultaneously no coincidence that its genesis coincides with the financial crisis of 2008, the economic and political uncertainty and austerity, that further catalysed a series of opportunistic economies.

The P2P economy exposes areas of impunity within the urban system—critical triggers that precipitate in tectonic shifts in cities:

- The generational swing of renting (leasing and borrowing) rather than possession, prioritizes "access" as opposed to "ownership." For the city and its architecture, this compels a rethinking of new centralities and transit nodes. Other

industries and technology services are transitioning from one-time purchase to long-term subscription models.
- The focus on under-utilized assets suggests the potential for a more efficient pattern of usage and occupation of objects, spaces, and cities.
- The P2P economy has usurped systems for valuation (and value) and how value is described and measured. Functions of "proximity," "likes," etc. now determine value.

These economies have prompted inventive if not radical application of logistical, commercial, spatial, and legal frameworks. Their expeditious uptake has also raised serious regulatory concerns—from confrontations with labour unions, monitoring minimum wage to safeguarding users and contractors. We have barely begun to understand the sharing economy and collaborative consumption.

Smart versus Collaborative

Collaborative consumption and its impact on a user, subscriber-generated perspective of the city.

It is vital to locate the sharing economy adjacent to the concept of "Smart Cities" which will also be a protagonist in the future city but rooted in a different set of assumptions and aspirations.

The "Smart City" has become a symbol and symptom of political change, of aspirational governance shifting one's gaze from space to data, and from civic to corporatization. Arguments against the smart city cite the following: that it is incompatible with the informal character of the city, that it subjects the city to corporate power and that it reproduces social and urban inequalities.[7]

The smart city as a proposition has become a hegemonic notion of urban governance, transforming and supplanting planning,[8] where the prevailing focus is infrastructure and not architecture or urban planning.[9] It is more than the movement of data. It is the exchange of capital.

Collaborative consumption is one attribute of the sharing economy, referring to events in which one or more persons consume economic goods or services in the process of engaging in joint activities with one or more others.[10] It involves not mere "consumers" but "obtainers" who may also be "providers,"[11] and stakeholders sharing resources.

Opportunism and desperation are perhaps two sides of the same coin. Surge pricing is a feature associated with Uber and other ride-sharing services. In essence, it is a supply-demand multiplier, that exponentially increases the rate at moments of bad weather, rush hour, and special events, for instance, may

cause unusually large numbers of people to want to ride, all at the same time.[12] This also encourages more services on the road. There are, of course, legitimate concerns around mobility services that adopt a model that exploits adverse circumstances.[13]

If we look past profiteering, this demonstrates an almost sentient connection with the city. It senses the city and can actively respond to it. Whether a sporting event or the disruptions to the city's public transport infrastructure, a user-generated data set mobilizes a heightened response.

The speed at which such information can form feedback loops is remarkable. The contention here is that this order of computing that can correlate and perhaps even anticipate is underestimated. The sharing economy has inadvertently stumbled on a smart city, one not created by governments or political interests, but by users, subscribers, and citizens. Can this be harnessed for social benefit?

Big Data

The city is a physical experience and a discarnate experience, citizens fluctuating between hybrid realities.

Big Data refers to complex data sets from new data sources that contain a greater variety that arrive in increasing volume and with more velocity, that traditional data processing software is inadequate. One scenario for discerning general trends in our city's usage and its social reality comes from a project that uses geolocated digital traces of mobile phone applications to map and speculate about a possible future for our cities.[14]

Through big data, we begin to understand an emergent city and architecture manifested through an operative, symbiotic entanglement between multiple agents simultaneously. These expansive protocols could include operative tunings in between ecological, biological, geological, and algorithmic variables.[15] Information now becomes experiential with technology that promotes a haptic informational interaction with humans that is intimate and multisensorial. This extends to an imminent possibility for hyper-computational processes to re-construct reality as another experience rather than as an abstraction of an experience.[16]

Pattern Recognition, System Complexity, and Medium Design

For us, of course, things can change so abruptly, so violently, so profoundly, that futures like our grandparents' have insufficient "now" to stand on. We have no

future because our present is too volatile. [...] We have only risk management. The spinning of the given moment's scenarios. Pattern recognition.
(William Gibson, *Pattern Recognition*)

The city encounters uncertainty and volatility that is, today, fast-tracked across all its operations. The abrupt shifts are often profound, where vast bureaucratic and political structures are not agile enough to respond to the fleeting, potentially violent momentary lapses that the contemporary city propels. Most actions involve immediate intervention, response and even risk management, and lengthy policy processes can be ineffectual in such matters.

The futility of lengthy intervention in a temporal and complex urban system is well epitomized by the city master plans of the twenty-first century. A central planner in dreaming of an urban future as a quest for an ideal state operates with a limited understanding of the result of system change within the city, oblivious to the impact and outcome of their designs, master plans are left hopelessly dependent, to their own detriment, on a specific time and place context.[17]

Today formulations on contemporary urbanism should stem from a necessity in engaging with tools in addressing and responding to the complexity of urban environments which by nature are temporal and in a constant state of flux. Methods of engagement, whose potential is not yet fully realized as repertoires of urban designers and planners, include:

Pattern recognition, a tool employed by sharing economy tech companies can help conceptualize change and negotiate the complexity evident in the dynamic city system. Pattern recognition can afford designers and planners with the ability to understand (Figure 7.1) and therefore intervene in the city system with an extended temporal dimension—allowing for their designs to unfold over time and remain in play.

Informal, unplanned urbanism, offers compelling capacity in their system adaptivity and evolutionary and endogenous processes.[18]

Keller Easterling's *Medium Design* offers an approach to bring awareness to the chain reactions and interdependencies, patterns of influence and political control to better understand, and influence the matrix of rules and relationships in which the city and its forms are suspended.[19]

Cesare Marchetti's analysis of anthropological and human behaviour uncovers an underlying city-human operational dynamic, instinctual rules of the game which shape our interaction with the built environment and influences the city's evolution over time.[20]

Frei Otto's analysis of growth and change in human settlement occupations and their connections provides an understanding of the broad intrinsic human and technological dispositions, inclinations, and rules for which the fabric of our modern city is suspended.[21]

FIGURE 7.1: Realtime Car Parking: Mapping patterns of car parking and city bike usage using real-time city data in Melbourne. The white circles indicate either occupied or unoccupied street parking, while the red circles indicate vacant or utilized bike parks. Credit: David Schwarzman and Ian Nazareth.

In their very essence, these approaches seek to better understand complexity in urban environments that are bound by the feature of temporality. Their contribution is not static or restricted to a time and place context, but rather aims to deepen efficacy in productive intervention and influence the trajectory of complex urban environments with an extended temporal dimension. At a time where conventional urbanism is slow and static, often based on top-down visions and unable to respond to rapidly changing social conditions the sharing economy has, as a

dynamic non-physical infrastructure navigated this complexity and inadvertently stumbled on a smart city. The legibility of this efficacy can be read in its ability to encourage such incredible dynamic occupation of space in the city not according to long-term planning rules or fixed set of criteria but rather according to ephemeral and temporal user demand and popularity (Figure 7.2)—a phenomenon highlighting the contrast between the city's static physical state and the dynamic social processes and human preferences which it orders.

FIGURE 7.2: Realtime Car Speeds: Mapping fluctuating vehicular traffic (shared and private) speed over time using real-time city data in Melbourne. The colour gradient of the street network indicates average vehicular speed—red to blue—slow to fast. Image Credit: David Schwarzman and Ian Nazareth.

As cities, just like natural systems, or any other complex adaptive system, will not settle into permanent structures, but rather remain in a constant state of flux and reconfiguration, formulations on contemporary urbanism should stem from engaging with tools that allow us to not only conceptualize change, just as the sharing economy has, but to navigate and ultimately harness the complexity and ephemerality of our urban environments.

Firmware

Disclosing the kinetic characteristics and behaviours of the city to architects and designers in the manner it manifests itself to open source and proprietary technology platforms.

Firmware is a design—research excursion on the city, approaching digital interfaces as physical environments. Firmware draws reference to a particular class of computer software that provides a standardized operating environment for the device's more complex operations. Without firmware, a hardware device would be non-functional.

This analogy is deployed to focus on the relationship between virtual applications, digital realms, and physical spaces in the city, as well as the implications they have on the temporal and permanent patterns of occupation, spaces, and typologies (Figure 7.3). It seeks to establish a platform through which virtual (and even real-time) data can be juxtaposed from multiple sources and spatialized.

This project is empowered by a process of data scraping—whereby geo-referenced information and data from web-based Application Programming Interfaces (APIs) can be extracted into design environments. Here raw information is co-referenced. The platform is thus a conduit between APIs and computer-aided design applications (Rhinoceros 3D) through an algorithmic visual programming language (Grasshopper).

The focus is to hybridize disparate datasets from public services and private entities who have a vested interest in the city. This convergence offers architects, planners, and other disciplines an insight into the behaviours of cities and networks (Figure 7.4) all captured through decentralized systems. These can record and reveal patterns and offer new ways of engaging with the city.

Using metropolitan Melbourne as a prototype, it can connect open-source city data, city-council-specific information, public transport, car park availability, alongside AirBnB listings, Uber movement, etc. Drawing from multiple insular datasets simultaneously, it offers a collective assessment of collaborative consumption.

In the Functional Mix (Figure 7.3), the city is simultaneously despatialized and dematerialized. It discloses a synchronous digital shadow and the legibility of the

PATTERN RECOGNITION—THE BIG SMART TRANSACTIONAL CITY

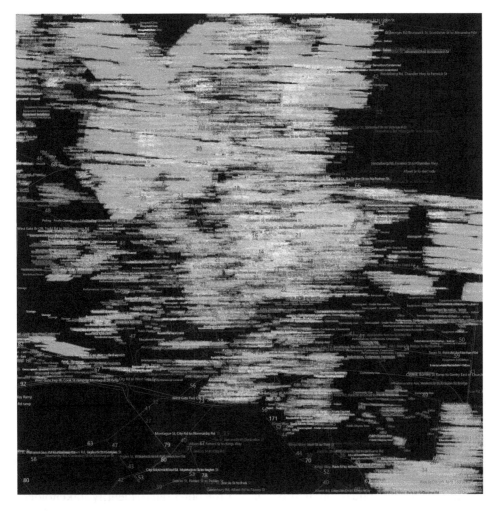

FIGURE 7.3: Melbourne Functional Mix: Mapping the functional, programmatic mix of Melbourne using open-source data from the City of Melbourne. Image Credit: David Schwarzman and Ian Nazareth.

virtual registers of the physical city. Devoid of geometry, a surreal landscape of data emerges, described explicitly by geo-located information. The multivalent systems, densities, behaviours, and inter-dependencies are perhaps indeterminate but unravel in real-time.

At present, these are analytical devices that reveal subliminal infrastructures of the city that could be pivotal to the future of the city. In the early phase of analysis, the project has demonstrated a range of new centralities that emerge, that are ironically a product of the decentralized economy. This has enabled a finer-grain focus on

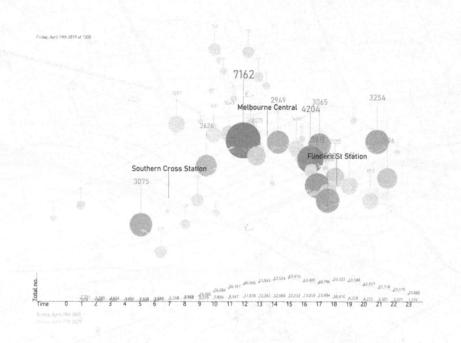

FIGURE 7.4: Realtime Crowd Sensing: Mapping and graphing fluctuating pedestrian flows through Melbourne using real-time data. Image Credit: David Schwarzman and Ian Nazareth.

such areas, that can be activated in future development, statutory planning, mobility strategies for cities, and so on. It also indicates the potential to identify stakeholders and commence engagement at an early phase of long-term strategic urban projects.

Participating in the future of the city today (due to its increasing complexity, the volume of data and variable use of its infrastructure, etc.) is not so much about the study of the physical but rather observing the rules, dynamics, interactions, potentials that the physical is suspended—real-time tools allow for our participation and observation of this—and can help our ability to participate in something which unfolds in a dynamic open-ended manner.

Projects

The subsequent projects operate in the domain of design research,[22] i.e. design as a medium for conducting research[23]—analysing, mapping, and reflecting on

architectural and urban projects and ideas, in conjunction with socio-cultural dynamics. It recognizes design speculation and modelling as potent tools to reveal and amplify critical observations and engage in procedural experimentation in the medium of architecture and urban design. The projects are located in Melbourne, Australia research leveraging the issues and potentials of the current city, and its future—where the medium and high-density developments proffer unique opportunities within specificities of its urban transformation for new typologies, intensities, and densities to be deployed.

Rearranging a liveable city

This project speculated about a possible symbiotic relationship between the fundamental structures and arrangement of the city (Figure 7.5) and real-time data that determines the transformative and transitionary nature of flows of people, products, and capital—proposing a repositioning and perhaps super positioning of the hierarchies and new centralities. Here generic binaries are replaced by more dynamic relationships—a spatio-temporal city. Seven domains or criteria—from housing affordability, employment, public transport, public open space, and walkability are primary determinants in prescribing a liveable neighbourhood. These are collocated with the relative growth of employment clusters and population density relative to centres. Mobility whether public transport or private car is understood in relation to distance travelled, carbon emissions, and finally, block level energy consumption and floor space usage densities. Considering scale and sprawl as a primary combinatory issue in Australian cities that are critical to address—walkability is highlighted, identified and reassessed as a particular programmatic output, and compared and alongside the urban grain, density of pedestrian infrastructures. Finally, the new networks consider how these various uses might in turn determine new morphologies and centralities for the city.

Urban performance measures

The qualitative attributes of cities are challenged by quantitative criteria and performance measures that produce a range of spurious metrics, rankings, and a standing of liveability, that seek to undermine or flatten any differential understanding of the built form or urbanism of a city. Potential sameness rather than plurality. This project seeks to unravel this through projecting a temporal lens to understand how cities can be recalibrated to better respond to and establish its own performance criteria. This is closely interrogated through land use mix (Figure 7.6), amenities, points of interest, density and its intersections, and mobility

FIGURE 7.5: Rearranging a Liveable City: Mapping Population distribution relative to the city centre and its change over time. Image Credit: Chaitali Bhanushali, Harshitha Mruthyunjaya & Shalome Pinto with Ian Nazareth and David Schwarzman, Firmware 2020.

and safety. Specific points in the CBD become the focus of further cartographies, further exploring more clearly defined comparatives. These include a typological array of facilities, amenities, and infrastructures understood in conjunction with

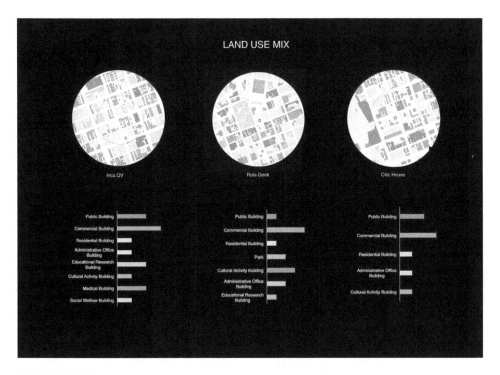

FIGURE 7.6: Urban Performance Measures: Analysing land use mix and densities in three locations across Melbourne. Image Credit: Zecong Tan, Mengzhen Li & Tszto Leung with Ian Nazareth and David Schwarzman, Firmware 2020.

density and floor area ratios within building envelopes. Here pedestrian activity near transport hubs, trip counts, and modality, are equated with accessibility and safety, vehicular traffic, crowding, intersection densities, etc. These benchmarks become indicators that get prioritized to maximize the benefit of recalibration, and currently under review for design outcomes that are catalysed by fine-grain analysis of datascapes.

Pestilential cities

The unpredictability and complexity of the city system could not be more well epitomized then by its rapid transformation into a pestilential city. This project responds to the physical distancing measures imposed by the local government in response to the COVID-19 pandemic and its impact on the function of the city. To understand the extent of the transformation the city's original patterns of occupation and movement are analysed and mapped against the status quo. The nature of the infectious disease and its inherent spatial consequence, the city's

spatial carrying capacity here is extracted and spatialized. Proposing spatial and non-physical interventions (Figure 7.7) this project aims to return the city to its function with minimal disruption and in doing so highlights the contrast between the city's static physical state and the dynamic social processes and human preferences which it orders.

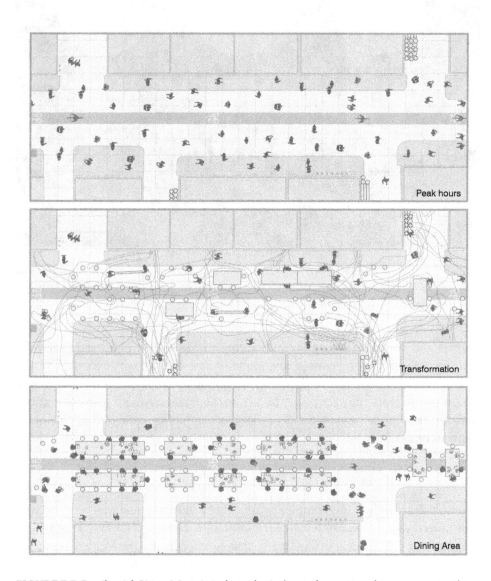

FIGURE 7.7: Pestilential Cities: Mapping a hypothetical transformation of street usage in China Town, Melbourne. Image Credit: Tess Nettlefold, Matthew Samson & Michael Cuccovia with Ian Nazareth and David Schwarzman, Firmware 2020.

Project summary

The projects aim to describe a relationship between areas of thoughts. It presents the proposition forces that demonstrably shape the city—focusing on technology and its implementation and imprint. Each project establishes a relation in the domain of architectural comprehension. Individually and collectively projects presuppose a way of understanding, staging a mode and model of relationships between external parameters and variables. They each extrapolate grains from the present, establish a relationship between data and physical structures, and provide evidence through speculation. The projects are models—a revisionistic tool, quantifying possibility.

Conclusion

The present is always invisible because its environmental. No environment is perceptible, simply because it saturates the whole field of attention.
(Marshall McLuhan *Mademoiselle*, 64, 1966: 114)

Through experiences and devices, we absorb space, data, and information in vast proportions. While many experiences are vicariously wrought through encoded and restrictive interfaces, they temper and influence our perception of reality and space. We are also active, sometimes reluctant contributors, patrons feeding the limitless system, fodder from advanced artificial intelligences to process, reconcile and make intelligible. We know physical from digital, work from leisure, near from remote, city from wilderness but it could all well be the same; collapsed into a seamless superstructure. The rational morphology of the city is superseded by an arbitrary logic of the temperamental, the real-time, the trending and yet an exaggerated blur. We are in control, or so it seems. The awareness of our existence is augmented. We have approached the "hyper urban."

With the pervasive reach of technology, we have arrived at a critical moment where ubiquitous computing, platform technology, and big data can effectively influence behaviour through suggestions and understanding of personal preferences. This, within a distributed landscape emerges as a city tuned to individual preferences.

British architectural critic Cedric Price, who sought to rethink architecture's relationship with society queried "Technology is the answer, but what was the question?" as the title of his 1979 lecture,[24] a polemic that remains relevant if not more acute in the post-critical era.

The themes, projects, and practice run analogous to over a decade of fundamental and perhaps subversive transformation of the potency of the architect and agency of architecture and its position within emergent power structures and differentiated value hierarchies. The architectural intervention, inventiveness, and typological fluidity—that each purport new modality (and positioning within self-regulated, post-capitalist paradigms) may well have been functional and purposeful. Now, even the act of construction and building—are "post-spatial"—where architectural novelty is discussed through alignment with decentralized models of procurement, finance, ownership, subscription, and management. The rapid rise of the peer-to-peer economy has already hinted at how technologies that bypass orthodoxies, might be embedded within the cognition of the city, and in equal measure their capacity for disruption. The infrastructures that enable P2P and collaborative consumption could be the pivot for resilience in future urban and architectural form. The future city needs to be adaptable and inclusive. The variants and typologies exist, and the new economic possibilities present a compelling armature. It is a question of capacity and redistribution. Millennials are already entrenched in a hybrid economic system each day.[25] The sharing economy is a prime variable, and these are futures for local and federal bodies to co-author with P2P platforms, to deliver social, economic, and ecological resilience in cities.

NOTES

1. Jeremy Rifkin, in E. Holodny, "A Key Player in China and the EU's 'Third Industrial Revolution' Describes the Economy of Tomorrow" (2017), *Business Insider Australia*. Accessed February 20, 2020. https://www.businessinsider.com.au/jeremy-rifkin-interview-2017-6?r=US&IR=T.
2. Kenneth Corey and Jean Gottmann, *The Coming of the Transactional City*, xi. University of Maryland Institute for Urban Studies, Maryland (1983).
3. Ibid.
4. Richard Florida, "The World Is Spiky." *The Atlantic Monthly* (2015), October 2005: 48–51. Accessed December 15, 2018. https://www.theatlantic.com/past/docs/images/issues/200510/world-is-spiky.
5. Rifkin, in Holodny, "A Key Player."
6. Ibid.
7. Maroš Krivý, "Towards a Critique of Cybernetic Urbanism: The Smart City and the Society of Control." *Planning Theory* 17, no. 1 (2018): 8.
8. Ibid.
9. Rahul Mehrotra, in D. Ratnam, "I Have No Idea What a Smart City Means: Rahul Mehrotra," *Live Mint, Hindustan Times*, August 22, 2015. Accessed March 21, 2018.

https://www.livemint.com/Politics/VFwRPtdqCtg6lyBeacEfZI/I-have-no-idea-what-a-smart-city-means-Rahul-Mehrotra.html.

10. Marcus Felson and Joe Spaeth, "Community Structure and Collaborative Consumption: A Routine Activity Approach." *American Behavioral Scientist* 21, no. 4 (1978): 614.
11. Myriam Ertz, Fabien Durif, and Manon Arcand, "Collaborative Consumption: Conceptual Snapshot at a Buzzword." *Journal of Entrepreneurship Education* 19, no. 2 (2016): 1. Accessed January 28, 2019. https://ssrn.com/abstract=2799884 or http://dx.doi.org/10.2139/ssrn.2799884.
12. "Uber: How Surge Pricing Works." Accessed January 28, 2019. https://www.uber.com/en-AU/drive/partner-app/how-surge-works/.
13. Anna Prytz, "$70 for 4km: Commuter Shock at Uber Surge Pricing during Train Chaos." *The Age* (May 3, 2018). Accessed January 28, 2019. https://www.theage.com.au/national/victoria/70-for-4km-commuter-shock-at-uber-surge-pricing-during-train-chaos-20180503-p4zd2s.html.
14. Ian Nazareth and David Schwarzman, "The Temporal City—The Agency of Big Data," in *The 8th International Conference on Architecture and Built Environment with AWARDs S.ARCH 2021*, Rome, Italy (September 22–24, 2021).
15. Manuel Gausa and Jordi Vivaldi, "Expansive Protocols," in *The Threefold Logic of Advanced Architecture: Conformative, Distributive and Expansive Protocols for an Informational Practice: 1990–2020*, by Manuel Gausa and Jordi Vivaldi (ACTAR Publishers, 2021), 221.
16. Ibid., 222.
17. Tom Verebes, "The Death of Masterplanning in the Age of Indeterminacy," in *Masterplanning the Adaptive City: Computational Urbanism in the Twenty-first Century*, ed. Tom Verebes (New York: Routledge, 2013), 92.
18. Ibid., 88.
19. Keller Easterling, *Medium Design* (Moscow: Strelka Press, 2018).
20. Cesare Marchetti, "Anthropological Invariants in Travel Behavior." *Technological Forecasting & Social Change* 47, no. 1 (1994): 75–88.
21. Frei Otto and Berthold Burkhardt, *Occupying and Connecting: Thoughts on Territories and Spheres of Influence with Particular Reference to Human Settlement* (Stuttgart: Menges, 2009).
22. Murray Fraser, *Design Research in Architecture: An Overview* (Farnham, UK: Routledge, 2013).
23. Leon van Schaik, *The Practice of Practice 2: Research in the Medium of Design* (Melbourne: RMIT University Press, 2003).
24. Cedric Price, "Technology Is the Answer, but What was the Question? Lecture Title, Audio with Slides." Pidgeon Digital, London. (1979). Accessed January 27, 2019. https://www.pidgeondigital.com/talks/technology-is-the-answer-but-what-was-the-question-/.
25. Rifkin, in Holodny, "A Key Player."

BIBLIOGRAPHY

Beilin, Ruth. "Conceptualising Change: Complexity, Post-Normal Science, Uncertainty and Risk." In *Reshaping Environments: An Interdisciplinary Approach to Sustainability in a Complex World*, edited by Helena Bender, 277–304. Port Melbourne: Cambridge University Press, 2012.

Corey, Kenneth, and Jean Gottmann. *The Coming of the Transactional City*. Maryland: University of Maryland Institute for Urban Studies, 1983.

Easterling, Keller. *Medium Design*. Moscow: Strelka Press, 2018.

Ertz, Myriam, Fabien Durif, and Manon Arcand. "Collaborative Consumption: Conceptual Snapshot at a Buzzword." *Journal of Entrepreneurship Education* 19, no. 2 (2016): 1. Accessed January 28, 2019. https://ssrn.com/abstract=2799884 or http://dx.doi.org/10.2139/ssrn.2799884.

Felson, Marcus, and Joe Spaeth. "Community Structure and Collaborative Consumption: A Routine Activity Approach." *American Behavioral Scientist* 21, no. 4 (1978): 614.

Florida, Richard. "The World Is Spiky." *The Atlantic Monthly* (2015), October 2005: 48–51. Accessed December 15, 2018. https://www.theatlantic.com/past/docs/images/issues/200510/world-is-spiky.

Holodny, Elena. "A Key Player in China and the EU's 'third industrial revolution' Describes the Economy of Tomorrow." *Business Insider Australia*, July 16, 2017. Accessed February 20, 2020. https://www.businessinsider.com.au/jeremy-rifkin-interview-2017-6?r=US&IR=T.

Johnson, Steven. *Emergence: The Connected Lives of Ants, Brains, Cities and Software*. London: Penguin, 2002.

Krivý, Maroš. "Towards a Critique of Cybernetic Urbanism: The Smart City and the Society of Control." *Planning Theory* 17, no. 1 (2018): 8

Marchetti, Cesare. "Anthropological Invariants in Travel Behavior." *Technological Forecasting & Social Change* 47, no. 1 (1994): 75–88.

Marshall, Steven. *Cities Design & Evolution*. New York: Routledge, 2009.

Otto, Frei and Berthold Burkhardt. *Occupying and Connecting: Thoughts on Territories and Spheres of Influence with Particular Reference to Human Settlement*. Stuttgart: Menges, 2009.

Price, Cedric, "Technology Is the Answer, but What was the Question?—Lecture Title, Audio with Slides." Pidgeon Digital, London, 1979. Accessed January 27, 2019. https://www.pidgeondigital.com/talks/technology-is-the-answer-but-what-was-the-question-/.

Prytz, Anna. "$70 for 4km: Commuter Shock at Uber Surge Pricing during Train Chaos." *The Age* (May 3, 2018). Accessed January 28, 2019. https://www.theage.com.au/national/victoria/70-for-4km-commuter-shock-at-uber-surge-pricing-during-train-chaos-20180503-p4zd2s.html.

Ratnam, D. "I Have No Idea What a Smart City Means: Rahul Mehrotra." *Live Mint, Hindustan Times*, August 22, 2015. Accessed March 21, 2018. https://www.livemint.com/Politics/VFwRPtdqCtg6lyBeacEfZI/I-have-no-idea-what-a-smart-city-means-Rahul-Mehrotra.html.

"Uber: How Surge Pricing Works." Accessed January 28, 2019. https://www.uber.com/en-AU/drive/partner-app/how-surge-works/.

Verebes, Tom. "The Death of Masterplanning in the Age of Indeterminacy." In *Masterplanning the Adaptive City: Computational Urbanism in the Twenty-first Century*, edited by Tom Verebes, 87–117. New York: Routledge, 2013.

8

Outsmarting the City— How Queer Subcultures in Queensborough Used Public Infrastructure for Community, Cruising, and Queering Car Culture, 1890–2000

Patricia Silva

Introduction

This chapter consolidates fragments of New York City history, personal experience, and the primary research that grounds Undisclosed Locations, a photographic project I began shortly after moving to Queensborough in the late 1990s. Undisclosed Locations uses contemporary and archival images to trace the networks where Queer people carved space for ourselves and each other in twentieth-century Queens. The year 2000 has been a logical marker for the scope of this project because it reflects the conditions of my access and engagement: (1) I frequented less Queer bars in Queens after 2004 than six years earlier; (2) nightlife information had solidly transitioned online but I didn't yet have online access at home in 2000.

The earliest photograph in my archive was made by an unknown photographer in 1890 along the same shoreline of my daily walks. What I do know is that a gender non-conforming person walked that route often for love and affection a couple of years after the photograph was made. Some of us have travelled long distances for love, but hours on foot across two boroughs, multiple times per week? I still feel a kinship with this person who used walking to learn about themself/ herself, in the same way that I rely on walking and cycling to learn about the history of Queerness before I arrived where I live. What I've learned is how the Queer spatialization of Queens varies greatly from the dominant register of NYC queer

narratives. The sites I've photographed have all formed along highways, revealing networks dependent on car culture for access and discretion. These locations present an urban story of pivoting constellations by the working-class Queer immigrants who built a thriving nightlife scene, support systems, and galvanized their own LGBTQIA+ movement with the first Queens Pride Parade in 1993.

The century's last decade filled New York City with hope, hardship, and mourning. A brief domestic economic boost for the middle and upper classes happened at the expense of defunded public services for the working classes and the poor. Policing, street surveillance, and racial profiling increased. The mourning that followed Queer people—due to hate crimes, police violence, and the loss of loved ones to AIDS—still loomed large in our communities. In Queens, New York City's largest borough, Queer activism was publicly mobilized during this era, after the brutal murder of Julio Rivera on July 2, 1990 in Jackson Heights, a case that became a turning point for the US hate crime law.[1] A teeming and thriving neighbourhood, Jackson Heights is also a renowned hub for queer bars and nightclubs in Queens, where working-class Queers work, dance, and mingle.

Until the Immigration Act of 1990, the United States was "the only country in the world with an explicit policy of excluding visitors and potential immigrants because of their sexual orientation."[2] Previously, the Immigration and Nationality Act of 1952 contained a provision that excluded anyone "afflicted with a psychopathic personality, epilepsy, or mental defect." The majority of US Courts interpreted "persons afflicted with a psychopathic personality" to mean people who identified as, or behaved as, homosexual. That same year, the American Psychiatric Association's very first Diagnostic and Statistical Manual of Mental Disorders (DSM) was published and classified homosexuality and other non-dominant orientations, as well as a variety of gender expressions, as forms of mental illness. This classification remained in circulation until 1973. Eight years prior to the declassification of Queerness as a mental illness, the Immigration and Nationality Act of 1952 was amended in 1965 to add "sexual deviation," but the 1990 Act removed provisions that prevented gay and lesbian persons from entering the United States.

When I moved to New York City in 1994 to study photography, I didn't know that the Immigration Act of 1990 no longer made me legally deportable, despite many people still being denied entry or deported due to the Act's "good moral character" requirement. The mid-1990s I witnessed were full of politically active Queers reading bell hooks and going to demonstrations, which I mostly avoided because of my own fears of deportation. It felt safer to go dancing so I did. The Pyramid Club was among the very first clubs I went to in New York City, and from there I also began frequenting Manhattan bars that catered to women. To learn about the city, reading nightlife ads in the then-weekly *Village Voice* was as important as reading Barthes' *Camera Lucida* for school. Once I moved to Queens,

I dotted my subway map with locations of bars and clubs now closer to me. I cut out an ad for Backstreet with Lady Bunny and kept it in a tiny notebook (Figure 8.1). That notebook became an address book, a directory of places to visit and I did just that as far as the subway would take me. My visual archive of Queer sites in Queens, titled Undisclosed Locations, began with this very small collection of addresses from nightlife listings, and a naîve will to discover a city so new to me. With school and work as primary responsibilities, my free time was sparse. Mostly, my efforts to find Queer spaces didn't result in anything at all. I would show up at an address expecting a club but only saw a row of abandoned warehouses.

FIGURE 8.1: Former site of Backstreet, now a strip club across from auto repair shop, 2019. Source: Patricia Silva Studio.

Looking back now, that may have been Queer culture functioning the way it was designed to be: with far less specificity I knew how to prepare for.

A Stream of Methodologies

Throughout this text I will refer to LGBTQIA+ history and culture as Queer, to broadly acknowledge western and non-western practices.[3] This text, and project, applies the term "Queer space" to sites with dominant narratives reduced to "gay." Though I specify known cultures for individual spaces (such as "gay bar," "lesbian club") I do refer to them collectively and individually as forms for Queer space. I prefer using "Queer space" to highlight how bars geared towards a particular orientation (gay, lesbian) are often havens for allyship, political coalitions, solidarity, for people who pass, and for those whose identities aren't safely outed there, or elsewhere. Though in New York City many gay bars have promoted a women's night, I work with the knowledge that gay male spaces can be mixed-use spaces depending on the hour, and historically (pre-Stonewall) have had to be mixed use by design, to divert suspicion.[4] To avoid detection by state agents, Queer people played games of "fooling the straights," a practice in which male presenting Queers walked arm in arm with female-presenting Queers in public—this alone disturbs the long-held assumption that women do not cruise each other in public. Of course they do, and have. It's just that these "experiences necessitate and offer a new spatial and temporal theoretical vocabulary."[5] A broader term like "Queer space" hopefully avoids the stereotypical traps, and historical slights, imposed on orientations beyond gay male traditions and leaves room for practices known and unknowable.

The practice of salvaging Queer history from historical erasure that informs my research is found in the academic contributions of Clare Hemmings, June Jordan, Maria Pramaggiore, Kenji Yoshino, George Chauncey, and Jack Halberstam. The idea of Queer Use is directly borrowed from Sarah Ahmed's writings about Use, and in particular, Ahmed's Kessler Award lecture in 2017 at the City University of New York's The Graduate Center, where Ahmed's rigorous studies of Use fortuitously expanded my own thinking about what I had been assembling with Undisclosed Locations. Thinking about space through the lens of use, rather than the specific identities associated with a space, broadened my scope for Queer use with the added benefit of dislodging the cis white male dominion of public and Queer spaces.

Primary research began with my own address book and over time expanded to include articles from the *Village Voice*, *New York Times*, and *Queens Chronicle*, with ephemera and other materials from NYC Municipal Archives, The Queens Library Archives, The New York Public Library, and The Wagner Archives at LaGuardia

Community College.[6] As of January 2022, there isn't a single academic book that historicizes the long-standing arcs of LGBTQIA+ lives in Queens,[7] where these histories are very socially diverse in terms of class, racialization, heritage, faith, and wit.

Photographic Approach

To understand Queer history where I live, I keep riding my bike in a borough made for cars and photographing only in available light. Early on, I decided to focus on buildings and public structures, without people, which has led me to consider the Queer undercurrents of a city in terms of models of itinerary. Undisclosed Locations isn't about mapping or cartography, it merely identifies a set of active networks that go in and out of public cognition and awareness, at different points in time. The 1990s photographic formality of Catherine Opie's Mini Malls in Los Angeles, and Zoe Leonard's Analogue series of Lower East Side shops provided visual inspiration for how to continue the photographic tradition of indexing urban streets through a non-male Queer lens that in New York began with Alice Austen and Berenice Abbott.

The photographs in Undisclosed Locations were originally taken with a Pentax 645N, a remarkably affordable autofocus medium format camera with a very loud shutter mechanism. In 2007, I spent a significant portion of my employee holiday bonus on a digital click-and-snap camera, the ultra-compact Leica D-Lux 2 from 2005. Though I had been roaming around the borough for some time, digital camera technologies enabled a faster photographic workflow that was also economical: no more film processing. With a smaller, faster camera made for street work, I began revisiting the addresses and making newer photographs, a process I began repeating again in 2012 after purchasing a used Canon 5D Mark II from a colleague. Eventually, the D-Lux 2 stopped functioning properly, so in 2018, I traded that model in for a newer one, a D-Lux 109 from 2015. The formal selections for Undisclosed Locations have all been created with the Canon and the Leica. My criterion for choosing a camera depends firstly on the environment: will I even dismount my bicycle? If not, it's the smaller Leica. If I can wander around safely, I pack the Canon.

Krash, 1997

Night class ended at 21:30 and 40 minutes later I should have arrived at my apartment share off 24th Avenue. The ride home seemed slower than usual. When the train started moving again I looked around a mostly empty train car filled with the sudden screeching of steel grinding on steel. That's when I realized I was on

the wrong train and would have to walk some twenty minutes home. Sleepy and annoyed, I exited the station at an inconvenient intersection, so I turned around. The image struck me immediately. Standing on the corner across from me, under the glow of street light was someone tall and taller in platform heels. Neon fishnet stockings, a mini skirt, and a little moto jacket to keep warm while smoking a cigarette. The traffic light turned red, cars stopped, and I crossed the street again. I hadn't seen an overtly gender non-conforming person in the neighbourhood before, and certainly not a Black femme presenting star with cheeks highlighted for the stage. I looked up and saw a sign I couldn't read in the dark, but now I knew it was a club. "Hey," I said as I passed. They smiled and nodded. I walked home elated as if my whole day had been spent dancing.

Was this sequence caught on camera? If so, whose? Since the Department of Transportation's instalment of red light street surveillance cameras in 1993, and the city's notorious Video Interactive Patrol Enhancement Response (VIPER) system's implementation in 1997, specifically within targeted communities, this particular corner would have been well monitored. Especially being two blocks from New York State Route 25A, which connects Queens to Manhattan via the Midtown Tunnel. Krash was also across from a car lot for P.C. Richards & Son, an electronics superstore, which would have had their own surveillance protocols in place. Any one of the adjacent businesses could have recorded my accidental discovery of Krash, but how long would this footage have lasted? Twelve hours before being erased?

Much of urban Queer life is inadvertently recorded this way: brief moments of mutual cognition and affirmation are too fleeting, too seemingly unrelated to be classified as connected. Subcultural bodies know how to generate meaning from randomness and chance but the intelligibility of such encounters isn't noticeable or recognized unless one participates in the encounter. Had it taken place fifteen years later, me and the person outside Krash would have been training algorithms (without our consent) to read us as two random people without shared interests. When I went to Krash, I didn't think too much of the name and didn't know that the location had been a car repair shop since the 1940s. Currently, the site is now a "gentleman's club" across the street from a lumber and hardware emporium one block from a fuel station. Though I don't remember seeing that performer again, I did return to Krash several times and made the mistake of thinking that this incredible dance space would be there for much longer.

Background: About Queens

By the turn of the twentieth century Queens was viewed as a lackluster borough of bedroom communities for working-class commuters and locals working in the

city's most diversified economy.⁸ It is the largest of New York City's five boroughs and the second most populated county in New York State. Queens holds the Guinness World Record for "most ethnically diverse urban area on the planet," where residents speak at least 140 documented languages and dialects. According to the 2019 US Census Bureau data,⁹ 55.7% of residents speak a language other than English at home, and First Nation residents comprise 1.3% of residents. Non-local Indigeneaty in Queens includes peoples from the Americas (Taíno, Carib, Garifuna, Aztec, Maya, Inca) as well as from international diasporic populations from Asia, Southeast Asia, the Balkans, Central Europe, the Middle East, North Africa, among more. As such, Indigeneaty in Queens is not a nostalgic timelapse, but a matrix of negotiations in the present time that extend beyond my capacity to address.

The borough's 280 km² (109 sq miles) rest on a marshy peninsula of unceeded land maintained by Munsee-speaking Lenape peoples of Mespat, Jameco, Reckowacky, Canarsie, and Matinnecoc heritage, prior to European settlement. This area was known as "Sewanacky," or the "island of seashells" for the hard clam shells collected by Lenape for wampum production. The bays, creeks, and ponds throughout Queens provided First Nation residents with fin fish, shellfish, and aquatic greenery while the forest offered game and migratory fowl. Corn and squash were harvested. Berries, grapes, chestnuts, walnuts, and paw-paws grew abundantly. As colonized territory, Queens became New Netherland under the Dutch in 1624, Yorkshire's West Riding under the British in 1664, and these settler communities included Quakers, French Huguenots, and freed Black people.[10] Each of these groups left their cultural imprint on broader American values, from ad hoc coalitions against religious tyranny to the farming-driven sustenance and industry that could not have thrived without centuries of efficient stewardship by First Nation peoples.[11] The European smallpox epidemic of 1662 that killed significant numbers of indigenous peoples in the borough prevented First Nation residents from participating in the borough's modern constructs long before geographic and legislative dispossession. New York City maps in the 1800s portray the borough as a completely verdant expanse but after 1900 the rubric for its urbanization was already set.

Flatlands for the Cruise

The history of LGBTQ+ cultural hubs is predominantly urban and Queer space is often relegated to the edges, where marginalized people can socialize without judgement or peril. The dominant LGBTQ+ history of New York City has been primarily focused on Manhattan, with a peripheral focus on Brooklyn, and

skimming over the oldest documented Queer community in all of New York City—Harlem. Neighbourhoods where scholars have centralized the dominant narratives of New York City's Queer histories (West Village, Chelsea in Manhattan; Brooklyn Heights, and Park Slope in Brooklyn) have become unaffordable to local residents with middle-class employment. Manhattan's historic queer spaces are bars, clubs, waterfront piers, theatres, public parks, public transport hubs, and Brooklyn follows a similar template. By contrast, Queens presents a constellation of queer bars situated at various thoroughfares and endpoints of parkways and highways.

When the Queensborough Bridge finally opened in 1909, the borough's isolation and dependence on water ferries ended. Queens Boulevard, a 12.1-km (7.5-mile) roadway, became a connecting artery for new residential hubs along existing routes to Central Queens (Figure 8.2). During the 1920s, Queens had a growth rate of 130 per cent as more bridges and highways were constructed. The 1939–40

FIGURE 8.2: Historic photograph, circa 1980, site of a Queer disco on Route 25A. Copyright: New York City Department of Records and Information Services.

world's fair elevated the borough to national conversation. The Fair was built on 1216 acres of park at Flushing Meadows, a site later used for the 1964–65 world's fair. According to the *New York Times*,

> The first fair laid out a glorious vision for the automobile: General Motors' Futurama exhibition [...] depicted the multilane highways of the future. The second fair arrived with that vision mostly realized—and the automobile near the pinnacle of its power and prestige.[12]

In preparation for the 1939 fair New York City's Mayor Fiorello LaGuardia closed down Queer bars and famed burlesque spots throughout the city. But the World's Fair grounds were a cruising site for Queer people long before the fair, and especially during. To an astute historian (like George Chauncey) the police reports reveal the covert presence of Queer life (Figure 8.3).

With the late nineteenth century's shift to electricity, machines, and faster modes of transport, the automobile became one of the symbols of the late Modern era. In Queens, the long-treaded routes of trade established by First Nation peoples and settler farmers became paved roads, boulevards, and motorways. The first US motorway constructed specifically for the automobile cut into Queens from Long Island in 1912. Known as the Vanderbilt Parkway, it was initially meant to be railroad heir William Kissam Vanderbilt II's private raceway. The smallest hills were flattened for fast tires and upper-class white men who could afford the practice of speeding for fun. William K. Vandervilt II declared in the *New York Times* that he wanted a parkway free from "interference from the authorities." Remnants of Vanderbilt Parkway can still be seen today at several spots known as cruising grounds for people of many orientations, but most notoriously for men seeking men. The Vanderbilt Parkway was eventually taken over by the City of New York (due to tax evasion) in 1938, just as public access to the 1939 world's fair was being developed.

FIGURE 8.3: World's Fair Marina grounds, 2015 and 2019. Source: Patricia Silva Studio.

Looking at a map today, it's easy to see how the former Vanderbilt Parkway connected the World's Fair grounds to places later identified as Queer sites. One of them is a small sliver of greenery off the Parkway. On June 20, 1969, a group of men took chainsaws and cut down several trees in this park (Figure 8.4), to prevent men from using this area for cruising.[13] According to the *New York Times*, 30 trees were destroyed, the site suffered $15,000 in damages, but no arrests. One perpetrator spoke to *The Times* using his full name and admitted that he was part of a group that banded together to shine flashlights in the faces of gay men to force them out. This source also admitted to police consenting to these actions. The perpetrators claimed to be protecting mothers and children, but one mother

FIGURE 8.4: Site of the 1969 vigilante attack, 2018. Source: Patricia Silva Studio.

spoke up and said that neither she, nor her children are out at 1am, and she didn't care what happened in the park at those hours. Most curiously, the article casually states that men drove from Pennsylvania and Connecticut to meet other men there. As some in the neighbourhood condemned this attack, the Stonewall Rebellion happened one week later, and this Queens protest faded out.

Close to this site is Utopia Parkway, an 8.2-km (5.1 miles) non-commercial boulevard running north–south connecting with other major motorways and roads (Figure 8.5). Interestingly, the Parkway begins north of the peninsula at the edge of Fort Totten and ends at Hillside Avenue in Jamaica. Fort Totten is a former Civil War battle site, a documented Queer cruising site for men seeking men, and for at least one trans woman who wrote about visiting her beaus at the Fort in the late 1800s. Tracing her route, I looked for photographs of what she might have seen on her walk to the Fort, and the only photograph I found with specificity was from 1890, which marks the beginning of this photographic archive.

Directly south of here in Jamaica[14] is where I've found the largest concentration of Black queer cruising spaces in Queens, though I presume there is so much more that isn't yet known, and much I haven't come across. Utopia Parkway becomes Homelawn Street and ends at Hillside Avenue. Turn one direction and you'll end up at a 1970s queer bar next to the Major Mark Park, where the Monument to Soldiers and Sailors is located. Turn the other direction, and you'll drive through 28 former LGBTQ sites along Hillside and Queens Boulevard culminating in an explosion of queer culture in Jackson Heights, Queens' most iconic LGBTQ+ neighbourhood and the starting point of the Queens Pride Parade.

FIGURE 8.5: Public park south of World's Fair grounds, 2020. Source: Patricia Silva Studio.

Hillside Avenue is also the site of a Queer bar, one that highlights the necessary labour required in reclaiming a historical record in the present time. For years, I had a name and an intersection for a queer bar in this section of Jamaica, which has historically been home to communities of Black, Caribbean, and West Indian heritage. In nightlife listings, this particular bar never listed its address, only an intersection near a subway: "Hillside and Parsons Boulevard." I visited this site multiple times in person, comparing the buildings to the lots I had seen on public records, trying to narrow down where this bar might have been. I logged rows of shops within a one-block radius of each possible direction but nothing was making sense. Then I read about a public cruising site nearby and began paying closer attention to the street leading directly there but again nothing stood out. Several years later, on a Zoom call during the 2020 pandemic, I was casually talking with friends about this project and one of them, Thierry, had grown up near Jamaica and remembered going to a queer bar on Hillside. Thierry didn't remember the name of the bar but remembered a red awning. By this time, NYC uploaded some of its archives online, and I spent some time looking at shop after shop searching for a red awning at that intersection. When I finally found a red awning halfway down the street I was searching on, it was not a bar, but the bar I had been looking for was just next door. The glass window featured the bar's name; Hide-A-Way. Looking at a miniscule picture online didn't feel glorious, but I had finally found one of the places I had known about the longest. Curiously, this bar is not at all at "Hillside and Parsons Boulevard," it's a whole block away, at another intersection. How curious, that a 1970s queer bar that was around until the mid-1990s, as Thierry confirmed, attracted clientele by printing the incorrect intersection and without a specific address. Without my friend's vague memory of its exterior, I would not have found it. Clearly, the Hide-A-Way clientele had protocols. You had to know someone to tell you the proper location, and still today, in the present time, I needed someone to tell me where it once was though it's no longer there.

Just off the end of Utopia Parkway, and one block south of Hillside is the former location of Salt & Pepper, a known disco for which I have little info other than an address that may or may not be complete. But the location of Salt & Pepper is right off one of Queens' oldest roads, a major New York City thoroughfare named New York Avenue in the 1850s and New York Boulevard by 1920. Intersecting a much older First Nation trade trail connecting the peninsula's east trade with the Midwest (now called Beaver Road), the New York Boulevard swiftly cut through South Jamaica directly towards 300 acres of verdant plains edging the water. These meadow lands became airfields, servicing the city as Idlewild Airport in 1948 and renamed to JFK Airport in 1963. West of these airfields is the old Ridgewood Aqueduct, decommissioned, but home to New York City's only thoroughbred horse racing facility since 1898, in Ozone Park. Close to the Aqueduct is the former

location of a queer bar called Pegasus, active from the 1970s through the 1980s. A bar named after a winged horse within walking distance from a racetrack and a short drive from the airport provided a perfect cover for an underground economy of queer gestures and games of glancing.

The most famous picture of Idlewild airport is of Christine Jorgensen returning to the United States in 1953 after undergoing gender realignment surgery in Denmark. But there must be photographs of Ms. Jorgensen performing at a cabaret in Jackson Heights at the time that this photo was taken in the 1950s. I've found nightlife listings from the 1950s advertising Ms. Jorgensen's shows in Jackson Heights, but the photographs have proved more difficult to find.

These are a few of the distinct connections I found between Queer culture and car culture in the borough. The cruising scene that was visible here from the 1920s on, did it begin with the unpoliced paths and overpasses of a parkway (Figure 8.6) without "interference"? Who were the men, often driving with male chauffeurs, who were arrested for having false license plate numbers? Later known as a route for transporting alcohol during Prohibition, the Vanderbilt Parkway carries all the signs of homosociality providing a cover for Queer behaviour. Is it an accident that a culture of cruising has formed around several of its remnants?

Conclusion

Before the 1969 Stonewall Rebellion, and after the 1995 rezoning laws that normalized anti-Queer violence,[15] Queer communities in Queens gathered mostly undetected by using heterosexual norms as a cover in geographically dispersed areas. These included: urban grids of car repair shops and fuel stations; zones without foot traffic after business hours; public parks off of highways and boulevards; within cabarets accessible by established routes of "deviancy"; bridges; beaches; bays; bathhouses, and in and around major transport hubs where new faces are the norm. Another layer to the spatial organization of avoiding detection is the practice of listing bars not by their actual street addresses, but by an intersection of major roads. In one instance, I found the exact bar one block away from where the bar advertised itself to be, and even so, I needed a former patron's loose memory to locate it. Several sites on my list are even more geographically vague. Although roadways were not designed for Queer people to find each other in cars, the Queens constellation of Queer spaces reveals extensive patterns of use for queering the urban road, presenting conditions that expand upon the dominant narratives of New York as a "gay city." These site-specific conditions have been ignored, as have the lives and struggles of Queers of colour who comprise the majority of Queer (and immigrant) life in Queens, on and off of the dancefloor (Figure 8.6).

FIGURE 8.6: Near remnants of Vanderbilt Parkway, highway underpass leading to the notorious park, 2017. Source: Patricia Silva Studio.

We often frame mechanisms of surveillance as being extensions of state control (which they are) but Queer bodies have long experienced forms of surveillance that depend not on technology but on moral servitude to the state apparatus. Vigilantes are forms of surveillance determined to keep Queer bodies off of parks, bars, and threaten the public safety of women, trans, and gender-nonconforming people. When I set out to make a visual project to understand a Queer present through histories of Queer use, I was not interested in a resolution, completeness, or unaffected accumulation. I wanted to investigate

what's possible to continue in the present time by shifting perceptions and expectations of places around me.

Though current research for Undisclosed Locations ends in the year 2000, public sites in Queens (and all over the city) were suddenly active, or more frequented, during the pandemic thanks to the connective power of mobile apps. Meeting in person has not become, will not become, obsolete. Space is indigenous, even when it's digital, and if location reveals nothing without patterns of context, can Big Data capture that which by design functions without detection, and always evolves to escape standard patterns of cognition? Queer bodies are the writers of a city's unwritten histories, fragmented narratives further obscured by social inequities, and requiring multiple literacies.[16] How can we trace these unwritten histories if our dependence on obsolescence (High Technology) continually increases? Given the absence of many Queer literacies in our cultural vocabulary, what can Big Data gather from Queer counterpublics that will reveal more of us to each other, to ourselves, and of our histories? And most importantly of all: where can we dance?

ACKNOWLEDGEMENTS

Undisclosed Locations is made possible (in part) by the Queens Council on the Arts with public funds from the New York City Department of Cultural Affairs in partnership with the City Council. Special thanks to Qiana Mestrich for continued support of this project; to Thierry Casias who helped identify The Hide-A-Way; to Pauline Park for the generosity of introducing me to Daniel Castellanos at Queens Pride House, where this project was first presented to the public in 2019; to Stephen Petrus at The Wagner Archives; to Syd Baloue, Elvis Bakaitis, Jasmine Sinanovic at The City University of New York's Center for Lesbian and Gay Studies for welcoming my presentation of Undisclosed Locations; and to Tamara Tavevska for providing feedback on a transitional draft of this text. I also want to specifically thank the organizers of Architecture Media Politics and Society's 2021 Urban Assemblage Conference at the University of Hertfordshire (UK), for providing me the opportunity to test my ideas among far more esteemed panellists at the virtual conference, and more recently, to our editor Silvio Carta for all the creative and administrative labour indispensable to assembling our ideas into this enriching book.

NOTES

1. For a look at the impact of Julio Rivera's murder on his Jackson Heights community, see Richard Shpuntoff's 2016 feature film *Julio of Jackson Heights*.

2. Shannon Minter, "Sodomy and Public Morality Offenses under U.S. Immigration Law: Penalizing Lesbian and Gay Identity." *Cornell International Law Journal* 26 (1993): 772.
3. I use the word Queer as an umbrella term for LGBTQIA+ identities, and as a manner of inclusion for gender nonconformers, and non-western forms of Queerness that inevitably occupied the borough from First Nation to the waves of Middle Eastern and Southeast Asian migrations. Though most of the materials I found specifically reference gay and lesbian culture, and conditions that may or may not have been drag as we know it today, I always presume that bisexual, asexual, trans, intersex, and other identities were present in the same spaces. As community terms (labels) evolve and change, I choose to use "Queer" in order to make my research framework inclusive of people who may not have wanted to out themselves even within gay and lesbian spaces due to their further marginalized identities and practices. I want to stress that my use of "Queer" stems from its use as a broad community term in relation to institutional power dynamics, and not as a signifier of individual identity.
4. And sometimes it's not even about diverting suspicion, it's how spaces operate. Martin Manalasan writes that "Gay travel guides feature maps where gay bars are indicated as points within various grids. However, this kind of mapping is too simplistic and does not take into account the various ways in which public spaces, particularly those 'out there' can be inflected by other identities." Manalasan goes on to describe how the straight patrons of one Filipino restaurant in Jackson Heights were habituated to the same restaurant becoming "home" to Filipino gay men after a certain time. Martin F. Manalasan, *Global Divas, Filipino Gay Men in the Diaspora*, 71.
5. Jen Jack Gieseking, *A Queer New York: Geographies of Lesbians, Dykes, and Queers*, 9. For further reading on the urban cruising styles of American lesbians, see Denise Bullock, "Lesbian Cruising: An Examination of the Concept and Methods," and Lillian Faderman, *Odd Girls and Twilight Lovers: A History of Lesbian Life in Twentieth-Century America*. It has been difficult to find a scholarly source detailing the cruising styles of nonmonosexual women and nonbinary people that actually emerges from within such communities.
6. Vincent Seyfried's books were essential to contextualizing the evolution of the borough, as were conversations with Richard Hourahan at The Queens Historical Society, and conversations with John Choe and Patrick Symes at the Old Quaker Meeting House in Flushing. Roxanne Dunbar-Ortiz's *An Indigenous Peoples' History of the United States* was indispensable.
7. Despite several books about Manhattan and a couple about Brooklyn's Queer past, there isn't a single academic book focusing exclusively on Queens. As a cultural center with limited infrastructure, Queens Pride House has focused on multilingual education and support for its constituents, maintaining group meetings, and a rich library of LGBTQIA+ books. The only publicly documented timeline I have found for the evolution of Queens Queer activism has been in the exhibition catalogue for *The Lavender Line, Coming Out in Queens*, a 2017 exhibition at the Queens Art Museum. See: Ciego-Lemur and Petrus, *The Lavender Line*, 10.

8. Health care, retail trade, manufacturing, construction, transportation, and film and television production.
9. "Quick Facts: Queens County (Queens borough), New York." United States Census Bureau Data. Accessed January 2021, https://www.census.gov/quickfacts/fact/dashboard/queenscountyqueensboroughnewyork/POP815219.
10. I learned much of this from Roxanne Dunbar-Ortiz's *An Indigenous Peoples' History of the United States*, and Vincent Seyfried's books.
11. As a response to Governor Stuyvesant's mandate that the Dutch Reform Church be the single religion practiced in New Netherland, Quakers reacted by producing the Flushing Remonstrance in 1657. This document is considered a precursor to the United States Constitution's provision on freedom of religion in the Bill of Rights. The Old Quaker Meeting House in Flushing is the oldest religious building in New York City, standing since 1694. On an informal conversation with Quaker Friend John Choe at the Old Quaker Meeting House in 2015, Choe explained how the presence of a Black middle class in Flushing emerged because Quakers helped liberate enslaved Black people and helped them set up farms. Not too far from the Meeting House is the key site of the Underground Railroad, the national secret network providing shelter and vital support to people escaping enslavement in the American South. According to the Queens Historical Society, the majority of Quakers had a history of protecting people escaping enslavement. James W. C. Pennington was a prominent teacher, writer, and abolitionist in Elmhurst before becoming Yale University's first Black student in the 1830s at the Divinity School. Pennington was forbidden to formally enroll, use the library, speak in class, or earn a degree, but was awarded an honorary Divinity degree from Heidelberg University, Germany in 1849, sixteen years before the US abolished slavery. This community in Elmhurst, set a pattern for future generations to form historically Black communities in Queens. Members of the Huguenots settlement at Flushing Landing taught Robert Prince the principles and practices of European horticulture, and when the Prince family opened the first commercial plant nursery in the United States in 1735, it quickly established Flushing as North America's destination for wholesale tree and plant nurseries. From the Underground Railroad to transit routes established for carrying trees all over the United States, these settler networks interacted with each other in mutually beneficial ways long before the arrival of the automobile, and the neoliberal implementation of commuting by car in service of The American Dream.
12. Phil Patton, "When Cars Ruled the World's Fair." *New York Times* (April 11, 2014), https://www.nytimes.com/2014/04/13/automobiles/collectibles/when-cars-ruled-the-worlds-fair.html. Last accessed October 19, 2023.
13. David Bird, "Trees in a Queens Park Cut Down as Vigilantes Harass Homosexuals." *New York Times* (July 1, 1969), https://www.nytimes.com/1969/07/01/archives/trees-in-a-queens-park-cut-down-as-vigilantes-harass-homosexuals.html. Last accessed October 19, 2023.
14. Writing about Jamaica in 1862, Queer American poet Walt Whitman described it as a "village [...] which is composed mostly of one long street, which is nothing else than

the turnpike." Whitman is also a former resident of Jamaica, 1838–40. Walt Whitman, "Brooklyniana: A Series of Local Articles, on Past and Present." *Brooklyn Standard* no. 36.

15. Lauren Berlant and Michael Warner, "Sex in Public." *Critical Inquiry* 24, no. 2 Intimacy (Winter, 1998): 547. See also: Hanhardt, *Safe Space*, 155.

16. In my experience, institutional Queer scholarship still lacks adequate historical inclusion of trans, bisexual, asexual, intersex, and other marginalized identities. Despite the increasing prominence of gay and lesbian history, and recent inclusion of trans studies, working class, poor, and non-western forms of gay, lesbian, and trans life are often excluded. And within each of these identities exist social inequities such as anti-Blackness, citizenship status, ablism, (trans)misogyny and (trans)misogynoir, the murderous policing of trans people's bodies, biphobia, and the bureaucratic disdain for gender fluidity. The spectrum of experience Queer bodies carry is a living script that hasn't been fully incorporated into the texts of the Academy with close attention to these (and more) structural conditions. Despite the growth of American, and European, Queer studies since the 1990s much remains excluded by policy, omission, erasure, white supremacy, classism, and hasty complacencies with the status quo.

BIBLIOGRAPHY

Ahmed, Sarah. *What's the Use? On the Uses of Use*. Durham, NC: Duke University Press, 2019.

Anon. *The History of Queens County New York with Illustrations, Portraits & Sketches of Prominent Families and Individuals*. New York City: W. W. Munsell & Co, 1882.

Bullock, Denise. "Lesbian Cruising: An Examination of the Concept and Methods." *The Journal of Homosexuality* 47, no. 2 (2004): 1–31.

Ciego-Lemur, Soraya, and Stephen Petrus. *The Lavender Line, Coming Out in Queens*. New York: LaGuardia and Wagner Archives, LaGuardia Community College/CUNY, 2018.

Chauncey, George. *Gay New York: Gender, Urban Culture, and the Making of the Gay Male World, 1890–1940*. New York: Basic Books, 1998.

Chisholm, Dianne. *Queer Constellations, Subcultural Space in the Wake of the City*. Minneapolis: University of Minnesota Press, 2004.

Faderman, Lillian. *Odd Girls and Twilight Lovers: A History of Lesbian Life in Twentieth-Century America*. New York: Columbia University Press, 2012.

Gieseking, Jen Jack. *A Queer New York: Geographies of Lesbians, Dykes, and Queers*. New York: New York University Press, 2020.

Hanhardt, Christina B. *Safe Space: Gay Neighborhood History and the Politics of Violence*. Durham, NC: Duke University Press, 2013.

Katz, Jonathan Ned. *Gay American History: Lesbians and Gay Men in the U.S.A*. Thomas Y. Crowell Company, 1976.

Kern, Leslie. *A Feminist City, Claiming Space in a Man-Made World*. New York: Verso Books, 2021.

Manalasan, Martin F. *Global Divas, Filipino Gay Men in the Diaspora*. Durham, NC: Duke University Press, 2003.

Minter, Shannon. "Sodomy and Public Morality Offenses under U.S. Immigration Law: Penalizing Lesbian and Gay Identity." *Cornell International Law Journal*, no. 26 (1993): 772.

Seyfried, Vincent. *300 Years of Long Island City 1630–1930*. New York: Edgian Press, 1974.

Seyfried, Vincent. *The Story of Queens Village*. New York: The Centennial Association, 1984.

Skal, George von. *The Illustrated History of the Borough of Queens*. New York City: F.T. Smiley Publishing Co., 1908.

Whitman, Walt. "Brooklyniana: A Series of Local Articles, on Past and Present." *Brooklyn Standard*, no. 36 (September 20, 1862).

9

The Influence of Artificial Intelligence on Autonomous Vehicle Design and Users' Lifestyle within Responsive Urban Environments

Marco Zilvetti, Matteo Conti, and Fausto Brevi

Introduction

Cities today can be regarded as living bodies, in which physical and digital realities overlap each other, changing the way users experience both private and shared spaces. The widespread use of information and communication technologies (ICTs) has enabled users to stay connected and access services through different web-based platforms and apps for multi-modal transport which empower travellers to use a range of shared and on-demand rental vehicles at any time.

As a natural evolution of this data-fuelled interactive reality, current road vehicles are gradually evolving into connected 'mobile spaces' where occupants totally or partially forego the role of driving, by relying on artificial intelligence (AI) and web-connected technologies.

Consequently, the ideation of innovative urban mobility products and services involves several intertwined factors such as physical context, ICTs, target users, travel patterns, vehicle typologies, and relevant services. This chapter suggests a set of recommendations for the design of the next-generation autonomous vehicles (AVs) founded on human-centred research and design rather than on the systematic implementation of innovative ICTs. The conducted research outputs involved both final users and experts' insights to better understand and respond to travellers' different lifestyles, needs, and issues in a smart mobility and city environment.

The smart urban environment

In the early 1990s, internet-led researchers predicted that cities would have declined in the future as technological advancements would have entailed the slow and irreversible "death of distance."[1] However, such forecasts did not come true considering that from 2008 more than 50% of the world population has been living in urban areas, with an expected 70% growth as 5 billion people living in cities by 2050.[2]

As Lukas Neckermann reports, Anne Hidalgo—Mayor of Paris—and Sadiq Khan—Mayor of London—in a 2016 joint statement declared that "if the 19th century was defined by empires and the 20th century by nation-states, the 21st century belongs to cities."[3] Current ICTs have become part of human interactions in this "age of networked intelligence."[4] Consequently, cities are becoming open-air computers that perform as testing grounds for the advancement of solutions supporting enhanced connectivity. As human web-based interactions take place, physical and digital realities tend to overlap each other, changing the way users experience both private and shared urban spaces.

The availability of pervasive mobile equipment has become a pivotal factor in what Mark Shepard[5] describes as a "sentient city": a responsive urban environment that senses, perceives, and elaborates data, as information processing becomes a distributed feature throughout the metropolitan spaces. This type of experience is increasingly mediated through digital technologies and smart cities become places for interaction where connected mobile devices and sensors generate a huge amount of information (Big Data). This data is then shared and analysed to implement, optimize, and update services as pervasive AI allows software and devices to become more accurate and rapidly respond to changing circumstances.[6] The widespread use of networked electronic sensors and wireless connectivity fostering the so-called Internet of Everything (IoE) is increasingly blurring the boundaries between the physical and digital world, with tangible consequences affecting how we interact and move around urban settings.

Urban mobility

Embedded ICT is key to the evolution of intelligent city environments; however, local administrators, planners, and engineers are called to apply research and design thinking in a more strategic and multi-disciplinary way to produce effective solutions to established wicked problems of "organized complexity"[7] around urban transport. This is necessary when planning and designing mobility services to provide more integrated, reliable, and connected transport systems, whilst making a positive impact on commuters' daily routine and the environment.

In this regard, a wide range of integrated mobility projects has been implemented over the last decade, with the clear intention of fighting against "car-centricity" to avoid congestion, reduce pollution, and optimize traffic flows. Key projects such as the new Nørreport Station in Copenhagen,[8] the MIND masterplan in Milan,[9] and the plan to create a low-traffic neighbourhood in the city centre of Paris,[10] include measures to improve the liveability and quality of life within the city centres like:

- Implementation of smart infrastructures to optimize traffic flows and avoid congestion by embedding sensors and predictive technologies.
- Reduction of traffic infrastructures and optimization of residential parking spaces.
- Creation of restricted areas within the city centre.
- Implementation of multimodal mobility services.

Implementation of smart infrastructures for traffic and parking spaces optimization

In recent years, the internet-based networked infrastructure has evolved becoming the nervous system of modern cities as sensors and cameras become inseparably interwoven within the urban fabric. The resulting symbiosis facilitates the conception of responsive urban spaces and innovative projects to optimize traffic flows and usage of parking spaces. The city of Hamburg's smart city initiative wisely incorporated Internet of Things (IoT) principles within its port infrastructures. As it represents a major economic driver for the region, the harmonization of its processes within the urban context becomes crucial. Consequently, the "SmartROAD" collaboration between Hamburg and Cisco improved traffic flow and resource management using information gathered through sensors for different operations, including the diversion of traffic around moveable bridges located in sensitive areas.[11] Barcelona Superblocks is a government-funded project that became part of global best practices due to the prioritization of people over cars with the participation of local communities in the plan development stages. The project identified and converted 120 intersections to reduce vehicular pollution and move towards more sustainable mobility. Using a scalable approach, this plan aims to transform one in three streets and create superblocks—503 in total—in which inner streets are only accessible to residents, public, emergency transport, bicycles, and other slow vehicles. This urban transformation provides other benefits such as the creation of pedestrian-safe public spaces.[12]

Examples of connected technology and sensors applied to the existing metropolitan infrastructures can be found in Helsinki, where a smart parking initiative

utilizes intelligent street lighting and monitoring systems to provide drivers with real-time information about available parking spaces. This reduces traffic and pollution but also optimizes the use of the available infrastructure.[13]

Creation of restricted areas within city centres

Local administrations around the world often struggle to find efficient measures to reduce traffic within urban boundaries. Restrictions rarely prove to be well-received by citizens and commuters, as they involve decreasing the number of cars permitted to flow into the city.

The London Congestion Charge was first introduced in 2003 to reduce traffic and its related impact within and around the charging area to ensure faster, more reliable journeys by public transport. This successful initiative reduced delays and traffic by approximately 30% and bus service disruptions by 60%.[14] Other cities around the world applied a similar approach to local restrictions and congestion charges. Milan, for instance, introduced its "Area C" in 2012 as an eighteen-month pilot programme due to the extremely high concentration of private-vehicle within the city[15] to tackle the persisting congestion-related issues and align with the local transport strategy to improve air quality. In 2019 local authorities introduced "Area B" which extended the restricted zone to about 72% of the urban area[16] demonstrating their intention to accelerate the transition to more sustainable and shared mobility solutions.

Multi-modal mobility and lifestyle

A multi-modal approach to mobility expects travellers to use more than one mode of transport to reach their destination by relying on ICTs that use real-time data to foster dynamic networks.[17] In the context of seamlessly web-connected technologies and responsive cities, car manufacturers should update their offering with mobility products that deliver a seamless integration with customers' lifestyle. As Jen-Hsun Huang, chief executive of Nvidia Corp, stated: "What happened with the mobile industry with the smartphone is about to happen with the car."[18] This suggests how the software (SW) running a vehicle's electronic systems is gaining relevance, turning cars into web-connected mobile products. Therefore, carmakers' investment in the field of electronics, AI, and user experience (UX) is necessary to ensure experimentation and constant improvements.

When designing shared urban mobility services, standardized interoperability across providers is an essential factor required to provide seamless access to a range of transportation options. As multimodal mobility is gaining relevance, urban planners and transport providers should offer services designed around

local specificities and include options for personal and shared mobility to bridge the existing gaps between private and public transport (Figure 9.1).

Mobility as a service

Pervasive technology influences the design of mobility-related products and services (e.g. Uber, Lyft, Sygic, RiDE, MVMANT, etc.) to align to local transport strategy plans. Such services take advantage of pervasive ICT, location-sensitive information, and internet-based technologies to enable real-time communication between vehicles and individuals, turning them into "active sensors" within urban boundaries.[19]

Mobility as a service (MaaS) is a transport concept that integrates various services using digital platforms to provide tailored solutions for flexible mobility within the city. This carries enormous potential to suit incidental trips through smartphone apps which make flexible multi-modal transport widely accessible. Prominent experts[20] in this field have outlined near-future scenarios in which private car ownership is expected to decline. However, combined

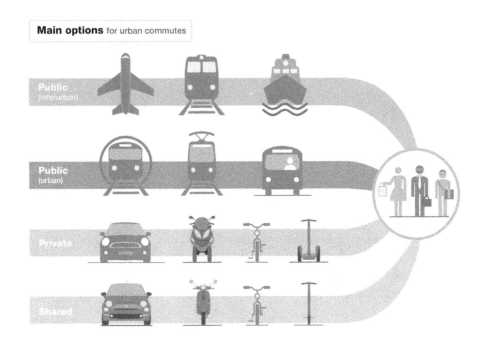

FIGURE 9.1: Options for urban commutes and multi-modal mobility. Marco Zilvetti, 2021.

discriminating factors must be considered when designing such services, as cost and levels of integration affect the successful application of MaaS to specific urban contexts.[21]

A wide range of services has been recently proposed including ride hailing, car sharing (peer-to-peer [P2P], one-way, etc.), bike sharing, moped, and scooter sharing. In all cases, four primary areas require consideration when designing mobility services:

- Commercial feasibility and market strategy (product-service appeal, target customers, tailored and commercially viable solutions).
- Attractiveness of MaaS solutions (service perception, travel optimization and appeal, impact on travel habits, private ownership vs. social inclusion).
- Accessibility (economically accessible service and user-friendly interface).
- Sustainability (service optimization and reduction of negative impacts on emissions, space occupancy, and ownership).

Efficiency is a crucial aspect, considering that a car is normally parked for 96% of its life cycle.[22] Many mobility experts suggest that soon urban car ownership will be replaced by shared options providing flexible and affordable solutions to reduce impacts and optimize travel times, in line with national and regional strategy plans.[23] Both hardware (HW) and SW are crucial for the successful application of shared-mobility services, as the vehicle should be safe, robust, easy to clean and hard to vandalize, while the platform should be reliable, intuitive and ensure continuity of service throughout the various stages of the journey, and accessible to all users.[24]

Autonomous Vehicles for Future Cities

Most of the vehicles meant to be shared within the city, are set to evolve into connected "mobile spaces" where the user totally or partially delegates driving tasks to the vehicle's onboard AI, which continuously exchanges information with the surrounding environment. Automated driving technologies promise to significantly improve road safety with predicted crash reductions between 80% and 90%. However, studies considering urban traffic and risks related to human–computer interaction concluded that AVs may actually prevent accidents by up to 34%.[25]

Although the relevant legislative framework is not yet in place, requiring fully autonomous vehicles to be supervised by human operators when moving on public roads, self-driving technology is rapidly evolving. SAE International, formerly

"Society of Automotive Engineers," developed a standard in 2016 to explain the key features of AVs and classify them using six levels which span from "no driving automation" (level 0) to "full driving automation" (level 5). As shown in Figure 9.2, a clear distinction lies between level 2—where the human driver performs part of the dynamic driving task (DDT)—and level 3, where the automated driving system (ADS) performs the entire DDT.[26]

Through current fast-paced innovations (e.g., AutoX, Baidu, Google, Tesla, Waymo, WeRide, etc.) a leap forward in AV manufacturing is expected soon as the United Kingdom (UK) government announced in 2021 that level 3 automated vehicles would become legal by the end of that year.[27] According to Fleet-News[28] AVs will constitute 40% of all new UK vehicle sales by 2035 based on a research report, conducted at the Connected Places Catapult, Element Energy and Cambridge Econometrics.[29]

As a result of technological advancements, designers should creatively re-think driverless car layout and interiors, making them more flexible and versatile as interactive components (such as virtual cockpit, digital exterior rear cameras, on-board computer touchscreens, augmented reality windshields, and wi-fi hotspots) are becoming common features. Therefore, companies in the field of SW and electronics, providing infotainment, connected services, and cyber-security, have increasingly penetrated the vehicle design field as they have been establishing partnerships with traditional carmakers to innovate both the HW and the SW of mobility products and undertake cross-sector research projects.

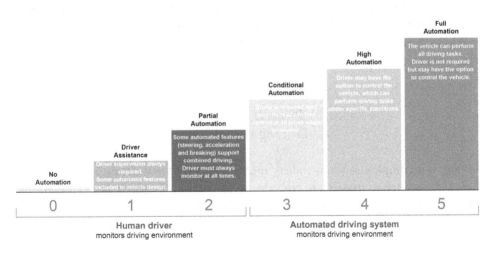

FIGURE 9.2: SAE levels of vehicle automation (adapted from SAE J3016 levels of automation for on-road vehicles). Marco Zilvetti, 2021.

Emerging Collaboration Methods in the Design Process

AVs capable of real-time interaction require technology also to address the needs and expectations of specific administrations and users, to foster democracy, justice, and equity. As Ben Green[30] underlines, this would create a "Smart Enough City" in which technology is not viewed as a panacea, where policy makers recognize social complexity and work to holistically apply innovative solutions to local problems.

Local specificities become a crucial factor when designing innovative mobility projects that meet commuters' expectations within specific urban environments.[31] Therefore, tapping into the so-called "wisdom of crowds" proves to be a strategic method to gain first-hand insights and envisage valid solutions for selected urban contexts, which then inform innovative solutions for private, public, and shared mobility.

The "wisdom of crowds" theory[32] plays a crucial role in contemporary society, as collaboration enables citizens' positive involvement in the process of conception and design of products and services. From a participatory design point of view, collective intelligence (CI) is a powerful practice that connects people and supports collaboration to solve problems by sharing ideas and creative endeavours.[33] This generates awareness about existing problems, provides insights about individual experiences, and how to improve products and services. In the contemporary scenario of digital innovation, crowdsourcing, decentralization, and peer production represent just some of the available real-time collaborative models to design new services, improve existing ones and coordinate urban activities.[34]

In the AV field, responsive technologies enable innovative approaches to car design and human-machine interaction (HMI), as the vehicle becomes a "mobile living space." Re-thinking the primary role of car interiors should also include the dialogical relationship between vehicles and streetscape.[35] These are valuable opportunities that can be exploited through multi-disciplinary research and design practice that enables collective creativity (CC) to work as a catalyst for collaboration and innovation.

The Research Project: Innovative Interiors for Self-Driving Urban Vehicles

Living in a complex modern society means that urban AV design also requires a holistic approach to research to consider users' commuting needs and expectations, alongside a multisensorial travel experience. It follows that involving people in the creative process is crucial to obtain insights that can then be translated into meaningful vehicle design features. As an exemplar activity, the "Mio project" which was launched in 2009 by Fiat in Brazil, was conceived to design a "crowdsourced" car by tapping into the digitally submitted ideas of more than 17,000 participants around the

world.[36] This case study represented a key reference for the research study undertaken within the Politecnico di Milano's Design School and completed as a PhD placement at the Royal College of Art in London, within the Intelligent Mobility Department (Figures 9.3 and 9.4). The main goal of this research project was to understand and define the main influences and features of AV interiors in 2030 for Milan and London.

FIGURE 9.3: Visual comparison between the urban assemblage of Milan (left) and London (right). Marco Zilvetti, 2021.

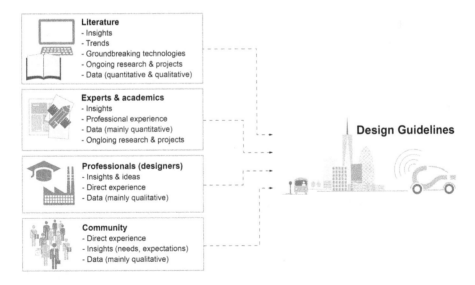

FIGURE 9.4: Research project process. Marco Zilvetti, 2021.

The study analysed both qualitative and quantitative insights generated through research activities as:

- **Literature review** to derive a trans-disciplinary overview of key trends in the field of car design, smart technologies, and urban personal mobility.
- **Interviews with experts** meant to elucidate issues relating to the design of future AVs, with a specific focus on the interior space and its use.
- **Workshops with designers** who provided key insights and visually interpreted the preliminary framework derived from the primary research.
- **Online survey** involving members of the public, from under 18 to 75+, both in Italy and in the United Kingdom. The intent was to obtain insights about their commuting and urban mobility experience.

Action Research Activity 1: Expert Interviews

Two rounds of semi-structured expert interviews involved 25 well-known professionals in the various fields of design, urban mobility, and technology/innovation, who were called to provide their opinions about key topics as:

- Urban mobility today and in the next ten to fifteen years.
- R&D priorities (urban mobility and car design).
- Relevance of local peculiarities.
- Driverless vehicles' key features.
- Vehicle sharing services.
- Other relevant topics (urban mobility and driverless technologies).

Insights derived from expert interviews

Looking at the future of urban mobility, the main interviewees' points and insights have been summarized as follows (Figure 9.5).

Experts' common view is that the development of fully driverless cars will be progressive, but with the likelihood that all vehicles will have a self-driving capability. The intermediate stages, prior to this endpoint, represent a "hybrid" solution, in which self-driven cars and traditional ones are available and used simultaneously. This situation is likely to persist for more than a decade with several interviewees considering 2030 as the earliest date by which AVs would be widely used with the necessary supporting infrastructure in place.

Most interviewed experts believe that by 2030 private transport will be mainly used for inter-urban journeys only: people living outside cities will still use private

Future urban mobility

Common aspects	Milan	London	Notes
Pervasive mobile tech • Significant & increasing use of technology. • Gradual progress with road infrastructure to deal with advance in technology. **Transport mix** • Public + private + shared. • Interoperability of systems. **Connections** • Between vehicles, spaces and people. • Create 'connected relationship' between users will be crucial. **Transition to driverless** • Intermediate stage with 'hybrid' solutions for more than a decade. • 2030 = Early stage in the car automation process. • Constraints for the initial phase: wheel, psychological aspects, car layout and settings, etc. **Time spent onboard** • Time optimisation is a must for multi-purpose vehicles. • Driverless will bring about optimised traffic flow and quicker commutes. **Private cars** • Will be a privilege mainly used for inter-urban journeys. **Car sharing** • Prominent service in the future. **Urban / inter-urban** • Recharging batteries will be key factor to consider (product & service design) • Cars & city need to adapt to each other. • Having flexible car is crucial.	**Inter-modality** • Crucial aspects in urban mobility. **Last-mile mobility** • Existing gaps need to be filled in. **Dedicated lanes** • For driverless cars today. • Situation will probably be different in foreseeable future. • Interesting solution for driverless buses. **Optimisation of public transport** • With links to key hubs. • Small (3 seats) taxi for sharing. **Ridesharing & cab sharing** • City admins must find effective ways to legalise service.	**Changes in car design schemes** • The car we know today has reached its limit. **Commuting priorities** • Different priorities according to specific location. • Solutions for goods deliveries and freight. **Commuting & cars** • People in London tend to walk a lot, and car solutions to be used instead of transport are seen as a threat to health. • The very rich ones will always want their private transport. **Existing gaps in mobility** • Driverless technologies must be used to improve current situation. **Privacy & brand** • People are reluctant to share their personal data. **Parking** • Driverless should lead to alternative and innovative parking & storage solutions.	**Transition** • Innvovation must deal with hybrid scenario (traditional & automated driving). • Psychological aspects related to automation (reluctance and fear of lacking control) to be considered. **Intermodal** • Conceive solutions to bridge different means of transport. **Dedicated lanes** • Keep in mind solutions that drive on dedicated lanes. **Privacy** • Keep in mind that people want their privacy. • People not always willing to share/exchange files with car. **Parking & storage** • Re-think process and relevant solutions applied to vehicles (HW/ SW/ Services).

FIGURE 9.5: Key future urban mobility insights in Milan and London (as derived from the expert interviews). Marco Zilvetti, 2021.

vehicles, while people within the city boundaries will use cars for long-distance journeys only. Inter-modality is also seen as a crucial factor underpinning the future of urban mobility in Milan, particularly around the connections between different modes of transport.

The next table presents insights about key design key aspects to consider in the development of future AVs (Figure 9.6).

An underlying theme is represented by the need to rethink the meaning of vehicles in their various uses to better address users' needs by going beyond the mass adoption of technology and making interiors desirable.

Another key topic to share is around the concept of car sharing and how future AVs and their related infrastructure should be designed (Figure 9.7).

What emerges from this study is that experts in the Milan area perceive AVs more as shuttles belonging to local car clubs, while in London the gathered insights suggest driverless vehicles as being part of a company fleet, to be used for commuting in the inner-city area.

Priorities in car design R&D

Common aspects

Interior vs exterior
- Innovation will mainly be focussed on interior space.
- Interior layout strongly influenced by activities.
- Exterior will be more fashion & trend oriented.

Objective factors to be fulfilled
- Legislation & technical aspects.

Car as a product
- Re-think the essence of cars.
- Relevance of startups.
- Key role of tech companies
- Car = commodity.

Life cycle
- Impact on production operations.
- Longer lifespan.
- Manufacturing needs to evolve.

Innovation
- Car architecture has been 'frozen' for decades.
- Cars are going to be more complex in the foreseeable future.
- Possible innovation in the field of quadricycles.

Layout
- Crucial to distinguish between shared & private vehicles.

Automation
- Manufacturers tend to follow general treds with no real innovation.
- Incremental improvements in foreseeable future.
- NO over-design is key.
- Good timing in marketing is key for innovation.

Cascade effect
- Crucial role for desirability.
- Convey idea of luxury & freedom.

Smartphone as a controller
- Integration is crucial.
- Full integration required.
- Central role of personal devices in the design of future cars.

Digital Environment
- Key systemic integration V2X.

App-based services
- Available through mobile devices.

Vehicle integration
- Augmented sensitivity.

Data security
- Data available through the car must be safe.

Safety & liability
- Consequences on insurance.

Involving users
- Involvement through social networks is crucial.
- It could be leat to mistakes.
- Field research must be well designed.
- Individuals (NO groups!) make great inventions.

Emotion & brand
- Car = architecture.
- Multisensorial domains must be considered as key factors.
- Differentiate image to stand out from other manufacturers.

Less car manufacturers
- Limited production with fewer companies in the future.

Energy supply & sustainability
- Sustainable solutions are absolute requirement.
- Combine natural materials with advanced technologies.

Disabled access
- Importance of accessibility, especially for public service vehicles.

Fair design
- Pricing should be consistent with car's intrinsic qualities.

The iPad car
- Simple & intuitive product
- Affordable & accessible.
- NOT perceived as something for impaired people.

Milan

Technical imperatives
- Multi-function.
- Flexible layout.
- Energy supply.
- Core innovation.

Customisation
- It should be soft and progressive.

London

Specific design features
- Incorporate specific features for driverless

Integration with public transport
- Seamless integration.
- Shared use vs corporate use.
- Room for soft customisation.
- Minimal design to ensure clean and sanitised interior space.

Notes

Innovative products
- Rethink the design process.
- Rethink the role of cars.
- Re-think the way the car is used.
- Possible innovation in the field of quadricycles could be easier to achieve.

Appeal
- When designing innovative products, it will be necessary to make something appealing & desirable, without over-designing.

Image
- Consider cars as mobile architectures with emotional and aesthetic relationship with the city.

Shared vs Private
- Considering vehicle as a space which can be shared with either restricted or wider public defines shape and details.

FIGURE 9.6: Priorities in car design R&D for the foreseeable future (as derived from the expert interviews). Marco Zilvetti, 2021.

Shared car design

Common aspects

Not a private car
- They must have universal appeal and customising to personal tastes is almost impossible.

Design for all
- Must satisfy multiple users.
- Versatile interiors is a key aspect to user satisfaction.
- As neutral as possible.
- NOT excessively pecialised.

Sharing vs private
- Younger generations don't seem to be obsessed with car ownership.
- Collapse of private ownership in the foreseeable future is possible.

Usefulness of the service
- Effortless use.
- No burden of owning & parking.

Free-floating vs Station-based
- Advantages in both schemes.
- Web-based technologies make free floating service a valuable option.
- Relocation is issue for free-floating.

Infrastructures
- City needs to have a certain level of infrastructures in place.
- Parking availability is crucial.

Tech integration
- Modifying a vehicle meant for car sharing is tricky.
- Future vehicles could be customised with smartphone-based technologies (screens & soft features).
- Management software is key.
- Full integration with personal devices is required.

Role of tech giants
- They will provide technologies & help car manufacturers' (research).
- Key role as software providers.
- Advertising will be key for tech companies (investments & revenues).

Privacy & data hacking
- Privacy must be a priority.
- Hacking is of considerable concern.
- Car will be part of interconnected system.

Joy of driving
- Controversial aspect for driverless cars.
- Retain control/ driving features?

Style
- Driverless entails potential depersonalisation, as usability & technology become priorities.
- Driverless cars can have multiple applications.
- Style will be priority AFTER fixing technial issues.

Visual interface for sharing
- It must limit the number of warning messages.
- Focus on user experience is key.

Materials & care
- Resistant.
- Washable & easy to clean.
- In line with target customers and type of service.

Taxi
- Inspired to London cab.

Private vs public service
- 2 different types of service with specific constraints.
- Differentiate through design.

Image
- Risk of being seen as unable to buy a private car (Hong);
- Generating something attractive is a Design imperative.

Civic sense
- Crucial aspect to consider when designing (vandalism).
- Use/ misuse may affect perception of a shared products.
- Misuse is an issue in cities.

Habits & networking
- Local differences in user habits & networking will not be relevant in the long term.

Milan

Car sharing in Milan
- Free floating = successful service.
- Opportunity for both investors and citizens.
- Growing number of providers.
- Reducing the need for private car.

Customisation
- It is key to create ad-hoc interface and equipment.

Time optimisation & parking
- Car sharing could remove several problems (restricted access, fees, stickers, tickets).

Cost issues
- Car sharing customers are small percentage of population, also due to cost reasons.
- It can replace public transport but it is more expensive.

Status symbol
- Shared vehicles will simply be used. NO status symbol.

London

Making it more appealing
- Vehicles nowadays are generally entry-level cars.

Image
- Some cars don't display a logo.
- Some users don't want to be seen using car clubs.

Developing the business
- Sharing represents a developing market.
- Opportunities for both basic and luxury service in the future.
- Profiling is crucial.

Last-mile mobility & business
- Driverless cars could integrate public transport.
- Integration could reduce urban congestion and pollution.

App-based
- Apps will be crucial for managing car sharing services in London.

Notes

Dedicated products
- Shared vehicles must be designed to appeal a wider range of people.
- Younger generations represent valuable target.
- Cars must be designed to avoid misuse, failure & vandalism (which would lead to money loss due to inactivity).

Use & efficiency
- Accessibility for all is a must.
- Shared vehicle must be versatile and easy to use.

Image & safety
- Products must appeal & inspire sense of reliability.
- Comfort is crucial factor.
- Perceived quality = relevant for success of service.

Materials
- Resistant & easy to clean.
- Consistent with price and level of service.
- Cost-effective solutions.
- Relevant to status, especially for premium services.

Customisation
- Soft, trough technology

Range
- Inclusive to attract wider range of customers.
- Family of vehicles made available to address different tasks.
- Designed to meet flexible needs and requirements.

FIGURE 9.7: Key aspects about car-sharing design (as derived from the expert interviews). Marco Zilvetti, 2021.

Action Research Activity 2: Survey Analysis

The proliferation of shared-use vehicle services over the last decade has shown how this kind of services could support a more flexible travel experience and reduce the need for private car ownership. Developing dedicated design solutions is crucial for the success of such a service, as vehicles are to be used by a high number of

customers, ensuring wear resistance and ease of maintenance, while responding to safety requirements. For this reason, the proposed research activity focused on outlining innovative solutions for shared mobility applied to urban services.

Ideal multi-modal solutions for shared driverless mobility

Participants to the survey and its related results provide an informative summary about the ideal urban car for 2030, as well as opinions around shared options and levels of automation:

- A significant percentage of people (48.7% in Milan and 44.9% in London) think that the ideal future urban car will be fully self-driving. Unexpectedly, many respondents (20.8% in Milan and 25.6% in London) think it will be a traditionally driving vehicle.
- When asked about their safety when using AVs, a slight majority of respondents (66.2% in Milan and 59.6% in London) preferred if such vehicles operated on dedicated lanes.
- Regarding the use of shared vehicles in the future, preferences in Milan and in London are remarkably similar, as most respondents believe that the ideal AV in 2030 will be shared and provided by either a taxi/cab network or a car-sharing company.
- Both in Milan and London people tend not to use car clubs (50.7% in Milan and 57.1% in London). If they use them, they do it rarely (18.2% in Milan do it once in a month, while in London 21.2% do it once in a year.)
- Connectivity is a crucial factor in urban cars' interiors, as pervasive wireless (5G) and wearable technologies become available. Car operating systems would be sharing information with occupants' smartphones and managing car functions (infotainment and personal preferences), and mirroring user pre-sets on the dashboard/ windshield (Figures 9.8 and 9.9.)

Through surveys and expert interviews, it was also possible to outline the list of possible AV roles in Milan and London. Most respondents, both in Italy and the United Kingdom, suggested that roads should feature dedicated lanes for automated-driving cars.

In addition, a set of specific questions identified the perceived relevance (on a 1–5 scale in order of importance) of specific technological features of driverless cars' interiors such as:

- General perception.
- Dashboard.

- Space and layout.
- Vehicle controls.
- Connectivity.
- Equipment, i.e. interactive surfaces and touchscreens.

Ideal use of driverless vehicles in urban context in 2030

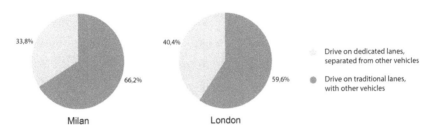

Ideal use/ ownership of the ideal urban car in 2030

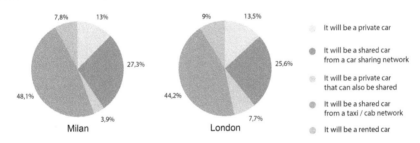

Level of automated driving in the ideal urban car in 2030

FIGURE 9.8: Key insights about ideal shared driverless cars (as derived from the survey). Marco Zilvetti, 2021.

The diagrams in Figure 9.8 clearly indicate that the public perception, in both cities, is similar even when it comes to car features as the average questions' score ranges between 2.9 and 4.1.

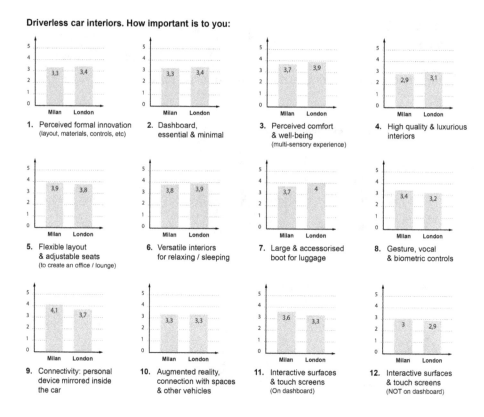

FIGURE 9.9: Relevance of key interior design features for 2030 driverless cars in Milan and London (as derived from the survey). Marco Zilvetti, 2021.

Action Research Activity 3: Sensorial Mood-Boards Workshop

Another activity was the generation of "sensorial mood-boards" to present comprehensive insights about the needs, desires, and expectations of potential users of driverless vehicles in 2030, through the interpretation of ten professional designers based either in Milan or London. In doing this, local peculiarities were crucial in defining the key aspects of future driverless cars' onboard experience and features of ideal AVs for urban spaces (Figure 9.10).

Together with the main insights derived from the previous components of the primary research, this activity provided keywords and observations that contributed to the definition of:

- Key typologies of vehicles for Milan and London (see Figure 9.11).
- Guidelines and recommendations for the two specific urban contexts.

THE INFLUENCE OF ARTIFICIAL INTELLIGENCE

 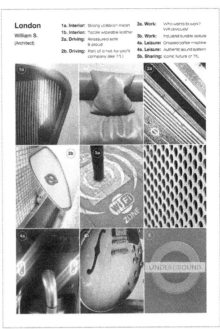

FIGURE 9.10: Examples of multisensorial mood-boards showing key designers' insights through keywords and multiple images collected by participants. Marco Zilvetti, 2021.

Key Findings and Recommendations

As a result of the proposed research activities, a set of guidelines has been generated for the conception of future AVs:

- Driverless cars could have a crucial role in last-mile mobility and other types of urban transport, with specific local applications.
- Ground-breaking internet-based technologies can support the development of innovative commuting solutions, in which personal general-purpose devices—such as smartphones—become the key element to manage and control the vehicle.
- Vehicle manufacturers must address safety concerns, but also comfort-related issues and total flexibility of interior layouts.
- Customization is nearly impossible for a limited number of vehicles (as in the case of car clubs), except for "soft" factors like finishing and minute details, due to industrial cost limitations.
- Driverless car layouts shall be conceived to maximize space and flexibility, to support a wide range of activities, especially when the car is meant for sharing.

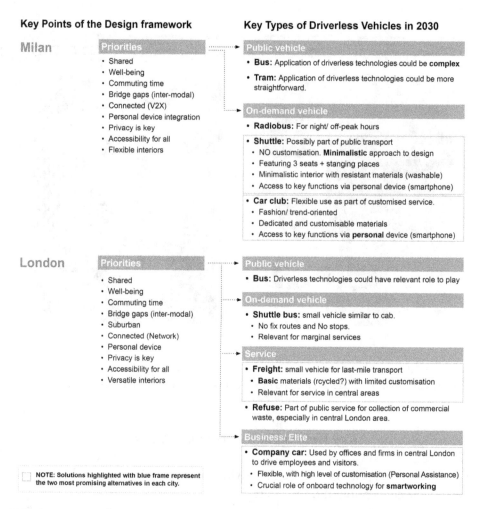

FIGURE 9.11: Key features and types of driverless vehicles in 2030. Marco Zilvetti, 2021.

- Materials and finishing for shared cars must address both needs of being aesthetically attractive and being resistant to vandalism and misuse.
- Data privacy is crucial, and the shared vehicle must ensure total protection of sensitive information, especially when personal devices are connected on-board.
- In mid-cities like Milan in which gaps of public transport are significant, conceiving solutions for last-mile and inter-modal mobility, capable of bridging those gaps is required.
- Small AVs would be a strategic solution in cities like Milan, to fill the existing gaps in the public transport network and address the issues related to inter-modal transport as shuttles for last-mile mobility.

- Milan and London, have strong differences, regarding their approach to private and shared mobility. The availability of a vastly different public transport system entails consequences in commuters' approach to car usage.

Such guidelines, together with insights derived from interviews and the survey, contribute to the creation of a design framework outlining key priorities to be considered in the design of driverless vehicles for 2030. As it is evident from the next figure, the study outlines specific types of transport which would thoroughly meet the needs and expectations of Milan and London, based on the conducted primary research.

The Role of Pandemic in Changing the Perception of Mobility

The outbreak of COVID-19 at the beginning of 2020 and the consequent state of the pandemic caused restrictions and disruptions to the labour market at a global level. It also altered the perception of physical proximity and the ways we travel and socialize for over two years. These unprecedented circumstances accelerated existing trends in the fields of remote work, virtual meetings, process automation, virtual transactions, and e-commerce. Some companies are now planning to bring onboard the experience accumulated during the pandemic and shift to more flexible arrangements for workspace, commuting, and business travel.[37]

Considering the multi-faceted impacts of the pandemic, a survey has been created and shared online between September 2021 and January 2022, with a total of 115 participants located in the United Kingdom and Italy. Feedback was gathered around targeted questions about personal preferences and effects of COVID-19 on values, preferences, and priorities related travel habits as well as key features of their desired future vehicle for a post-pandemic scenario (Figure 9.12).

Reaching the workplace is still the main reason for travelling (43.5%) as before the pandemic, followed by food-shopping-related needs (27.8%). However, the duration of average trips appears to have reduced and most of the respondents (86%) now travel less than one hour per day.

Private transport remains the favourite choice, with an overall 70.2% (+9.6%) now choosing it as the first option, while public transport has lost ground with a −27.5% reduction if compared to the pre-COVID-19 period. Surprisingly, neither cleanliness or safety—which show a +100% and +200% growth respectively—are the main reasons leading to specific transport choices during the pandemic: speed and flexible access (which combined show a −19.8% reduction) still rank first (Figure 9.13).

THE PHYSICAL AND THE DIGITAL CITY

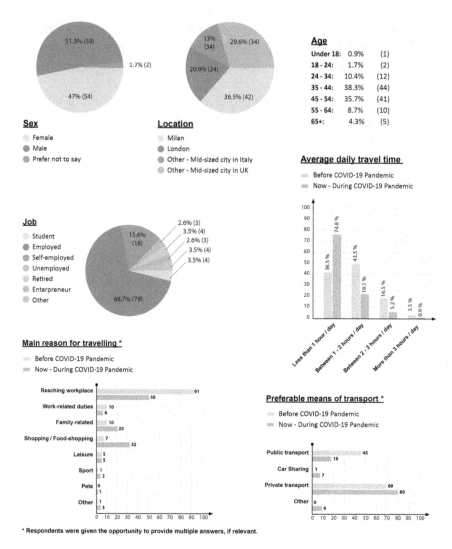

FIGURE 9.12: Information about respondents to the survey and travel habits. Marco Zilvetti, 2022.

The questions about how COVID-19 has changed the approach to mobility confirm that the perception of private, shared, and public transport has evolved, and this is identifiable in key areas of interest such as:

- The overall approach to the use of transport has changed to various degrees because of the circumstances generated by the pandemic. Remote working and online meetings are widely mentioned as key factors for the reduction of daily mileage and commuting.

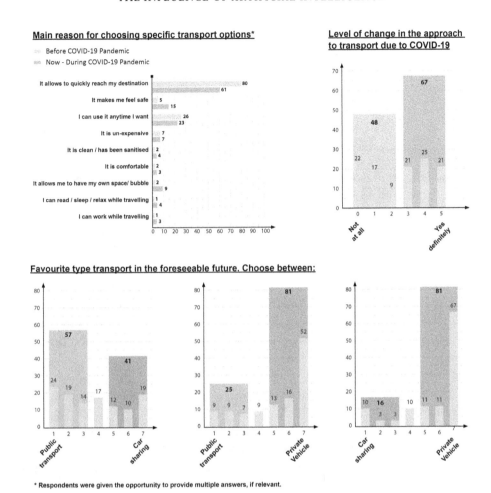

FIGURE 9.13: Key insights about vehicle preferences and use (as per survey). Marco Zilvetti, 2022.

- When describing the key changes in the approach to transport, several respondents (18.3%) claim that they avoid public transport—especially during rush hours. However, a relevant part of respondents still prefers public transport to car-sharing. In this regard, space—which allows for distancing—and reliability of service have been mentioned as key selection criteria.
- Private vehicle remains the favourite alternative for travelling in the city in Milan and in mid-sized cities, while public transport is the preferable alternative in London, where the tube and buses are easily accessible but expensive.
- Car-sharing tends to be perceived—especially in Milan and London—as too complicated and not reliable. Some respondents underline that car clubs and

ridesharing would affect the sense of privacy and pleasure of travelling due to the presence of strangers in a limited space.
- The use of owned bikes—and even walking—have been identified as valuable alternatives to the use of private and public transport during the pandemic.

Key Conclusions of the Research Study

Inter-modality represents a critical parameter underpinning the future of urban mobility in both investigated cities, especially in Milan, where connections between different modes of transport and attention to last-mile mobility are crucial across the whole metropolitan area and not just in the city centre. Local differences have relevance and participants to both surveys and interviews underlined the need for the creation of vehicles with distinctive identities. Although people tend to be individualist, as highlighted in the interviews, the use of private cars in the future is to be considered mostly as a privilege for inter-urban trips. This confirms the set of priorities of the current transport strategies in both cities. Even with differences in the application to urban vehicles designed for specific contexts, common features that represent key priorities include:

- Driverless vehicles are meant to be mostly shared and applied to specific local services.
- Efficiency is key and the vehicle should be used intensively to avoid visual and spatial "static pollution" derived from being parked.
- Smartphone/ personal devices should be used to access, set up, and control the vehicle by providing key information about the passenger in charge, their preferences, and destinations.
- Integrated commands with digital controls designed to make the vehicle extremely user friendly, accessible, and intuitive. A typical dashboard can be replaced by projected information on the windshield.
- Augmented reality—using windshield and windows—to advertise and inform others about the surroundings, giving passengers the opportunity to selectively disable specific features or contents.
- As wellbeing is critical, AI should be used to reduce stress and enhance user experience onboard.

Looking at future mobility scenarios of fully autonomous vehicles, passengers' attention will no longer be focused on driving but on a variety of tasks or recreational activities which will empower users and provide them with increased levels of quality time during travel. This constitutes an unprecedented opportunity to re-think the primary

role of AVs interiors from scratch. If we also consider today's wicked problems around traffic congestion and longer commuting times in relation to time poverty and well-being, it is self-evident to comprehend the intrinsic benefits AVs can offer. This represents one of the latest challenges that society faces in the multifaceted area of smart mobility, which requires novel cross-disciplinary approaches to design thinking and concept development to make a positive impact on tomorrow's fast-evolving society.

NOTES

1. Frances Cairncross, *The Death of Distance. How the Communication Revolution Is Changing Our Lives* (Boston: Harvard Business School Press, 1997).
2. United Nations (UN)—Department of Economic and Social Affairs, Population Division, "World Population Prospects: The 2008 Revision," in *A Vision of Smarter Cities. How Cities Can Lead the Way into a Prosperous and Sustainable Future*, Susanne Dicks and Mary Keeling (Somers: IBM Global Business Services, 2009), 3.
3. Lukas Neckermann, *Smart Cities, Smart Mobility. Transforming the Way We Live and Work* (Leicester: Matador, 2017), 16.
4. Violeta Sima, Ileana G. Gheorghe, Jonel Subić, and Dumitru Nancu, "Influences of the Industry 4.0 Revolution on the Human Capital Development and Consumer Behavior: A Systematic Review." *Sustainability* 12, no. 10 (2020): 4035, https://doi.org/10.3390/su12104035.
5. Mark Shepard, *Sentient City: Ubiquitous Computing, Architecture and the Future of Urban Space* (Cambridge, MA: MIT Press, 2011).
6. Sara Brown, "Machine Learning, Explained," accessed June 29, 2022, https://mitsloan.mit.edu/ideas-made-to-matter/machine-learning-explained.
7. Farah Habib and Ali Shokoohi, "Classification and Resolving Urban Problems by Means of Fuzzy Approach." World Academy of Science, Engineering and Technology, Open Science Index 36, *International Journal of Civil and Environmental Engineering* 3, no. 12 (2009), 501–08.
8. "The New Nørreport Station: Rethinking and Doubling Bicycle Parking." Cycling Embassy of Denmark, accessed June 29, 2022, https://stateofgreen.com/en/news/the-new-norreport-station-rethinking-and-doubling-bicycle-parking/.
9. "MIND—Milano Innovation District." MIND, accessed June 30, 2022, https://www.mindmilano.it/en/.
10. Simon MacMichael, "Centre of Paris to Become a Huge Low Traffic Neighbourhood," accessed June 30, 2022, https://road.cc/content/news/centre-paris-become-huge-low-traffic-neighbourhood-283357.
11. "Port of Hamburg Paves the Way with Europe's First 'smartROAD'," Cisco Systems, accessed June 30, 2022, https://newsroom.cisco.com/c/r/newsroom/en/us/a/y2015/m06/port-of-hamburg-paves-the-way-with-europe-s-first-smartroad.html.
12. Ronika Postaria, "Superblock (Superilla) Barcelona—A City Redefined," accessed July 12, 2022, https://www.citiesforum.org/news/superblock-superilla-barcelona-a-city-redefined/.

13. "Smart Cities Initiative: Smart Parking for Better Services." Philips Lighting, accessed July 12, 2022, http://www.philips.com/smartcities.
14. "C-Charge Celebrated Successful First Year." Transport for London, accessed July 12, 2022, https://tfl.gov.uk/info-for/media/press-releases/2004/february/ccharge-celebrates-successful-first-year#:~:text=Congestion%20Charging%20%2D%20February%202004,are%20faster%20and%20more%20reliable.
15. "Area C Milano." Comune di Milano, accessed June 30, 2022, https://www.areacmilano.it/en.
16. "Area B." Comune di Milano, accessed June 30, 2022, https://www.comune.milano.it/aree-tematiche/mobilita/area-b.
17. Mario Gerla and L. Kleinrock, "Vehicular Networks and the Future of the Mobile Internet." *Computer Networks* 55, no. 2 (2011): 457–69, 10.1016/j.comnet.2020.10.10.015.
18. Mike Ramsey, "Self-driving Cars Could Cut Down on Accidents, Study Says." *The Wall Street Journal* (March 15, 2015), https://www.wsj.com/articles/self-driving-cars-could-cut-down-on-accidents-study-says-1425567905. Last accessed November 16, 2023.
19. Monika Büscher et al., "Intelligent Mobility Systems: Some Socio-Technical Challenges and Opportunities." *Communications Infrastructure: Systems and Applications in Europe*. EuropeComm 2009. Lecture Notes of the Institute for Computer Sciences, Social Informatics and Telecommunications Engineering, vol. 16, 140–52. Berlin, Heidelberg: Springer. https://doi.org/10.1007/978-3-642-11284-3_15.
20. Steve Melia, *Urban Transport Without the Hot Air. Volume 1: Sustainable Solutions for UK Cities* (Cambridge: UIT Cambridge, 2015).
21. Anne Durand, Lucas Harms, Sascha Hoogendoorn-Lanser, and Toon Zijlstra, "Mobility-as-a-Service and Changes in Travel Preferences and Travel Behaviour: A Literature Review." Mobility-as-a-Service Research Programme for the Dutch Ministry of Infrastructure and Water Management, October 2018, 10.13140/RG.2.2.32813.33760.
22. Stephen Moss, "End of the Car Age: How Cities are Outgrowing the Automobile." *The Guardian* (April 28, 2015), http://www.theguardian.com/cities/2015/apr/28/end-of-the-car-age-how-cities-outgrew-the-automobile?CMP=share_btn_tw. Last accessed November 27, 2023.
23. "Future of Mobility: Urban Strategy. Moving Britain Ahead." Department for Transport, March 2019, accessed June 30, 2022, https://assets.publishing.service.gov.uk/government/uploads/system/uploads/attachment_data/file/846593/future-of-mobility-strategy.pdf.
24. John Loeppky, "Ride-Sharing Services and Accessibility." accessed July 13, 2022, https://www.accessibility.com/blog/ride-sharing-services-and-accessibility.
25. Todd Alexander Litman, *Autonomous Vehicle Implementation Predictions: Implications for Transport Planning* (Victoria, British Columbia, Canada: Victoria Transport Policy Institute, 2020), http://www.vtpi.org/avip.pdf. Last accessed November 27, 2023.
26. Jennifer Shuttleworth, "SAE International News: J3016 Automated-Driving Graphic Update," July 1, 2019, https://www.sae.org/news/2019/01/sae-updates-j3016-automated-driving-graphic.
27. https://www.traffictechnologytoday.com/news/autonomous-vehicles/self-driving-vehicles-to-become-legal-in-uk-in-2021.html. Last accessed November 27, 2023.

28. Fleet News Media House, "Self-Driving Vehicle Report Suggests Widespread Use Within 15 Years." *Fleet News* (January 14, 2021), https://www.fleetnews.co.uk/news/latest-fleet-news/connected-fleet/2021/01/14/self-driving-vehicle-report-suggests-widespread-use-within-15-years. Last accessed November 27, 2023.
29. Department for Transport and Centre for Connected and Autonomous Vehicles, *Connected and Automated Vehicles: Market Forecast 2020* (study conducted on behalf of the UK Government Department for Transport), https://www.gov.uk/government/publications/connected-and-automated-vehicles-market-forecast-2020. Last accessed November 27, 2023.
30. Ben Green, *The Smart Enough City. Putting Technology in Its Place to Reclaim Our Urban Future* (Cambridge, MA: The MIT Press, 2019).
31. Roberto M. F. Rivera, Marlene Amorim, and João Carlos Gonçalves dos Reis, "Public Transport Systems and Its Impact on Sustainable Smart Cities: A Systematic Review," in *Industrial Engineering and Operations Management. IJCIEOM. Springer Proceedings in Mathematics & Statistics* 367 (2011): 33–47, https://doi.org/10.1007/978-3-030-78570-3_3.
32. James Surowiecki, *The Wisdom of Crowds* (New York: Knopf Doubleday Publishing Group, 2005).
33. Thomas W. Malone, Robert Laubacher, and Chrysanthos Dellarocas, "The Collective Intelligence Genome." *IEEE Engineering Management Review* 38, no. 3 (March 2010): 38–52, 10.1109/EMR.2010.5559142.
34. Germaine R. Halegoua, *Smart Cities* (Cambridge, MA: The MIT Press, 2020).
35. Daimler Communications, "The Mercedes-Benz F 015 Luxury in Motion: Forerunner of a Mobility Revolution," March 2015, https://group-media.mercedes-benz.com/marsMediaSite/en/instance/ko/The-Mercedes-Benz-F-015-Luxury-in-Motion-Forerunner-of-a-mobility-revolution.xhtml?oid=9906573. Last accessed November 27, 2023.
36. Marlei Pozzebon and Fabio Prado Saldanha, "Fiat Mio: The Project that Embraced Open Innovation and Creative Commons in the Automotive Industry." *Harvard Business Review* 13, no. 1 (2015). https://www.hbsp.harvard.edu/product/HEC095-PDF-ENG. Last accessed November 27, 2023
37. Susan Lund et al., "The Future of Work after COVID-19." McKinsey Global Institute, February 2021, https://www.mckinsey.com/featured-insights/future-of-work/the-future-of-work-after-covid-19.

BIBLIOGRAPHY

Bandini Buti, Luigi. *Ergonomia Olistica: Il Progetto per la Variabilità Umana*. Milan: Franco Angeli Editore, 2011.

Barth, Matthew, and Susan A. Shaheen. "Shared-Use Vehicle Systems: Framework for Classifying Carsharing, Station Cars, and Combined Approaches." *Transportation Research Record Journal of the Transportation Research Board* 1791, no. 1 (2002): 105–12, https://doi.org/10.3141/1791-16.

Belli, Laura, Antonio Cilfone, Luca Davoli, Gianluigi Ferrari, Paolo Adorni, Francesco Di Nocera, Alessandro Dall'Olio, Cristina Pellegrini, Marco Mordacci, and Enzo Bertolotti. "IoT-Enabled Smart Sustainable Cities: Challenges and Approaches." *Smart Cities* 3, no. 3 (2020): 1039–71. https://doi.org/10.3390/smartcities3030052. Last accessed November 27, 2023.

Burkacky, Ondrej, Johannes Deichmann, and Jan Paul Stein. *Automotive Software and Electronics 2030: Mapping the Sector's Future Landscape*. July 2019. https://www.mckinsey.com/industries/automotive-and-assembly/our-insights/mapping-the-automotive-software-and-electronics-landscape-through-2030.

CB Insights. "Corporations Working on Autonomous Vehicles." Accessed June 12, 2021. https://www.cbinsights.com/blog/autonomous-driverless-vehicles-corporations-list/. Publication date: December 16, 2020.

Cupchik, Gerald, and Michelle Hilscher. "Holistic Perspectives on the Design of Experience." In *Product Experience*, edited by Hendrik N. J. Schifferstein and Paul Hekkert, 241–55. Amsterdam: Elsevier, 2008.

European Directorate-General for Communication. "Special Eurobarometer 422a / Wave EB82.2: TNS Opinion & Social." Accessed July 26, 2021. https://data.europa.eu/data/datasets/s2017_82_2_422a_422b?locale=en. Published February 24, 2015.

FleetOwner. "TuSimple among Autonomous Truck Companies to Join Self-Driving Coalition." Accessed August 15, 2021. https://www.fleetowner.com/technology/autonomous-vehicles/article/21152006/tusimple-among-autonomous-truck-companies-to-join-selfdriving-coalition. Published January 11, 2021.

Frost & Sullivan. *Future of Sharing Market to 2025*. August 2, 2016. https://store.frost.com/future-of-carsharing-market-to-2025.html.

Lyft. "It's Your City. Let's Discover It All Over Again." https://www.lyft.com/rider.

Marek, Ogryzek, Daria Adamska-Kmieć, and Anna Klimach. "Sustainable Transport: An Efficient Transportation Network—Case Study." *Sustainability* 12, no. 19 (2020): 8274, https://doi.org/10.3390/su12198274.

McKinsey & Company. "Smart Cities: Digital Solutions for a More Livable Future." Accessed August 15, 2021. https://www.mckinsey.com/business-functions/operations/our-insights/smart-cities-digital-solutions-for-a-more-livable-future.

MVMANT Group. "Public Transport Operators." https://www.mvmant.com/sustainable-mobility-partners/.

Resch, Bernd, Rex Britter, and Carlo Ratti. "Live Urbanism: Towards Senseable Cities and Beyond." In *Sustainable Environmental Design in Architecture. Impacts on Health*, edited by Samantha Th. Rassia, and Panos M. Pardalos, vol. 56, 175–84. New York: Springer Optimization and Its Applications, 2012.

Reynolds, Emily. "Elon Musk: Apple Is a Graveyard for Fired Tesla Employees." *Wired.co.uk*, October 9, 2015, https://www.wired.co.uk/article/elon-musk-apple-tesla-graveyard. Last accessed November 27, 2023.

Robert Bosch GmbH. "Bosch Teams Up with Microsoft to Develop Software-Defined Vehicle Platform for Seamless Integration." Bosh. Accessed March 23, 2021. https://www.bosch-presse.de/pressportal/de/en/bosch-teams-up-with-microsoft-to-develop-software-defined-vehicle-platform-for-seamless-integration-between-cars-and-cloud-224832.html. Published February 18, 2021

SAE International. "Taxonomy and Definitions of Terms Related to On-Road Motor Vehicle Automated Driving Systems J3016_201401." SAE International. Accessed March 24, 2021. https://www.sae.org/standards/content/j3016_201401/ Published January 16, 2014.

Singh, Sarwant. *New Mega Trends: Implications for Our Future Lives*. New York: Palgrave Macmillan, 2012.

Sygic. "Sygic GPS Navigation: The World's Most Popular Offline Navigation App, Trusted by More than 200 Million Drivers." https://www.sygic.com/.

Tuominen, Anu, Antti Rehunen, Juna Peltomaa, and Kirsi Mäkinen. "Facilitating Practices for Sustainable Car Sharing Policies—An Integrated Approach Utilizing User Data, Urban Form Variables and Mobility Patterns." *Transportation Research Interdisciplinary Perspectives* 2 (2019): 100055. https://doi.org/10.1016/j.trip.2019.100055.

Universal Technical Institute. "Main Components of a Car and Their Function." Accessed August 12, 2021. https://www.uti.edu/blog/automotive/car-components.

Weiser, Mark. "The Computer for the 21st Century—Specialized Elements of Hardware and Software Connected by Wires, Radio Waves and Infrared Will Be So Ubiquitous That No One Will Notice Their Presence." *Scientific American* (1991): 94–104. https://www.ics.uci.edu/~corps/phaseii/Weiser-Computer21stCentury-SciAm.pdf. Last accessed November 27, 2023.

Winston, Clifford. "Improving Urban Mobility Through Technological Advance of Motor Vehicles." New Cities Foundation. https://newcities.org/improving-urban-mobility-technological-advance-motor-vehicles/. New Cities. Published February 27, 2014.

Yao, Richard. "The Shift Towards Multimodal Transportation & The Future of Mobility." Accessed May 17, 2021. https://medium.com/ipg-media-lab/the-shift-towards-multimodal-transportation-the-future-of-mobility-d0c7c25d4a06. Medium Published July 12, 2018.

10

Understanding Postmetropolis in the Latest Virtual City: Urban Analysis of Night City in *Cyberpunk 2077*

Yulin Li

The long-awaited, open-world video game *Cyberpunk 2077* was released in September 2020 and has generated heated discussion among players and commentators. Night City, the "remarkable virtual metropolis"[1] in which stories of *Cyberpunk 2077* take place, is created under the cooperation of game-level designers and environmental artists, as well as architects and urban planners who rationalize the urban structure and regional details. Nowadays, a number of virtual products have created solid spatial and social experience. Metaverse, the concept of the integrated virtual world, is now a frequently mentioned milestone for the recent future. Under this trend, Night City of *Cyberpunk 2077* is an outstanding creation on the halfway towards the creation of an integral virtual experience. This chapter applies the urban theory of Edward Soja to analyse the spatial and social characteristics of Night City. Through comparative analysis of Night City with the real urban forms, socio-economic trends and postmodern cultures and ideas, this chapter reveals that the current virtual space has already possessed the qualities of a city—it creates social structure and spatial experience equivalent to a real city, and casts impacts to people's understanding and feeling of urban experience.

Introduction of Night City: Similes and Metaphors of Real Urban Qualities

Night City is an unreal creation based on real geography and politics. It is located in Morro Bay—a real coastal region between San Francisco and Los Angeles

(LA). Night City's weather and natural geography reveal typical west-Californian features—hilly, torrid, deserted. However, the central urban area of Night City is built, in its own storytelling, on the non-existing land reclaimed from the bay. This major part of Night City is also unrealistically overloaded—it accommodates around 10 million people[2] within the size of 75.42 km^2.[3] Night City's urban history is set on the real timeline and is closely associated with real geopolitics: its establishment dates back to the United States's early-1990s recession, with its aim to be self-sufficient, corporate-operated, and independent from all existing political powers.[4] Therefore, Night City exist both within the real social history context and independent from the outside environment.

Being realistically virtual, the urban plan and appearance of Night City contain similes of the urban and social features of real cities (Figure 10.1). Commentators have spotted features of Night City in the intricate highways and suburban wastelands of Dallas,[5] in the neon-lighted, dense and hybrid buildings in Hong Kong,[6] and in the unplanned urban sprawl and coastal Californian climate of LA.[7] In particular, the layout of urban districts and landmarks in Night City and LA reveal a series of similarities: Both of them have an urban centre with high-rise corporate buildings and hybrid cultures and communities, suburban hills distributed with luxurious dwellings and headquarters of international businesses, coastal industrial ports and recreations, and peripheral wastelands with abandoned mass construction of industrial building and housing by the government.

FIGURE 10.1: North Oak Sign in Night City of the game *Cyberpunk 2077*. CD Projekt Red, 2020.

The landmarks such as Chinatown, Little Tokyo, and Hollywood of LA are reappropriated and reassembled as Japantown, Little China, and North Oak in Night City. And within such an urban context are the similar demographic and social characters of ethnic diversity, weak political governance, occupation of gangs, and autonomy of districts.

Besides this projection of reality, Night City is also a collection of the cyberpunk metaphors of urban problems. The name, social history and urban layout of Night City draw directly from the pen-and-paper role-playing game *Cyberpunk*, released in 1988, and its following version *Cyberpunk 2020*, released in 1990.[8] The aesthetics of brutalist architecture, dispersed neon lights and media panels, the atmosphere of mixed population and the dilapidated urban environment reveal direct similarities with the film *Blade Runner*, directed by Ridley Scott. The typical "cyberpunk verticalities" of Night City reflect the twentieth-century science fiction literatures[9] that depict the high-rise buildings with stratified population according to their social classes. In these ways, Night City is a collection of urban and social metaphors in the cyberpunk culture, which include the "strong contrast between the highly developed human civilization and the real life of the bottom people,"[10] the dominant position of capital magnates in politics and the society, the prevailing use of cyberwares, the blend of real and virtual experience, and the "deepening inequalities and social and class distinctions" caused by "militarization, privatization, and control of the surface."[11]

Therefore, the integrity and representativeness of Night City should qualify itself as an object for urban studies. In the current era when virtual space is becoming part of people's living environment, Night City could be studied as a new city formed over the past century, driven by the transforming urban features, social structures and ideological trends, especially the cyberpunk culture that emerged since the 1960s.

Literature Review: Perspectives to Unpack Night City

Night City, as a typical cyberpunk creation, is characterized by the postmodern "bricolage"[12] or "pastiche"[13] of images and cultural resources from the past. Many of Night City's architectural styles, names and features of urban districts, as well as the storytelling of its historical events, could be traced from the real sites, film images and literature narratives that emerged during the past century, especially those related to LA—the hub of media creation and precedent of a postmodern urban form. Coming into being since the 1960s, the cyberpunk science fictional genre is a fictional manifestation of the formation and development of the postmodernism ideology.[14] Based on the earlier arts and theories that critically delineate the

end or transformation of modernity, postmodern aesthetics and politics reveal the impacts of milestones of social change within the past century—the development of imaging and communication technology and media, the globalization of economy and culture, the weakening and transformation of modernistic urban forms developed in the early twentieth century. As the latest creation of the cyberpunk genre, Night City is not only a collage of the history, the postmodern world-view and the cyberpunk aesthetics. Moreover, it reveals how the recent social transformations—the trend into metaverse, the tendency of working and living virtually, as well as all the other contemporary living experiences—impact the postmodern understanding and cyberpunk description of the social structure and urban experience.

This chapter unpacks Night City primarily as a city, while also as an art creation and technological product. These three aspects correspond to three branches of postmodern theories—the postmodern aesthetics of simulacra and simulation, the posthumanism understanding of the human experience extended and blurred by technology, and the LA School of Urbanism, which discusses the postmodern urban forms and phenomena that appeared with the post-Fordist economy and the postmodern social-cultural changes.

In the twentieth century, much of the urban research, as well as the urban plan of global cities, have been "predicated on the precepts of the concentric zone, sector, and multiple nuclei theories of urban structure," which were associated with the Chicago School of Urbanism "flourished in the 1920s and 1930s."[15] Since the 1960s, LA has revealed its important position in global economics, and its industrial and urban structures distinctive from the Chicago format.[16] Since the 1980s, the LA School of Urbanism was formed and quickly developed, which focused on the urban characters of Los Angeles as "a suggestive prototype—a polyglot, polycentric, polycultural pastiche that is somehow engaged in the rewriting of the American social contract" that would "quickly overtake Chicago."[17] The LA School widely refer to theories of postmodernism and backgrounds of the postmodern economy, socio-politics, and global relationships developed in the information age. Its formalization of LA's "social polarization and fragmentation, hybridity of culture and auto-driven sprawl"[18] was detailed and visualized in the Cyberpunk culture as representative cyberpunk urban features. Based on the close relationship between the LA School of Urbanism and the cyberpunk culture, and the similarities between Night City and the real and science-fictional LA, this chapter analyses the urban features of Night City with a comparative reading of the "six discourses on the postmetropolis,"[19] put forward by the representative LA School scholar Edward Soja. The six discourses—Flexcity, Cosmopolis, Exopolis, Metropolarities, Carceral Archipelagos, and Simcities—conclude and outline six layers of LA's socio-economic structures and their manifestation in the urban layout and citizens' lifestyles.

While this study focuses on similarities of Night City with reality justify the urban qualities of the game experience, the differences between Night City and real cities are also important for the studies of a virtual environment. The environmental and socio-cultural features within cyberpunk visual creations are the simulacra of reality, which are detached from the real historical backgrounds and recombined as a new cultural creation.[20] In this way, the postmodern aesthetics of simulation and simulacra, and the linguistics of signifier and signified are used to facilitate the understanding of the architectural styles and details of Night City, which differentiate it from reality. And to understand Night City in its unique background of the semi-cyber space, it is also necessary to understand the ideological history that explores the present and prospect of human experience integrated with digital media and cybernetic machines. Ideas concerning the experience transformed by technologies and imaging media could be traced back to Martin Heidegger and Marshall McLuhan, while the wider discussion over life experience that cannot be detached from machines and cyberwares then developed into the viewpoints of posthumanism, and its variants, such as Transhumanism, Metahumanism, and New Materialisms.[21]

While the theoretical foundation behind Night City is grand and complicated, this chapter focuses on the comparative analysis between the "six discourses of postmetropolis" and the Night City, and adopts other closely related theories to facilitate the understanding of Night City as an urban product. This analysis details how *Cyberpunk 2077* provide an integral and sensible urban experience, and reveals the driving forces behind the creation of Night City and the popularity of *Cyberpunk 2077*—the globalized and fragmentized economy and culture, and the deconstruction and reconstruction of the resources in history, culture, ideology, and reality.

Flexcity *and* Cosmopolis

Soja's concept of the *Flexcity* refers to the post-Fordist theories about a flexible industrial structure. Facing the rapidly changing market demands and fashions, corporations transformed from mass production of a certain product into conglomerates that produce items at smaller scales but with wider scope.[22] Single-ended production lines are combined and re-organized into production networks, each brand now incorporates multiple smaller-scale production units, and subcontracts are established within production units and among different firms. The flexibility of industry on the one hand led to the global labour division, while on the other hand causes globalization within a single city. Unlike New York or London which become pure economic centres in global labour divisions, LA developed into an important metropolis with its variety of industries and populations.

Under these backgrounds, the *Cosmopolis* could be read in two ways. As a driving force, the advanced information and electronic industries in LA become fundamental trades in the post-Fordist economy, and therefore have led to the rise of LA as an international metropolis. While as a result, LA compresses the global elements into its metropolitan area. Central LA is "the financial centre of global finance," which is "a first-world island floating on the sea of third-world population."[23] Surrounding the economic centre, there are the "postmodern hyperreal spaces"[24] such as the Latino Central Market, Chinatown, and Little Tokyo, which create the cultural and social environment of the other regions over the world. In this sense, the *Cosmopolis* is a social spatialization of the global industrial structure. Such cosmopolitan characteristics of the city enables the formation of the *Flexcity*—a city that contains in itself the flexible industrial system and the fluid workers.

The Night City in *Cyberpunk 2077* highlights the characteristics of *Flexcity* and *Cosmopolis* in LA, and detailed Soja's narrative of these two discourses as continuing urban processes.

The structural and spatial agglomeration, and the stratification of industries that characterize Soja's *Flexcity* are depicted in Night City's economic history and corporate organization. Although Night City's history began in the 1990s, its development can be related to the rise of LA over the past century. The initial construction of Night City was based on three fictional corporations: Arasaka, a comprehensive manufacturing company from Japan; the Euro Business Machines which produces electronic and information products; and the Petrochem which focuses on the petrochemical industry. These three companies are reduced reflections of LA's initial boom in the 1920s that saw the rise of manufacturing, information services and the petroleum industry, and they form the LA-style urban sprawl with world immigration and global companies in Night City. After decades of competition and conflict amongst the corporations depicted in Night City's history, companies have consolidated into megacorporations, acquiring enterprises of more diverse industries as subsidiaries. For example, the Biotechnica company in 2077 takes the place of Petrochem with its high-tech and cheap-labour production mode and its wide range of services based on its core technology of bioengineering and the synthetic fuel CHOOH2.[25] In Soja's description of the re-industrialization process in *Flexcity*, "producer-oriented services and technology"[26] become a significant new industry. In correspondence, the Arasaka, which in 2077 focuses on services for corporate security, manufacturing, and banking, has won over all the other corporations and become the most influential corporations in the world.[27]

The cosmopolitan cultural features of LA are revealed in the naming and visual design of different districts. The representative names such as Little Tokyo and Chinatown in LA are recombined into the Japantown and Little China in Night

City. The visual identifiers of the two different Asian cultures are also mixed and recombined. The Japanese market in Night City, for example, is located in Little China. Similar to *Blade Runner*, the Asian districts in Night City combine nostalgic and noir architectural styles of the early twentieth-century Chinatown and Little Tokyo and the "East Asian Eclectic architecture"[28] and intermingled cultural scenarios that were reconstructed in these districts of LA at the end of the twentieth century (Figure 10.2). According to Giuliana Bruno's discussion of postmodernity in *Blade Runner*, the mixed cultural elements are the postmodern pastiche of cultural languages. Through abstraction and reorganization, "the pertinence and uniqueness of architecture to specific places, cultures, and times has been lost in postmodernism," and they together form the culture of the new cosmopolitan city.[29]

Night City's fictive urban history also strengthens this postmodern detachment from the traditional contexts: Night City is detached from world politics because it has maintained its autonomy and independence from governmental control since its initiation. It is also detached from the real natural and cultural geography because the city of 2077 was rebuilt after the nuclear destruction of all previous urban structures. The reconstructed Night City is located on the land fill in the bay instead of on the original coastal plain. Night City's identity is therefore built through the abstraction and reorganization of global urban resources into a new and blank context. This new urban style developed from the pastiche

FIGURE 10.2: Japantown in Night City of the game *Cyberpunk 2077*. CD Projekt Red, 2020.

of architectural languages, in Charles Jencks' words, "can be described as radical eclecticism or adhocism. Various parts, styles or sub-systems are used to create a new synthesis."[30]

These historical and visual narratives of Night City facilitate the understanding of the postmodernity contained in Soja's *Flexcity* and *Cosmopolis*. The *Flexcity* that contains the networked industrial system and *Cosmopolis* that holds its global features both emphasize the self-sufficiency of the city—the simulation of the global economic and cultural structure onto the urban scale. The megacorporations in *Cyberpunk 2077* build up the city's industrial system and reflect the global industrial system. The postmodern pastiche of global urban features of varied locations and times generates the city's complex connections to the world, as well as its independence and individuality. Night City's abstracted and reorganized history, geography, and economy support Soja's proposal to "radically rethink and perhaps deeply restructure—that is, deconstruct and reconstitute—our inherited forms of urban analysis."[31]

Exopolis *and* Metropolarities

According to Soja, *Exopolis* and *Metropolarities* are the two major social and spatial consequences following the formation of *Flexcity* and *Cosmopolis*. While the first two discourses depict the reproduction of global economic and cultural geography on an urban scale, *Exopolis* depicts the simulation of urban qualities in the subdistricts. In LA, the continuous influx of migrants and agglomeration of industries generated subdistricts with their own industrial systems, residences, and infrastructures.[32] As a result, autonomous districts and independent counties spread on the urban sprawl of LA. This unique "sprawling centrifugal form" of LA makes it "a city without a centre […] a collection of suburbs in search of a city."[33] In this way, the traditional division between suburb and centre has been changed. Therefore, the "exo-" prefix in Soja's discourse on the one hand refers to the "outward" heterogeneous agglomerations of urban qualities, and on the other hand, indicates the city that dispels the "traditional qualities of citiness."[34]

Metropolarities refers to the new kinds of social polarization and stratification that happens in the formation of *Flexcity* and *Exopolis*. The flexible production system leads to a need for flexible employment: it demands "core workers" with interdisciplinary skills and "peripheral" manual labours that can accommodate flexible working schedules and tolerate economic uncertainty. The two kinds of workers tend to reside in different regions of the city. Core professionals migrated to the newly developed suburbs, and the time-flexible blue-collar workers immigrated into urban centres to quickly respond to labour demands. Although the

population was mobilized and redistributed, social hierarchies were only reinforced instead of being weakened. The autonomous subdistricts reinforced the segregation of different ethnicities, and the rich and poor population: "Sometimes in poor neighbourhoods a network is protection against the insecurities of employment, in others it constitutes the source of information by which new jobs are found."[35]

Night City (Figure 10.3) vividly displays the formation of *Exopolis* in the vertical stratification of the urban centre, which, similar to how Hewitt and Graham describe the urban structure in sci-fi literatures, are "vertical spatial and architectural metaphors to symbolise, posit and expose deepening inequalities and social and class distinctions."[36] Night City's central urban districts contain a vertical articulation and hybrid of different styles and levels of deterioration. They are built upon each other and are interconnected with formal or informal commuting space, visualizing a time sequence that new urban layers overlay onto the traditional urban landscape. The noir slums, bleak retail stores, and vendors are often located underground, populated by the exotic, cheap manual labours. The dark, incarcerate environment with no windows or a narrow leak of daylight from above generates the repressive atmosphere of the bottom life. The ground level often prospers with restaurants and bars, as well as the dense residences of ethnic communities who operate these businesses. Corporate mansions are built above these lower constructions, with newly burgeoning

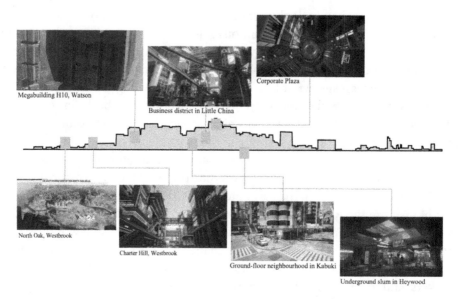

FIGURE 10.3: The location of different neighbourhoods on the elevation of Night City. Graphic created by the author. Pictures credited to CD Projekt Red, 2020.

companies on top of the old, declined ones. Corporates metabolize, compete, and evolve as the buildings grow over each other. As the corporate buildings annex smaller enterprises and grow taller, they become more interconnected horizontally, suggesting interconnected industrial networks. Buildings of the dead corporates are soon occupied by the lower crowded communities in need of space and resources.

While the city centre has extreme density and vertical complexity, the suburb with business headquarters and the residence of rich people are often spacious and single-layered. The Corporate Plaza, which is the economic centre of Night City, has a ground-level memorial park surrounded by the headquarters of the dominant corporates, which are the tallest megabuildings of the city, and the independent buildings that do not stack over each other. Another form of integral high-rise building in Night City is the massive housing complex that dots all districts of the city. While the game designers aim to name all the urban entities, these buildings are deliberately named generically as Megabuilding H1 to H12. Taking the concepts of arcology and structuralism, these buildings "are functioning like cities within a city,"[37] producing a self-contained society for the urban middle class with residential housing, entertainment, food, and other services common in shopping mall experiences. The third type of cityscape without vertical hybridity reflects Soja's "urbanized suburb" or "Outer Cities"[38]: districts like Westbrook contain mainly the technology core of wealthy corporations, corporate elites and media celebrities—the upper class in capital competition, cybernetic social system and mass media. The North Oak, for example, could be easily identified as a combination of the Beverly Hill villas and the Hollywood landscape. Different from the dense inner city, there are very few tall buildings in these areas. These places are depicted as the best place to live and have fun in Night City, with adequate open ground and clear sky view.

These three architectural styles with unified vertical structure problematize the metaphor of the vertical hierarchy in sci-fi literatures. In the corporate centre, towers function more as symbols of economic-political power than a practical necessity. In Koolhaas' words, the tower "claims the superiority of mental construction over reality."[39] In contrast, the numbered housing megabuildings deny the corporates' simile of height to social status. The height of the housing megabuildings is, instead, the compelled solution to fulfil the basic demand for space of the large number of poor citizens. The myth of height is dissolved and becomes a critical response to "the militarisation, privatisation and control of the surface."[40] The suburban elite districts with adequate space and no high-rise buildings, being a voluntary choice of the wealthy classes, help to critique the metaphorical alignment between the spatial level and social hierarchy, which is created and reinforced by the capital powers.

Night City combines contradicting social-spatial metaphors to problematize the understanding of multi-scaled urban entities and social stratification in *Exopolis* and *Metropolarities*. While the city is in general growing taller and taller, the poor population agglomerate in the centre, while the core industries and core workers move to the outskirts of the city. The higher corporate buildings symbolize the bigger economic and political power of the elite capital owners, while the higher residential buildings indicate the less resource and freedom of the major population. These opposing movements of population and contradictory driving forces of the upward growth of buildings achieve a dynamic balance of the urban system, while also reveals the increasing income gaps and social polarizations.

Carceral Archipelagos *and* Simcities

Carceral Archipelagos and *Simcities* are described by Soja as the societal response to the former four discourses. Represented by the description of LA in the *City of Quartz*, walled-in communities, fortress, and surveillance are enforced as social complexity and conflicts increase.[41] In response to the turbulent flexible economy and the cosmopolitan urban heterogeneity, the people, communities, and the metropolis as a whole, are increasingly reliant on informational technology and hyperreality to both reinforce the safeguard and to surpass the community border and reach the wider world. With the promotion of information technology and digital media, the "urban imaginary" precedes the urban reality to define social regulation, or the "new regimes of capitalist accumulation," which are described in *Flexcity* and *Cosmopolis*.[42] In this way, the societal responses to the new urban processes in return devote to the formation of the postmetropolis.

These two discourses are most obviously and widely adopted in the game: within the game environment, the communities of different regions are under the jurisdiction of different gangs, and the industrial parks, corporate centre and top residences of elites are safeguarded with high-tech monitors and robots. Cyberware is a necessity for every virtual citizen, and trespassing the monitored gates is the primary mission of gaming.

Moreover, the essence of Night City as a video game setting adds another layer to the understanding of *Carceral Archipelagos* and *Simcities*. We, the players, could not only build and break gates within the game but also could cross the boundary between the virtual world and reality by seeing from our screens what the protagonist sees in his/her similar cyberware (Figure 10.4). In this sense, characteristics of Simcity and Carceral Archipelago in Night City are not only produced for citizens within the virtual city but also for gamers who observe Night City as an outside

FIGURE 10.4: The processed reality seen by the protagonist "V." Screenshot from the game *Cyberpunk 2077*. CD Projekt Red, 2020.

manipulator. These similarities problematize the boundary between the gamer and the protagonist "V," and between the virtual world and reality.

Conclusion and Further Thoughts

This chapter analysed the sources and driving forces in modern and contemporary history that supported the creation of Night City in *Cyberpunk 2077*. With reference to Edward Soja's analytical structure, the constitutors and contributors to Night City are divided into three parts: the economic structure, its revelation in the socio-spatial patterns, and the further trends coming into form in the society and the urban environment. The development of communication and information technology promoted the globalization of industry and created a segmented and interconnected economic structure. The economic transformation generated changes in culture, social structure, and urban forms, such as the destructed and recombined cultural icons, the redefinition of boundary, location and identity, the social polarization caused by the growth of capital power, and the reformed urban structure that manifest and support the socio-economic transformation. The simultaneously increasing social disintegration and invisible interconnection push forward the development of cyberspace. After the weakening of geographical

boundaries promoted by globalization since the twentieth century, further developments in society and in technology are blurring the boundaries between real and virtual experience.

By tracing the source of Night City in real urban history, scientific urban aesthetics, and socio-cultural trends, this chapter finds that the formation of the virtual urban space in Night City is also founded on the continuous urban, social and cultural history in reality. As a creation with international developers and customers, Night City draws widely from global urban features and socio-cultural symbols. Therefore, compared with real cities, Night City contains more postmodern qualities: it gets rid of traditional definitions of geographical location and political belonging, and simulates the global economic and social structures within the scale of a small city, and transforms the real social phenomena and living experience into the pastiche of visual simulacra and virtual gaming experience.

The analysis of Night City in this chapter is based on the urban prototype presented by Edward Soja in the late 1990s. Under the impact of Lefebvre's theories on the relation among space, social science and humanities, the basic causality within the six discourses of postmetropolis is that the city is a result and manifestation of the social driving forces.[43] In the 2010s, Soja reviewed his concepts of the postmetropolis and discussed the new developments of urban studies in the twenty-first century: the city is not only regarded as the result of social transformation, but more importantly, as an "important driving force shaping human history," "a generative force that is the primary cause of economic development, technological innovation, and cultural creativity."[44]

With reference to this further thought of Soja, this chapter could also suggest how Night City, as an interactive urban space, could impact people's social life and living experience as a driving force of social transformation. In *Cyberpunk 2077*, being a member of the city and act according to the chosen social identity is the core story and major task for the player. And judging the comments online, navigating through the city, interacting with the NPCs, and feeling to be a member of the city have become the major enjoyment of many players of the game. From the emergence of Cyberpunk novels until now, the virtual cities are gradually becoming more accessible and immersive. They are no longer simply the metaphor of reality but are becoming the valid space that could contain human activities and impact human life. While Night City is limited by its sheer volume of data that cannot be used for multiplayer online interaction, it presents a detailed urban model to exemplify the existence of urban structure in a digital platform. Many other games and social platforms have already created their online and offline societies with their virtual urban prototypes and social structures, even though they are not as visible as Night City. Therefore, this chapter tries to start a further discussion regarding the impact of virtual space towards real society.

In the end, these analyses and findings about Night City further suggest the possibility and necessity to study the urban qualities of virtual spaces with reference to the theories of urban and social space. The future design, development, and transformation of virtual spatial creations should also be discussed together by the academia of urban sociology, human geography, and by the professionals that design and plan for the human environment.

NOTES

1. Andy Kelly, "Watch This Atmospheric Tour of *Cyberpunk 2077*'s Night City." *PC Gamer*, December 9, 2020, https://www.pcgamer.com/watch-this-atmospheric-tour-of-cyberpunk-2077s-night-city/.
2. "Population Growth and Density of Night City." Reddit, accessed March 28, 2022, https://www.reddit.com/r/cyberpunkgame/comments/7x3eoi/population_growth_and_density_of_night_city/.
3. "Night City Cyberpunk Wiki." Cyberpunk Fandom, accessed March 18, 2021, https://cyberpunk.fandom.com/wiki/Night_City.
4. Cyberpunk Fandom, "Night City Cyberpunk Wiki."
5. Matthew Gault, "*Cyberpunk 2077*'s Dystopian Cities Are Already Here." Vice.Com, December 17, 2020, https://www.vice.com/en/article/88amav/cyberpunk-2077s-dystopian-cities-are-already-here.
6. Tats Miyagawa, "*Cyberpunk 2077*: Hong Kong Edition." YouTube, August 11, 2019. https://www.youtube.com/watch?v=ns1AT7A1VSA.
7. Quora, "Will Los Angeles Eventually Turn into 'Night City' from *Cyberpunk 2077* Like Some People Suggest? How Might This Happen?" December 12, 2021, https://www.quora.com/Will-Los-Angeles-eventually-turn-into-Night-City-from-Cyberpunk-2077-like-some-people-suggest-How-might-this-happen.
8. Gareth Damian Martin, "The Origins of *Cyberpunk 2077*." *PC Gamer*, June 18, 2018. https://www.pcgamer.com/the-origins-of-cyberpunk-2077/.
9. Lucy Hewitt and Stephen Graham, "Vertical Cities: Representations of Urban Verticality in 20th-Century Science Fiction Literature." *Urban Studies* 52, no. 5 (2015): 1–15, https://doi.org/10.1177/0042098014529345.
10. Honghai Zhang and Zhang Mengruo, "Research on Cyberpunk Images in the Visual Digital Media." *2020 International Conference on Computer Vision, Image and Deep Learning*, 2020, 39, https://doi.org/10.1109/CVIDL51233.2020.00015.
11. Hewitt and Graham, "Vertical Cities,"12.
12. Amelia A. Rutledge, "SF, Postmodernism, and Cyberpunk." George Mason University, last modified 2005. http://mason.gmu.edu/~rutledge/neur_pomo.htm.
13. Giuliana Bruno, "Ramble City: Postmodernism and *Blade Runner*." *October* 41 (1987): 66. http://www.jstor.org/stable/778330.

14. Veronica Hollinger, "Cybernetic Deconstructions: Cyberpunk and Postmodernism." *Mosaic* 23, no. 2 (1990): 29–44, http://www.jstor.org/stable/24780626.
15. Michael Dear and Steven Flusty, "Postmodern Urbanism." *Annals of the Association of American Geographers* 88, no. 1 (1998): 51. http://www.jstor.org/stable/2563976.
16. Edward W. Soja, "Beyond Postmetropolis." *Urban Geography* 32, no. 4 (2011): 464, https://doi.org/10.2747/0272-3638.32.4.451.
17. Dear and Flusty, "Postmodern Urbanism," 53.
18. Roger W. Caves, *Encyclopedia of the City* (Florence: Taylor & Francis Group, 2005), 296.
19. Edward W. Soja, "Six Discourses on the Postmetropolis." *Cartas Urbanas* 5 (1996): 6–20, http://hdl.handle.net/10553/11574.
20. Bruno, "Ramble City," 61–74.
21. Francesca Ferrando, "Posthumanism, Transhumanism, Antihumanism, Metahumanism, and New Materialisms." *Existenz* 8, no. 2 (2013): 26–32. https://existenz.us/volumes/Vol.8-2Ferrando.pdf.
22. Michael Savage and Alan Warde, *Urban Sociology, Capitalism and Modernity* (London: Macmillan, 1993), 56.
23. Vic Lockwood, Edward W. Soja, and Kenneth Thompson, "Los Angeles—City of the Future?" Filmed 1991 at BBC2, video. https://randomarchitecturememories.com/home/los-angeles-city-of-the-future.
24. Ibid.
25. Fandom, "Night City Cyberpunk Wiki."
26. Soja, "Six Discourses," 11.
27. Fandom, "Night City Cyberpunk Wiki."
28. "EXPLORING CHINATOWN Past and Present." *Los Angeles Conservancy* (2016): 9. https://www.laconservancy.org/sites/default/files/files/documents/LAC_Chinatown_Final_0.pdf.
29. Bruno, "Ramble City," 66.
30. Charles Jencks, *The Language of Post-Modern Architecture* (London: Rizzoli, 1991), 90.
31. Soja, "Six Discourses," 7.
32. Tom Sitton and William Deverell, *Metropolis in the Making: Los Angeles in the 1920s*, 1st ed. (University of California Press, 2001), 4.
33. Carey McWilliams, *Southern California Country, an Island on the Land* (New York: Duell, Sloan & Pearce, 1946), 232.
34. Soja, "Six Discourses," 14.
35. Savage and Warde, *Urban Sociology* 60.
36. Hewitt and Graham, "Vertical Cities," 4.
37. Fandom, "Night City Cyberpunk Wiki."
38. Soja, "Six Discourses."
39. Rem Koolhaas, *Delirious New York: A Retroactive Manifesto for Manhattan*, ed. Mau Bruce (New York: Monacelli Press, 1994), 20.

40. Hewitt and Graham, "Vertical Cities," 12.
41. Mile Davis, *City of Quartz—Excavating the Future in Los Angeles* (London: American Council of Learned Societies, 2006); Soja, "Six Discourses," 16.
42. Soja, "Six Discourses."
43. Soja, "Beyond Postmetropolis," 452; Henri Lefebvre, *State, Space, World: Selected Essays*, trans. G. Moore, N. Brenner, S. Elden and ed. N. Brenner and S. Elden (Minneapolis and London: University of Minnesota Press, 2009), 185.
44. Soja, "Beyond Postmetropolis," 452.

REFERENCES

Bruno, Giuliana. "Ramble City: Postmodernism and *Blade Runner*." *October* 41(1987): 61–74. https://doi.org/10.2307/778330.

Caves, Roger W. *Encyclopedia of the City*. Florence: Taylor & Francis Group, 2005.

Davis, Mike. *City of Quartz: Excavating the Future in Los Angeles*. London: American Council of Learned Societies, 2006.

Dear, Michael, and Steven Flusty. "Postmodern Urbanism." *Annals of the Association of American Geographers* 88, no. 1 (1998): 50–72. http://www.jstor.org/stable/2563976. Last accessed November 16, 2023.

"EXPLORING CHINATOWN Past and Present." *Los Angeles Conservancy* (2016). https://www.laconservancy.org/sites/default/files/files/documents/LAC_Chinatown_Final_0.pdf. Last accessed November 16, 2023.

Fandom. "Night City Cyberpunk Wiki." Accessed March 18, 2021. https://cyberpunk.fandom.com/wiki/Night_City. Last accessed November 16, 2023.

Ferrando, Francesca. "Posthumanism, Transhumanism, Antihumanism, Metahumanism, and New Materialisms." *Existenz* 8, no. 2 (2013): 26–32. https://existenz.us/volumes/Vol.8-2Ferrando.pdf. Last accessed November 16, 2023.

Gault, Matthew. "*Cyberpunk 2077*'s Dystopian Cities Are Already Here." Vice.Com, December 17, 2020. https://www.vice.com/en/article/88amav/cyberpunk-2077s-dystopian-cities-are-already-here. Last accessed November 16, 2023.

Hewitt, Lucy, and Stephen Graham. "Vertical Cities: Representations of Urban Verticality in 20th-Century Science Fiction Literature." *Urban Studies* 52, no. 5 (2015): 1–15, https://doi.org/10.1177/0042098014529345.

Hollinger, Veronica. "Cybernetic Deconstructions: Cyberpunk and Postmodernism." *Mosaic* 23, no. 2 (1990): 29–44. http://www.jstor.org/stable/24780626. Last accessed November 16, 2023.

Jencks, Charles. *The Language of Post-Modern Architecture*. London : Rizzoli, 1991. http://www.jstor.org/stable/24780626. Last access: 16 November 2023

Kelly, Andy. "Watch This Atmospheric Tour of *Cyberpunk 2077*'s Night City." *PC Gamer*. December 9, 2020. Accessed March 1, 2021. https://www.pcgamer.com/watch-this-atmospheric-tour-of-cyberpunk-2077s-night-city/.

Koolhaas, Rem. *Delirious New York: A Retroactive Manifesto for Manhattan*. Edited by Mau Bruce. New York: Monacelli Press, 1994.

Lefebvre, Henri. *State, Space, World: Selected Essays*. Translated by G. Moore, N. Brenner, S. Elden and edited by N. Brenner and S. Elden. Minneapolis and London: University of Minnesota Press, 2009.

Lockwood, Vic, Edward Soja, and Kenneth Thompson. "Los Angeles: City of the Future?" Filmed 1991 at BBC2, video. https://randomarchitecturememories.com/home/los-angeles-city-of-the-future.

Martin, Gareth Damian. "The Origins of *Cyberpunk 2077*." *PC Gamer*, June 18, 2018. https://www.pcgamer.com/the-origins-of-cyberpunk-2077/.

McWilliams, Carey. *Southern California Country, an Island on the Land*. New York: Duell, Sloan & Pearce, 1946.

Miyagawa, Tats. "*Cyberpunk 2077*: Hong Kong Edition." YouTube, August 11, 2019. Accessed July 14, 2024. https://www.youtube.com/watch?v=ns1AT7A1VSA.

Quora. "Will Los Angeles Eventually Turn into 'Night City' from *Cyberpunk 2077* Like Some People Suggest? How Might This Happen?" December 12, 2021, https://www.quora.com/Will-Los-Angeles-eventually-turn-into-Night-City-from-Cyberpunk-2077-like-some-people-suggest-How-might-this-happen. Last accessed November 16, 2023.

Reddit. "Population Growth and Density of Night City." 2019. Accessed March 28, 2022. https://www.reddit.com/r/cyberpunkgame/comments/7x3eoi/population_growth_and_density_of_night_city/.

Rutledge, Amelia A. "SF, Postmodernism, and Cyberpunk." George Mason University. 2005. Accessed March 15, 2022. http://mason.gmu.edu/~rutledge/neur_pomo.htm.

Savage, Michael, and Alan Warde. *Urban Sociology, Capitalism and Modernity*. London: Macmillan, 1993.

Sitton, Tom and William Deverell. *Metropolis in the Making: Los Angeles in the 1920s*, 1st ed. London, UK: University of California Press, 2001.

Soja, Edward W. "Six Discourses on the Postmetropolis." *Cartas Urbanas* 5 (1996): 6–20.

Soja, Edward W. "Beyond Postmetropolis." *Urban Geography* 32, no. 4 (2011): 451–69, https://doi.org/10.2747/0272-3638.32.4.451.

Zhang, Honghai, and Mengruo Zhang. "Research on Cyberpunk Images in the Visual Digital Media." *2020 International Conference on Computer Vision, Image and Deep Learning*, 2020, 39–43, https://doi.org/10.1109/CVIDL51233.2020.00015.

11

Parkour, the City, and Mediated Subjectivities

Fidelia Lam

Introduction

A provocation: move from point A to point B in as straight a line as possible, reconfiguring your body as necessary. Parkour is a movement practice and discipline that involves running, jumping, vaulting, swinging, and flipping around, across, and through obstacles as they are encountered in the urban landscape. Its practitioners navigate the city in unexpected and subversive ways, imagining new political possibilities of existence with their movement. While most parkour scholarship has discussed the practice in terms of its spatial, political, and philosophic dimensions as a self-contained metaphor and object,[1] little scholarship has looked at the cultural productions of parkour itself. As a dynamic and relatively young movement practice, parkour has evolved alongside the development of digital camera technologies and online social media, and as such, has a rich media culture that reflects parkour's unique relationship to movement and urban space. As camera technologies have become smaller, lighter, mobile, and more affordable, parkour's practitioners and the community have leveraged these emerging technologies to create new assemblages of media, bodies, and urban architectures that are easily shared via online platforms such as Instagram, YouTube, and TikTok. How do these movements, visions, and technologies inform our perceptions of public life and public space? What implications do these apparatuses hold for our understanding of these assemblages? Following Jacques Rancière's articulation of aesthetics as a "specific regime for identifying and reflecting on the arts: a mode of articulation between ways of doing and making, their corresponding forms of visibility, and possible ways of thinking about their relationships,"[2] I examine the aesthetics of first person (FPV), 360 camera, and drone perspectives as well as the editing practices and narrative trends of parkour media productions to offer

a parkour subjectivity of the city, one that understands the city as dynamic, relational, material, in-process, and embodied.

Cities, Media, Subjectivities

Urban space and representational media have had a longstanding relationship, from late eighteenth-century panoramic paintings of London and early cinematic works like Dziga Vertov's Soviet urban montage *Man with a Movie Camera* (1929) to Ridley Scott's futuristic dystopian Los Angeles in *Blade Runner* (1982) to newer digital social media genres of urban exploration and ambient urban walks. Representational media of cities has provided a rich analytic space for tracing the underlying concepts that inform historical modes and understandings of being in the world, and indeed numerous texts and edited collections[3] highlight the complex and interconnected processes that influence the formation of subjectivities of and within urban space and media. For instance, in her seminal text *Atlas of Emotion: Journeys in Art, Architecture, and Film*, Giuliana Bruno traces the entangled history of art, architecture, and film, describing how filmic architectures come into form and are experienced through a process of "cinematic mapping" mobilized by emotion and embodiment. She argues "film is a modern cartography: its haptic way of site-seeing turns pictures into an architecture, transforming them into a geography of lived, and living, space." Bruno describes how camera cinematography in early city travelogues reproduced the daily practices of being in public urban space, articulating how cinema as an architectural practice has been instrumental in shaping how we not only cognitively understand, but affectively experience urban space.[4]

This haptic and embodied mode of experiencing space through media builds on work by feminist film scholars such as Vivian Sobchack whose seminal work on the phenomenology of film articulates how the subject encountering these representations is also deeply implicated in the process. She argues

> cinematic and electronic screens differently demand and shape our "presence" to the world and our representation in it. Each differently and objectively alters our subjectivity while each invites our complicity in formulating space, time, and bodily investment as significant personal and social experience.[5]

Orienting around existential phenomenology, which is concerned with the experiential and perceptual field in which humans make sense of the temporal, spatial, and bodily structures of the world, Sobchack argues that cinematic and technological modes of representation mediate our engagement with the world, with others, and with ourselves in such a way that actively and perceptually transforms how

we see, sense, and make sense of ourselves in the world as different prior to cinematic and electronic mediation and engagement.

This attention to subjectivities through the embodied experience of cinematic and technological representation is further taken up by media scholars such as Dustin Greenwalt and William Uricchio. Greenwalt analyses the use of sound, lighting, duration, and movement in user-generated videos of urban exploration in Detroit to consider the formation of affective maps through urban media representation.[6] His analysis emphasizes the haptic and multisensory nature of these videos as they are created and circulated online, observing how affective experiences and conceptions of Detroit are in part shaped through these videos. Similarly, Uricchio observes a series of representational trends in pre-cinematic and post-cinematic depictions of the city to highlight not only "*what* is stored in the various image systems under consideration, but [...] [also] *how* [...] cultural trends in urban representation can lead to insights into the broader encounters between historical subjects and their self-fashioned environment."[7] His analysis of panoramic painting and films, city symphonies, and the world of Sims in terms of their representational strategies emphasizes the specific historical, technological, and aesthetic affordances and contexts to offer an approach that "encourag[es] us to reflect upon a body of representation in terms of its metaphoric capacities [...] [and] offers a way to move beyond what is seen in order to consider a way of seeing or being in the world."[8] By highlighting the specific elements of these representations, Greenwalt and Uricchio also point to the production contexts out of which they emerge, suggesting that the embodiment of the production process must also be considered alongside its reception and viewing.

Thus, in looking at parkour cultural media productions and its aesthetics, I consider both the embodied nature of production as well as reception to offer a parkour "way of seeing or being in the world"—a parkour subjectivity of the city. While parkour often appears in a variety of popular cultural forms such as video games and Hollywood films, this chapter focuses primarily on the media productions emerging from the parkour community and made by parkour practitioners. The rest of the chapter is structured as follows: I first discuss FPV, 360 and drone camera perspectives as they are used in the productions of parkour media before turning to a discussion of editing practices and narrative trends within these productions to suggest a parkour understanding of bodies and urban architectures through media practice.

First Person (FPV)

First-person parkour shots are used to mimic the subjective experience of the camera operator as they move through urban space, and indeed constitute

a whole subgenre of parkour videos on their own. Through their movements, parkour practitioners understand urban space as both material and dynamic, an embodied perceptual process of unfolding. According to media semiotician Ruggero Eugeni, the first-person shot represents a transformation of the classical point of view shot, or "subjective shot" found within traditional audiovisual forms such as film and television.[9] While I cannot rehearse the extended histories and theorizations of these perspectives[10] due to space, I want to briefly situate the FPV in parkour in relation to Eugeni's conceptualization of the first-person shot, who argues that it "represents the sight of located, embodied, enworlded, active, dynamic, and hybrid agents [...] an intermedia figure directly exhibiting the dynamic grasp of the world [...] and consequently its perceptual, practical, emotional, living and ongoing experience."[11]

FPV shots are often captured via an action camera held in the mouth using a specially designed mouth mount and are subject to the haptic feedback of the body-in-motion which emphasizes the phenomenological and embodied nature of both parkour and of the first-person perspective. The jostling and jiggles that result from the camera-in-mouth work towards what Alexander Galloway calls the "subjective shot," a more volatile first-person perspective that mimics the physiology of human vision and more intimately places the viewer in the subjectivity of the camera operator.[12] This subjective intimacy is further conveyed through the heavy breathing and grunting that results from the camera being held in the mouth as the body exerts physical effort, highlighting the material and embodied dimensions of how these shots are produced. In addition, though parkour is widely understood as a physical sport and discipline, it also pushes its practitioners' mental limits, forcing confrontations with fear and other mental barriers.[13] By echoing the perspective of the parkour practitioner, FPV parkour shots showcase this aspect and can phenomenologically induce similar feelings of fear, particularly for videos that include parkour across rooftops and jumping roof gaps (Figure 11.1).

Additionally, the position of the camera-in-mouth results in the fragmentation of the body; various limbs come in and out of view but the body of the camera operator is never seen in full. Other parkour bodies may come in and out of frame as they collectively traverse the landscape, though because bodies are continuously in motion, they are collectively dis-located and dis-placed[14]; there is no situating within a particular location, site, or place (aside from what information is given in the video title and description, or what can be inferred from the footage). Space is not fixed, but rather, the body and urban landscape work together to continuously and collectively recompose and reconstitute themselves through movement.

FIGURE 11.1: Parkour athlete jumping over a gap while recording with an FPV camera in their mouth, 2021. Image used with permission from the copyright holder. Source: Scott Bass.

360-degree cameras

360-degree cameras create pre-rendered spherical videos that are most often used for immersive virtual reality films and applications. In these videos and experiences, the camera position itself is largely fixed and unmoving, while the user changes their particular perspective and view by looking around using the head-mounted display (HMD), which is generally limited to a 90-degree field of view.[15] In 360 VR, the illusion of "being there" is solid—the world is stable and follows our expectations of its traditional video predecessors.[16] These videos have traditionally been created using camera arrays that are bulky and expensive, requiring specialized knowledge and access to generate full spherical images. However, with the development and release of action-360 cameras such as GoPro MAX and Insta360, 360 cameras and spherical videos have become much more financially accessible and physically mobile, allowing for more dynamic filmmaking.

Yet 360 VR requires an HMD to be "immersed" in the scene, an additional apparatus that (while increasingly common) limits who can experience the footage and how. Because parkour media is most easily and often shared on online social video platforms like YouTube and Instagram, 360 video is often remediated into more familiar video formats that can be viewed on screen-based apparatuses.[17] Editing 360 footage for screen allows media producers to make decisions about where and how the gaze is directed as well as stylistic choices regarding the

perspectival distortion that results from spherical video capture. Thus unlike the "immediacy" of VR, which seeks to erase or deny any form of mediation,[18] the use of 360 in parkour media reflects a hyperawareness of the multiple layers of mediation involved in representing parkour, space, and movement, what Bolter and Grusin term a "remediation of the self."[19]

While most discussions of 360 video focus on its VR applications,[20] looking more closely at the visual content of remediated 360 parkour media reveals alternative implications for understanding these assemblages of bodies, urban space, and media. As mentioned above, the development of action-based 360 cameras allows for greater camera mobility and movement, and due to the spherical nature of these shots, editing 360 video into screen-based formats often results in dynamically distorted views (Figure 11.2). Rather than employing a static camera position where events happen around the camera, which traditionally has suggested a neutral subjectivity, in 360 parkour content the camera often traverses the terrain with and in close proximity to the parkour practitioner, foregrounding the relational compositions of media, body, and space. Combined with the distortion of the remediated spherical video, parkour and parkour media render the body and landscape at unfamiliar orders of magnitude, continuously constructing unfamiliar views of the site and body through motion and destabilizing conceptions of place and site. For the viewer then, 360 perspectives engender a continuous process of situating and attending to the relational dynamics between the camera, body, and objects that constitute the urban space.

FIGURE 11.2: Parkour athlete using a 360-degree camera to record a line, 2021. Image used with permission from the copyright holder.

Drones

The use of drones and aerial cameras in parkour media foregrounds the narrative of the body-in-motion, highlighting the relational nature of parkour as well as the non-normative movements and trajectories that the parkour body cuts across the landscape. Showcasing the transgressive paths within the broader urban context also points to the political dimensions of parkour, as parkour practitioners elide the prescribed paths of the built environment in favour of creative traversals that leverage overlooked architectural features in such a way that challenge notions of public and private space and who is permitted to move through space and how.

The smaller consumer microdrones and racing drones used in parkour media allow for greater manoeuvrability that results in dynamic perspectives of body and landscape. This is in contrast to the dominant contexts and discourses of aerial and drone aesthetics, which discuss the perspectives from larger macro drones in two different contexts: (1) the sweeping aerial and panoramic shots of cinema, used to establish a setting and situate the viewer within the location, and (2) the drone aesthetics of geopolitics, war, and surveillance. These discourses emphasize the role and impact of distance in aerial representation, which suggests a totalizing neutral and objective perspective from above that extends the scopic regime of modernity, fixes its subjects, and establishes an asymmetrical power relation between the operator and viewing subject.[21] At the same time, in their discussion of coronavirus pandemic drone videos, Patricia Zimmerman and Caren Kaplan observe that "distance is relational and historical."[22] In other words, distance is situated and is not only spatial but temporal as well. Attending to the production contexts of drones in parkour media emphasize the situated and continuously relational nature of drone, drone operator, site, and body-in-motion, foregrounding the collaborative compositions of parkour.

The technological affordances of smaller drones also impact how these shots are produced, holding additional implications for how we understand these elements together. Unlike distant impersonal views of cinema and drone warfare which abstracts and depersonalizes,[23] drones used in parkour contexts operate at closer distances so that the primary focus is the body and how it moves across the site, moving between multiple scales of distance. Because of the prioritization of the body-in-motion, parkour media also has a common cinematographic trope of the body not staying in frame or view, often entering and leaving the frame in a single shot, suggesting an inability to be completely contained by the camera's "capture." Furthermore, the increased manoeuvrability of these smaller drones also means that the perspective and angle of the shot can dynamically change, emphasizing the multi-dimensionality of these compositions and the continuously relational nature of drone, body, and landscape all in motion together.

Additionally, the drone operator must remain proximate to the drone itself, meaning that unlike the drone operators of military airstrikes, the operator is on-site and on the ground, working in tandem with the parkour practitioner and landscape to create and capture the shot. In the particular context of parkour media productions, the drone operator is often a parkour practitioner themselves, and has an embodied understanding of the movements they work to capture and showcase. In short, these shots are often produced through an intricate collaborative choreography between the mover, the terrain, the drone, and the drone operator, disrupting the binary logics of "us" and "them," "here" and "there," "machine" and "human" found within dominant drone discourse[24] and suggesting a different, dynamic set of relations between the body, city, and camera.

Editing practices + narrative trends turning to trends in editing practices and narrative trends, I want to highlight three aspects that reflect a parkour subjectivity of the city: a material and spatial attention to the site, an emphasis on process and progression, and fragmentations and recombinations of time and space.

While most narratives of parkour describe its engagement with the environment as a continuous free-flowing movement that spans the city, contemporary parkour practice most often occurs in and at "spots," architectural arrangements and structures that lend themselves to parkour-style movement. Depending on one's capability and experience, these spots might range from configurations of ramps, rails, stairs, ledges, walls, etc. in parking lots and building entryways, to rooftops and alleyways, to sculptures and landmarks, or maybe even something as simple as a curb. In parkour, a site's significance is demarcated not by its discursive specificity (i.e. historical, political, social factors), but rather through the specific configuration of elements—the material nature of features to its spatiality (distance, height, angle, etc.) and the affordances of movement. This way of seeing and experiencing space is often called "parkour vision."[25]

This way of seeing is reflected not only in the cinematography of parkour media productions, which are instrumental in providing new interpretations and subjectivities of the city[26] but also in the narrativizations of parkour in vlogs, whose creators often highlight the specific material features and arrangements when introducing a spot. For example, in one parkour vlog, professional parkour athletes STORROR express delight at the brick at a spot in Pimlico, an area in London, stating "come check this brick out […] the apple of my eye […] this is golden brick, you get a little bit of slip, a little bit of grip, you get a bit of everything […] unbelievable settings here."[27]

Parkour media also often emphasizes process, displaying and narrativizing affirmative relationships with fear and failure. One way this is shown is through edits that display the failed repeated attempts that precede the successful take of particular movement challenges. Rather than hiding failures and only showing

"successes," "failure" is understood as a rich and essential part of parkour. In this context, "failure" is temporally understood not with a sense of finality or closure, but rather as part of an information-gathering process that often informs the next attempt. Furthermore, by showing repeated (failed) attempts, parkour practitioners display the ongoing physical and mental exertions that contribute to the dialogic process between the practitioner and the environment.

Another common way of showcasing the process is through narrativizing the process of constructing lines, which are sequences of parkour movements strung together in a spot intended to be completed in one take. These narratives describe the thought process of parkour practitioners as they move through the spot and identify what features and movements they are drawn to, as well as what aspects might make particular movements challenging or scary, articulating localized and material psychogeography. For example, in a training vlog at Castle Park, Bristol, parkour athlete Ed Scott describes his thoughts when attempting a tic-tac[28] off a light post to the top of a garbage bin:

> I'm just scared at the moment of just the foot placement and the fact that the bin has got a hole in it, like if I go to bounce it and my feet go too low I could put my feet inside the bin and it would just end bad ... But I've done this before ... and I remember it being okay once I've done it, it's just really scary to commit to. So those are things that I'm working through at the moment, but I think it's just a case of having a go ...

A few attempts later, Scott notes to the camera "it needs to happen on this go because I'm getting myself scared now."[29] He commits to the move, successfully making it to the top of the bin before bouncing off due to force and impact. Scott comments, "Ugh, that took far too long."[30]

Parkour and its media productions understand space and time as fragmented, recombinant, and affective. The process of creating lines in a spot continuously reorders space, as numerous sequences can be composed, combined, and modified in various ways according to the imagination and capabilities of the practitioner, and the different lines across a spot change the affective experience of the space. Furthermore, as Scott's commentary reveals, the experience of being in a spot is affectively situated, not only in terms of its spatiality but also its temporality—that is, how one is feeling (physically, emotionally, mentally), on that particular day in that particular moment. Despite having done this particular challenge before, the site activates an affective response that influences how Scott engages with his environment. In this sense, progress in parkour is understood as non-linear, a process of ongoing embodied attunement, effort, and engagement.

While I have separated the apparatuses above for the sake of organization and clarity, the shots created by these apparatuses are often edited together to

show parkour movement from multiple angles, foregrounding the elements of the urban landscape that often go unattended and offering a way to see site and movement from many perspectives at once. Showcasing these movements from multiple perspectives also results in temporal fragmentation as the movements are repeatedly shown, often at varying speeds, disrupting any singular linear notion of time. These spatial and temporal fragmentations of parkour media acknowledge the mediated nature of vision and experience and extend post-Cartesian, post-perspectival, and post-cinematic modes of subjectivity.[31]

To discuss some of the implications this mode of perception, what I have been calling a "parkour subjectivity," holds, I want to briefly turn to a discussion of two popular action films that feature extensive parkour sequences: Martin Campbell's *Casino Royale* (2006) and Michael Bay's *6 Underground* (2019). *Casino Royale* features Daniel Craig's debut as James Bond in a reboot of the series, and is the twenty-first instalment of the James Bond film series, grossing $599 million at the box office. Produced by Netflix, *6 Underground* stars Ryan Reynolds as the head of an ensemble cast, and is one of the studio's most expensive films to date with a budget of $150 million. Both films feature sweeping locales across the globe as well as high-intensity action and parkour sequences. The shift is intended not to set up a divide between parkour cultural media productions coming from the parkour community and those coming from "outside" that space, but rather to identify some of the norms and expectations of bodies and space within visual moving media in order to highlight how the context of these media works to differently influence how assemblages of bodies, space, and media are represented. I choose these two films as they reflect both popular and institutionalized representations of parkour-oriented assemblages of bodies, space, and media found within Hollywood and the popular film industry and culture. More specifically, I want to focus on how the narrative frame and its prioritization in these films present a different understanding and treatment of bodies, movement, geographies, and temporality from what this chapter has discussed so far.

Early on in *Casino Royale*, Bond is tasked with capturing a bombmaker in Madagascar. He locates his target at an animal ringfight, before the bombmaker, played by Sébastian Foucan, catches on and begins to make his escape. The following seven-minute chase sequence moves across the urban and jungled landscape, including an active construction site and two towering cranes, before ending in a bombtastic gunfight at an embassy. The scene cuts between the bombmaker, who deftfully jumps, climbs, vaults, and threads his way through the landscape and Bond, who at one point commandeers a bulldozer to catch up to Foucan.

In *6 Underground*, parkour is emblematized in the character of "Four" (aka "Billy"), who is given the nickname "The Skywalker" (played by Ben Hardy) due to his rooftop-traversing, parkour-based abilities. Each member of the eponymous

"six" have become "ghosts," faking their deaths and cutting ties with their past lives in order to become part of Reynolds' ("One") plan to stop a dictatorship and enact a coup in the fictional country of Turgistan. In his past life, Four was a thief who "died" while stealing jewellery in Ukraine. The scene chronicling his death and subsequent recruitment into One's crew includes a chase sequence through and across Kiev's rooftops with four other members of his heist crew, whilst they are chased by Ukrainian police.

Each of these narratives and scenes establishes a chase-based context for parkour to be showcased that already pre-figures a relation between the bodies in frame: those doing the chasing and those being chased. One party is necessarily "behind" while the other is "ahead," one creates a trajectory, while the other follows (and tries to catch up). Chase scenes build anticipation, intent on culminating in a high-stakes conclusion that inevitably has consequences for the narrative arc of the film. In describing the film and editing techniques of the action sequence, film historian Ken Dancyger remarks

> action sequences are scenes at the edge of emotional and physical survival. The achievement of one character's goals may well mean the end of another character. This is why the action sequence so often plays itself out as a matter of life or death [...]. The audience must be at the edge of physical survival with the character; if they are not, the action sequence fails in its strength: excitation, deep involvement, and catharsis.[32]

For Dancyger, the editing principles and practices of action sequences arise from shaping this experience for the audience. Dancyger identifies four particular "issues" that film directors and editors attend to in the editing decisions of the sequence: identification, excitation, conflict, and intensification, and his text describes how each of these becomes activated by leveraging the formal qualities of cinematography and editing.

With this in mind, the parkour sequences in *Casino Royale* and *6 Underground* are crafted in such a way that serves the narrative frame and the goals of the sequence as described by Dancyger—there is a discursive context that particularly situates how the assemblages of bodies, geographies, and movement are presented to and received by the audience. While this may appear obvious, I want to note that this discursive context is fundamental to understanding the relationships between how bodies and subjectivities are represented, how geographies are leveraged, and how we position and implicate ourselves as viewers within media. This context orders the temporality, which in contrast to narrativized Hollywood films, is actively destabilized and reconfigured within parkour media cultural productions.

Conclusion

In sum, parkour has a rich media culture that reflects the practices' dynamic understandings of urban assemblages of bodies, space, and media. This chapter has discussed the use of newer camera technologies of first-person, 360, and drone camera apparatuses as well as the editing practices and narrative trends found in parkour media productions to suggest a parkour subjectivity of the city, one that foregrounds an embodied, material, in-process, and relational experience of urban assemblages.

A parkour subjectivity also has broader ontological implications that I have alluded to but have not had the time or space to discuss in detail, and it is also worth noting the political dimensions of parkour as a practice that were briefly mentioned but not discussed in full. Finally, while the technologies discussed here are more consumer friendly than their predecessors, there are still social and financial limitations on who can access these technologies, which impacts what particular parkour subjectivities are foregrounded.

AUTHOR'S NOTE

This work also appeared in video essay form presented at the 2021 *AMPS Urban Assemblage: The City as Architecture, Media, AI and Big Data* and won Best Video Award.

NOTES

1. See for example, Michael Atkinson, "Heidegger, Parkour, Post-Sport, and the Essence of Being," in *A Companion to Sport*, ed. David L. Andrews and Ben Carrington, Blackwell Companions in Cultural Studies 15 (Hoboken: Wiley-Blackwell, 2013); Christoph Brunner, "Nice-Looking Obstacles: Parkour as Urban Practice of Deterritorialization." *AI & SOCIETY* 26, no. 2 (2011): 143–52, https://doi.org/10.1007/s00146-010-0294-2; Maria Daskalaki, Alexandra Stara, and Miguel Imas, "The 'Parkour Organisation': Inhabitation of Corporate Spaces." *Culture and Organization* 14, no. 1 (2008): 49–64, https://doi.org/10.1080/14759550701659029; Sophie Fuggle, "Le Parkour: Reading or Writing the City?" in *Rhythms: Essays in French Literature, Thought and Culture*, eds. Elizabeth Lindley and Laura McMahon, *Modern French Identities*, vol. 68 (Oxford: Peter Lang, 2008), 159–70; Jeffrey L. Kidder, "Parkour, the Affective Appropriation of Urban Space, and the Real/Virtual Dialectic." *City & Community* 11, no. 3 (2012): 229–53, https://doi.org/10.1111/j.1540-6040.2012.01406.x; Matthew Lamb, "Miseuse of the Monument: The Art of Parkour and the Discursive Limits of a Disciplinary Architecture." *Journal of Urban Cultural Studies* 1, no. 1 (2014): 107–26; Matthew Lamb, "Self and the City: Parkour,

Architecture, and the Interstices of the 'Knowable' City." *Liminalities* 10, no. 2 (2014): 1–20; Bill Marshall, "Running across the Rooves of Empire: Parkour and the Postcolonial City." *Modern & Contemporary France* 18, no. 2 (May 1, 2010): 157–73, https://doi.org/10.1080/09639481003714872; Oli Mould, "Parkour, the City, the Event." *Environment and Planning D: Society and Space* 27, no. 4 (2009): 738–50, https://doi.org/10.1068/d11108; Jimena Ortuzar, "Parkour or 'l'art Du Déplacement': A Kinetic Urban Utopia." *TDR* (1988-) 53, no. 3 (2009): 54–66.

2. Jacques Rancière and Slavoj Žižek, *The Politics of Aesthetics: The Distribution of the Sensible* (2004), 10.

3. See for example, Christoph Lindner, ed., *Urban Space and Cityscapes: Perspectives from Modern and Contemporary Culture* (London: Routledge, 2006); Kevin Lynch, *The Image of the City, Publications of the Joint Center for Urban Studies* (Cambridge: MIT Press, 1960); Barbara Caroline Mennel, *Cities and Cinema*, Routledge Critical Introductions to Urbanism and the City (Milton Park, Abingdon, Oxon: Routledge, 2008); François Penz and Richard Koeck, eds., *Cinematic Urban Geographies*, 1st ed., 2017 edition (New York: Palgrave Macmillan, 2017); Francois Penz and Andong Lu, *Urban Cinematics: Understanding Urban Phenomena through the Moving Image* (Bristol: Intellect, 2011); Jr Warner, *Imaging the City: Continuing Struggles and New Directions*, 1st edition (New Brunswick, NJ: Routledge, 2001); Andrew Webber and Emma Wilson, eds., *Cities in Transition: The Moving Image and the Modern Metropolis*, Illustrated edition (London: Wallflower Press, 2007).

4. Giuliana Bruno, *Atlas of Emotion: Journeys in Art, Architecture, and Film* (New York: Verso, 2002), 31 (ebook).

5. Vivian Sobchack, *The Address of the Eye: A Phenomenology of Film Experience* (Princeton, NJ: Princeton University Press, 2009), https://doi.org/10.1515/9780691213279, 138.

6. Dustin A. Greenwalt, "User-Generated Videos of Urban Exploration and the Production of Affective Space." *Explorations in Media Ecology* 14, no. 1–2 (2015): 125–39, https://doi.org/10.1386/eme.14.1-2.125_1.

7. William Uricchio, "Imag(in)ing the City: Simondes to the Sims," in *Cities in Transition: The Moving Image and the Modern Metropolis* (London: Wallflower Press, 2008), 102.

8. Uricchio, "Imag(in)ing the City," 111.

9. Ruggero Eugeni, "First Person Shot: New Forms of Subjectivity between Cinema and Intermedia Networks," 2012, 20, https://doi.org/10.7238/a.v0iM.1499.

10. See Edward Branigan, *Point of View in the Cinema: A Theory of Narration and Subjectivity in Classical Film*, Reprint 2010, Approaches to Semiotics 66 (Berlin: Mouton, 1984), https://doi.org/10.1515/9783110817591; Dominique Chateau, *Subjectivity: Filmic Representation and the Spectator's Experience, Key Debates Subjectivity* (Amsterdam, Netherlands: Amsterdam University Press, 2011); Vivian Sobchack, *The Address of the Eye: A Phenomenology of Film Experience* (Princeton, NJ: Princeton University Press, 2009), https://doi.org/10.1515/9780691213279.

11. Eugeni, "First Person Shot", 24.

12. Alexander R. Galloway, *Gaming: Essays on Algorithmic Culture*, Electronic Mediations; vol. 18 (Minneapolis: University of Minnesota Press, 2006), 43.
13. Stephen John Saville, "Playing with Fear: Parkour and the Mobility of Emotion." *Social & Cultural Geography* 9, no. 8 (2008): 891–914, https://doi.org/10.1080/14649360802441440.
14. Eugeni, "First Person Shot", 27–28.
15. In the web version of 360, supported on platforms like YouTube and Vimeo, the user can click and drag the video screen to change which part of the spherical video they see, or if on a mobile device, use their device's onboard sensors to control where the virtual camera is directed.
16. William Uricchio, "VR Is Not Film: So What Is It? By William Uricchio." *Medium*, September 21, 2017, https://immerse.news/vr-is-not-film-so-what-is-it-36d58e59c030.
17. It is worth noting here that while this work separates out these apparatuses and perspectives for purposes of organization and clarity, they are often used and edited in concert with each other, a point I will discuss in more detail in the section on editing practices and narrative trends.
18. J. David Bolter and Richard A. Grusin, "Remediation." *Configurations (Baltimore, Md.)* 4, no. 3 (1996): 344. https://doi.org/10.1353/con.1996.0018.
19. Bolter and Grusin, "Remediation", 356.
20. See Uricchio, "VR Is Not a Film"; Homay King and Shari Frilot, "VIRTUAL REALITY IN REAL TIME: A CONVERSATION." *Film Quarterly* 71, no. 1 (2017): 51–58, https://doi.org/10.1525/fq.2017.71.1.51.
21. Grégoire Chamayou, *A Theory of the Drone* (New York: The New Press, 2015); Kyle Grayson and Jocelyn Mawdsley, "Scopic Regimes and the Visual Turn in International Relations: Seeing World Politics through the Drone." *European Journal of International Relations* 25, no. 2 (2019): 431–57, https://doi.org/10.1177/1354066118781955; Joanna Tidy, "Visual Regimes and the Politics of War Experience: Rewriting War 'From Above' in WikiLeaks' 'Collateral Murder'." *Review of International Studies* 43, no. 1 (2017): 95–111, https://doi.org/10.1017/S0260210516000164.
22. Patricia Zimmerman and Caren Kaplan, "Coronavirus Drone Genres: Spectacles of Distance and Melancholia." *Film Quarterly* (April 30, 2020), https://filmquarterly.org/2020/04/30/coronavirus-drone-genres-spectacles-of-distance-and-melancholia/.
23. See for instance James Bridle, *Dronestagram*, 2012.
24. Katherine Fehr Chandler, "A Drone Manifesto: Re-Forming the Partial Politics of Targeted Killing." *Catalyst (San Diego, Calif.)* 2, no. 1 (2016): 1–23, https://doi.org/10.28968/cftt.v2i1.28832.
25. Saville, "Playing with Fear", 901; Wen Bin Loo and Tim Bunnell, "Landscaping Selves through Parkour: Reinterpreting the Urban Environment of Singapore." *Space and Culture* 21, no. 2, 145–58, https://doi.org.10.1177/1206331217720073.
26. Penz and Lu, *Urban Cinematics*, 16.
27. STORROR, "Incredible Parkour spots! STORROR clothing SS21GB", May 31, 2021, vlog, 17:30–17:45, https://www.youtube.com/watch?v=Oi_dUPn843Y. Accessed June 14, 2024.

28. A tic-tac is a move that involves running and pushing off an object to change trajectories.
29. One of the mental aspects to parkour is presented in the notion of "committing" to a move, which generally includes suppressing the body's fear response to protect itself and putting full mental and physical commitment into the move.
30. Storm Freerun, "Pushing Mental Barriers", May 13, 2021, vlog, 02:04–03:20. https://www.youtube.com/watch?v=25jiNchBX6w. Accessed June 14, 2024.
31. Anne Friedberg, *The Virtual Window: From Alberti to Microsoft* (Cambridge: MIT Press, 2006), 7.
32. Ken Dancyger, *The Technique of Film and Video Editing: History, Theory, and Practice* (Oxford: Routledge, 2011), 299.

BIBLIOGRAPHY

Atkinson, Michael. "Heidegger, Parkour, Post-Sport, and the Essence of Being." In *A Companion to Sport*, edited by David L. Andrews and Ben Carrington, Blackwell Companions in Cultural Studies 15. Hoboken: Wiley-Blackwell, 2013.

Branigan, Edward. *Point of View in the Cinema: A Theory of Narration and Subjectivity in Classical Film*, Reprint 2010, Approaches to Semiotics 66. Berlin: Mouton, 1984. https://doi.org/10.1515/9783110817591.

Bolter, David J, and Richard A. Grusin. "Remediation." *Configurations (Baltimore, MD)* 4, no. 3 (1996). https://doi.org/10.1353/con.1996.0018.

Brunner, Christoph. "Nice-Looking Obstacles: Parkour as Urban Practice of Deterritorialization." *AI & SOCIETY* 26, no. 2 (2011): 143–52. https://doi.org/10.1007/s00146-010-0294-2.

Bruno, Giuliana. *Atlas of Emotion: Journeys in Art, Architecture, and Film.* New York: Verso, 2002.

Chamayou, Grégoire. *A Theory of the Drone.* New York: The New Press, 2015.

Chandler, Katherine Fehr. "A Drone Manifesto: Re-Forming the Partial Politics of Targeted Killing." *Catalyst (San Diego, CA)* 2, no. 1 (2016): 1–23. https://doi.org/10.28968/cftt.v2i1.28832.

Chateau, Dominique. *Subjectivity: Filmic Representation and the Spectator's Experience*, Key Debates in Subjectivity. Amsterdam: Amsterdam University Press, 2011.

Dancyger, Ken. *The Technique of Film and Video Editing: History, Theory, and Practice.* Oxford: Routledge, 2011.

Daskalaki, Maria, Alexandra Stara, and Miguel Imas. "The 'Parkour Organisation': Inhabitation of Corporate Spaces." *Culture and Organization* 14, no. 1 (2008): 49–64. https://doi.org/10.1080/14759550701659029.

Eugeni, Ruggero. "First Person Shot: New Forms of Subjectivity between Cinema and Intermedia Networks," 2012, 20. https://doi.org/10.7238/a.v0iM.1499.

Friedberg, Anne. *The Virtual Window: From Alberti to Microsoft.* Cambridge, MA: MIT Press, 2006.

Fuggle, Sophie. "Le Parkour: Reading or Writing the City?" In *Rhythms: Essays in French Literature, Thought and Culture*, edited by Elizabeth Lindley and Laura McMahon, Modern French Identities, vol. 68, 159–70. Oxford: Peter Lang, 2008.

Galloway, Alexander R. *Gaming: Essays On Algorithmic Culture, Electronic Mediations*, vol. 18. Minneapolis: University of Minnesota Press, 2006.

Grayson, Kyle, and Jocelyn Mawdsley. "Scopic Regimes and the Visual Turn in International Relations: Seeing World Politics through the Drone." *European Journal of International Relations* 25, no. 2 (2019): 431–57. https://doi.org/10.1177/1354066118781955.

Greenwalt, Dustin A. "User-Generated Videos of Urban Exploration and the Production of Affective Space." *Explorations in Media Ecology* 14, no. 1–2 (2015): 125–39. https://doi.org/10.1386/eme.14.1-2.125_1.

Kidder, Jeffrey L. "Parkour, the Affective Appropriation of Urban Space, and the Real/Virtual Dialectic." *City & Community* 11, no. 3 (2012): 229–53. https://doi.org/10.1111/j.1540-6040.2012.01406.x.

King, Homay, and Shari Frilot. "Virtual Reality in Real Time: A Conversation." *Film Quarterly* 71, no. 1 (2017): 51–58. https://doi.org/10.1525/fq.2017.71.1.51

Lamb, Matthew. "Miseuse of the Monument: The Art of Parkour and the Discursive Limits of a Disciplinary Architecture." *Journal of Urban Cultural Studies* 1, no. 1 (2014): 107–26.

Lamb, Matthew. "Self and the City: Parkour, Architecture, and the Interstices of the 'Knowable' City." *Liminalities* 10, no. 2 (2014): 1–20.

Lindner, Christoph, ed. *Urban Space and Cityscapes: Perspectives from Modern and Contemporary Culture*. London: Routledge, 2006.

Loo, Wen Bin, and Tim Bunnell. "Landscaping Selves through Parkour: Reinterpreting the Urban Environment of Singapore." *Space and Culture* 21, no. 2, 145–58. https://doi.org/10.1177/1206331217720073.

Lynch, Kevin. *The Image of the City: Publications of the Joint Center for Urban Studies*. Cambridge: MIT Press, 1960.

Marshall, Bill. "Running across the Rooves of Empire: Parkour and the Postcolonial City." *Modern & Contemporary France* 18, no. 2 (May 1, 2010): 157–73. https://doi.org/10.1080/09639481003714872.

Mennel, Barbara Caroline. *Cities and Cinema*, Routledge Critical Introductions to Urbanism and the City. Abingdon: Routledge, 2008.

Mould, Oli. "Parkour, the City, the Event." *Environment and Planning D: Society and Space* 27, no. 4 (2009): 738–50. https://doi.org/10.1068/d11108.

Ortuzar, Jimena. "Parkour or 'l'art Du Déplacement': A Kinetic Urban Utopia." *TDR (1988–)* 53, no. 3 (2009): 54–66.

Penz, François, and Andong Lu. *Urban Cinematics: Understanding Urban Phenomena through the Moving Image*. Bristol: Intellect, 2011.

Penz, François, and Richard Koeck, eds. *Cinematic Urban Geographies*, 1st ed., 2017 edition. New York: Palgrave Macmillan, 2017.

Rancière, Jacques, and Slavoj Žižek. *The Politics of Aesthetics: The Distribution of the Sensible*. New York: Continuum, 2004.

Saville, Stephen John. "Playing with Fear: Parkour and the Mobility of Emotion." *Social & Cultural Geography* 9, no. 8 (2008): 891–914. https://doi.org/10.1080/14649360802441440.

Storm Freerun. "Pushing Mental Barriers," May 13, 2021, vlog, 02:04–03:20, https://www.youtube.com/watch?v=25jiNchBX6w. Last accessed October 19, 2023.

STORROR. "Incredible Parkour spots! STORROR clothing SS21GB" May 31, 2021, vlog, 17:30–17:45, https://www.youtube.com/watch?v=Oi_dUPn843Y. Last accessed October 19, 2023.

Sobchack, Vivian. *The Address of the Eye: A Phenomenology of Film Experience*. Princeton, NJ: Princeton University Press, 2009. https://doi.org/10.1515/9780691213279.

Tidy, Joanna. "Visual Regimes and the Politics of War Experience: Rewriting War 'From Above' in WikiLeaks' 'Collateral Murder'." *Review of International Studies* 43, no. 1 (2017): 95–111. https://doi.org/10.1017/S0260210516000164.

Uricchio, William. "Imag(in)ing the City: Simondes to the Sims." In *Cities in Transition: The Moving Image and the Modern Metropolis*. London: Wallflower Press, 2008.

Uricchio, William. "VR Is Not Film: So What Is It? By William Uricchio." *Medium*, September 21, 2017. https://immerse.news/vr-is-not-film-so-what-is-it-36d58e59c030. Last accessed October 19, 2023.

Warner, Jr. *Imaging the City: Continuing Struggles and New Directions*, 1st edition. New Brunswick, NJ: Routledge, 2001.

Webber, Andrew, and Emma Wilson, eds. *Cities in Transition: The Moving Image and the Modern Metropolis*, Illustrated edition. London: Wallflower Press, 2007.

Zimmerman, Patricia, and Caren Kaplan. "Coronavirus Drone Genres: Spectacles of Distance and Melancholia." *Film Quarterly* (April 30, 2020). https://filmquarterly.org/2020/04/30/coronavirus-drone-genres-spectacles-of-distance-and-melancholia/. Last accessed October 19, 2023.

12

Apple Town Square: Digital Placemaking and Digital Transformation of Urban Public Spaces

Isabel Fangyi Lu

Introduction

Curiously, discussions on digital town squares tend to depict something "virtual": networks, platforms, augmented space, and data flows. We pay particular attention to the processes that are less "tangible," like how collated data can predict public behaviour, twist public debates and exploit decision-making.[1] Concerns about privacy, security, and censorship heightened after Elon Musk purchased Twitter in April 2022. Many commentators lament that the commercial nature of Twitter makes it unlikely to become a "digital town square," an open and safe place "where matters vital to the future of humanity are debated."[2]

However, another type of digital transformation persists, hailed as urban redevelopment before inciting public suspicion and contention. Over the past years, we have seen a global trend for tech companies to propose urban innovation solutions and transform urban public spaces. One high-profile example was the Quayside project from Sidewalk Lab, an urban planning and infrastructure subsidiary of Google. Having proposed to build a smart precinct in Toronto, the project was abandoned in 2020 amongst citizen protests against urban surveillance and data abuse, citing "financial uncertainty during the pandemic." Less examined are these multidimensional "turf wars" between global tech corporates and urban public spaces.

Of all examples, Apple "town squares" can be considered the most civically ambitious, albeit short-lived. Apple's media release described an Apple town square as a hybrid of a retail store and an education centre that delivers workshops for photography, music, gaming, and app development. The town square was inspired

by Starbucks's success in creating a third space, a place where people would like to gather and hang out. Starting with Apple Union Square, Apple began to redesign its flagship stores by adding large glass doors, incorporating open spaces, and redefining store zones since 2016. The town square plan (ca. 2016–19) was borne out of the redesigning scheme and reflected Apple's attempt to rebrand its retailing business. Angela Ahrendts, then Senior Vice President of Retail at Apple, expressed in an interview that "I'll know we've done a really, really great job if the next generation, if Gen Z says: 'Meet me at Apple. Did you see what's going on at Apple today?'."[3] So far, Apple has proposed a few global town squares, including Apple Carnegie Library in Washington DC, Apple Michigan Avenue in Chicago, Apple Piazza Liberty in Milan, Apple Kungsträdgården in Stockholm, and Apple Federation Square in Melbourne.[4] While some town squares successfully opened to the public, Stockholm and Melbourne rejected the town square plan. With Angela Ahrendts leaving Apple in February 2019, the Apple town square lost tractions, yet the event programming remained through Today at Apple. Unlike Google's approach to smart cities, Apple town squares are oriented less towards harnessing data but more towards redesigning experience and community life. In other words, Apple has proposed a new mode of digital placemaking by positioning itself at the centre circle of placemakers.

With the shelved Apple Federation Square case, this chapter examines Apple town square as digital placemaking through an urban assemblage lens. In the following sections, I will unpack the concepts of urban assemblage and placemaking, map out the participating actors of Apple Federation Square, deconstruct various issues at the core of the Apple controversy and reassemble the notion of digital placemaking. This chapter argues that digital placemaking can be viewed as a dynamic site of contestations and collaborations over various issues amongst multiple actors. By exploring tech companies' involvement in placemaking, this work offers an alternative perspective on urban digital transformation.

Urban Assemblages and Placemaking

Urban assemblage thinking takes intellectual inspiration from Giles Deleuze and Felix Guattari, Farías and Bender, and Bruno Latour.[5] In *A Thousand Plateaus*, Deleuze and Guattari use the term *agencement* (meaning assemblage in French) to highlight the connections of human and nonhuman components in a rhizomatic network.[6] A rhizomatic network accommodates multiple and non-hierarchical culture organizations rather than fetishizing hierarchies and binaries.

Urban planner and theorist Kim Dovey defines an urban assemblage as the interconnectivity and flows between constituent parts. Different components, such

as urban life, traffic, goods, money, plans, policies, nature, and infrastructure, come together to give the street intensity and an emergent sense of place.[7] These components are in constant processes of "coming together (territorialisation)" and potentially "falling apart (de-territorialisation)."[8] In this way, urban assemblage depicts the contingent processes of how heterogeneous flows and exchanges cohere, sustain, dissipate, and disintegrate.

Urban assemblage thinking understands place and placemaking as inseparable and relational processes. It does not view places as physical sites but as productions through actions. Human geographer Jon Anderson contends that a surfed wave exists through practices and concerted efforts of all actors, including the surfer's body, the ocean waves, the board and the cord that attaches to the surfer, the weather, the surfers' luck and the unpredictable currents.[9] Anderson further suggests that the coastline coheres and stabilizes as a place over time, through many ocean waves, many surfers, and their actions of surfing. Urban assemblage thinking considers not only "the material, actual and assembled" but also "the emergent, the processual and the multiple."[10] An assemblage lens rejects seeing place and placemaking on separate terms. Place and placemaking intertwine through actions and processes, i.e., repeated practices and incessant labour.[11]

Placemaking is a process of shaping public spaces to create meaningful experiences "(in, of, and for) people."[12] Unlike traditional planning discourse that deems placemaking as clearly defined projects, urban assemblage thinking sees placemaking as open-ended and contingent. In this line, placemaking can be traced through the amalgamation and disintegration of heterogeneous actors and actions in a place's life cycle: designing, planning, managing, maintenance, programming, and demolishing. Each assemblage reveals different sets of associations, relations, and issues. No one assemblage triumphs over the other. The domination of one industry over the other requires reconsideration. Urban planning, designing, development, governance, and dwelling can be seen as embedded in the synergist morphology of the placemaking assemblages, adding complexity and nuance to each other's existence.[13] Similarly, the discursive thread of the "large scale," "worldwide," and the "broader implication" of the global hierarchy does not diminish the lure and vitality of the "local," the "informal," and the "microspatialities."[14]

Investigating the concrete placemaking examples through an assemblage lens helps us map out the participating actors, processes, and issues of a specific placemaking conflict, giving visibility to latent actors and emerging concerns. On the one hand, an assemblage lens accommodates a sociomaterial way of understanding heterogeneous urban elements that tend to be compartmentalized and dealt separately, such as urban structure and infrastructures (buildings, streets, plazas, shops, institutions, laws, rules); human actants (both as individuals and as collectives);

as well as technological practices and transformations.[15] On the other hand, an assemblage lens can assist inquiries into emerging urban configurations rather than applying existing hierarchical and normative assumptions. More specifically, an assemblage lens can facilitate an understanding of heterogeneous and dynamic urban environments.

Apple Federation Square: Assemblages and Oligoptica

In December 2017, Apple Inc. announced its town square plan for Federation Square, a high-profile public space in the centre of Melbourne, Australia (Figure 12.1). Federation Square's governing body, the State of Victoria, and its managing body, Federation Square Pty Ltd (FSPL), endorsed the plan. They deemed an extra Apple flagship store as a tourism booster, a local job creator, and an addition to the event programming of Federation Square and its cultural tenants. Nonetheless, the decision lacked community consultations mandated for land-use decisions and placemaking processes in most Australian state and local government jurisdictions. Both the Melbourne City Council and the public communities voiced discontent, which evolved into online petitions and urban activism ("Our City, Our Square").[16] In April 2019, Apple withdrew its plan as the demolition request for the site was denied by the Victorian heritage authority and Federation Square was incorporated into the Victorian Heritage Register in August 2019. Soon after, FSPL hosted a civic design hack (Hack Fed Square) and invited public groups to brainstorm Federation Square's future direction.[17] Subsequently, the State of Victoria launched a review to examine FSPL's overall condition (the State Review).[18] The above accounts are by no means a series of separate accounts but a complex placemaking controversy involving many actors, actions, and consequences. Rather than reducing the Apple controversy to a binary of a failed business proposal or

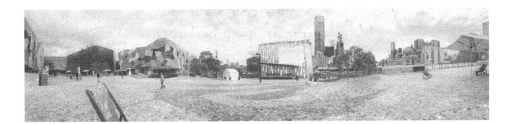

FIGURE 12.1: A panorama of Melbourne's Federation Square, a prominent public meeting place, 2020. The irregular building to the left of the large digital screen, the Yarra Building, was once proposed to be demolished to make way for an Apple flagship store in 2017. Author's photo.

a public triumph, I use assemblage thinking to break down the key processes and clarify major participating actors.

Since urban assemblage thinking accommodates heterogeneous elements outside institutional boundaries, placemaking processes and controversies can be reassembled. Matthew Carmona's "place-shaping continuum" defines four place-shaping processes: the "knowing" design and development phases and the "unknowing" use and management phases.[19] I propose to explore the Apple controversy through three interlocking placemaking assemblages: activist, organizational and governmental assemblages. These assemblages are organized around place use and activism, management, and governance. This view enables a trans-industrial discussion of placemaking rather than confining discussions to one compartmentalized placemaking industry. It further highlights the significance of place managers, whose work of infrastructural maintenance, events programming and financial operations can appear mundane yet indispensable to producing places through constant labour.

Each assemblage acts as a Latourian oligopticon, a special site where the micro-structures of macro-phenomena are assembled and crafted. For Bruno Latour, an oligopticon is a tool to see, understand, or exert control within a minimal scope, producing a "sturdy, but narrow view."[20] Parliaments, courtrooms, offices, even a photo and a map, are examples of oligoptica. The activist, organizational and governmental assemblages reflect the views of—but are not limited to—the activists, place managers, and governments relevant to Federation Square. For example, the activist assemblage differs from an activist group. The former does not observe strict group boundaries and includes all those who are activist-minded and support the initiative. The nomenclature is relevant to my understanding of the Apple controversy and its resolution as an intricate mode of politics that arises from the fluidity and the synergies of different assemblages. The sense of politics as absolute opposition between irreconcilable enemies can be renewed as the clash of different concerns, connective styles, and *modi operandi*.

At its most reductive interpretation, an activist assemblage is constantly performed and embodied through the entanglement of networked corporeality. It combines traits of urban protests and networked activism that underpins personal connections and frames. The activist assemblage can be captured by the eighteen-month "Our City, Our Square" campaign that involved networks of activists, campaign volunteers and content contributors, the general Melbourne public, heritage advocates, and City of Melbourne councillors. Concerned with aesthetic incoherence, privatization of public space, secret decision-making and Apple's socio-spatial impact, the campaign adopted a hybrid strategy that combined conventional activist techniques with performative elements in online and offline realms. With Federation Square being added to Victoria State Heritage register,

the campaign contributed to the discontinuation of the Apple plan, and blurred formal and informal placemaking processes, offering citizens ways of participating in space and claiming rights.

An organizational assemblage is tasked with maintaining physical and digital urban infrastructures through constant labour to achieve place vibrance and economic sustainability through establishing a feasible business model. The organizational assemblage can be captured by the design hackathon Hack Fed Square that involved FSPL, urban marketing agencies, and business partners. A civic hackathon is an event where predefined problems are solved in a limited time frame. In the wake of the thwarted Apple deal, FSPL invited 60 members of the public to compete in a mock pitch contest to rejuvenate Federation Square. Hack Fed Square allowed to FSPL strategically reconsider its future directions and restore Federation Square's reputation after the year-long public discontent by portraying itself as an open and fun place that constantly engaged with the communities. It also subtly revealed FSPL's three existential threats (the reasons why FSPL endorsed an Apple plan): financial deficit due to an unsustainable business model, growing maintenance costs out of infrastructural deterioration, and difficulties in finding strategic cultural collaborators. Hack Fed Square was an assembling force to bring people and resources together and mobilize different kinds of labour. SPL's placemaking labour maintained Federation Square's physical architecture and potentiated a public *agora*. Although some actions of FSPL can be criticized as market-driven, they cannot be reduced to a neoliberal frame. The evaluation of urban hackathons should consider the multi-layered urban complexities and highlight the importance of placemaking organizations and their labour.

The governmental assemblage aims to achieve actionable consensus by strategically managing urban projects and balancing the interests of a vast range of stakeholders. The governmental assemblage can be captured by the State Review that involved the Victorian government, the City of Melbourne, public engagement consultation firms, communities, and various other internal and external stakeholders of FSPL. The State Review examined the public usage of Federation Square's physical assets and the financial and governance model of FSPL. With inputs from more than 1,700 people, the State Review made three major findings, including adopting a new community-informed vision and objectives for Federation Square, ensuring the built environment supports the new vision and rearranging Federation Square's governance structure and business model. The Victorian government accepted the State Review's recommendation by instigating two structural changes that aligned with public opinions, namely respecting Federation Square's heritage status and acknowledging it as a state-owned creative organization. However, as Apple Federation Square has shown, contemporary placemaking controversies are no longer bound within state borders as internal

issues or local affairs due to techno-capitalism's global expansion. The review failed to reveal and respond to this trend.

Deconstructing the Apple Controversy

The Apple controversy can be broken down into three entangled issues with different temporalities in public life and political trajectories. To explain the political trajectories, I refer to Bruno Latour's Political Circle which describes five different stages of political issues.[21] Political-1 refers to "new associations between humans and nonhumans." Political-2 refers to a moment when an issue becomes a problem and unsettles the public. Political-3 refers to the stage when the government turns the problem into a public-facing question to be dealt with through established government institutions. Political-4 refers to the formation of deliberative assemblies that aim at debating and solving the issue. Political-5 refers to the governmental incorporation of the issue as part of the daily administration. Political-1 and political-5 are considered apolitical by most people and scholars.

Three issues were most prominent: the architectural issue, the business model issue and the digital issue. The architectural issue focuses on whether physical changes to Federation Square should be allowed to make way for the Apple town square. This issue was contended by the activist assemblage and resolved when Federation Square's heritage status was recognized. The architectural issue was fully intervened, performed, acted out, and deliberated by the public and civil society. It can be said that the architectural issue went through the full political circle, from the political-1 to the political-5. The Apple proposal could potentially change the Federation Square site (political-1) and triggered public discontent (political-2). The Victorian Heritage Council called for and accepted public submissions (political-3 and political-4) and enlisted Federation Square to the State Heritage Register (political-5).

The second issue concerns the business model of FSPL. Specifically, both the organizational and the governmental assemblages sought ways for Federation Square to be self-sustained while delivering community value. Before the State Review, FSPL was self-funded as a private company that managed public assets and programmed public culture. Initiatives like the Apple town square reveal the underfunded Victorian arts and cultural sector. Apple was brought in as a commercial tenant to alleviate FSPL's financial pressure. This issue has skipped political-1 and political-2 since many members of the public were unaware of FSPL's financial difficulty nor the fact that Federation Square was not an official cultural institution before 2020. This issue was raised in the State Review process (political-3) and discussed in the stakeholder engagement sessions (political-4).

Including Federation Square as a state-owned cultural institution concluded the identity crisis of Federation Square (political-5). The business issue was settled as the Victorian State recognized FSPL as a state cultural institution, which meant immediate capital injection and a stable funding stream for Federation Square.

The third issue, the digital issue, concerns the platforms and tech companies' capability to transform urban socio-spatial structures. This issue is still emerging through the activist and the organizational assemblages while unrecognized by the governmental assemblage. The activists have begun to reflect on and articulate their trepidations about Apple's socio-spatial and technopolitical impact. The Federation Square management has sought ways to leverage FSPL's digital capital for self-sustainability and reproductivity. However, this level of concern disappeared in the governmental assemblage. During the review, digital technologies have only been used as instruments to effectively gather public opinion and visualize public needs regarding urban space change. Urban governments have yet to respond to tech giants like Apple and address potential problems like privatization, exclusion, privacy breach, and platform urbanism. Platform inquiries worldwide tend to focus on content rather than urban environments. How tech companies can shape placemaking industries, change urban political processes, and corporatize civic life has been ignored.[22] Interestingly, the digital issue started as a ubiquitous urban reality (political-5) without being questioned. The activists and placemakers only began to notice this new phenomenon and its profound structural impact (so I consider this in-between political-1 and political-2).

Conclusion: Reassembling Digital Placemaking

With the case of Apple Federation Square, this chapter shows digital placemaking as sites of contestations and collaborations over various issues amongst multiple actors. That is to say, digital placemaking is a whole-of-society complexity that cannot be reduced to one actor or a single issue.

First, digital placemaking is built on the global trend of urban digital transformation. Digital technologies are taken as pre-formed and built into the urban public environments without being properly questioned. Not only in accelerated digital placemaking and smart city initiatives driven by governments, developers, and tech companies, but also in the natural digital placemaking process.[23] Smartphones, urban screens, smart wayfinding apps, VR artworks, and online engagement portals are everyday manifestations of the societal incorporation of digital technologies as part of placemaking activities.

In addition, digital placemaking also contributes to a global movement against big tech companies' transforming urban public space when people organize their

actions through digitally enabled methods. Recent examples include public rejection of the Google campus in Berlin and Amazon's proposed headquarter in New York City. Both cases fought against tech companies' gentrification, displacement, and privatization of public space. The public start not only started to reflect on tech companies' ambition to reproduce urban public space, but they also manifested new dynamics and formed pathways through which the public contention is exercised. These collective actions have been preliminarily rewarded. In 2017, the mayor of London released a first-of-its-kind urban document draft, the London Plan, to tackle the growing corporate control of civic spaces, parks, and squares. The plan ensured the urban public realms would remain open and free for all public use.

Further, digital placemaking creates new wealth and power centralization opportunities that potentiate a renewed evaluation of *place*. David Harvey has explicated how neoliberal devices of privatization, financialization, crisis management, and state redistribution dispossess the public and private entities of their wealth or land.[24] In the new spatial orders of urban digital transformation, the logic of accumulation is no longer limited to physical geography. New evaluations of the place emerge that test public values and rapidly change the urban landscape. For example, while governments defunded arts institutions and retailers closed stores during the pandemic, tech companies, and digitally native brands have rediscovered the lure of brick-and-mortar places as a contributing factor to brand value. These new retailers no longer measure stores on a sales-per-square-foot basis but think of stores as a media node for advertising and a hub for customer acquisition.[25] Embedded in intricate sociotechnical networks, a physical place like Apple town square materializes Apple's aesthetics, products, and service rather than merely boosting transactions. As neoliberal as it may sound, this new evaluation method can provide rationales behind funding arts and creative placemaking initiatives.

Last, digital placemaking comprises trajectories of various debatable issues, some of which are yet to be incorporated into a governance framework. In the case of the Apple controversy, the architectural and business model issues have been accepted as "policy material" within established political institutions. When concerns are raised, they follow existing procedures and protocols for resolution, i.e., Victorian urban policy and cultural policy. In contrast, the digital issue is yet to find a policy document and a guiding principle in an urban context. Although the Australian government has created a blueprint for critical technologies, it focuses on national security rather than urban and community interests. Urban governments should realize that digital transformation for urban public spaces is ongoing and open. Rights to the digital city, such as security, dignity, prosperity, and the ability to choose and change urban technologies, should be embedded in policy considerations.

The implications of such digital placemaking processes remain to be seen. Public service and urban infrastructures are increasingly managed as corporates or public–private partnerships.[26] Combined with the push of technocapitalist logic in urban reproduction, public civic, and cultural institutions face two new concerns. First, lacking funding and revenue, how would they respond when global corporates like Apple offer partnership in exchange for a role that assumes public cultural function? Second, what are the consequences of public cultural sectors becoming more corporatized and goal-oriented? When we talk about urban digital transformation, we talk about using specific technological tools, such as mobile phones and social media; about extracting, wrangling, and interpreting urban big data, surveillance, AI ethics, and privacy.[27] We also talk about how the digital has transformed the urban rather than using the digital as tools for analysing or representing "place."[28] However, we should also inquire into the complex sequences and trajectories of objects, actions, and values embedded in the increasingly corporatized and commodified public life.[29] In this line, not only the technological applications and data policies but also the value systems should be the concerns of urban governments.

ACKNOWLEDGEMENT

This study has been produced through research funded by the Australian Research Council (ARC DP170102796).

NOTES

1. For an excellent analysis particular in an Australian context, see Peter Lewis and Jordan Guiao, *The Public Square Project* (Melbourne: Melbourne University Press, 2021). Also see Mark Andrejevic and Kelly Gates, "Big Data Surveillance: Introduction." *Surveillance & Society* 12, no. 2 (2014): 185–96.
2. Monica Potts and Jean Yi, "Why Twitter Is Unlikely to Become the 'Digital Town Square' Elon Musk Envisions." *FiveThirtyEight*. 2022. https://fivethirtyeight.com/features/why-twitter-is-unlikely-to-become-the-digital-town-square-elon-musk-envisions/. Last accessed October 19, 2023.
3. Angela Ahrendts expressed Apple's ambition of becoming the meeting place of the twenty-first century. "Starbucks figured it out, for being a gathering place. You know, 'Meet me at Starbucks.' And I've told the teams, I'll know we've done a really great job if the next generation, if gen Z says: 'Meet me at Apple. Did you see what's going on at Apple today?'" See https://futurestoreseast.wbresearch.com/blog/apple-is-creating-the-town-square-of-tomorrow-today. Despite Apple's enthusiasm, the idea of a meeting place holds sacredness in the Australian psyche. From the First Nations custodians of the Australian land to the

European descendants who cherish the political ideal of an *agora*, to the contemporary citizens living in a functional liberal democracy, the notion of a gathering place is entrenched with the awareness of sovereignty, access, ownership, and freedom.

4. After public contention, the Stockholm City Council vetoed the plan, which was meant to build an Apple flagship store in *Kungsträdgården* (The King's Garden). It is one of the city's oldest parks, the venue for public events from Pride parades to election debates, political protests to winter ice-skating. Apple Carnegie Library opened in May 2019. The store locates in Carnegie Library, a 114-year-old building located across the street from the Washington Convention Centre in Mount Vernon Square.
5. Felix Guattari and Gilles Deleuze, *A Thousand Plateaus: Capitalism and Schizophrenia* (Minneapolis: University of Minnesota, 1987). Ignacio Farías and Thomas Bender, eds. *Urban Assemblages: How Actor-network Theory Changes Urban Studies* (New York: Routledge, 2012). Bruno Latour, *Reassembling the Social: An Introduction to Actor-Network-Theory* (Oxford: Oxford University Press, 2005).
6. John Philips argues that the English translation of the terminology "assemblage" is too static to be satisfactory. John Phillips, "Agencement/Assemblage." *Theory Culture Society* 23, no. 2–3 (2006): 108–109.
7. Kim Dovey, "Informal Urbanism and Complex Adaptive Assemblage." *International Development Planning Review* 34, no. 4 (2012): 349–68.
8. Guattari and Deleuze, *A Thousand Plateaus*, 406.
9. Jon Anderson, "Relational Places: The Surfed Wave as Assemblage and Convergence." *Environment and Planning D: Society and Space* 30, no. 4 (2012): 570–87.
10. See Farías (2009), 15.
11. Jill Sweeney, Kathy Mee, Pauline McGuirk, and Kristian Ruming, "Assembling Placemaking: Making and Remaking Place in a Regenerating City." *Cultural Geographies* 25, no. 4 (2018): 571–87.
12. Dominique Hes and Cristina Hernandez-Santin, eds. *Placemaking Fundamentals for the Built Environment* (Singapore: Palgrave Macmillan, 2020).
13. This is not to deny dominance, but to pursue an analysis which does neither presume dominance nor ignore it.
14. Dovey, "Informal Urbanism and Complex Adaptive Assemblage", 348.
15. Anna MacLeod, Paula Cameron, Rola Ajjawi, Olga Kits, and Jonathan Tummons, "Actor-network Theory and Ethnography: Sociomaterial Approaches to Researching Medical Education." *Perspectives on Medical Education* 8, no. 3 (2019): 177–86.
16. https://ourcityoursquare.org/. Last accessed October 19, 2023.
17. https://fedsquare.com/events/hack-fed-square. Last accessed October 19, 2023.
18. https://engage.vic.gov.au/federation-square-review. Last accessed October 19, 2023.
19. Matthew Carmona, "The Place-shaping Continuum: A Theory of Urban Design Process." *Journal of Urban Design* 19, no. 1 (2014): 2–36.
20. Latour, *Reassembling the Social*, 181.

21. Bruno Latour, "Turning around Politics: A Note on Gerard de Vries' paper." *Social Studies of Science* 37, no. 5 (2007): 811–20. Bruno Latour, *An Inquiry into Modes of Existence* (Cambridge, MA: Harvard University Press, 2013).
22. One may argue this is also due to local governments' difficulty in regulating the transglobal tech companies and platforms. In other words, one of the tensions/controversies that is in play is the limits of the Westphalian model of sovereignty and governance.
23. Marcus Foth, "Some Thoughts on Digital Placemaking." *Media Architecture Compendium: Digital Placemaking*, 203–05. 2017.
24. See David Harvey, *The New Imperialism* (Oxford: Oxford University Press, 2005), especially the concept of "accumulation by dispossession."
25. Pamela Danziger, "Measuring the True Value of the Store: Here's the New Math." *Forbes* (2020). https://www-forbes-com.cdn.ampproject.org/c/s/www.forbes.com/sites/pamdanziger/2020/08/10/measuring-the-true-value-of-the-store-heres-the-new-math/amp/.
26. Steve Graham and Simon Marvin, *Splintering Urbanism: Networked Infrastructures, Technological Mobilities and the Urban Condition* (London: Routledge, 2002).
27. For examples, see Graham Cairns, *Digital Futures and the City of Today: New Technologies and Physical Spaces* (Bristol: Intellect Books, 2016); Sarah Barns, *Platform Urbanism: Negotiating Platform Ecosystems in Connected Cities* (Springer Nature, 2019); Yang Wang, *Digital Media in Urban China: Locating Guangzhou* (MD: Rowman & Littlefield International, 2019); Dietmar Offenhuber and Carlo Ratti, *Decoding the City: Urbanism in the Age of Big Data* (Birkhäuser, 2014); Rob Kitchin, Tracey P. Lauriault, and Gavin McArdle. *Data and the City* (Routledge, 2017).
28. See Scott McQuire, *Geomedia: Networked Cities and the Future of Public Space* (New York: John Wiley & Sons, 2017); Nikos Papastergiadis, ed. *Ambient Screens and Transnational Public Spaces* (Hong Kong: Hong Kong University Press, 2016).
29. Robert Hassan, *The Condition of Digitality: A Post-Modern Marxism for the Practice of Digital Life* (London: University of Westminster Press, 2020), 212.

BIBLIOGRAPHY

Anderson, Jon. "Relational Places: The Surfed Wave as Assemblage and Convergence." *Environment and Planning D: Society and Space* 30, no. 4 (2012): 570–87.

Andrejevic, Mark, and Kelly Gates. "Big Data Surveillance: Introduction." *Surveillance & Society* 12, no. 2 (2014): 185–96.

Barns, Sarah. *Platform Urbanism: Negotiating Platform Ecosystems in Connected Cities*. Springer Nature, 2019, Palgrave Macmillan Singapore. https://link.springer.com/book/10.1007/978-981-32-9725-8.

Cairns, Graham. *Digital Futures and the City of Today: New Technologies and Physical Spaces*. Bristol: Intellect Books, 2016.

Carmona, Matthew. "The Place-Shaping Continuum: A Theory of Urban Design Process." *Journal of Urban Design* 19, no. 1 (2014): 2–36.

Dovey, Kim. "Informal Urbanism and Complex Adaptive Assemblage." *International Development Planning Review* 34, no. 4 (2012), 349–68.

Farías, Ignacio, and Thomas Bender, eds. *Urban Assemblages: How Actor-network Theory Changes Urban Studies*. Routledge, 2012. https://www.routledge.com/Urban-Assemblages-How-Actor-Network-Theory-Changes-Urban-Studies/Farias-Bender/p/book/9780415692052.

Foth, Marcus. "Some Thoughts on Digital Placemaking." In *Media Architecture Compendium: Digital Placemaking*, edited by Luke Hespanhol, M. Hank Häusler, Martin Tomitsch, and Gernot Tscherteu, 203–05. Media Architecture Compendium—Digital Placemaking, 2017.

Graham, Steve, and Simon Marvin. *Splintering Urbanism: Networked Infrastructures, Technological Mobilities and the Urban Condition*. London: Routledge, 2002.

Guattari, Felix, and Gilles Deleuze. *A Thousand Plateaus: Capitalism and Schizophrenia*. Translated by B. Massumi. Minneapolis: University of Minnesota, 1987.

Harvey, David. *The New Imperialism*. Oxford: Oxford University Press, 2005.

Hassan, Robert. *The Condition of Digitality: A Post-Modern Marxism for the Practice of Digital Life*. London: University of Westminster Press, 2020.

Hes, Dominique, and Cristina Hernandez-Santin, eds. *Placemaking Fundamentals for the Built Environment*. Singapore: Palgrave Macmillan, 2020.

Phillips, J.W.P. "Agencement/Assemblage." *Theory, Culture & Society* 23, no. 2–3 (2006), 108–09, https://doi.org/10.1177/026327640602300219.

Kitchin, Rob, P. Lauriault Tracey, and Gavin McArdle. *Data and the City*. London, New York: Routledge, 2017.

Latour, Bruno. *Reassembling the Social: An Introduction to Actor-Network-Theory*. Oxford: Oxford University Press, 2005.

Latour, Bruno. "Turning around Politics: A Note on Gerard de Vries' Paper." *Social Studies of Science* 37, no. 5 (2007): 811–20.

Latour, Bruno. *An Inquiry into Modes of Existence*. Cambridge, MA: Harvard University Press, 2013.

Lewis, Peter, and Jordan Guiao. *The Public Square Project: Reimagining Our Digital Future*. Melbourne: Melbourne University Publishing, 2021.

MacLeod, Anna, Paula Cameron, Rola Ajjawi, Olga Kits, and Jonathan Tummons. "Actor-network Theory and Ethnography: Sociomaterial Approaches to Researching Medical Education." *Perspectives on Medical Education* 8, no. 3 (2019): 177–86.

McQuire, Scott. *Geomedia: Networked Cities and the Future of Public Space*. New York: John Wiley & Sons, 2017.

Offenhuber, Dietmar, and Carlo Ratti. *Decoding the City: Urbanism in the Age of Big Data*. Basel, Switzerland: Birkhäuser, 2014.

Papastergiadis, Nikos, ed. *Ambient Screens and Transnational Public Spaces*. Hong Kong: Hong Kong University Press, 2016.

Sweeney, Jill, Kathy Mee, Pauline McGuirk, and Kristian Ruming. "Assembling Placemaking: Making and Remaking Place in a Regenerating City." *Cultural Geographies* 25, no. 4 (2018): 571–87.

Wang, Yang. *Digital Media in Urban China: Locating Guangzhou*. Lanham, Maryland: Rowman & Littlefield International, 2019.

13

Decoding the Phygital Space: Exploring How Youths Produce New Urban Festival Spaces through Social Interactions

Rebecca Onafuye

Introduction

The rise of digital technology usage in festival landscapes is undoubtedly altering the characteristics of physical and virtual space. The interplay between the spatial elements and digital features causes a shift in the space-making paradigm, and as a result formulates a homogenous visual of a new dimensional space (Kirsch 1995; Salinas 2014a).[1] In that, the questions arise: how can physical and digital social spaces interact synchronously? How can we begin to visualize and dwell within said space? What does the intersection between physical elements, digital features, and sociocultural norms look like? While festival spaces are an integral theoretical concept in various research fields (Stevens and Shin 2012),[2] the influence of digitalization and societal norms has resulted to festival spaces no longer being described merely as a physical construct. Works conducted by Ciolfi (2004),[3] Benedikt (1992),[4] Dyson (1998),[5] and others have argued that physical and digital models do not seamlessly interlock with one another. However, the unique characteristics of festivals spaces' unique characteristics, the sociocultural connotations surrounding youths, and how they use social media within them, suggests otherwise. Based on this insight, this chapter suggests how both dimensions of space and its youths can coexist and interact within a multi-facetted environment. Additionally, it provides an agenda for further research on the production of hybrid festival space, revealing that the relationships between all three aspects (physical, digital, and sociocultural) lead to what we call "phygital space." Building upon Henri Lefebvre's triad of space, the findings from this qualitative and quantitative study propose a framework for understanding and visualizing the production

of new phygital space. In an attempt to depict the contemporary interactions of youth's usage of digital media, new notions of space and culture emerge as the forefront of such communication. In that, it suggests that phygital space is socially produced, whilst providing

The Structure of Spatial Experiences in Festivals

From the late 1960s urban festivals have played a significant part in the social lives of individuals all over the world, from different cultures and societies. Although, not a new phenomenon, it has become an integral social fact as a space for sensory experience and temporary escape from external social relations (Gardiner 2010).[6] These forces are moulded by the distinctive behaviours, social interactions of the festival-goers, and by physical settings (Stevens et al. 2017).[7] The newly formed role of urban festivals increases sensation, influences interaction, and produces memorable expressions within new spaces. This is achieved by the compression of youth festival-goers, their behaviours, and activities in a restricted space. Willems-Braun (1994)[8] debates that festival landscapes can act as a medium to heighten communication and community building through "the transformation of urban spaces characterized by rationalization and efficiency into 'festival spaces' marked by intersubjectivity" (1994: 78). Braun's suggestion of intersubjectivity insinuates that festivals infuse a personal connection between individuals, the spatial arrangement, activities, and other social components. Supplementarily, the subjective and objective breakdown of festivals further insinuates the notion of liminality being imbedded into the festivals physical and social constructs (Taylor et al. 2014).[9] The qualities of liminal space help to frame the understanding of youth's intimate but temporal connection to festival space, as it reveals the hidden physical, digital, and sociocultural qualities that aid different interactions within the landscape. Rohr (2020)[10] describes liminal space as an area "where we are betwixt and between the familiar and completely unknown. There alone is our world left behind […]. This is the sacred space where the old world is able to fall apart, and a bigger world is revealed." His association with liminality and words such as "betwixt," "sacred," and "a bigger world" not only insinuates a grander perspective of such reconstruction, but it redefines the dynamics of the space from an intimate and subjective angle.

 Rohr's (2002) findings confirm that festival spaces can be reconceptualized as nuanced and multi-dimensional by considering the modern forms of digital and physical interaction. Whilst existing literature using the idea of festivals as case studies has focused on the activities that take place within the physicality of the space, and as a result has failed to pay attention to the possibilities of space

expansion and reproduction through digital advancements. Digital attributes of social media manifests in physical space, and through this shared commitment and "ritual" of physical and digital interaction, it creates an avenue for youths to transform the space into almost anything at any given time. Lefebvre's (1974)[11] idea of representational space enlightens how social space is not fixed and can reflect relationships of power and agency. He states, "nothing disappears completely [...]. In space, what came earlier continues to underpin what follows [...]. Pre-existing space underpins not only durable spatial arrangements but also representational spaces and their attendant imagery and mythic narratives" (1974: 230). This research acknowledges Lefebvre's idea of representational space as the space for youths—a space where the objects within the festival are interacted with, associated with the social engagements of youth and used to build different spatial experiences. The new constructions of festivals through youth's physical and digital experiences and interactions reveal its subverted and social nature, and therefore begin to illustrate the social modes of production.

The main spatial aspects of festival settings are centred around its physical, digital, and cultural characteristics. Whilst these social settings have a deeper connection to both the attendees and the environment that they are situated in (Cudny et al. 2012),[12] the majority of the work conducted, lacks the modern understanding of British Nigerian youth's ways of exploring, experiencing, and socializing within the urban environment. Stevens and Shin's (2012)[13] study on the dynamics of social life within the local space revealed two spatial parameters of festival space—*axiality* and *permeability*—characteristics that frame ways in how festival attendees introduce new uses within local space. Such discovery can be tailored to the urban festivals that youth's dwell in—their modern ways of engaging youths physically and digitally present at festivals reveals an alternative method of physically experiencing space. For example, new social media trends that are practised within the festival landscape, automatically weave digital and sociocultural dynamics into the festival space, thus creating an intersection between both worlds. Urban festivals consist of multiple areas that house different programmes and social activities that contribute to the overall perception and experience of the space.

Looking at the physical form of urban festivals, it is clear that these landscapes promote togetherness and interaction, in the exchange of ideas and social conversation; whilst creating a sense of place. Oldenburg's (2001) work can be used to introduce a new theme—festivals as third space, a concept that Soja (1996)[14] defines as "a particular way of thinking about and interpreting socially produced space." Here Soja suggests that festivals, like third space, encompass social extracts and objective and subjective qualities that convey a social message that can be tailored to suit individual and communal experiences. The spatial objects of festivals contribute to the youth's primary perception of space, whilst their music tastes

and contemporary forms of communication (explained in the previous section) become secondary and produce a sociocultural layer. These new arrangements and understandings of festival space—new physical and digital objects, interaction, and so on, encourage the space to *talk* and be reproduced over time. Similar to third space, the concept of liminal space in festival landscapes aids youths to comprehend how a shared purpose, shared experiences and shared culture at urban festivals create a sense of community amongst them. This joint force of physical and digital social activity strengthens the foundation of new space, and invites phygital affordances within the landscape, through youth's use of digital technologies, most especially social media. For instance, different youths are interested in showcasing different aspects of the space—some desire to socially engage with the celebrities and showcase their exchanges, whilst others a more inclined to display the physical activities on site. Not only does this afford a new stream of technology into the festival space, but exposes the behaviours and builds connections between the youth physically present, and those watching at a distance. Heim indicates that youth's desire and "marriage to technology" stem from the "aesthetic fascination" (1991: 60)—its simple but complex forms create an easy experience for youths to navigate and build adaptable connections between like-minded youths, therefore causing a deeper and an intimate relationship with digital technologies; what Heim describes as something that "not only fascinates our eyes and minds, it captures our hearts" (1991: 61). Heim's idea of *third-person bodies* suggests that youths are not the primary occupants of such space—in disagreement with this concept, British Nigerian youth's version of digital space is a representation of their morals, values, shared likes and dislikes, and other communal trends. It is only right that they become the sole occupants of such space as they understand the digital dynamics, navigation, and overall modes of dwelling within the landscape. Their love affair with social media runs deeper than the surface-level concepts presented in current literature—youths are constantly searching for spaces where they can materialize their trends, discuss their worries, and socially be in the presence of their peers.

The examinations of social behaviour in this chapter seek to focus specifically on how youth's spatial experiences, digital behaviours, and sociocultural norms influence hybrid space production. Lefebvre (1974)[15] and Pauly (1986)[16] support this triadic cultural division by insinuating that our experiences in space are governed by the different cultures we encounter during our past, our present, and even our future. Youth's experiences within space are dependent on a variety of attributes; one of which are the social and cultural norms formed them. Each norm is expressed through the behaviours and is powered by the sounds they hear, the forms of the structures around them, the garments worn to the festivals, and the multiple social groups sharing the same space. Through these attributes, different behaviours emerge and contribute to the cultural aspect of youths and how they

communally share and manifest their social cultures inside the festivals. Relph's (1976)[17] body of work persistently emphasizes that places are constructed through bodily and perceptual experience and are anything but void. According to him, space is a "isometric plane or a kind of container that holds places" (Hubbard et al. 2008: 44). He argues that, for the relationship of place to be seen through the experiences of individuals, the study of space must be done in the same manner. Although Relph explains the multiple types of spatial experience—"a continuum that has direct experience at one extreme and abstract thought at the other" (1976: 9), he carefully identifies two modes of space: the first, which is an inherent, bodily, and instant mode of spatial experience—pragmatic space, perceptual space, and existential space, whilst the second cerebral, ideal, and tangible mode—planning, cognitive, and abstract space.

Methodology: The Phygital Framework

The fieldwork for this research had three stages: The first stage was a two-part participant observation of multifaceted social behaviours occurring within the physical and digital public spaces; during the selected festivals for this study. The second, using online hashtags (#) was to collect and analyse a series of online Twitter and Instagram data from all three festivals. Using the Twitter API, metadata such as (1) the username of individuals associated to the tweet; (2) geolocation; (3) the message attached to the hashtag; and (4) the date and time were collected to highlight patterns in the online conversations. The third stage was in-depth interviews with the youths at the festivals. All methods were set to expose the relationships between the physical and digital public realms, and the social interactions of youths. The analysis sought to formulate a clear framework for new productions of urban and local space. It revealed the conservations surrounding each festival, and explored the impact of sociocultural influences amongst youth and how they perceived and experienced the space. Additionally, it exposed their modes of interaction based on their physical and digital movements; thus, enabling significant relationships between the physical, digital, and sociocultural characteristics. Together, these aspects illustrated the phygital space triad that suggests the role festivals play in the hybrid space-making paradigm.

This research focused on three relatively new festivals: (1) Days Like This, (2) AfroNation, and (3) No Signal/Recess. Each festival was initiated between 2018 and 2021, where the vast majority of attendees were local youth residents in London, United Kingdom. The overarching aim of this research was to demonstrate a significant shift in social space-making through digital channels. To successfully achieve this, each festival had to have a physical and digital aspect, to build

connections between the physicality of the space and the digital interactions; which in turn, suggest the premise of space reproduction. Days Like This was chosen to predominately analyse the physical (and partly digital) interaction, AfroNation, both the physical and digital, whilst No Signal/Recess emphasized the digital (and partly physical) exchanges between youth present. All festivals were selected based on the social, geographical, and cultural contexts surrounding each festival. With this, the main purpose was to focus on the empirical realities of how youths acted within the spaces specially arranged for these festivals and its wider local context. The duo-examination of all three festivals began to illustrate the scope of youth's spatial experiences during the festivals, thus, exposing a range of ways in which the spatial arrangements influenced online interactions and vice versa. This relationship provided an opportunity to frame and further examine a new notion of hybrid space—phygital—a space of spectacle where physical arrangements host digital penetrations and expose cultural foundations.

Fieldnotes, photographs, videos, site analysis, Twitter, and Instagram data from the live physical and digital observations were complemented by literal studies/reports/journals from previous researchers. Physical and digital observations took place before, during, and after the festival to explore the physical, digital, and sociocultural impacts at different scales. They focused on the following central interests.

Festival space (physical aspect)

- Organization of the festival objects—stage, barriers, public and private areas.
- Festivals' contextual impact on the existing local space—activities, events, etc.
- How youths create and navigate the digital festival space.
- How festivalgoers (youth) use and interact with the physical space.

Festival behaviour (digital aspect)

- Social interactions and relationships between the different youth groups.
- Behaviour stimulated by the course of events within the space.
- Activities occurring within the space and online.
- How youths integrate social media within the space.

Festival culture (sociocultural aspect)

- The different youth cultures exposed at the festival.
- The manifestation of online cultures being practised within the physical festival space and how it impacts online/physical interactions.
- Intensive displays of social norms and cues within the physical and digital space.

By closely observing youth's sensory perceptions, behaviour, and social interactions during the festivals, the fieldwork and analysis produced sought to anticipated to shed light on how youth's social realities are structured around the distinctive spatial arrangements of the festival. The analysis of the data collected, focused on the topological, material, and representational features of the physical and digital settings of these events. Observing youth's actions, behaviours, and cultures illustrated the youth's role of hybrid space production and further exposed the key factors which were the foundations of this new space, and that were identified in the literature review: festival activities, digital culture, security, and intimacy. The ethnographical study examined the distinct sensations, bodily actions, and cultural norms associated with the festival, to enable a deeper understanding of how phygital spaces are produced and perceived by youths.

Towards a Definition of Phygital Space

The intensity and diversity of interactions amongst the present and online festivalgoers at all festivals have established that phygital space is socially produced. Fundamentally, when discussing the social production of new space, it is important to understand that whilst it is built upon an existing landscape and its spatial practices, it can only be produced through the lived practices and interactions of youths at festivals. Despite this, the analysis of raw social media data, spatial observations and direct interviews with youths present, have openly challenged, developed, and reconfigured a handful of ideologies that discuss youth digital culture, space-making, and other concepts that are like that of this research. Moreover, it has presented a new sociocultural angle to look at social space-making, particularly festival spaces and community forming within hybrid spaces. In addition, this study has explored the numerous counteracting and supporting arrangements of phygital spaces, and it should therefore be noted that although this new hybrid space is unique and easily produced, it bears a significant level of power to adjust the social experiences of youths. Whilst studies by Boyd (2008, 2014),[18] Gardner and Davis (2013),[19] Turkle (1996),[20] and others, have suggested that social environments have a significant impact on how youths interact, this research has argued that the spatial and digital interactions of youth, can in fact, manipulate, reconfigure and reproduce the spaces they are in. Having said that, the phygital framework of such space must be able to be applied to both physical/digital space and sociocultural practices, to offer an in-depth relationship between spatial dynamics, social practices, and phygital space-making.

Festival Activities

Festival activities were identified as the most influential factor, across all three case studies. From the three datasets (spatial, digital, and interviews), musical performances from celebrity artists and local youth, were the activity that generated the most positive data, and stimulated the majority of the interactions and conversations that were retrieved. As well as these activities shaping the spatial experiences of youths present, it also highlighted the pragmatic realities of how youth act within specially arranged environments, and the groups of communities they build based on shared cultural norms. Although only three festivals were analysed for this study and are unable to summarize the spatial experiences of youths, in its entirety, the key themes explained gives an incline to the various ways that the special arrangements of festivals activities, shape youth's experience and produce spaces of meaning and social value. At Days Like This festival the first three DJ's at the first festival invited all youths present to approach the dance floor and perform certain dance moves. Similar instances were presented at Afro Nation Ghana and Recess; however, the most popular celebrity artists were deliberately scheduled as the last activity, to encourage youths to stay till the end of the festival.

Additionally, another significant aspect that was discovered at the DLT Brunch festival was the brunch activity. The shared love of cultural food, drink, and the overall ambience generated a range of conversations between the youth and encouraged them to share different perceptions, thoughts, and ideas based on their interests, thus introducing a sense of agency. Afro Nation Ghana used heritage and social and digital culture as tools of inspiration, for youths to construct multi-dimensional spaces where they were free to adjust their social routines, to fit the new constructs of phygital space. On the other hand, No signal and Recess, celebrated the relationships between different social classes, societies, and location-based communities. The obscure blend of youths from different areas produced a homogenous space, where each individual could interact and experience other local cultures, based on the activities arranged by the festival organizers. Whilst this proved the flexibility and power of phygital space, it also demonstrated that this hybrid landscape is socially produced, with elements that break biased boundaries, and can be produced within multiple social settings.

Digital Culture

The sociological thread that connected all three case studies, was the digital culture that youths continuously practised through their new methods of communication. Colloquial language, gifs, hashtags, and other online trends—also known

as *signs*, were used to celebrate certain instances taking place at each festival. The general consensus of them was that the digital behaviours expressed by the youth were a replicate of their human behaviour. Physical actions they performed at the festivals were applied to the digital landscapes in the form of layers and will be explained in the next section. The digital observations for DLT Brunch set the tone for understanding the ecosystem of phygital culture. Most of the messaging and ways of communication were almost identical, which unveiled the sense of uniformities and grouped them as a single entity. However, Afro Nation Ghana with its own cultural connotations highlighted the importance of one's heritage and its impact on public behaviours. That said, No Signal/Recess came from a different digital perspective, and underlined online pop-cultures level of influence on the way youths experienced the digital world. Whilst each social media trend differed based on the spatiality of the physical context, it visually explained what Papadimitriou (2012) calls a *high-context culture*. Developed in the early 1970s, all the interactions, messages, images, and so on, were implicitly decoded in the same manner. Youths could easily act and behave in the same manner, across all three festivals because they shared similar languages, expressions, sociologies, and methods—which provided a solid base for phygital layers to be built upon.

Comparatively to Hjorth and Richardson (2017)[21] who used the digital phenomenon *Pokémon GO* to reflect on the intricacies of location-based mobile applications, and Raressens' (2006)[22] and Mäyrä's (2012)[23] study on playful identities and the affectivity of digital culture, youths within the phygital culture chose to engage with one another, as opposed to youths from other localities. This detection was observed at all three case studies but was categorically explained at the last festival of No Signal. The notion of universality demonstrated youth's ability to connect and define themselves differently, through their relationship with others. Their high levels of comfort and interactions with other individuals of the same descent materialized Papadimitriou's (2012) concept, but at the same time, embraced a sense of individuality. Although patterns within the data examined the concept of togetherness and unity within shared cultures, the data collected introduced an ounce of individualism within the collective phygital culture.

Security and Intimacy

Security and intimacy, two opposing but complementary determinants, created a hidden sentimental component to the overall structure of phygital space. Its flexibility to influence within physical and digital environments proved its importance on youth's phygital footprint in festival spaces. To begin, security in conjunction with privacy, involved youth's eagerness to share instances of the festival, and

their personal thoughts and feelings about it. Additionally, their proclamation of the festival was dependent on their capability to control what was being distributed, and who was interacting with their tweets, videos, gifs, and so on (Belanger et al. 2002; Eastlick et al. 2006).[24] This factor emerged from the Chorus TV/Mosquito data (the locations of some youths were non-existent) at Afro Nation Ghana, whilst reasons behind it, were expressed during the interviews. Many youths expressed their thoughts about maintaining a certain level of privacy on social media, whilst others counteracted these feelings, by declaring their opinions of security and intimacy.

Boyd (2008),[25] Lee and Chang (2016),[26] and Jarvis (2011)[27] perceive security as a form of protection. In their individual studies, they collectively argue that youth's new sense of publicness changes the way they experience and interact and create real relationships. Whilst this research initially began with this argument, the data proved different—it showed that youth's sudden need to be public (and at the same time private) is a ploy to invite a sense of security and create intimate relationships. Their social methods of "don't show, don't tell" and other modes of interaction within their social culture, and in real space, strengthened their connections, and enhanced the last level of phygital space. To add weight to this point, Gardner and Davis (2013)[28] presented a new generation that approached intimacy, identity, and imagination. Through their extensive studies, they concluded that social media opens a new way of observing the youth world; one of which this research proves that youth are producing with the help of festival spatial dynamics. Both arguments are relevant to this topic as they cooperatively propose the requirement of a new social realm, where youths are free to privately or publicly dwell in a space that enables the feeling of security and intimacy.

The strategic selection of case studies, and the physical, digital, and sociocultural factors examined, demonstrate the imaginable characterization of phygital space. Each influential group of determinants represents one of the main pillars (as a developed alternative of Lefebvre's [1974] triad of space)[29] that depicts the underlining layers needed when producing a new hybrid space. It is through this categorization that youth's new modes of interaction can be validated to suggest the tools needed in socially cohabiting within these landscapes. The visual imagery (Figures 13.1–13.3) is a series of illustrations, aimed to visualize phygital space, act as a framework to understand the structural, digital, and sociocultural aspects of phygital space, and to provide opportunities for future research in this area. Each set diagrammatically clarifies the existing festival landscape, youth's interaction, a factor of influence, and demarcation of hybrid space; and at the same time offers a complex understanding of each layer's qualities and its social practices. All layers of information have been plotted as a result of the direct observation conducted at the festival.

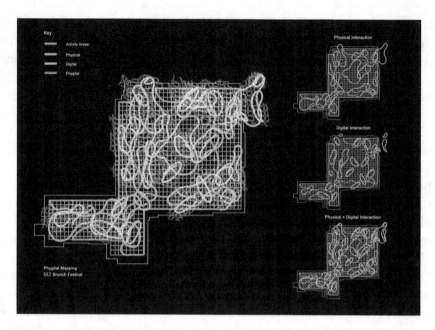

FIGURE 13.1: Visual diagram of phygital space (middle left), and the dissection of physical interaction (top right), digital interaction (middle right), and the intersection of physical and digital within the festival landscape (bottom right). Rebecca Onafuye, 2021.

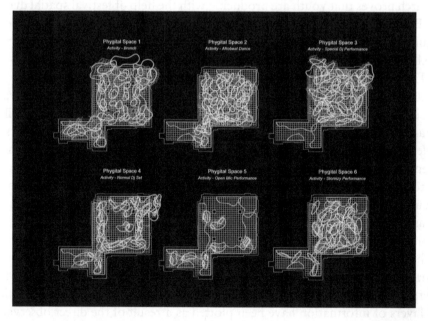

FIGURE 13.2: Mapping of physical interaction within the festival landscape. Rebecca Onafuye, 2021.

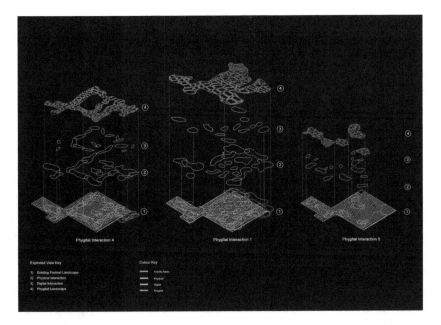

FIGURE 13.3: Exploded visual of phygital space—highlighting that phygital space is a series of layers—layers of physical and digital interaction. Rebecca Onafuye, 2021.

Phygital spaces are built upon existing landscapes, youth's social cues, taste cultures, and other factors of social dwelling, whereby physical and digital traditions are dwelt through the festival interaction and youth's lived experiences (Lefebvre 1974),[30] and therefore transformed into information and then, new space. However, this research has argued that the production of phygital space must also take into consideration, the lived and adopted cultures of its inhabitants; in this context youth festivalgoers. Their experiences, social backgrounds, and needs as a collective tribe require careful understanding, with an effort to create intimate spaces of value and solace. Subsequently, the ways in which new modes of interaction are represented, should reflect and act on the regular interactions of youth in festival spaces; to centralize the lived behaviours and experiences of British Nigerian youths. The diagrams of physical and digital interaction above represent the phygital experience in its physical and digital form.

Conclusion: A New Sense of Festival Space

By describing and analysing the physical, digital, and sociocultural factors that influenced social behaviours and contemporary interactions amongst youths, this

chapter identified and visually illustrated key determinants that dissected the physicalities, digital constructs, and the sociocultural qualities that make up the phygital world. Festival activities, digital culture and security, and intimacy were the three factors that ran through all three case studies—which enacts the festival space by suggesting its countercultural history brings together youth, purpose, and solidarity. As all factors encouraged diverse interactions amongst the cohort, it disrupted the traditional constructs of urban festivals by introducing modern forms of digital communication—colloquial language, social media trends, and other informal behaviours and constructed a unique creative culture that empowered youths. This chapter through the visual images and diagrams outlining the interactions, showed that phygital space forms peculiar societies that express different levels of freedom and agency. Its major and crucial quality is the idea of remoulding its phygital pillars to suit the social dynamics of the communities that dwell within the festival space. Through this, this research has clarified that spaces of youthful festival spaces are more than ordinary landscapes; they are environments of worship, inspiration, mystery, spectacle, tradition, and transition. The relations of body and space or the notion of spatial identity contribute to the social production and reproduction of phygital spaces, and demonstrate multiple shifts in its physical structure.

The shifting landscapes of the festival space are to be seen as the physical representations of shifts in youth's values and priorities, and represent a change in their concerns and social consciousness. Their subjective and objective attachment to the physicalness and digitalness of festivals embraces the individualistic and communal qualities of new space. This research elaborates a new notion of space in the field of architecture and space-making—phygital. It includes physical perceptions of space, digital media, and sociocultural understandings of youth culture and community, and has articulated in detail a concise framework for the production of phygital space. Additionally, this research exposes a need for further studies into the adaptable perceptions and experiences of architecture, and to observe whether the concept of phygital space can be established in other social settings.

NOTES

1. D. Kirsh, "The Intelligent Use of Space." *Artificial Intelligence* 73, no. 1–2 (1995), 31–68.
   L. Salinas, "Digital Public Space(s): Redefining Publicness," in *Social Media and the Transformation of Public Space* (Amsterdam, 2014).
2. Q. Stevens and H. Shin, "Urban Festivals and Local Social Space." *Planning Practice and Research* 29, no. 1 (2012): 1–20.
3. L. Ciolfi, "Understanding Spaces and Places: Extending Interaction Design Paradigms." *Cognition, Technology & Work* 6, no. 1 (2004): 37–40.

4. M. Benedikt, *Cyberspace*. Cambridge, MA: MIT Press, 1992.
5. E. Dyson, *Release 2.1: A Design for Living in the Digital Age*. New York: Broadway, 1998.
6. M. Gardiner, "Everyday Utopianism: Lefebvre and His Critics." *Cultural Studies* 18, no. 3 (2010): 228–54.
7. M. Stevens, T. Rees, P. Coffee, N. Steffens, S. Haslam, and R. Polman, "A Social Identity Approach to Understanding and Promoting Physical Activity." *Sports Medicine* 47 (2017): 1911–18.
8. B. Willems-Braun, "Situating Cultural Politics: Fringe Festivals and the Production of Space of Intersubjectivity." *Environment and Planning D: Society and Space* 12, no. 1 (1994), 75–104.
9. J. Taylor, A. Bennett, and L. Woodward, *Festivalisation of Culture*, 1st ed. (Surrey: Ashgate Publishing Ltd., 2014).
10. R. Rohr, *Between Two Worlds—Center for Action and Contemplation* ([online] Center for Action and Contemplation, 2020). Accessed January 21, 2020. https://cac.org/between-two-worlds-2020-04-26/.
11. H. Lefebvre, *The Production of Space*, trans. Donald Nicholson Smith (Oxford, UK: Basil Blackwell Ltd., 1974).
12. W. Cudny, P. Koree, and R. Rouba, "Resident's Perception of Festivals: The Case Study of Lodz, Sociológia." *Slovak Sociological Review* 44, no. 6 (2012): 704–28.
13. Q. Stevens and H. Shin, "Urban Festivals and Local Social Space." *Planning Practice and Research* 29, no. 1 (2012): 1–20.
14. E. Soja, *Thirdspace*. Malden: Blackwell, 1996.
15. Lefebvre, *The Production of Space*.
16. J. J. Pauly, "The Use of Tone: On Rereading Richard Hoggart." *Critical Studies in Mass Communication* 3, no. 1 (1986): 102–06.
17. E. Relph, *Place and Placelessness*, 1st ed. (London: Pio Limited, 1976).
18. D. Boyd, *Taken Out of Context: American Teen Sociality in Networked Publics*, PhD dissertation (Berkeley, CA: University of California Berkeley, 2008). D. Boyd, *It's Complicated the Social Lives of Networked Teens* (New Haven, Connecticut: Yale University Press, 2014).
19. H. Gardner and K. Davis, *The App Generation: How Today's Youth Navigate Identity, Intimacy, and Imagination in a Digital World* (Yale University Press, 2013).
20. S. Turkle, *Life on the Screen: Identity in the Age of the Internet*, 1st ed. (London: Weidenfeld & Nicholson, 1996).
21. L. Hjorth and I. Richardson, "*Pokémon GO*: Mobile Media Play, Place-Making, and the Digital Wayfarer." *Mobile Media & Communication* 5, no. 1 (2017): 3–14.
22. J. Raessens, "Playful Identities, or the Ludification of Culture." *Games & Culture* 1, no. 1 (2006): 52–57.
23. F. Mäyrä, "Playful Mobile Communication: Services Supporting the Culture of Play." *Interactions: Studies in Communication & Culture* 3, no. 1 (2012): 55–70.

24. F. Belanger, J. Hiller, and W. Smith, "Trustworthiness in Electronic Commerce: The Role of Privacy, Security, and Site Attributes." *The Journal of Strategic Information Systems* 11, no. 3-4 (2002): 245-70.
25. Boyd, *Taken Out of Context.*
26. T. Lee and P. Chang, "Examining the Relationships Among Festivalscape, Experiences, and Identity: Evidence From Two Taiwanese Aboriginal Festivals." *Leisure Studies* 36, no. 4 (2016), 1-15.
27. J. Jarvis, *Public Parts: How Sharing in the Digital Age Improves the Way We Work and Live*, 1st ed. (New York: Simon & Schuster, 2011).
28. Gardner and Davis, *The App Generation.*
29. Lefebvre, *The Production of Space.*
30. Ibid.

BIBLIOGRAPHY

Belanger, F., J. Hiller, and W. Smith. "Trustworthiness in Electronic Commerce: The Role of Privacy, Security, and Site Attributes." *The Journal of Strategic Information Systems* 11, no. 3-4 (2002): 245-70.

Benedikt, M. *Cyberspace*. Cambridge, MA: MIT Press, 1992.

Boyd, D. *Taken Out of Context: American Teen Sociality in Networked Publics*. PhD dissertation. Berkeley, CA: University of California Berkeley, 2008.

Boyd, D. "Social Network Sites as Networked Publics: Affordances, Dynamics, and Implications." In *Networked Self: Identity, Community, and Culture on Social Network Sites*. Edited by Zizi Papacharissi, 39-58. 2010.

Boyd, D. *It's Complicated: The Social Lives of Networked Teens*. New Haven, Connecticut: Yale University Press, 2014.

Ciolfi, L. "Understanding Spaces as Places: Extending Interaction Design Paradigms." *Cognition, Technology & Work* 6, no. 1 (2004): 37-40.

Cudny, W., P. Korec, and R. Rouba. "Resident's Perception of Festivals: The Case Study of Lodz, Sociológia." *Slovak Sociological Review* 44, no. 6 (2012): 704-28.

Dyson, E. *Release 2.1: A Design for Living in the Digital Age*. New York: Broadway, 1998.

Eastlick, M., S. Lotz, and P. Warrington. "Understanding Online B-to-C Relationships: An Integrated Model of Privacy Concerns, Trust, and Commitment." *Journal of Business Research* 59, no. 8 (2006): 877-86.

Gardiner, M. "Everyday Utopianism: Lefebvre and His Critics." *Cultural Studies* 18, no. 3 (2010): 228-54.

Gardner, H., and K. Davis. *The App Generation: How Today's Youth Navigate Identity, Intimacy, and Imagination in a Digital World*. New Haven, Connecticut: Yale University Press, 2013.

Hjorth, L., and I. Richardson. "*Pokémon GO*: Mobile Media Play, Place-Making, and the Digital Wayfarer." *Mobile Media & Communication* 5, no. 1 (2017): 3-14.

Jarvis, J. *Public Parts: How Sharing in the Digital Age Improves the Way We Work and Live.* 1st ed. New York: Simon & Schuster, 2011.

Kirsh, D. "The Intelligent Use of Space." *Artificial Intelligence* 73, no. 1–2 (1995), 31–68.

Lee, T., and P. Chang. "Examining the Relationships Among Festivalscape, Experiences, and Identity: Evidence from Two Taiwanese Aboriginal Festivals." *Leisure Studies* 36, no. 4 (2016), 1–15.

Lefebvre, H. *The Production of Space.* Translated by Donald Nicholson Smith. Oxford, UK: Basil Blackwell Ltd., 1974.

Mäyrä, F. "Playful Mobile Communication: Services Supporting the Culture of Play." *Interactions: Studies in Communication & Culture* 3, no. 1 (2012): 55–70.

Oldenburg, R. *Celebrating the Third Place: Inspiring Stories about the "Great Good Places" at the Heart of Our Communities.* 1st ed. Chicago, IL: Da Capo Press, 2009.

Pauly, J. J. "The Use of Tone: On Rereading Richard Hoggart." *Critical Studies in Mass Communication* 3, no. 1 (1986): 102–06.

Raessens, J. "Playful Identities, or the Ludification of Culture." *Games & Culture* 1, no. 1 (2006): 52–57.

Relph, E. *Place and Placelessness.* 1st ed. London: Pio Limited, 1976.

Rohr, R. *Between Two Worlds—Center for Action and Contemplation.* [online] Center for Action and Contemplation, 2020. Accessed January 21, 2020. https://cac.org/between-two-worlds-2020-04-26/.

Salinas, L. "Digital Public Space(s): Redefining Publicness." In *Social Media and the Transformation of Public Space.* Amsterdam, 2014.

Soja, E. *Thirdspace.* Malden: Blackwell, 1996.

Stevens, M., T. Rees, P. Coffee, N. Steffens, S. Haslam, and R. Polman. "A Social Identity Approach to Understanding and Promoting Physical Activity." *Sports Medicine* 47 (2017): 1911–18, https://doi.org.10.10007/s40279-017-0720-4.

Stevens, Q., and H. Shin. "Urban Festivals and Local Social Space." *Planning Practice and Research* 29, no. 1 (2012): 1–20.

Taylor, J., A. Bennett, and I. Woodward. *Festivalisation of Culture.* 1st ed. Surrey: Ashgate Publishing Ltd., 2014.

Turkle, S. *Life on the Screen: Identity in the Age of the Internet.* 1st ed. London: Weidenfeld & Nicholson, 1996.

Willems-Braun, B. "Situating Cultural Politics: Fringe Festivals and the Production of Spaces of Intersubjectivity." *Environment and Planning D: Society and Space* 12, no. 1 (1994), 75–104.

14

Airbnb Plus Filter: Creating Strategic and Photogenic Interiors

Esra Duygun and Duygu Koca

Introduction

As a peer-to-peer accommodation provider, Airbnb has a transformative impact on the current temporary hospitality industry. Since 2010, the impact has been discussed in many different fields. When the studies on the disruptive innovation created by Airbnb in the accommodation sector are examined, two approaches can be mentioned, mainly based on economics and psychology. However, little has been done to theorize the impact of Airbnb on the domestic space.

In current literature, it is noted that studies in this area have shown its existence in recent years. Studies on the relationship between Airbnb and interior design are generally based on the analysis of home photos presented within Airbnb. As an example of these studies; Rahimi et al. (2016) listed the photos of Airbnb homes in ten major cities to explore geographical differences in interior styles. The photos were analysed according to elements such as colour, comfort, spaciousness, orderliness, warmth and cosiness, the existence of a personal identity, theme, and cultural components. This study reveals that globalization has blurred the design.[1] Nguyen et al. (2018) conducted a multimedia search to understand how the featured photos on the Airbnb platform affect the first impressions of potential customers. The study provides important data to determine whether there will be a consistent breakdown of home interior photos or whether they can be grouped according to their physical characteristics.[2] In the research of Mat Nawi et al. (2019), it was determined that physical environmental elements such as ambiance, decoration, and layout have a positive effect on the behavioural intentions and preferences of potential Airbnb customers.[3] In another detailed study of the geo-located images of indoor living spaces listed on Airbnb, Liu et al. (2019) focused on wall art, colour, plants, books, and decorative objects blessed with

Airbnb Plus status. It is noted that these elements are used in statistically different ways globally, but common usage trends are presented.[4] In the studies on existing literature shows that the determining factors are; colour, decor, lighting, ambience, cultural components, and room types. One different study in the literature is Murialdo's (2019) work. This study describes that "Airbnb platform is not just a technological device to list and organize information, but a two-way mechanism (instrument) able to change the cultural and material role of interiors."[5] Although most of these assessments are made from a customer-centric perspective in general terms "Is it possible to talk about a common decoration trend?" or "Can Airbnb interior images be categorized?"

In these studies, the influence of Airbnb and tips on interior design and decoration to attract more customers were not included in the field of inquiry. In fact, the house is a personal space that the user or the host can customize and revise according to their character or wishes. It is interesting that in Airbnb, the house is open to an anonymous user worldwide. Some design steps are given to attract global users who are not related to the host in terms of interior architecture and design discipline. This chapter looks at the process of designing Airbnb houses from the perspective of interior architecture and design discipline. Do the interior design ideas of Airbnb affect the design process, content, and context of the future of interiors?

Accordingly, in the first part of the section, the hierarchical order created during the operation of Airbnb and the main factors are defined. In the second part, Airbnb Plus status, which is the subject of the study and where Airbnb's criteria for interior design ideas is visible, has been evaluated. These criteria, namely Plus standards, are shared on globally with interior design and home decoration tips given on both Airbnb's own website and the social networking platform Pinterest. These posts, which include strategic tips, are mainly based on illustrations and "example house photos" as a visual reference. In this direction, in the final part, Airbnb-Pinterest cooperation is discussed. Airbnb's Pinterest posts are examined and the "strategic" and "photogenic" qualities of the interiors are defined through formal and discursive analysis.

In addition, in line with the given clues; it is seen that the roles, hierarchies, and contexts of space and its objects have changed. The underlying element of this transformation is that the clues are generally focused on "creating an environment" and "visual perception" through one style. As a result, interior design turns into a total mental practice of global social praxis mediated by the production and consumption of images, devoid of professional understanding, ethics, and methods. This situation minimizes the discipline of interior design to an image devoid of depth and content and provides a basis for professional discussion.

Methodology

This chapter considers Airbnb as a space with multiple meanings, reflecting the transitional nature of standardization on a global scale, where spatial criteria, roles, and hierarchies are redefined. In this chapter, interior design and home decoration tips for Airbnb Plus status acting as "verified design" and "new tier of homes" through the social networking platform Pinterest were examined and the "strategic" and "photogenic" qualities of the interiors are tried to be defined. The services provided by the Airbnb Plus programme are supported by tips provided by the Airbnb and Pinterest website through "sample houses" as visual references and illustrations. In this respect, it is important to define the terms in the clues, to identify the selected themes, and then to assess the interior design in the context of these guidelines. Sharing illustrations and photos play an essential role in transmitting clues to an anonymous global audience in a message. For this reason, the (visual) clues—space and form of representation—were evaluated through formal analysis, with a priority in the study. Clue-led posts that appeared as editorial content are evaluated discursively, as well as the formal evaluation of the spatial organization, materials, connections, and objects, as well as perceptions and emotions conveyed by the Airbnb language.

Airbnb Background

Airbnb is an online platform where people can rent their home as accommodation, through descriptions and photos of owners and home space. Airbnb has reached a global scale by constantly updating its hosting and rental applications, strengthening its technological infrastructure, and making effective use of social media. Many studies have considered the technological infrastructure, which played an active role in the rise of Airbnb, as the major ability to create an atmosphere of trust between hosts and guests.[6]

Ert and Flesher (2019) describe the three main indicators of trust: "reputation, host identity—verified identification, and certification."[7] However, in order to create an atmosphere of confidence, this system does not only promote the service offered, the host, and the house as a product. It also shapes the reasons for the potential guest's choice and defines the formulas and standards of desirability for homes at the Airbnb Help and Resource Center, along with the information provided on how this community can live together within Airbnb. The standards set are supported by Airbnb's strategic tips.

With these applications, Airbnb has created both a marketing strategy and a hierarchical order determined by evaluation scores and Airbnb approval. This

order is composed of Standard Hosts, Superhosts, and Airbnb Plus hosts, respectively. Homeowners who want to change their class, rearrange, and present both their behaviour and the spatial configuration of the house in a "strategic" and "artificial" way. Likewise, Airbnb provides some clues as a "directing" and "determining" actor as well as being a guide to the hosts and presents likes and role models with examples. These tips essentially make the interior design of the house an important focal point besides hospitality. On the Airbnb platform, the home phenomenon is treated as a communication and interaction environment and has a unique appearance. The homes where this look is most evident are undoubtedly Airbnb Plus homes, created with the idea of launching "verified design" and a "new tier of homes."[8]

Verified new home tier: Airbnb Plus

Airbnb Plus is a classification programme that recognizes host lists with outstanding quality, comfort, and style. To qualify for Plus status, hosts must meet the standards set by Airbnb. Plus standards are generally determined by three criteria: style, comfort, and hospitality.[9] These criteria are presented to homeowners under the name Home checklist created by Airbnb in collaboration with the Home Operations Team, which focuses on objective criteria such as maintenance and amenities, and the Environments Team, which focuses on subjective criteria such as interior design.[10] Standard design guidelines were developed by the research of the Airbnb Environments Team. This research provides an opportunity to exchange ideas on what elements make the home space unique and what special details should be emphasized.[11] Thus, "The Airbnb platform is not just a technological device to list and organize information, but a two-way mechanism (instrument) able to change the cultural and material role of interiors."[12] In this direction, the home interior becomes an important criterion in order to create and develop the Airbnb global mindset.

The lead interior designer of the Environments Team says that the design process of the Airbnb home started with a couple of questions. The questions are:

> What is the architectural style and how is the home furnished? What details and thoughtful touches were brought in to show off the character of the host or location? How do these elements affect the overall function and feel of the space for a guest? What would it look like if we had a collection if houses we checked for aesthetics and thoughtful amenities?[13]

Besides, the Airbnb platform defines itself as hospitality company where houses and experiences are their "products." In this direction, it offers some tips on how

to design the interior space, or in other words, the representation of interiors as a product, both on its website and Pinterest.

Airbnb-Pinterest Collaboration

It makes sense that Airbnb uses the Pinterest platform, which is used as a visual source of creative ideas in today's world, where we are more connected with the technology in our daily lives. Thus, Airbnb transmits Plus house ideas to everyone with "visual-oriented" shares via Pinterest. Airbnb shares have been created in two ways. These are illustration and photography which are elements of visual communication. Visual material or technical illustrations and photographs in the transfer of ideas are editorial content where all the details of the Plus House idea are carefully organized, created with an original language, and allows the target audience to receive the message in the easiest way.

Home building process with illustration

Sharing illustrations begins with the introduction of style and theme to create harmony and integrity. With these shares, a "basic style guide" is created for homeowners to get the ideal appearance. The sample styles refer both an art movement and a certain lifestyle like Art Deco and 80's Pop Style (Figure 14.1a). For both shares, if decorative elements such as shapes, colours, and materials of this particular style, are used, the space will look "ideal" remarkable or cool. Thus, art movements have been treated formally by being reduced to an "appearance," regardless of ideological, conceptual, functional meanings and the elements that they have acquired in the design process of an architectural entity.

Likewise, the other sharing based on a particular lifestyle are Farmhouse and Bohemian style. In this sharing, it has been stated that the environment obtained by using specific colour, material, and texture will offer a relaxed, shabby, or warm atmosphere. In fact, just like art movements, life styles in these sharing has been reduced to a pure view by referring to furniture, fittings, and decorative objects.

Another share of the Airbnb Plus is about the living room. The share titled "Tips for arranging a living room" offers an illustration that is similar to a plan drawing (Figure 14.1b). A very "rational" language is used in this sharing while giving ideas on how to place furniture and households in the living room. Accordingly, the tips given are mostly related to the household items and the layout of furniture in the living room.

In fact, these shares contain areas that enable to display the status or identity of the host (Figure 14.1c). One of these areas is the fireplace where the placement of

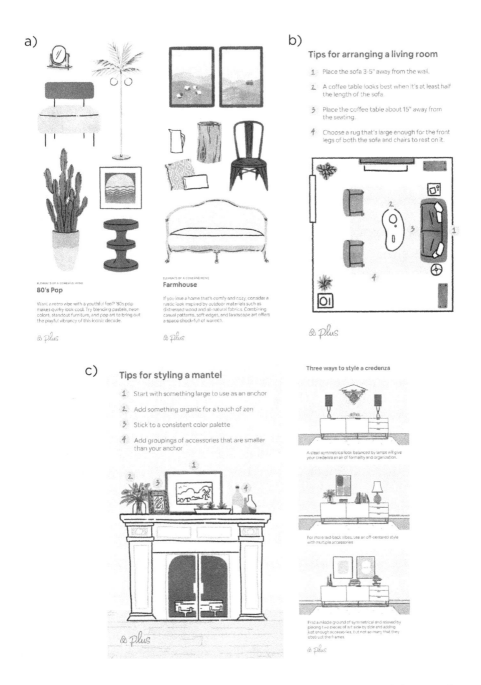

FIGURE 14.1a–c: (a) Pinterest, "Elements of Cohesive Home: 80's Pop [left] / Farmhouse [right]," n.d. © Airbnb Incorporated. (b) Pinterest, "Tips for arranging a living room," n.d. © Airbnb Incorporated. (c) Pinterest, "Tips for styling a mental [left] / Three ways to style a credenza [right]," n.d. © Airbnb Incorporated.

a large picture is defined as a work of art. Later, the compatible elements with this selection like decorative objects and plants are placed. Another display area is the credenza. The emphasis is mostly on the decorative objects to be placed on or above the credenza. It is stated that decorative objects give a "comfortable," "formal," and "symmetrical" appearance if arranged in accordance with their dimensions, location, and relationship with each other. Actually, there are certain elements used in three given styling ways. The most striking of them is that the wall behind the sideboard should be filled with objects such as paintings and crafts and never be left empty.

According to Airbnb suggestions, any decorative touch on the walls adds value to the space. In this spirit, Airbnb gives tips about how to transform walls into a space for visual composition (Figure 14.2a). In this sharing focusing on stylizing the gallery wall, the behind wall of the seat and the bed, ideas are similar with the previous wall arrangements. The important issue is to choose paintings according to the position, length, and shape of furniture. Painting called art is an important in player used to design the surfaces. Another player used to create a visual composition is pillows (Figure 14.2b). In Plus home ideas; the position, colour, form, and texture of the pillows are given great importance. This sharing is an indication of the classified views as eclectic, layered, symmetrical, and traditionally in Airbnb's design language and understanding.

There are other elements in the Airbnb Plus shares that should be transformed or edited to fit certain or scenery (Figure 14.2c). One of these elements is the sofa which makes a great contribution to the space in terms of visual perception and functional organization. However, unlike other posts, the item addressed in that post is not sofa directly, but sofa legs and the relationship between legs and the style. Another detailed approach is on curtains. In this post, it is intended to teach the hosts tips on how to place the curtain, how to stylize it, and how to draw the edges. When we look at these posts, we can see that Airbnb puts emphasis on creating a visual composition on furniture and surfaces. However, this situation reduces the importance of the idea of designing a volume in architecture. A three-dimensional (3D) volume is reduced to a two-dimensional (2D) frame with the posts of Airbnb about design.

Home building process with photograph

The photographs that convey the first impressions of the home experience are very important on the Airbnb Platform. Plus house photos are a kind of photographic proof of how the Plus house looks when all visually oriented ideas and tips are applied.

The most shared and underlined aspect of the Design Essentials series is the visual effect (Figure 14.3a). The common feature in the post handled within the scope of Design Essential: visual impact is the wall–artwork relationship, which is

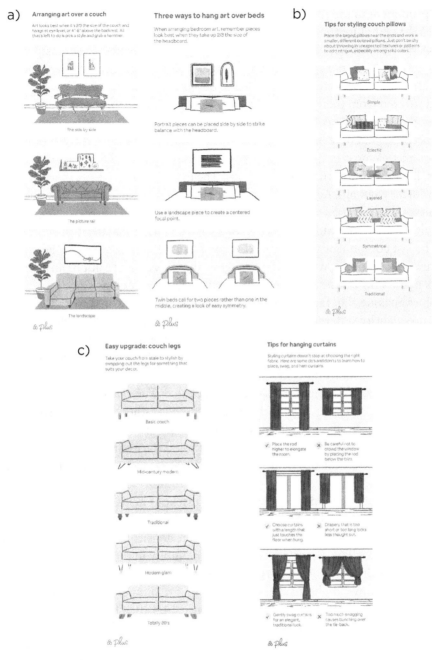

FIGURE 14.2a–c: (a) Pinterest, "Arranging art over a couch [left] / Three ways to hang art over beds [right]," n.d. © Airbnb Incorporated. (b) Pinterest, "Tips for styling couch pillows," n.d. © Airbnb Incorporated. (c) Pinterest, "Easy upgrade: couch legs [left] / Tips for hanging curtains [right]," n.d. © Airbnb Incorporated.

also prominent in the illustrations. According to Airbnb, the pictures should not be just art. What matters is the added value of this image to the space. For example, Airbnb states that 2D surfaces containing visual elements such as pictures, drawings, and photographs, which refer to daily life or other qualities, can also be used. Just like architecture left the idea of designing a volume, the visual elements are separated from their content. The only focus is that the visual material has to reflect the correct ratio, colour, and texture in the defined frame instead of what the picture is, made, what it says or where it stands in the spatial volume.

Another element in the Design Essentials series is the qualified material used in walls, floors, and furniture (Figure 14.3b). The materials in the posts share the same fate with the paintings. Again, they are manipulated only by appearance. The quality of the material is only used to add a visual value to the space regardless of its essence. As a result, "the material and its essence is reduced to an image, making it an indicator."[14]

The last component we examined in the Design Essentials series is personality (Figure 14.4a). In fact, while Airbnb suggests that there should not be any personal items in the Plus houses, it is quite interesting that the emphasis on individuality becomes an issue.[15] In fact, what Airbnb wants to say to the hosts with these posts is to use identity differentiate themselves from other homes through this value. However, what is at stake here is not a representation of personal identity, but a criterion for the rental house to distinguish itself from the similar. The phenomenon of producing something different, new, individual, or special on the Airbnb platform emerges as a major concept for raising market value. The visuals refer to the image created by the elements used in global popular trends rather than the personality of the host or the main character of the space. Thus, as a marketing strategy, the personality becomes "an illusory identity specified in the interface of reality and imagery."[16]

The common point of Airbnb Plus house ideas is that after determining a "style" in general, they add a "spirit," "style," and "vitality" to the space by adding the recommended and appropriate household items or decorative objects in harmony and integrity. In line with this view, Airbnb shares a sample home photo as an answer to the question "how to create an Airbnb Plus look" with some touches and additions. In the post titled "Turn Nudity in the Bedroom into Plus," the "nude" bedroom space was transformed a Plus bedroom by adding decorative objects, pillows, lighting element, cover, plant, and personalized objects—to increase the "vitality" level of the space (Figure 14.4 b). This post is a summary of Airbnb's Plus interior design process. As shown in Table 14.1, the strategic home tips of Airbnb can be categorized as areas, harmony and integrity, and visual impact. These categories indicate a surface rather than a volumetric spatial relationship. In fact, Airbnb, which reveals a "surface design" rather than interior design, offers a kind of "home model" of today's "image" world to the target audience with the ideas it shares.

a)

Alternative art
Design Essentials | Visual Impact

Art is everything and everything is art. Ok, not exactly, but you know what we mean. Try featuring old photos, black and white photography, pencil sketches, graphic posters, maps, or old charts for an alternative take on art.

Find art everywhere
Design Essentials | Visual Impact

You don't need to go to a gallery to find artwork, though that's a great place to start. Find unusual pieces at a flea market, abstracts at a student show, or posters at a museum.

b)

Paint with paper
Design Essentials | Quality Materials

Wallpapers add visual impact and texture to an otherwise bland room. Bold patterns are best for smaller spaces like hallways and closet interiors, while simpler prints work well in larger rooms. When choosing a design, think about how it will complement other elements in the room.

Groundwork
Design Essentials | Quality Materials

Flooring is underratedly important, and sets the groundwork of a room. Solid woods are full of character and get better with age, while ceramic tile and concrete add an industrial look to kitchens and bathrooms.

FIGURE 14.3a–c: (a) Pinterest, "Design Essentials | Visual Impact: Alternative art [left] / Find art everywhere [right]," n.d. © Airbnb Incorporated. (b) Pinterest, "Design Essentials | Quality Materials: Paint with paper [left] / Groundwork [right]," n.d. © Airbnb Incorporated.

a)

b)

FIGURE 14.4a–c: (a) Pinterest, "Design Essentials | Personality: Elements of surprise [left] / Gallery wall [right]," n.d. © Airbnb Incorporated. (b) Pinterest, "Bare to Plus / Bedroom," n.d. © Airbnb Incorporated.

TABLE 14.1: Strategic tips of Airbnb for spatial considerations through illustration and photography.

Strategic Tips	Areas			Harmony and Integrity		Visual Impact			
	Regional	Surface	Detail	Style/Themes	Placement	Color	Material	Decorative objects	Personality
Illustration									
Photograph									

The table is categorized into two rows—illustrations, photographs—and three columns: areas, harmony and integrity, and visual impact. From left to right the three columns are classified according to their scope as follows:

- Areas: Regional, Surface, Detail.
- Harmony and integrity: Style/Themes, Placement.
- Visual Impact: Color, Material, Decorative objects, Personality.
  Coloured areas indicate existing clues.

Conclusion

Airbnb Plus model is "no reference to the context, and interiors are presented as dioramas, a multitudinal sequence of images, a series of parallel interiors, expressive of parallel lives and societies, regardless of location and inhabitation."[17] In the Airbnb Plus Filter, objects, colours, and materials have become "images" with symbolic and "visual" oriented references. The role of Airbnb has assumed; as an "effective critic," to teach this "image repertoire" to the target audience and to give ideas about its adaptation to the home space. However, this situation has led to the reduction of the space as a 3D volume to a 2D frame. The indispensable aspect in these shares is the scenery created on surfaces rather than the relationship between the emphasized elements with the space volume. The interior design, on the other hand, is based on imitating a mounted image sequence in this process.

With its design-related posts, Airbnb has led to the reduction of space as a 3D volume to a 2D frame. Thus, Airbnb's tips are not for the process of designing an interior, but for the process of designing a 2D surface, namely, a frame. Plus Houses, which presents a model of Airbnb's—and perhaps the future—interior design approach, can be called a "Photogenic Home" that resembles a formative, photographic, and popular lifestyle peculiar to today's world.[18] However, the global scale of photogenic house formation can cause to develop new understanding and application for the discipline of interior architecture.

As can be seen in the house photos produced with the Airbnb Plus filter, the resulting product does not present a spatial and volumetric difference, even though the colour, texture, and form of objects used are different (Figure 14.5). What is

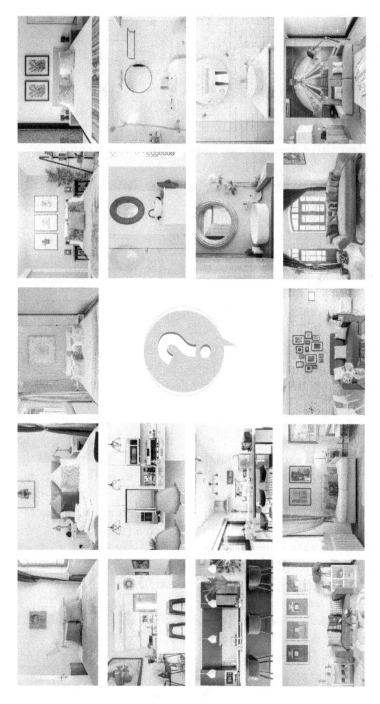

FIGURE 14.5: Duygun, "Airbnb Plus Filters: Interior Fragments," 2021, Ankara. © Airbnb Incorporated.

emphasized in this study is that with Airbnb's strategic clues, the design process deals with a 2D frame and brings a uniformity issue to the agenda by defining global standards for design. When we look at Airbnb photos, this whole process makes us think about the future of design. Is there any sort of standardization in question? Will all houses look alike? Will a plus living space emerge when everyone applies the Plus home criteria? What will Airbnb say about the interior space when everyone's home reaches Plus standards? Where does the field of interior architecture stand in this process? What should the design discipline do? Does the discipline have to be renewed? This study tries to make a contribution by asking questions about the future of interior architecture and the design discipline.

NOTES

1. Sohrab Rahimi, Xi Liu, and Clio Andris, "Hidden Style in the City: An Analysis of Geolocated Airbnb Rental Images in Ten Major Cities" (paper presented at the *UrbanGIS '16: Proceedings of the 2nd ACM SIGSPATIAL Workshop on Smart Cities and Urban Analytics*, Burlingame, CA, October 2016).
2. Laurent Son Nguyen et al., "Check Out This Place: Inferring Ambiance from Airbnb Photos." *IEEE Transactions on Multimedia* 20, no. 6 (2018): 1499–1511, https://doi.org/10.1109/TMM.2017.2769444.
3. Nor Maizana Mat Nawi, Hashim Nik, and Hamid Rasidah, "Airbnb Physical Environment Attributes and Customer Behavioral Intention: A Proposed Study." *The International Journal of Academic Research in Business and Social Sciences* 9, no. 8 (2019): 144–51, https://doi.org/10.6007/IJARBSS/v9-i8/6230.
4. Xi Liu et al., "Inside 50,000 Living Rooms: An Assessment of Global Residential Ornamentation Using Transfer Learning." *EPJ Data Science* 8, no.1 (2019), https://doi.org/10.1140/epjds/s13688-019-0182-z.
5. For an excellent discussion of the reality and representation of interiors offered by online platforms like Airbnb, see Francesca Murialdo, "The New Digital Interiorscape and the Edited Airbnb Interior," in *Interior Futures: Vol.1 Habituated | Mediated*, ed. Graeme Brooker et al. (CA: Crucible Press, 2019), 180.
6. Daniel Guttentag, "Airbnb: Disruptive Innovation and the Rise of an Informal Tourism Accommodation Sector." *Current Issues in Tourism* 18, no. 12 (2015): 1192–1217, https://doi.org/10.1080/13683500.2013.827159; Ert Eyal et al., "Trust and Reputation in the Sharing Economy: The Role of Personal Photos in Airbnb." *Tourism Management* 55 (2016): 62–73, https://doi.org/10.1016/j.tourman.2016.01.013; Stephan Reinhold and Sara Dolnicar, "The Sharing Economy," in *Peer to Peer Accommodation Networks: Pushing the Boundaries*, ed. Sara Dolnicar (Oxford: Goodfellow Publishers, 2017), 15–26 http://dx.doi.org/10.23912/9781911396512-3600.
7. See Eyal Ert and Aliza Fleischer, "The Evolution of Trust in Airbnb: A Case of Home Rental." *Annals of Tourism Research* 75 (2019): 279–87, https://doi.org/10.1016/j.annals.2019.01.004.

8. See "Plus Personality." Airbnb Incorporated, accessed April 30, 2021. https://airbnb.design/plus-personality/.
9. See "Airbnb Plus Program Terms." Airbnb Incorporated, accessed May 4, 2021. https://www.airbnb.com.tr/help/article/2195/airbnb-plus-program%C4%B1-%C5%9Fartlar%C4%B1.
10. See note 8.
11. See "Wordly Workspace." Airbnb Incorporated, accessed May 4, 2021. https://airbnb.design/worldy-workspaces/.
12. See note 5.
13. See note 8.
14. Jean Baudrillard, *The System of Objects*, trans. Oğuz Adanır (Istanbul: BUPRESS, 2014), 49.
15. See note 8.
16. See Duygu Koca, "Remapping Contemporary Housing Production in Turkey: A Case Study on Housing Patterns and Marketing Strategies" (PhD dissertation, Middle East Technical University, 2012), 171, http://etd.lib.metu.edu.tr/upload/12614423/index.pdf.
17. See note 5.
18. See note 14.

BIBLIOGRAPHY

Airbnb Incorporated. "Airbnb Plus Program Terms." Accessed May 4, 2021. AirBnB Design.

Airbnb Incorporated. "Plus Personality." Accessed April 30, 2021. https://airbnb.design/plus-personality/. AirBnB Design.

Airbnb Incorporated. "Wordly Workspace." Accessed May 4, 2021. AirBnB Design. https://airbnb.design/worldy-workspaces/. AirBnB Design.

Buadrillard, Jean. *The System of Objects*. Translated by Oğuz Adanır. Istanbul: BUPRESS, 2014.

Ert, Eyal, Aliza Fleischer, and Nathan Magen. "Trust and Reputation in the Sharing Economy: The Role of Personal Photos in Airbnb." *Tourism Management* 55 (2016): 62–73. https://doi.org/10.1016/j.tourman.2016.01.013.

Ert, Eyal, and Aliza Fleischer. "The Evolution of Trust in Airbnb: A Case of Home Rental." *Annals of Tourism Research* 75 (March 2019), 279–87. Accessed September 3, 2021. https://doi.org/10.1016/j.annals.2019.01.004.

Guttentag, Daniel. "Airbnb: Disruptive Innovation and the Rise of an Informal Tourism Accommodation Sector." *Current Issues in Tourism* 18, no. 12 (2015): 1192–1217, https://doi.org/10.1080/13683500.2013.827159.

Koca, Duygu. "Remapping Contemporary Housing Production in Turkey: A Case Study on Housing Patterns and Marketing Strategies." PhD dissertation, Middle East Technical University, 2012.

Liu, Xi, Zixuan Huang, Clio Andris, and Sohrab Rahimi. "Inside 50,000 Living Rooms: An Assessment of Global Residential Ornamentation Using Transfer Learning." *EPJ Data Science* 8, no. 1 (2019): 4, https://doi.org/10.1140/epjds/s13688-019-0182-z.

Murialdo, Francesca. "The New Digital Interiorscape and the Edited Airbnb Interior." In *Interior Futures: Vol.1 Habituated | Mediated*, edited by Graeme Brooker, Harriet Harriss, and Kevin Walker, 176–90. CA: Crucible Press, 2019.

Nawi, Normaizana Mat, Nik A. A. N. Hashim, Zurena Rena Shahril, and Hamid Rasidah. "Airbnb Physical Environment Attributes and Customer Behavioral Intention: A Proposed Study." *The International Journal of Academic Research in Business and Social Sciences* 9, no. 8 (2019): 144–51. https://doi.org/10.6007/IJARBSS/v9-i8/6230.

Nguyen, Laurent S., Salvador Ruiz-Correa, Marianne Schmid Mast, and Daniel Gatica-Perez. "Check out This Place: Inferring Ambiance from Airbnb Photos." *IEEE Transactions on Multimedia* 20, no. 6 (2018): 1499–1511, https://doi.org/10.1109/TMM.2017.2769444.

Rahimi, Sohrab, Xi Liu, and Clio Andris. "Hidden Style in the City: An Analysis of Geolocated Airbnb Rental Images in Ten Major Cities." Paper presented at *UrbanGIS '16: Proceedings of the 2nd ACM SIGSPATIAL Workshop on Smart Cities and Urban Analytics*, Burlingame, CA, October 31, 2016.

Reinhold, Stephan, and Sara Dolnicar. "The Sharing Economy." In *Peer to Peer Accommodation Networks: Pushing the Boundaries*, edited by Sara Dolnicar. 15–26. Oxford: Goodfellow Publishers, 2017.

15

The Smart City in the Smaller Context: Digital Subjectivities and Smart City Development in Rural Conditions

Daniel Koch

Introduction

That there are challenges translating the "smart city" to rural contexts is already established,[1] as is discourse on whom the "smart city" is for.[2] In an era of sudden change, and in locations of noticeable demographic transformation, some of these challenges become particularly noticeable. Sometimes—at least in popular media and discourse—understood as conflicts between those who adapt and adopt, and those who resist or reject. While, indeed, conflicts do emerge, they are much less clear-cut, and need to be understood in a more nuanced way. This is where this work makes its contribution, building its argument from a research and innovation project in Duved, outside of Åre, Sweden.[3] I say that it builds its argument because while it takes some observations to explore how they relate to ideas, ideals, and processes of digitalization and smart city development, the intent is not to give a representative account of Duved (as site, society, individual or collective actors, or research and innovation project), but to learn from some of Duved's sites of contestation and conflict as forces of different scale operate on, in and through the local context—where *conflicts* should be understood in the full range from (silent or open) confrontation to the meetings of difference that in their chafing interaction drive potentials of deepened mutual understanding, social change, and development.[4]

The local context: Duved

Duved (Figure 15.1) is a small society of about 700 inhabitants near the larger municipal centre Åre in western Jämtland, Sweden. Both are heavily based on the

FIGURE 15.1: Duved's main street and centre, 2009. Photo: Matti Paavola (CC).

tourist industry that is largely focused on the ski slopes in winter season. Åre is a more developed tourist resort with dominance of hotels and chain stores, whereas Duved as of yet retains a more local character with a strong sense of local identity. At the same time, Duved has a recent history of continuous demographic change: a growth and influx of people complemented by a loss of long-term inhabitants has followed a similar pattern for at least over a decade. This process has been accelerated through the COVID-19 pandemic where remote working has become a more viable alternative for increasingly many people.[5] In this situation, Duved has become attractive for an additional range of potential inhabitants, who can now live and work primarily in Duved while only occasionally going to their workplaces, which tend to be located in Östersund or Stockholm—and the municipality also sees this as a potential to develop Duved.[6]

As a result, Duved has seen accelerated demographic change; a process that was already ongoing with high levels of both in- and outflux of inhabitants has grown stronger. Statistics from the municipality's latest demographic report (Figure 15.2)[7] do not in and of themselves show whether these patterns are due to people moving to Duved and then out into the rest of the municipality or if it is rather a process of displacement. And, to the extent it is displacement, they do not say if

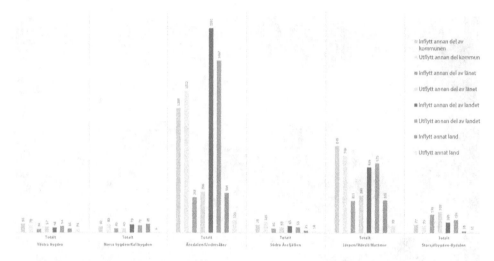

FIGURE 15.2: Demographic change in Åre municipality per administrative unit (2012–17) with Duved part of the third set. The chart shows in- and outflows of people ordered in pairs to and from other contexts, where the more saturated/darker bars per pair show incoming population and lighter show people moving out. The two categories with a surplus concern "other parts of the country" (red/orange, third pair) and "other country" (greys, fourth pair). The yellow/first pair and green/second pair concern the municipality and region, respectively. Åre kommun, 2017.

locals are pushed out because their homes are bought or grow too expensive, or an indirect process where the homes that become available or built are acquired by people moving into Duved, leaving little (physical, financial) room for people from Duved who need a *new* home to go anywhere but elsewhere. What can be said is that the area has a surplus of immigrants from Sweden outside of the region and internationally, but a deficit to the municipality and the region, and that property prices are rising fast.[8] Immigrants to Duved tend to come from far away and have comparatively noticeable amounts of economic capital.

This creates a diverse population with a mix of long-time locals and recent immigrants, and recently, of immigrants who are living there part-time. Here, shifting demographics lead to shifting habits and shifting expectations of what Duved is to be, while the notion of *remaining Duved* can be as strong in recent immigrants as in long-time locals.[9] Some youths have begun wearing carpenter's clothes on their spare time as a marker of not belonging to the recently arrived mobile distance working population, while at the same time there seems to be something shared across such potential lines of conflict: recurrent use of the terminology "not Åre."[10] However, while many wish to preserve Duved's character and avoid transforming into "Åre" (metonymically used to stand for an over-commercialized tourist destination), it

needs to be acknowledged that the influx of people allows for things to happen that long-time locals have long wanted, and can secure or re-establish services such as local stores and a local healthcare centre.[11] That Duved largely originates from the tourist industry further complicates the relation between a "too touristy" Åre and a more "authentic" Duved.[12] Additionally, Åre is of central importance to many aspects of life in Duved, from providing services that Duved is too small to carry on its own, to work for, for instance, small construction companies and other small businesses in Duved, or providing employment opportunities. One way or the other, most people in Duved regularly make use of Åre to live their lives. This conflicted relation to Åre can also be found in the answers to an online PPGIS questionnaire performed in the project, amongst other questions asking respondents to note places they visit often, and places they avoid: Åre is one of the most heavily pointed out in both of these categories (Figure 15.3).[13]

In the same study, it is also clear how many of the qualities—places highly valued by the population—are spread over a larger area. What makes up the value of "Duved" is thus not only Duved but includes a large portion of its context. These are also places that only partially match the places reportedly used often, further demonstrating the complex relation between identity, types of values, and the pragmatics of everyday life.

Here, one can draw a careful parallel to Sharon Zukin's and Ervin Kosta's *Bourdieu Off-Broadway*,[15] noting the positional claim of quality of some stores of being located on *not Broadway* (i.e. "not mainstream"), while absolutely dependent on the proximity to Broadway for their existence. There is the "mainstream" Åre, that which has given in too much to the tourist industry and for instance chain stores and restaurants, which Duved is *not*—but Duved would also not be able to exist without the proximity to it. Paradoxically, it may be that the only way "Duved" *could* be fully independent from "Åre" would be by, at least in part, becoming it. Most people are clearly also aware of this interdependency, and such

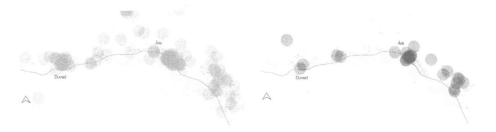

FIGURE 15.3: "Places I use a lot" (left) and "places I avoid" (right) in the Duved-Åre valley. The highest concentration of both is found in Åre, whereas Duved has noticeably fewer places that are avoided compared to places used often. Maps by Ann Legeby, 2021.[14]

positioning should primarily be understood as one of identity differentiation and not of rejection in practice. That being said, the "not-Åre" identification has the capacity to act as a unifying concept shared by different positions amongst inhabitants, part-time inhabitants and visitors to Duved, cutting across differences in forms of capital and reasons to want to "not become Åre." In some situations, the "not-Åre" positioning unifies (some) privileged and underprivileged resistance identities.[16]

The Smart City as Ideology

The "smart city," and digitalization, partially enters here in a rather specific form given an extra push by the COVID-19 pandemic: the potential of remote working. This has enabled more people—many of them from Stockholm—to try a life where they mostly live in Duved while performing work that they used to do elsewhere. For many of them, it is also convenient enough to go to Stockholm or Östersund every now and then for the parts of work that *do* need it, or for other reasons. By and large, this is also the type of subject around which large portions of the smart city concept is constructed: given that there are different definitions of what a "smart city," or a "smart society" is,[17] they all tend to concern societies where intentional, active subjects make use of the city through dual mobility in navigating physical and virtual space.[18] From being able to spend leisure time or perform work in a variety of locations which can be found, supported, or facilitated by digital technology, to services, activities, and workplaces being facilitated and provided via digital interfaces be they virtual, remote, or guided to.

This ideology, in the form of how inhabitants and their activities, intents, and relational ecologies to each other and their environment are conceptualized, must be understood as being built around notions of the mobile subject.[19] The mobile subject, here, further understood not as the subject which moves around—but as the subject which *can* do so, where *can* takes many forms; it of course relates to having the economy to be mobile, but also to consider the environment and one's use of and life in it from certain points of view.

Digitalization, data labour, tech labour

Before moving further, it is important to understand how this is a relation to the environment that not everyone can share equally, and that is built on the labour of many who cannot. Reaching from the fact that it depends on cables, chipsets, IT-products from handhelds to laptops to switches to routers,[20] it also

depends on furniture, food, clothes, and many other things which are produced in very decidedly place-based economies,[21] as well as the workers who clean, cook, facilitate, and maintain the infrastructure being cruised by the digitized cosmopolitan, from the café clerk to the cleaner or repairperson.[22] Many of these economies are not mobile in any sense of the word, be it because they concern production or extraction of raw materials, involve machinery with their involved expertise, require masses of matter to be performed, or depend on economies of scale. In different ways, this means that those *working with them* are not particularly mobile in the sense considered here, even in the cases they could afford it economically—or commute long distances as daily routine.[23] The mobile subject depends on the relatively lower wages of the labour underpinning the mobile life.

Additionally, the general notion of the smart city is built on comparative information abundancy for subjects comparatively lacking knowledge. That is, where on the one hand, *the environment is so complex that there are always new possibilities to find through relatively sparse information systems,* and on the other, *any individual has little enough knowledge of this environment that they can make such discoveries.* Information abundancy is thus not a fact but a relative concept, where it must feel like there is *more to know,* and that the smart system *can help you find it out.* In reality, most digital systems contain very little information compared to the "real world,"[24] and environments are easily identifiable where it is easier to simply know the local context than to browse any supportive app or system. If everyone knows the one local restaurant, who would ever need a restaurant finding service?

This scalar problem is emphasized by the fact that data is always *made.*[25] Even if we accept that some of it is accumulated by tracking (the use of which privacy concerns can call to a screeching halt in small societies like Duved), this wouldn't work unless the data is made—put into the system *by someone.*[26] Again, in dense, sprawling environments this laborious part of smart systems disappears because there are economic interests for actors to register themselves in the system, there is economy for the municipality and other services to do more of that work, and the input in "crowdsourcing" data works because only a comparatively small part of the population need to contribute with a comparatively small effort to provide enough for the system to overcome the perceived information abundancy threshold.[27] In less dense environments, with fewer inhabitants, the fact that information systems require *work* to be useful becomes much more readily apparent, as does the fact that the smart city's information abundancy is built on free labour. This does not mean digital systems cannot provide quality contributions in rural settlements, it is to say what qualities they can contribute with need to be rethought.

Relational Ecologies and Spatial Capitals

Looking at these challenges combined—the different possibilities to relate to the world as mobile subjects or not, the more pragmatic question of being tied to local conditions or not, and the need of smart systems to have both data and tech labour put into them—some of the challenges of Duved's transformation can become clearer. They can be made especially clear, I believe, by being considered from the points of view of *spatial capital*, as discussed by Jacques Levy[28] and Lars Marcus.[29] The strength of Levy's concept is the identification of two types of spatial capital and their interrelation—the *position* ("contextual") capital in the local environment and *situation* ("personal") capital that allows one to overcome deficiencies in the position capital—whereas the strength of Marcus' discussion is how concretely analysable it makes "position" capital as well as the conceptual depth and clarity therein. Marcus' work further elaborates on how capital is created by how *access* is structured through architectural space—providing a richer and more nuanced understanding of how it operates to differentiate down to very local scales. It thereby also more clearly integrates "space" as a form of capital in its own right. Many of the aspects identified by Marcus have been investigated in the project in the work package focusing on the living environment, analysing distances to and densities of ranges of different amenities and services.[30]

Situation capital, the possibility to overcome distance challenges, has been further developed by for instance Patrick Rérat discussing mobility as capital, and how spatial capital can be drivers of gentrification and segregation.[31] Rérat is clear that it is not so easy as to say that people with more spatial capital live further away; just like Bourdieu's concept of types and distribution of capital,[32] spatial capital in this sense is complex and both positional and situational capital can be valuable. Some identifiable "gentrifiers" in urban development, for instance, are those who can afford to live in locations with much positional capital—with much of what they seek in close vicinity—so that they can afford a lifestyle without car ownership and by frequenting mostly local stores and services. Similarly, lack of both types of capital can be understood as the major disadvantageous form of spatial segregation. This again becomes a complex question in a location like Duved where the balance between potential "gentrifiers" making it more possible for everyone to live more locally (by supporting and increasing position capital) and economic displacement is at the very least difficult to identify. Digitalization here provides a new challenge: while it offers place-based economies many possibilities including online retail and direct-to-consumer services, and a broader reach in e.g. customer engagement for tourism, and so on, the constitution of "situational capital" is being rapidly and fundamentally transformed; most clearly, the way digitalization currently operates, the capacity for *some* to overcome distance

through digital means, allowing them to work from "anywhere," changes how economic forces operate in and on Duved faster and more powerfully than the digitalization gains of local businesses.

In relation to the "cosmopolitan subject" then, it is worth at least considering the cosmopolitan not only as the *mobile subject*, but as *the subject which can overcome distance* (or lack of contextual spatial capital), in whatever form it does so. But, furthermore, that it is a position that relates to the environment in general—including the local context—in this mobile way; the always-existing potential to be elsewhere *also locally* to, for instance, work on one's laptop. To an extent, this collapses digital and physical mobility into different capacities of overcoming distance, which, I argue, is of critical importance. Not the least because it captures how the Smart City subject is considered *in both physical and digital realms of action*. That is, it is a subject that not only can use the digital world to navigate or overcome difficulties in the physical world, but a subject that has the same relation to digital spaces, be they communities, sites, tools, fora, platforms, or any other form through which the digital world is navigated. The "ideal" smart city inhabitant is a cosmopolitan in both realms.

Here we can note that the majority of employers in Duved-Åre (the geographical unit which statistics are made for) do not believe that their personnel can work significantly more from home in the future.[33] To an extent, this can be understood by how many of them are businesses like carpenters, builders, hotel- or restaurant owners, and other types of services that are performed on-site. In the project's questionnaire, furthermore, a notable share of respondents provides the same perspective for how they see their future. Of note, while the number of responses is too low to draw any more than anecdotal conclusions, *no* respondent currently studying in high school or university saw themselves working mostly from home in five years. Neither the local population nor local business environment identify with ideas of Duved being, or becoming, the home of distance workers.[34]

Un-homing with words: Duved with a little help from my (middle-class) friends

From such an understanding it is important to consider how one works with planning and development in an area undergoing significant transformation. It is not only a question of what would make life better or worse, or what services are needed or not, but about whom the development is for—beyond the pragmatics of housing costs. As Sara Westin points out, the discourse on who is "supposed" to inhabit a place can drive displacement by generating senses of belonging or non-belonging to what is "meant to be."[35] Unless differences in such positioning are acknowledged, efforts meant to bring together and include may rather have the effect of exclusion and polarization. Engaging in various forms of local activities is

also, as Blokland points out, different if it is a cosmopolitan act—it is interesting and highly engaging while doing it, but I can leave to somewhere else tomorrow—or if it is engaging in a place you are more permanently tied to.[36]

Conflict and polarization are, of course, not necessary results of these processes: on the contrary, Blokland points to the importance to embrace the challenge and learn from real examples of when the intention of bridging and bonding *works*—and that *how* one enacts activities like these are pivotal for how they develop the social relations of those involved. One should, however, not rush to conclusion regarding demographic change. That there is "displacement"—as in that long-term residents move out and new residents move in—is not necessarily synonymous with long-term residents being pushed out,[37] and it is important to be careful in assuming a process directly similar to that in (global north) cities.[38] Without identifying these challenges, however, it is difficult to even understand the (social, physical, virtual) sites of contestation and potential production of conflict or displacement at work, and to write off resistance as simple conservatism.

Some Preliminary Conclusions

Approaching conclusion, I wish to reiterate that this chapter does not provide a complete or representative picture of Duved and the challenges involved in its development, nor of the research and innovation project. Figures and observations are used to drive the discussion forward, and are not descriptions of particular individuals or groups. So, when examining how the emergence of resistance identities relates to ideas of digitalization and smart cities, and what we can learn from this to understand, critically discuss, and evolve concepts of "smart digital solutions" to be more inclusive and adaptable for contexts for which they are not developed, the claim is not that there is a dichotomous situation or open conflict between locals and non-locals, or easily drawn lines between "digitized" and "none-digitized" individuals, or any one side or the other. On the contrary, such lines and positions are demonstrated to form tangled messes that require further research to unpack, which involves not only relations to digital technologies but to a range of other types of capital. But within these tangled messes, there are conflicts between the ideal cosmopolitan subject of the "smart city," the relative amount of labour needed to provide an environment where such a subject can be enacted—from registering data to the diverse and multiple sets of services that allow such "cruising" of the local environment—the simple lengths of cables and amounts of other infrastructure needed, and the local subjectivities that have found other ways of relating to themselves, others, and the environment in other ways. While provisional, these considerations thus also demonstrate how digitalization and smart systems need to engage with local practices

and subjectivities; to adapt and transform not only particular solutions but mode of operation. But also, they suggest that these uncovered positions exist also in cities where the cosmopolitan subject can operate more easily. There may be practical reasons the general ideas of smart solutions cannot be applied, but also reasons of mental, social, and environmental ecologies stemming from both history and from the ways in which life in sparse settlements is or can be lived. At this stage, it is about *critically theorizing* the implications of such phenomena, to enable further empirical studies to come, and to equip research and innovation with a better understanding of sites of possible or probable conflict and contestation.

ACKNOWLEDGEMENTS

This chapter has been produced through researched funded by Vinnova, Sweden's innovation agency, project no 2020-01851.

NOTES

1. André Torre et al., eds., *Smart Development for Rural Areas* (London: Routledge, 2021); Lucia Naldi et al., "What is Smart Rural Development?" *Journal of Rural Studies* 40 (2015); Veronika Zavratnik, Andrej Kos, and Emilija Stojmenova Duh, "Smart Villages: Comprehensive Review of Initiatives and Practices." *Sustainability* 10, no. 7 (2018).
2. Johan Colding, Magnus Colding, and Stephan Barthel, "The Smart City Model: A New Panacea for Urban Sustainability or Unmanageable Complexity?" *Environment and Planning B: Urban Analytics and City Science* 47, no. 1 (2020); Jennifer Gabrys, "Programming Environments: Environmentality and Citizen Sensing in the Smart City." *Environment and Planning D: Society and Space* 32, no. 1 (2014); Katherine S. Willis, "Whose Right to the Smart City?," in *The Right to the Smart City*, ed. Paolo Cardullo, Cesare Di Feliciantonio, and Rob Kitchin (Bingley: Emerald Publishing Limited, 2019); Miltriadis D. Lytras and Anna Visvizi, "Who Uses Smart City Services and What to Make of It: Toward Interdisciplinary Smart Cities Research." *Sustainability* 10, no. 6 (2018), 1998.
3. See www.duvedmodellen.se/english/ and the report from the project's digitalization work package: Daniel Koch, *Digitalisering och landsbygdsutveckling: Lärdomar från Duvedmodellen för lokalsamhällen 2.0* (Stockholm: KTH, 2022).
4. See e.g. Sharon Zukin, *The Cultures of Cities* (Oxford: Blackwell, 1995); Talja Blokland, "Gardening with a Little Help from Your (Middle Class) Friends: Bridging Social Capital across Race and Class in a Mixed Neighbourhood," in *Networked Urbanism: Social capital and the city*, ed. Talja Blokland and Mike Savage (Farnham: Ashgate, 2008).
5. "Inrikes omflyttning mellan län efter kön och län. År 2000 - 2021." SCB, 2021, accessed May 20, 2022, http://www.statistikdatabasen.scb.se/pxweb/sv/ssd/START__BE__BE0101__BE0101J/InOmflytt/table/tableViewLayout1/.

6. Mia Wahlström and Sarah Bragée, *Lokalekonomisk analys för Duved* (Stockholm: Tyréns, 2021).
7. *Åre kommun, Kommuntäckande översiktsplan* (Åre: Åre kommun, 2017).
8. Ibid.; Länsstyrelsen Jämtland, *Bostadsmarknadsanalys 2020: En lägesbild över bostadsmarknaden i Jämtlands län* (Östersund: Länsstyrelsen i Jämtlands län, 2020).
9. The trend of an inflow from, especially, Stockholm has been growing for the last two decades, but has seen an extra push over the last few years. Statistiska Centralbyrån, "Inrikes omflyttning mellan län efter kön och län. År 2000–2021;" Wahlström and Bragée, *Lokalekonomisk analys för Duved*.
10. Paula Westberg, "Här formas framtidens landsbygd." *Dagens Nyheter* (Stockholm), November 27, 2021, Ekonomi. However, it is worth noting that while this is said by many today, the report from the citizen dialogue in 2012 rather states that participants wished for Åre and Duved to grow into one comprehensive settlement. Åre kommun, *Inledande medborgardialog: Underlagsrapport översiktsplan Åre kommun* (Åre: Åre kommun, 2012).
11. Karin Fjaervoll, "Duved får hälsocentral: 'Det här har varit världens sämst bevarade hemlighet'." *Östersundsposten* (Östersund), November 19, 2020.
12. See e.g. Jordbruksdepartementet, *Åre: Utvecklinsplan för ett svenskt rekreationsområde* (Stockholm: Jordbruksdepartementet, 1971); Länsstyrelsen Jämtland, *Länsplanering 1974: Förslag till länsprogram* (Östersund: Länsstyrelsen Jämtland, 1974).
13. Ann Legeby, Daniel Koch, and Christina Pech, *Betydelsefulla platser: kartenkät i Åre kommun 2021* (Stockholm: KTH, 2021).
14. Ibid.
15. Sharon Zukin and Ervin Kosta, "*Bourdieu Off-Broadway*: Managing Distinction on a Shopping Block in the East Village." *City & Community* 3, no. 2 (2004). 101–14
16. I here tie to the understanding of resistance identities discussed by Mitch Rose. Mitch Rose, "The Seductions of Resistance: Power, Politics, and a Performative Style of Systems." *Environment and Planning D: Society and Space* 20 (2002). Observations along similar paths of the complex relations between part-time and permanent residents have also been made by, e.g. Chris Paris, "Second Homes, Housing Consumption and Planning Responses," in *The Routledge Companion to Rural Planning*, ed. Mark Scott, Nick Gallent, and Menelaos Gkartzios (London: Routledge, 2019).
17. Colding, Colding, and Barthel, "The Smart City Model"; Michael Batty, *The New Science of Cities* (Cambridge, MA: MIT Press, 2013). See also Paul Cowie, Leanne Townsend, and Koen Salemink, "Smart Rural Futures: Will Rural Areas Be Left behind in the 4th Industrial Revolution?" *Journal of Rural Studies* 79 (2020).
18. See e.g. Tsugio Makimoto and David Manners, *Digital Nomad* (Chichester: Wiley & Sons, 1997); Lytras and Visvizi, "Who Uses Smart City Services and What to Make of It."
19. e.g., Alberto Vanolo, "Smartmentality: The Smart City as Disciplinary Strategy." *Urban Studies* 51, no. 5 (2014). Relational ecologies here built on Felix Guattari's work of mental, social and environmental ecologies, related to how Thomas A. Markus formulates it as relations of self-to-self, self-to-others, and self-to-the-other. Félix Guattari, *The Three*

Ecologies [*Les trois écologies*], trans. Ian Pindar and Paul Sutton (London: Athlone Press, 2000); Thomas A. Markus, *Buildings and Power: Freedom and Control in the Origin of Modern Building Types* (London: Routledge, 1993).

20. Shannon Mattern, "Maintenance and Care." *Places Journal*, no. November 2018 (2018). Jennifer Gabrys, *Digital Rubbish: A Natural History of Electronics* (Ann Arbor, MI: University of Michigan Press, 2011); Adriá Carbonell, "The Solid Matter(s) of Digital Natures: Multiscalar Technologies of World Urbanisation," in *Proceedings: Space and Digital Reality: Ideas, Representation/Applications and Fabrication*, ed. Jüri Soolep, Kadi Karine, and Andres Ojari (Tallinn: Estonian Academy of Art, 2020).

21. Daniel Koch, "On Architectural Space and Modes of Subjectivity: Producing the Material Conditions for Creative-Productive Activity." *Urban Planning* 3, no. 3 (2018).

22. Hannes Frykholm, "Inside the Backside: On Labour and Infrastructure of the Casino Lobby," in *Civic Spaces and Desire*, ed. Charles Drozynski and Diana Beljaars (London: Routledge, 2019); Erin Hatton, "Mechanisms of Invisibility: Rethinking the Concept of Invisible Work." *Work, Employment and Society* 31, no. 2 (2017).

23. Daniel Koch and Monica Sand, "Rhythmanalysis—Rhythm as Mode, Methods and Theory for Analysing Urban Complexity," in *Urban Design Research: Method and Application—Proceedings of the International Conference* held at Birmingham City University, December 3–4, 2009, ed. Andreas Wesener and Mohsen Aboutarabi (Birmingham: Birmingham City University, 2009).

24. Lars Marcus and Daniel Koch, "Cities as Implements or Facilities—The Need for a Spatial Morphology in Smart City Systems." *Environment and Planning B: Urban Analytics and City Science* 44, no. 2 (2017); Shannon Mattern, "A City is Not a Computer." *Places Journal* February 2017 (2017).

25. Lisa Gitelman, ed., *"Raw Data" Is an Oxymoron* (Cambridge: MIT Press, 2013).

26. Gabrys, "Programming Environments"; Imanol Arrieta-Ibarra et al., "Should We Treat Data as Labor? Moving beyond 'Free'." *AEA Papers and Proceedings* 108 (2018). See also the short story "The Skeleton Crew" by Janelle Shane, and the accompanying reflection by Melissa Valentine; Janelle Shane, "The Skeleton Crew." *Slate* June 26 (2021); Melissa Valentine, "The Ghost Work Behind Artificial Intelligence." *Slate* June 26 (2021).

27. See for instance Felix Stalder, *The Digital Condition* (London: John Wiley & Sons, 2018).

28. Jacques Lévy, "Inhabiting," in *The SAGE Handbook of Human Geography*, 2v, ed. Roger Lee et al. (London: SAGE, 2014); Jacques Lévy, *L'espace légitime: sur la dimension géographique de la fonction politique* (Paris: Presses de la Fondation nationale des sciences politiques, 1994).

29. Lars Marcus, "Spatial Capital: A Proposal for an Extension of Space Syntax into a More General Urban Morphology." *Journal of Space Syntax* 1, no. 1 (2010).

30. Ann Legeby and Christina Pech, *Kartläggning av platsens betydelse: Hållbar utveckling av lokalsamhällen* (Stockholm: KTH, 2022).

31. Patrick Rérat, "Spatial Capital and Planetary Gentrification: Residential Location, Mobility and Social Inequalities," in *Handbook of Gentrification Studies*, ed. Loretta Lees (Cheltenham: Edward Elgar, 2018). See further John Urry, *Mobilities* (Cambridge: Polity, 2007).

32. Pierre Bourdieu, *Distinction: A Social Critique of the Judgement of Taste* [*La distinction: critique sociale du jugement*], trans. Richard Nice (Cambridge: Harvard University Press, 1984).
33. Åre kommun, *Näringslivsundersökning Åre kommun 2020* (Åre: Åre kommun, 2020).
34. For an in-depth discussion on youths' relations to mobility and "Stockholm" in northern Sweden, see further Sara Forsberg, "'The Right to Immobility' and the Uneven Distribution of Spatial Capital: Negotiating Youth Transitions in Northern Sweden." *Social and Cultural Geography* 20, no. 3 (2019).
35. Sara Westin, "Un-Homing with Words: Economic Discourse and Displacement as Alienation." *Cultural Geographies* 28, no. 2 (2021).
36. Blokland does not specifically discuss the cosmopolitan subjectivity but the root of her discussion is the relational construct between people and the site and activity. Blokland, "Gardening with a Little Help from Your (Middle Class) Friends."
37. Roger Marjavaara, "The Displacement Myth: Second Home Tourism in the Stockholm Archipelago." *Tourism Geographies* 9, no. 3 (2007).
38. Francesco Indovina and Oriol Nel·lo, "Gentrification: Disaster, Necessity, Opportunity? Notes for a Critical Use of the Concept," in *Gentrification as a Global Strategy: Neil Smith and Beyond*, ed. Abel Albet and Núria Benach (New York: Routledge, 2018).

BIBLIOGRAPHY

Åre kommun. *Inledande Medborgardialog: Underlagsrapport Översiktsplan Åre Kommun.* Åre: Åre kommun, 2012.

Åre kommun. *Kommuntäckande Översiktsplan.* Åre: Åre kommun, 2017.

Åre kommun. *Näringslivsundersökning Åre Kommun 2020.* Åre: Åre kommun, 2020.

Arrieta-Ibarra, Imanol, Leonard Goff, Diego Jiménez-Hernández, Jaron Lanier, and E. Glen Weyl. "Should We Treat Data as Labor? Moving Beyond 'Free'." *AEA Papers and Proceedings* 108 (2018): 38–42.

Batty, Michael. *The New Science of Cities.* Cambridge, MA: MIT Press, 2013.

Blokland, Talja. "Gardening with a Little Help from Your (Middle Class) Friends: Bridging Social Capital across Race and Class in a Mixed Neighbourhood." Chap. 8. In *Networked Urbanism: Social Capital and the City*, edited by Talja Blokland and Mike Savage, 147–70. Farnham: Ashgate, 2008.

Bourdieu, Pierre. *Distinction: A Social Critique of the Judgement of Taste* [*La distinction: critique sociale du jugement.*] Translated by Richard Nice. Cambridge: Harvard University Press, 1984.

Burns, Ryan, and Max Andrucki. "Smart Cities: Who Cares?" *Environment and Planning A: Economy and Space* 53, no. 1 (2021): 12–30.

Carbonell, Adriá. "The Solid Matter(s) of Digital Natures: Multiscalar Technologies of World Urbanisation." In *Proceedings: Space and Digital Reality: Ideas, Representation / Applications*

and Fabrication, edited by Jüri Soolep, Kadi Karine, and Andres Ojari, 44–53. Tallinn: Estonian Academy of Art, 2020.

Colding, Johan, Magnus Colding, and Stephan Barthel. "The Smart City Model: A New Panacea for Urban Sustainability or Unmanageable Complexity?" *Environment and Planning B: Urban Analytics and City Science* 47, no. 1 (2020): 179–87.

Cowie, Paul, Leanne Townsend, and Koen Salemink. "Smart Rural Futures: Will Rural Areas Be Left Behind in the 4th Industrial Revolution?" *Journal of Rural Studies* 79 (2020): 169–76.

Fjaervoll, Karin. "Duved Får Hälsocentral: 'Det här har varit världens sämst bevarade hemlighet'." *Östersundsposten (Östersund)*, November 19, 2020.

Forsberg, Sara. "'The Right to Immobility' and the Uneven Distribution of Spatial Capital: Negotiating Youth Transitions in Northern Sweden", *Social and Cultural Geography* 20, no. 3 (2019): 323–43.

Frykholm, Hannes. "Inside the Backside: On Labour and Infrastructure of the Casino Lobby." In *Civic Spaces and Desire*, edited by Charles Drozynski and Diana Beljaars, 53–67. London: Routledge, 2019.

Gabrys, Jennifer. *Digital Rubbish: A Natural History of Electronics*. Ann Arbor, MI: University of Michigan Press, 2011.

Gabrys, Jennifer. "Programming Environments: Environmentality and Citizen Sensing in the Smart City." *Environment and Planning D: Society and Space* 32, no. 1 (2014): 30–48.

Gitelman, Lisa, ed. *"Raw Data" Is an Oxymoron*. Cambridge: MIT Press, 2013.

Guattari, Félix. *The Three Ecologies* [*Les trois écologies.*] Translated by Ian Pindar and Paul Sutton. London: Athlone Press, 2000.

Hatton, Erin. "Mechanisms of Invisibility: Rethinking the Concept of Invisible Work." *Work, Employment and Society* 31, no. 2 (2017): 336–51.

Indovina, Francesco, and Oriol Nel·lo. "Gentrification: Disaster, Necessity, Opportunity? Notes for a Critical Use of the Concept." In *Gentrification as a Global Strategy: Neil Smith and Beyond*, edited by Abel Albet and Núria Benach, 54–65. New York: Routledge, 2018.

"Inrikes omflyttning mellan län efter kön och län. År 2000 - 2021." SCB, 2021. Accessed May 20. 2022, http://www.statistikdatabasen.scb.se/pxweb/sv/ssd/START__BE__BE0101__BE0101J/InOmflytt/table/tableViewLayout1/.

Jordbruksdepartementet. *Åre: Utvecklinsplan för ett svenskt rekreationsområde*. Stockholm: Jordbruksdepartementet, 1971.

Koch, Daniel. "On Architectural Space and Modes of Subjectivity: Producing the Material Conditions for Creative-Productive Activity." *Urban Planning* 3, no. 3 (2018): 70–82.

Koch, Daniel. *Digitalisering Och Landsbygdsutveckling: Lärdomar Från Duvedmodellen För Lokalsamhällen 2.0*. Stockholm: KTH, 2022.

Koch, Daniel, and Monica Sand. "Rhythmanalysis—Rhythm as Mode, Methods and Theory for Analysing Urban Complexity." In *Urban Design Research: Method and Application—Proceedings of the International Conference* held at Birmingham City University, December 3–4, 2009, edited by Andreas Wesener and Mohsen Aboutarabi, 61–72. Birmingham: Birmingham City University, 2009.

Jämtland, Länsstyrelsen. *Länsplanering 1974: Förslag till Länsprogram*. Östersund: Länstyrelsen Jämtland, 1974.

Jämtland, Länsstyrelsen. *Bostadsmarknadsanalys 2020: En lägesbild över bostadsmarknaden i Jämtlands län*. Östersund: Länsstyrelsen i Jämtlands län, 2020.

Legeby, Ann, and Christina Pech. *Kartläggning av platsens betydelse: Hållbar utveckling av lokalsamhällen*. Stockholm: KTH, 2022.

Legeby, Ann, Daniel Koch, and Christina Pech. *Betydelsefulla platser: Kartenkät i Åre kommun 2021*. Stockholm: KTH, 2021.

Lévy, Jacques. *L'espace Légitime: Sur La Dimension Géographique De La Fonction Politique*. Paris: Presses de la Fondation nationale des sciences politiques, 1994.

Lévy, Jacques. "Inhabiting." In *The Sage Handbook of Human Geography*, 2v, edited by Roger Lee, Noel Castree, Rob Kitchin, Victoria Lawson, Anssi Paasi, Christopher Philo Philo, Sarah Radcliffe, Susan M. Roberts, and Charles W. J. Withers, 46–68. London: SAGE, 2014.

Lytras, Miltriadis D., and Anna Visvizi. "Who Uses Smart City Services and What to Make of It: Toward Interdisciplinary Smart Cities Research." *Sustainability* 10, no. 6 (2018): 1998.

Makimoto, Tsugio, and David Manners. *Digital Nomad*. Chichester: Wiley & Sons, 1997.

Marcus, Lars. "Spatial Capital: A Proposal for an Extension of Space Syntax into a More General Urban Morphology." *Journal of Space Syntax* 1, no. 1 (2010): 30–40.

Marcus, Lars, and Daniel Koch. "Cities as Implements or Facilities—The Need for a Spatial Morphology in Smart City Systems." *Environment and Planning B: Urban Analytics and City Science* 44, no. 2 (2017): 204–26.

Marjavaara, Roger. "The Displacement Myth: Second Home Tourism in the Stockholm Archipelago." *Tourism Geographies* 9, no. 3 (2007): 296–317.

Markus, Thomas A. *Buildings and Power: Freedom and Control in the Origin of Modern Building Types*. London: Routledge, 1993.

Mattern, Shannon. "A City Is Not a Computer." *Places Journal*, February 2017 (2017).

Mattern, Shannon. "Maintenance and Care." *Places Journal*, November 2018 (2018).

Naldi, Lucia, Pia Nilsson, Hans Westlund, and Sofia Wixe. "What Is Smart Rural Development?" *Journal of Rural Studies* 40 (2015): 90–101.

Paris, Chris. "Second Homes, Housing Consumption and Planning Responses." In *The Routledge Companion to Rural Planning*, edited by Mark Scott, Nick Gallent, and Menelaos Gkartzios, 273–86. London: Routledge, 2019.

Rérat, Patrick. "Spatial Capital and Planetary Gentrification: Residential Location, Mobility and Social Inequalities." In *Handbook of Gentrification Studies*, edited by Loretta Lees, 103–18. Cheltenham: Edward Elgar, 2018.

Rose, Mitch. "The Seductions of Resistance: Power, Politics, and a Performative Style of Systems." *Environment and Planning D: Society and Space* 20 (2002): 383–400.

Shane, Janelle. "The Skeleton Crew." *Slate*, June 26 (2021).

Stalder, Felix. *The Digital Condition*. London: John Wiley & Sons, 2018.

Torre, André, Stefano Corsi, Michael Steiner, Frédéric Wallet, and Hans Westlund, eds. *Smart Development for Rural Areas*. London: Routledge, 2021.

Urry, John. *Mobilities*. Cambridge: Polity, 2007.

Vanolo, Alberto. "Smartmentality: The Smart City as Disciplinary Strategy." *Urban Studies* 51, no. 5 (2014): 883–98.

Valentine, Melissa. "The Ghost Work behind Artificial Intelligence." *Slate* (Washington), 2021.

Wahlström, Mia, and Sarah Bragée. *Lokalekonomisk analys för Duved*. Stockholm: Tyréns, 2021.

Westberg, Paula. "Här Formas Framtidens Landsbygd." *Dagens Nyheter (Stockholm)*, November 27, 2021, Ekonomi, 36–38.

Westin, Sara. "Un-Homing with Words: Economic Discourse and Displacement as Alienation." *Cultural Geographies* 28, no. 2 (2021): 239–54.

Willis, Katherine S. "Whose Right to the Smart City?" In *The Right to the Smart City*, edited by Paolo Cardullo, Cesare Di Feliciantonio, and Rob Kitchin. Bingley: Emerald Publishing Limited, 2019.

Zavratnik, Veronika, Andrej Kos, and Emilija Stojmenova Duh. "Smart Villages: Comprehensive Review of Initiatives and Practices." *Sustainability* 10, no. 7 (2018): 2559.

Zukin, Sharon. *The Cultures of Cities*. Oxford: Blackwell, 1995.

Zukin, Sharon, and Ervin Kosta. "*Bourdieu Off-Broadway*: Managing Distinctionon a Shopping Block in the East Village." *City & Community* 3, no. 2 (2004): 101–14.

Contributors

JUSTIN AGYIN is an architect at Amsterdam-based architecture office Space Encounters, which works on architecture at various scale levels, ranging from interior design and furniture to large scale housing and inner-city densification projects. Concurrently, he was an editor and programme maker at the Architecture Institute Rotterdam (AIR), which organizes public debates on architecture and the city. Moreover, he is a member of the editorial board of *OASE Journal for Architecture*, a co-organizer of the research group Critical Intermediate Affairs (CIA), a founding-member of the Curatorial Research Collective (CRC), and co-founder of The Architecture Circus that through small-scale provocative design and research projects explores a fascination for how spatial design in general and architecture in particular shapes the human condition.

*****

FAUSTO BREVI is an associate professor at Politecnico di Milano School of Design. His teaching activities are mainly focused on design representation techniques, both traditional and digital. He is specialized in digital three-dimensional (3D) modelling and visualization for concept design, mainly in car design world. In 2014–15 he has been visiting professor at Stanford University; from 2015 he is visiting professor at Alma Mater Studiorum—Università di Bologna. Since 2009 he is the director of the post-graduate Master Course in Transportation & Automobile Design (TAD) at Politecnico di Milano. He managed a five-year research project in collaboration with Volkswagen Group Design entitled "Moving Milano 2010–2015: Urban Mobility Culture associated to EXPO 2015" focused on developing electric concept cars for urban mobility. Currently he is managing the research project "From Sign to the Shape," focused on innovative contents and methods for teaching the project representation techniques in the university industrial design courses, funded by FARB—University Fund for Basic Research of Politecnico di Milano, and one of the Design Dept. teams involved in the research project "BASE-5G: Broadband Interfaces and Services for Smart Environments

enabled by 5G Technologies," funded by the Lombardy Region and coordinated by Politecnico di Milano.

*****

DR DAVID CAPENER is an architect, artist, and writer. In collaboration with the multidisciplinary design group ANNEX he recently co-curated and designed *Entanglement*, the Irish Pavilion at the Venice Biennale 2021. He is a lecturer at Belfast School of Architecture at Ulster University. His practice critically examines the spaces produced by our contemporary technological condition. He is co-editor of the book *States of Entanglement* published by Actar (2021) and has written for *The Irish Times*, *The Guardian*, *The Sunday Times*, and numerous other print and online publications.

*****

MATTEO CONTI is a senior lecturer in design innovation, and a specialist in industrial and transportation design practice with a particular research focus on smart mobility, e-mobility, and low carbon vehicles (LCVs). As he leads the MA/MSc Multi-Disciplinary Innovation course at Northumbria University, Matteo focuses on ongoing industrial and academic collaboration for research purposes alongside commercial value for business through contracted studio and consultancy projects. This is achieved through creative solutions using strategic innovation to solve real world, complex challenges to social, organizational, and commercial issues. As an expert in "usability aesthetics in smart mobility" Matteo has developed a track record of completed live projects in the low carbon vehicles (LCVs) sector (mainly through the High Value Low Carbon design entity) and autonomous vehicles (AVs). As a former senior tutor at the RCA in MA Vehicle Design, Matteo has acquired considerable experience in coordinating and leading external advanced design projects at the highest level within the automotive industry as well as contributing to postgraduate teaching and research. Previously, he worked in the marine industry, utilizing his design and business capabilities to establish and manage a design consultancy providing a tailored design service to clients, mainly in the yachting area.

*****

ESRA DUYGUN is a PhD student at Hacettepe University, Department of Interior Architecture and Environmental Design. Her Master's thesis is about the image-oriented design of the Airbnb platform titled as "Photogenic Space: Airbnb and

Transformation of the House." She continues her doctoral studies on the effects of media on space design and organization. She makes her designs and artworks as a freelance designer.

* * * * *

DR EMILY EYLES does quantitative analysis on several UK Applied Research Collaboration West (ARC West), including those relating to risk factors for hospital admissions for people with dementia, and hospital bed demand. Emily also has a range of prior research experience in a variety of contexts using both qualitative and quantitative methods.

* * * * *

DR JOHN EYLES is a distinguished university professor at McMaster. After receiving his PhD in science and working in the University of London, he came to McMaster in 1988. Based in Geography and Earth Sciences, he holds appointments in clinical epidemiology and biostatistics, Sociology and the Centre for Health Economics and Policy analysis. His main research interests lie in environmental influences on human health and access to health care resources. He has published widely in these areas. He has served on several advisory committees at the local, provincial, and national levels, primarily with the role of science in public policy. He has recently begun (again) working internationally in South Africa and India.

* * * * *

LIZ FELTON is a PhD student with the Institute of Artificial Intelligence at De Montfort University, in the United Kingdom. She graduated from the University of Birmingham in 2014 with a B.Sc. in artificial intelligence, and with an M.Sc. in intelligent systems and robotics from De Montfort University in 2019. Liz's PhD research focuses on computational methods to handle uncertainty in affective computing, and forecasting emotional change with fuzzy time-series analysis. She also acts as the staff liaison to the student-led robotics club.

* * * * *

CALVIN HILLIS is a doctoral student in media design & innovation at Toronto Metropolitan University (TMU). His research interests include mixed-reality applications such as Augmented Reality (AR) and Virtual Reality (VR), as well as robotics and artificial intelligence. Calvin is currently the Project Manager

for TMU's Explanatory Journalism Project, and an emerging researcher at the Responsible Artificial Intelligence research team at TMU. He achieved his Master of Arts from McMaster University with the Major Research Project *Bad Faith Cycles in Algorithmic Cultivation,* a discussion-based examination of personalized content algorithms through the media effects lens Cultivation Theory, that is concerned with sociological concepts such as agency and continental philosophy approaches to identity.

* * * * *

DUYGU KOCA is an associate professor in the Department of Interior Architecture and Environmental Design at Hacettepe University, Turkey. She received her B.Arch, March and PhD in architecture from Middle East Technical University, Faculty of Architecture. She has worked on the mutual relationship between image production/ identity /residential architecture in Turkey in her PhD She both teaches architectural design, residential architecture, and design/research methods and also practised as an architect. She has published in various international and national journals and has delivered multiple conference papers. She has two books and awards from national and international architectural competitions.

* * * * *

DANIEL KOCH is a docent in architecture and researcher in urban design and urban theory at the KTH School of Architecture, and practising architect at Patchwork Architecture Laboratory. He is co-director of the interdisciplinary master's programme in sustainable urban planning and design. His research builds on the relation between space, social structures, and the formation of subjectivities, engaging with questions of spatial configuration, power, and architecture as material communication. Aside from the project in Duved from which the chapter in the current volume comes, Daniel's research has more recently engaged with digitalization and smart cities through projects in the Senseable Stockholm Lab and Digital Futures.

* * * * *

FIDELIA LAM 林安慈 is a new media artist, researcher, and facilitator. Their current research praxis teases the tensions within contemporary techno-cultural and aesthetic imaginaries and practices of digital technologies as they are undergirded by histories + logics of gendered and racialized capital, spectacle, capture, display, and labor within North America and across the transpacific, with particular

relation to Hong Kong. Their work has been exhibited and presented at Human Resources Los Angeles, Geidai Games Online at Tokyo University of the Arts, *Architecture, Media, Politics, Society* (London), TongLau Space (Hong Kong), American Studies Association (Montreal), ISEA (Barcelona), *Arts for the Society of the Present* (Los Angeles), Flow 34 @ International Association for Media and Communication Research (Nairobi), among other venues. They hold a PhD in Cinematic Arts, Media Arts + Practice from the University of Southern California, an MA in Media Arts from the University of Michigan, Ann Arbor, and are currently Assistant Professor in Critical Computational Media in the department of Digital Futures at OCAD University in Tkaronto, Canada.

* * * * *

YULIN LI is a graduate student, researcher, and editor in the field of urban studies and planning. During her studies of the Master of Philosophy degree in the University of Cambridge, she developed her research projects focusing on the transformation of urban form and experience under the impact of digital technology and social network. She is now pursuing the direction of historic preservation planning in Cornell University, with her research interest in the geographical and virtual networks of migrants, and their impact on the urban processes. She also widely contributes to urban research and preservation planning projects in China, and was the leading editor and content producer in the architectural intellectual media Global Knowledge Leifeng.

* * * * *

ISABEL FANGYI LU is a Melbourne-based interdisciplinary researcher. Having obtained her PhD from The University of Melbourne, she researches digital engagement in the realms of arts and culture, digital placemaking and disinformation operations, focusing on Australia, China and Taiwan. She has contributed to *Visual Culture Wars at the Borders of Contemporary China* (Palgrave Macmillan), *Art and the Global City (Peter Lang), Journal of Urban Affairs, Global Media and China*, and *Convergence*. She also manages research projects and art projects. She can be contacted via https://www.isabelfangyilu.com/.

* * * * *

IAN NAZARETH is an architect, researcher, and educator. Ian is the director of TRAFFIC—a design and research practice working across architecture, urbanism, and computation, co-director of the Urban Futures Office (UFO) and an academic at

the School of Architecture and Urban Design, RMIT University Melbourne. He also contributes extensively to architectural media and critical design discourse internationally and is the series editor for The Practice of Spatial Thinking (ACTAR). Ian was previously the programme director and head of urban design at RMIT.

* * * * *

REBECCA ONAFUYE is a respected figure in design and academia, with a unique blend of expertise and passion to the creative realm. With a PhD in Digital Architecture and Design, along with an MA and a BA in Interior Architecture and Design, Dr. Onafuye has accumulated extensive experience spanning over a decade. She is dedicated to nurturing young design talent within the diaspora, with a strong commitment to building equality, diversity, and inclusivity within the classroom. Dr. Onafuye's research work further underscores her dedication to inclusive and equitable urban development. Specialising in urban planning, digital placemaking, social placemaking, and spatial data visualisation, she explores how these disciplines can enhance public engagement in urban planning processes and building phygital social landscapes. Her innovative research aims to create more interactive and participatory platforms for community involvement, ensuring that urban development reflects the diverse needs and aspirations of all its inhabitants.

* * * * *

KAI REAVER is an American/Norwegian dual citizen with a background from architectural design and technology research. He is a PhD researcher at AHO, The Oslo School of Architecture and Design, and guest professor at HEAD in Geneva. He is architectural policy author at NAL, the Norwegian Association of Architects, and also runs Udaru, a research consultancy working across design, technology and planning. He serves on the board of Europan and AHO, in addition to several government advisory panels. His work concerns the digitialization of the built environment, and developing theory and methods for understanding the phenomenology of human spatial experience beyond the confines of materialism. He has previously worked at Snøhetta, Planeta, and Zago architecture and has taught with architects such as SO-IL, Sergison Bates, Jun Igarashi, Go Hasegawa, and Rafael Zuber.

* * * * *

TOBY REED is a director of Nervegna Reed Architecture, an interdisciplinary architecture practice working on projects across architecture, urbanism, and media. NR's Projects are widely published and include the Arrow Studio, the Melbourne Quakers

Centre, the Precinct Energy Project Dandenong, large-scale urban design in China and the recently completed Maryborough Central Goldfields Art Gallery on Dja Dja Wurrung Country, exhibited in the Australian pavilion at the 2023 Venice Architecture Biennale. Reed's PhD at RMIT University formed the basis of Screenness in this publication. Reed extends his architectural design discourse through teaching, writing, magazines, and architectural documentaries and video installations.

* * * * *

DAVID SCHWARZMAN is an architect at UNStudio in Amsterdam and Academic at RMIT University in Melbourne Interested in the relationships between the built environment, human behaviour and data. He holds a BA of environments from The University of Melbourne and MA in architecture from RMIT and completed part of his masters at The Royal Danish Academy of Fine Arts in Copenhagen in the CITA (advanced computation in architecture) programme.

* * * * *

PATRICIA SILVA is a Lisbon-born, Queens-based photographer, video artist, and educator. Over the past nine years since graduate studies, they have experimented with cross-disciplinary narratives for photographs, printed photo books, and video works. They are adjunct faculty at The School at the International Center of Photography in New York City, and the recipient of a 2019 Queens Council on the Arts New Works Grant, and two ICP Director Fellowships. Their photographic work has been published in the *New York Times*, *Diva UK*, *The Times of Israel*, *Out Magazine*, *The Advocate*, *Der Grief*, and in several art books. Their writings on photography and visual culture have been published in *The Gay & Lesbian Review*; *Dodge & Burn: Decolonizing Photography*; *Queering the Collection*; *Daylight*; and in *Memories Can't Wait: Conversations on Accessing History and Archives Through Artistic Practices*.

* * * * *

DR DAVID HARRIS SMITH is associate professor in the Department of Communication Studies and Media Arts at McMaster University. His research and creative works in emerging media technologies, include the practices and applications of artificial intelligence, robotics, virtual worlds, and mixed reality environments. Dr Smith's cultural robotics project with Dr Frauke Zeller, hitchBOT the hitchhiking robot, received extensive international media coverage.

* * * * *

DEBORA SILVA DE JESUS is a communications professional and multimedia designer. She holds a master's degree in Communication and New Media from McMaster University and a bachelor's degree in Communication and Multimedia from the Pontifical Catholic University of São Paulo. Her Master's thesis focused on the use of 3D virtual worlds for participatory urban planning, with a focus on the experience of citizens living with disabilities. Currently, Debora is the manager of diversity, inclusion and belonging content and communications at Canadian Tire Corporation.

*****

DR HÜSNÜ YEGENOGLU is an architect, researcher, and educator. He holds a MA of Architecture from the Darmstadt University of Technology, and a PhD from the Eindhoven University of Technology for his thesis on the social and architectural transformation of a social housing area in Amsterdam. He is an assistant professor at the Eindhoven University of Technology and lectures in architectural analysis, typology, and design. He was a member of the Aesthetics Committee of Amsterdam, the Dutch Architecture Foundation in Rotterdam, and until 2019, member of the editorial board of the architectural journal *OASE*. Since 2020, he is co-organizer of the research group Critical Intermediate Affairs (CIA) that critically examines inscriptions of cultural and power-related alterations in architectural and urban space driven by data technology, ecological intelligence, and the culture of self-pleasure.

*****

DR MARCO ZILVETTI is a PhD-qualified product designer with doctoral degree in transportation design from the Politecnico di Milano. As part of his pluriannual collaboration with Politecnico, Marco has been teaching 3D modelling and virtual prototyping applied to product design, while also collaborating as a tutor for the Master in Transportation and Automobile Design (TAD). Since 2010 Marco has held positions with several major multinational companies, working on several projects in the fields of product, interior, and communication design. After obtaining his doctoral degree in 2017, he has actively collaborated with both academia and industry, focusing his activity on the fields of urban mobility and smart cities, exploring the boundaries of different disciplines and the strategic relationship between urban studies and interior design. Since 2019 Marco is a full-time lecturer at Northumbria University—School of Design, Arts and Social Sciences—where he works for the Interior Design Programme and the Year in International Multidisciplinary Innovation Programme. As part of his activity, and

driven by his passion for the subjects, he has been involved in research projects that explore the potentials of technologies applied to both smart ports and product-service design for urban innovation.

*****

DR FRAUKE ZELLER is professor of HCI & Creative Informatics at Edinburgh Napier University in Scotland. She completed her Habilitation (the highest academic degree in Germany) at Ilmenau University of Technology, working on computational methods to analyse online communities. She received her PhD (Dr.phil.) from Kassel University, Germany, in English linguistics and computational philology. Frauke has received funding for various international and national projects on Germany, Canada and the United Kingdom. One of her projects focused on participatory planning for urban universities, combining HCI and social sciences approaches. Other projects focused on human–machine communication and human–robot interaction (HRI) studies combining her backgrounds in the humanities, social sciences, and HRI. She is the co-creator of hitchBOT, with Dr David Harris Smith, Canada's first hitchhiking robot.

Printed in the USA
CPSIA information can be obtained
at www.ICGtesting.com
JSHW060813180924
69884JS00003B/5